Writing:
Process to Product

Writing: Process to Product

John F. Parker

ML McDougal, Littell & Company
Evanston, Illinois
New York   Dallas   Sacramento   Columbia, SC

Copyright © 1991 by McDougal, Littell & Company
Box 1667, Evanston, Illinois 60204
All rights reserved. Printed in the United States of America

ISBN 0-8123-7111-0

WARNING: No part of this book may be reproduced or transmitted in any form or by any means, electronic or mechanical, including photocopying, recording, or by any information storage and retrieval system, without permission in writing from the Publisher.

90 91 92 93 94 - DCI - 15 14 13 12 11 10 9 8 7 6 5 4 3 2 1

The author wishes to thank his wife, Mary, for her understanding and encouragement throughout the writing process; the teachers and consultants who worked on pilot testing portions of the text, but especially Steve Pearse and his students at Shorewood High School in Seattle for their many contributions; and finally Barbara-Anne Eddy and Karen Klaushie for their help in research.

PILOT TESTING

Portions of this textbook were pilot tested by the following teachers. Our thanks to them and to their students, who contributed many of the compositions.

Michael Bruner
Pikesville High School
Pikesville, Maryland

Kathy H. Eder
Independence High School
San Jose, California

Nadine G. Feiler
Parkville High School
Parkville, Maryland

Dorothy E. Hardin
Hereford High School
Parkton, Maryland

Jerry Hay
Pleasure Ridge High School
Louisville, Kentucky

Steve Kelly
Shorewood High School
Seattle, Washington

Mary Susan Nickerson
Danvers High School
Danvers, Massachusetts

Joseph W. Peacock
Shawnee High School
Louisville, Kentucky

Steve Pearse
Shorewood High School
Seattle, Washington

Mary A. Pietrini
Danvers High School
Danvers, Massachusetts

Jan Richardson
Southern High School
Louisville, Kentucky

Ralph Riola
Somers High School
Somers, Connecticut

Janet Sanchez
Independence High School
San Jose, California

George O. Walsh
Shorewood High School
Seattle, Washington

Contents

PREFACE — x

The Writing Process — 1

    Steps of the Writing Process — 2
    Using *Writing: Process to Product* — 3
    Introductory Assignment — 4

Assignments

    ABOUT THE ASSIGNMENTS SECTION — 20
1. Narrative Paragraph — 21
2. Descriptive Paragraph — 30
3. Expository Paragraph — 37
4. Informative Essay — 48
5. Argumentative Essay — 55
6. Narrative Essay — 63
7. Autobiographical Essay — 71
8. Biographical Essay — 78
9. Review — 87
10. Literary Essay — 97
11. Short Research Paper — 110
12. Long Research Paper — 118
13. Feature Article — 126
14. Set of Instructions — 132

15	Demand Essay (Answering Questions on an Essay Test)	139
16	Memo	150
17	Proposal and Report	156
18	Personal Letter	164
19	Business Letter	173
20	Letter to the Editor	182
21	Résumé and Cover Letter	190

First Workshop: Content and Organization

	HOW TO USE THE FIRST WORKSHOP	200
	PREWRITING	
22	Journal Writing and Instant Writing	201
23	Brainstorming	208
24	Thesis Statements and Topic Sentences	234
	DRAFTING	
25	Beginnings and Endings	243
26	Unity	248
27	Coherence	264
	EDITING AND REVISING	
28	Self-Editing, Peer-Editing, and Teacher-Editing	270
29	Unwriting—Paraphrase, Précis, Outline	282

Second Workshop: Style

	ABOUT THE SECOND WORKSHOP	292
30	Style	294
31	Sentence Variety	305
32	Rhetorical Devices	315
33	Figurative Language and Allusions	320
34	Slant	330
35	Satire	336
36	Research Skills and Documentation	343

Appendix

A. Proofreaders' Marks and Other Symbols for Peer Editing — 364

B. Literature Selections

Fiction
- "Their Mother's Purse" by Morley Callaghan — 367
- "The Censors" by Luisa Valenzuela — 371
- "Kong at the Seaside" by Arnold Zweig — 373

Poetry
- "Out, Out—" by Robert Frost — 379
- "A Man Said to the Universe" by Stephen Crane — 380
- "Shining" by Michelle Malan — 380
- "Ruth" by Pauli Murray — 380
- "Guitarreros" by Americo Paredes — 381
- "Not Waving But Drowning" by Stevie Smith — 381
- "Small Wire" by Anne Sexton — 382
- "For Poets" by Al Young — 383

Drama
- "Dentist and Patient" by William Saroyan — 384

C. Suggested Topics for Writing Literary Essays — 388

GLOSSARY — 391
INDEX — 397
ACKNOWLEDGMENTS — 400

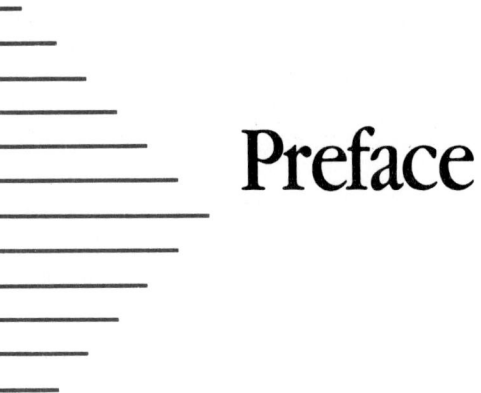
Preface

Are these statements true or false?
- Good writers have a "special talent" for writing that ordinary people do not have.
- Good writers always know what they are going to say before they sit down to write.
- Good writers have the ability to turn out a perfect product at one sitting.
- All good writers follow exactly the same procedures when they sit down and write.

Most good writers and teachers of writing would say that all these statements are false. First, the major difference between good writers and other people is that good writers write—a great deal! Second, most good writers do not sit down and turn out perfect products in one sitting. During their writing process, they are willing to experiment, make mistakes, and learn from their mistakes. They frequently discuss their work with other people. Above all, they revise their material over and over until they are satisfied that it works.

There is no magic formula that will automatically produce good writers. But you can become a better writer by concentrating on your writing process through a variety of meaningful assignments. *Writing: Process to Product* provides many opportunities for you to develop your writing process.

Writing: Process to Product will help you to discover *your own* writing process in several ways:

a) by providing a series of writing assignments, with strategies to assist you at each stage of the writing process—specifically, prewriting, drafting, and editing and revising
b) by encouraging you to write for a real purpose to a specific audience
c) by encouraging and helping you to approach the writing process positively
d) by encouraging revision and offering suggestions for you and your classmates to help each other in editing and revising your writing
e) by providing workshop sections with exercises to help you improve your writing skills and express yourself in a variety of ways
f) by offering opportunities for you to become an independent, confident writer

"Who am I, what am I, how did I come to be? What shall I make of the life around me, what celebrate, what reject?"

RALPH ELLISON

The Writing Process

Steps of the Writing Process

The writing process involves three steps. But writers do not necessarily go straight from step one to step two to step three, ending up very comfortably with a perfect product. They often backtrack, go forward, and backtrack again. Even so, familiarity with the steps will help you develop your personal writing process.

Step One: Prewriting
The writing process begins with prewriting, or producing ideas and supporting details. For example, you might

    a) develop an idea that you have been thinking about
    b) brainstorm a topic by talking with other people
    c) read until an idea of your own comes to mind
    d) watch a show, game, or other event and then write about it
    e) write about something in which you have been involved
    f) simply write until an idea comes to mind
    g) be given a general topic

At some point during prewriting, you should begin to control and limit your piece of writing according to seven writing variables: topic, audience, purpose, format, voice, situation, and point of view. These variables are discussed on pages 5–8.

Writing: Process to Product provides you with specific prewriting suggestions for every assignment. Additionally, you will have opportunities to enrich your prewriting process in three workshop chapters: "Journal Writing and Instant Writing," "Brainstorming," and "Thesis Statements and Topic Sentences."

Step Two: Drafting
Drafting means composing your writing assignment, shaping it so that it communicates exactly what you want to say. At this stage, you organize your information and think about your sentence structure and word choice.

Writing: Process to Product provides specific suggestions for drafting each assignment. In addition, you will find special drafting help in three workshop chapters: "Beginnings and Endings," "Unity," and "Coherence." Finally, you can refer to other workshop chapters when you require help with a specific writing technique or style.

Step Three: Editing and Revising
Revision is an ongoing process. Most writers revise their work many times both before and after they show it to others for editorial comments and suggestions.

Although you can and should revise your work by yourself, research shows that receiving comments from your peers—other students in your class—is more helpful. At first you may be reluctant to show other students your writing. But you will soon discover that this kind of sharing can create a happy working situation. Not only do you learn a great deal from your peers, but you can also share with them what you know.

Every assignment in *Writing: Process to Product* provides a checklist of editing and revising questions for you and your peers. Therefore, you will always have guidance when you edit a paper. In addition, the First Workshop offers two chapters of specific information to make your editing and revising process as smooth as possible: "Self-Editing, Peer-Editing, and Teacher-Editing" and "Unwriting—Paraphrase, Précis, and Outline."

Going through the steps of the writing process will enable you to produce a publishable paper. *Publishable* means simply that your paper is ready to present to a final reader. If the reader finds it hard to understand what you have written, the writing process is not over. You may have to take more time to revise and bring your paper to the publishable stage.

Using *Writing: Process to Product*

Besides this introductory section, *Writing: Process to Product* has one assignment section and two workshop sections.

Assignments. The assignment section is designed to use with the assistance of your teacher/editor and your peers. This section involves you in many projects, all with strategies to shape your writing at each stage of the writing process. Because writing simply for the sake of writing often produces bad results, you should always have an audience and a purpose in mind when you write.

Before you complete any of the writing assignments in the assignment section, do the Introductory Assignment on this page. This assignment familiarizes you with the writing variables and takes you through the steps of the writing process.

First Workshop: Content and Organization. This section deals with all the steps of the writing process. If you are having difficulty with any step (prewriting, drafting, editing and revising), look up the chapters dealing with that step and do the exercises with a partner. The partner can be a classmate at school or a friend or relative at home.

Second Workshop: Style. This section is also designed to work on with a partner. Most of it deals with specific techniques that will improve your writing style. In addition, each chapter in this section ends with a special writing assignment that you can do *for* your partner. You can work on the chapters in any order and complete only those portions of a chapter that you need to work on to help you refine a particular technique of style.

Introductory Assignment

Because the best way to learn something is to *do* it, you can learn about the writing process by working through this assignment. As you work, remember:

1. The point of doing this assignment is to become familiar with the writing process. Concentrate more on each part of the process than on the finished product.

2. Plan to complete the assignment in a specific period of time. If you work in the classroom, your teacher may set time limits for each step. If you work at home, you should set up your own time limits.

3. Be prepared to try new things.

4. Relax. Modern research indicates that a knowledge of the writing process makes writing easier and more interesting. By working through the steps of this assignment, you are on the way to becoming an independent writer.

ASSIGNMENT ▶ Write a 125-word composition about some activity in which you have taken part.

As you progress through this assignment, you will also be able to see how Ben Chavez, another student, worked through the assignment.

Prewriting Process

1. To discover a topic quickly, focus your attention on activities that you like and dislike. To help you think more systematically, draw two columns on a sheet of paper: "Like" and "Dislike." Jot down specific activities in which you have participated, putting them in the appropriate column. Include as many activities as you can remember.

Here is what Ben Chavez jotted down:

Like	*Dislike*
going to movies	seeing a play
playing racquetball	eating breakfast
debating	visiting a dentist
break dancing	watching a demolition derby
jogging	boxing
fishing	hunting
people-watching	writing an essay

2. Decide which activity you most like or most dislike. This can be your **broad topic** for the assignment. On another piece of paper, write your broad topic.

Ben wrote:

Broad topic: playing racquetball

The fact that you have decided on your broad topic does not mean that you are ready to write your paper. Before you begin to write, you should consider the other writing variables: audience, purpose, format, voice, situation, and point of view. Your variables will help you control the development of your paper.

3. Consider your **audience**, your intended reader or readers. Will your audience be real or fictitious? Weak writing occurs when writers have no sense of their audience, when they write to no one in particular or to everyone in general. If you have no real person or persons to whom you want to write, choose an imaginary audience. (Think of your teacher as one of your editors, but not as your final audience. Assume you are writing for some reason other than simply getting a grade.)

For his intended audience, Ben considered the following: his girlfriend, his favorite racquetball opponent, his twelve-year-old brother, an imaginary world champion racquetball player, and classmates who have never played racquetball. (Can you see why Ben would have to change his writing style to satisfy each intended audience?) Finally he wrote:

Audience: Classmates who have never played racquetball. Real. I intend to let them read it.

Just below your broad topic, write down your intended audience as Ben has done, saying whether your audience is real or imagined.

4. By thinking about your reason for writing about a particular activity, you will discover your **purpose**. (Writing a paper simply to earn a grade will probably produce a weak piece of work.)

Ben considered the following reasons for writing to classmates who have never played racquetball: to describe a racquetball game, to explain how to play racquetball, to persuade his readers to learn to play racquetball, to argue that racquetball is the best court game. (Can you see how each purpose would result in a different piece of writing?) Finally he wrote:

Purpose: to persuade my audience to learn to play racquetball.

Just below audience, write down your purpose.

5. Consider your **format**. Because you are doing this assignment to familiarize yourself with the writing process, feel free to write a paragraph, an essay, a letter, or a piece of writing that follows some other appropriate format. The only restriction is length; your writing should be short, not much more than 125 words.

Ben thought about writing a self-contained paragraph, a poem, or an advertisement. Finally he wrote:

Format: self-contained paragraph.

Just below your purpose, write down your format.

6. Consider the **voice** you intend to adopt. Voice reveals the kind of person a writer is. In many cases writers write in their own voice, as themselves. But writers can use another voice by adopting a **persona**—that is, by imagining they are someone else, perhaps a fictitious person. For example, you might consider writing about your activity from the persona of a six-year-old or of a creature from another planet.

Ben thought about using the persona of someone who has never played racquetball, of an experienced racquetball teacher, or of an advertiser of a newly opened racquetball club. (Can you see why each persona would result in a different piece of writing?) Finally he decided to use his own voice. He wrote:

Voice: my own.

Just below your format, write down your voice. If you decide to use a persona, provide as many details as possible—for example:

Voice: persona of a Martian with extremely keen vision who has never seen a racquetball game before.

7. **Situation** includes feelings, attitudes, and relationships. To write effectively, you must consider both your situation (how you feel about your topic and your audience) and your audience's situation (how they feel about your topic and you). If you want to be a good writer, you must forget that you are a student writing this assignment for a grade. Assume instead that you are writing for strong personal reasons to a real audience and have every intention of publishing—that is, of giving your finished piece to your audience. Only by approaching your writing process with this positive outlook can you give serious consideration to both your situation and that of your audience. Remember that both situations will influence your writing.

Ben had decided he was writing for a real audience, his classmates. He thought about his situation and wrote:

Situation: I am a good racquetball player. I enjoy the sport and I like my classmates. They have never seen a racquetball game, let alone played one. Because I am informed about my topic and my readers are uninformed, I should avoid technical terms (kill shot, lob, love, etc.) and use clear, general terms. Because my readers are my peers, I should use a style that appeals to them—informal language and fairly short sentences.

Just below your information on voice, write down what you decide about situation. The following suggestions should help you record your information.

a) Make sure you indicate whether your situation is real or imagined. If you are using a persona, the situation of the persona should be imagined as well. If you have an imagined audience, you will have to invent an imagined situation for them.

b) The more you write about the way the situation will affect your writing style, the easier your drafting process will be.

8. You have already chosen a broad topic for your assignment. Once you have decided about your other variables (audience, purpose, format, voice, and situation), you should have no difficulty in focusing on a **limited topic**.

After Ben reviewed his prewriting notes, he considered the following possibilities for his limited topic: how to play a racquetball game; racquetball is a good way to exercise; racquetball is fun; racquetball is easy to play. Finally he settled on:

Limited topic: benefits of playing racquetball.

Just below your information on situation, write your limited topic.

9. Once you have limited your topic, you should think about **point of view**. To understand point of view, think of the difference between addressing an audience from a lecture platform and talking to a friend who is sitting across the table. Each point of view requires a different choice of words. Point of view has a great deal to do with the pronoun you use most in your writing: first person [I, we], second person [you], or third person [he, she, they]. For example, you would probably use third person when writing formally to a large audience but second person when writing informally to a friend.

Ben is writing to persuade students in his class to learn racquetball. He wrote:

Point of view: I must write with confidence and authority, but I must also sound friendly and inviting. I want my audience to think I am close to them and writing directly to them. Therefore I will use the second person (you) whenever possible.

Record your point of view.

10. What you have been doing up to now is often called brainstorming. Throughout this book, brainstorming is used to name two ways of providing ideas and supporting details for ideas. You can brainstorm in two ways—either alone or with other people. When you do it alone, you probe your mind for ideas and details to support them. When you do it with others, you probe the minds of those in your "think tank" for their ideas and details. Although both ways are valuable, two or more minds working together will usually produce a larger number of ideas for you to consider. Furthermore, in a group brainstorming session, you may be able to see the flaws in your thinking and improve your ideas.

All of Chapter 23 is devoted to brainstorming techniques. If you study it, you will have these techniques at your command. In the meantime, use the following brainstorming technique, known as Aristotle's Topics, by yourself or with a few of your classmates.

Notice how Ben used these topics and recorded his brainstorming notes.

Aristotle's Topics	*Brainstorming Notes*
Definition	Racquetball is a court game. Played with short rackets and a single ball. Object is to hit the ball to the end wall and make it bounce on the floor twice before your opponent can return the ball. It's a fast game.
Comparison and Contrast	It's like squash and handball. But it's faster than handball and slower than squash. It's easier to play than both. I think it's more fun than both. Keeping score is the same for all three games. You can play doubles in racquetball as you can in handball and squash.
Cause and Effect	Racquetball is such a fast game that you couldn't possibly be aware of any outside problems. There is no time to be aware of anything but the game. No time to feel depressed. Racquetball is a great way to have a good workout. I'm sweating after five minutes. Game is easy to learn but hard to play. Enthusiasts say that racquetball takes minutes to learn but a lifetime to perfect.
Supporting Evidence	Racquetball is popular. Fastest growing court game in the last ten years. Most players play three or four times a week. Racquetball provides exercise, play, and fun. The more experienced players learn to kill a shot, zigzag serves, and play the back wall. They dive for the ball before it has a chance to bounce on the floor twice. It's a fast sport.

Now record your own brainstorming notes.

If you do not have many supporting details after using Aristotle's Topics, choose another brainstorming technique from Chapter 23 and work up another set of notes. Record and keep all your notes. Do not be too concerned about how you record your information. Notice that Ben's notes include both full sentences and fragments.

11. Brainstorming will help you discover what you want to use as your **thesis statement**, a sentence stating the main idea of your piece of writing. Thesis statements are discussed in detail in Chapter 24. However, the following information will help you with this assignment.

A thesis statement should clearly focus on the idea in your limited topic. It should not be so vague that your readers do not know what idea you are developing or should not contain so many ideas that you provide enough suggestions for many papers. A thesis statement should be specific, limited, and precise. It should be a complete sentence with both a **subject** and a **predicate**. What you are writing about (the subject) should be linked to what you want to say about it (the predicate).

After you read Ben's thesis statement, write your own.

Ben's Thesis Statement

Subject	Predicate
Racquetball	**is an easily learned game that provides exercise and fun.**

Now that you have composed a workable thesis statement that controls and limits your main idea, you can begin your first draft. As you write your first draft, you may find that more significant ideas emerge. If you discover a new insight or approach to your topic, use it as the basis for another piece of writing and begin the prewriting process again. Never dismiss good ideas.

Drafting Process

1. Whereas you may receive a great deal of help during your prewriting and revising stages, you will draft your piece of writing alone. The more familiar you become with the contents of this book, the easier your drafting stage will become. Many chapters of the book will help you improve your organization, style, and sentence structure. Still others will help you choose vocabulary to reflect the right meaning and exact slant you want.

2. Throughout the drafting stage, keep your writing variables in front of you as you write. Stick to your limited topic, write to your audience,

consider the situation, keep your purpose clear, maintain your format, and keep your voice and point of view consistent.

3. Include a version of your thesis statement—your main idea—in your draft. For this assignment, you might like to present your main idea near the beginning of your paper. For future assignments, you should study Chapter 24 for other ways of placing thesis statements effectively.

4. Think about ways of organizing the information that supports your thesis statement. Chapter 25 presents many methods of organization. Use a method that is most appropriate to your material.

5. As you write, be careful to make your thoughts clear to your audience. Present details to help your readers see what you see and feel what you feel.

6. Conclude your piece by summing up your main idea in a way that you think will interest your readers.

7. Write a clean, double-spaced draft with an appropriate title. This draft will be used in an editing session.

Ben's first draft is on page 12. As you read it, think about what you would suggest to help him revise his paragraph.

**Ben's Variables
And Thesis Statement**

Broad topic: playing racquetball

Limited topic: benefits of playing racquetball

Audience: Classmates who have never played racquetball. Real. I intend to let them read it.

Purpose: to persuade them to play racquetball

Format: self-contained paragraph

Voice: my own

Situation: I am a good racquetball player. I enjoy the sport and like my classmates. They have never seen a racquetball game, let alone played one. Because I am informed about my topic and my readers are uninformed, I should avoid technical terms (kill shot, lob, love, etc.) and use clear, general terms. Because my readers are my peers, I should use a style that appeals to them—informal language and fairly short sentences.

Point of view: I must speak with confidence and authority, but I must also sound friendly and inviting. I want my audience to think I am writing directly to them. Therefore, I will use second person (you) whenever possible.

Thesis statement: Racquetball is an easily learned game that provides exercise and fun.

Ben's First Draft

Play Racquetball

Everyone should exercise, and if you can have fun at the same time, it would give you an extra bonus. Racquetball is an easily learned game that provides exercise and fun. It is also a relatively new court game. So, if you feel out of sorts or depressed, play a game of racquetball every three or four days. Do you know how to play squash or handball? Racquetball is slower than squash, but faster than handball. But racquetball is easier to learn to play than either squash or handball. Most beginning players of racquetball need no more than one lesson to learn how to play. From then on, you'll be able to play, exercise, and have fun learning how to perfect your technique. Then you'll be able to kill a shot in the corners, take a ball off the back wall, slam one from the back wall to the front, in fact, theirs nothing you won't try. Racquetball fanatics say "Racquetball takes minutes to learn, but a lifetime to perfect".

Editing and Revising Process

Professional writers depend on their editors to help them in the revising process. You can use your peers and your teacher for this important step. Modern research shows that when students learn to edit each other's work, their own writing improves significantly.

Editing:

If you have never engaged in a peer-editing session, this introductory assignment is an ideal opportunity for you to learn the basics of editing someone else's writing.

1. Form a peer group of three. Group members will then exchange completed drafts and lists of writing variables. When you edit another group member's draft, first read it quickly to get a sense of the writing variables and content.
2. Read the draft again. This time write your reactions directly on the paper. To help you make worthwhile comments, keep in mind all the writing variables. For example, a composition intended for a twelve-year-old should be very different from one addressed to a senator.
3. Whenever appropriate, use the proofreader's symbols on pages 364–366. They provide editors and writers with a common language and help speed up the editing process.
4. While editing, don't forget to praise what you like about the writing.
5. Check the organization of the paper to make sure that the meaning is clear. If it is not clear, make suggestions for adding, deleting, changing, or moving sentences or paragraphs. You may feel reluctant to suggest major changes, but such suggestions are far more helpful than pointing out a few spelling or punctuation errors.
6. Consider the following questions while editing your peer's composition. When appropriate, write your comments on the paper.

   a) What do you like least about the paper? What do you think the writer can do about it? (Even if you do not know how to correct a problem, telling a writer that you became confused may be extremely helpful. By talking it through after the editing session, the writer and editor can suggest possible revisions.
   b) Are there any problems with spelling, punctuation, capitalization, or sentence structure? Correct any error you see or just comment, "I don't think this is right. How about checking it?"
   c) Do the sentences flow smoothly and logically from one to the other? If not, offer as much help as you can.

14 WRITING: PROCESS TO PRODUCT

    d) Are there enough connecting or transitional words to keep the reader on track? (Are there too many? Should some be deleted?)

    e) Is the title interesting?

When you have edited one paper from your peer group, you should read and edit the other papers. Read the previous editor's comments as well. Feel free to agree or disagree with those comments as well as to add your own.

Read below what two of Ben's peers wrote about his paper. Do you agree or disagree with their comments? What would you have said?

Ben's First Draft and His Peer Editors' Comments

Play Racquetball

Everyone should exercise, and if you can have fun at the same time, it would give you an extra bonus. Racquetball is an easily learned game that provides exercise and fun. It is also a relatively new court game. So, if you feel out of sorts or depressed, play a game of racquetball every three or four days. Do you know how to play squash or handball? Racquetball is slower than squash, but faster than handball. But racquetball is easier to learn to play than either squash or handball. Most beginning players of racquetball need no more than one lesson to learn how to play. From then on, you'll be able to play, exercise, and have fun learning how to perfect your technique. Then you'll be able to kill a shot in the corners, take a ball off the back wall, slam one from the back wall to the front, in fact, theirs nothing you won't try. Racquetball fanatics say "Racquetball takes minutes to learn, but a lifetime to perfect."

Peer editor comments (left margin):
There's something wrong here. Is "it," with "should," and "would"?

I think your thesis is good but I think you should give more details.

Couldn't you join these sentences?

You have shifted your subjects. Stick to "you."

I think I know how to do this, but will the readers?

Isn't that "hit hard"?

I think this is a pretty good paragraph. When you revise it, I would like to see it again.

Peer editor comments (right margin):
Change your title. I agree — make it stronger.

I think the problem is with "Everyone" & "you." Stick to "you."

Isn't it spelled rackitball? No, he's right.

Isn't that expensive?

Will your audience know what this means?

I don't think this is right. Shouldn't one be a semicolon?

After reading this I don't know anything about racquetball. Shouldn't I know more than it's easy to learn and moderately fast? I'd like to see what you do to make it better.

INTRODUCTORY ASSIGNMENT   15

Revising:

Once you have had your first draft edited by two peer editors, read the comments. If there is anything you do not understand or agree with, talk to your peers so that you can revise your paper before you submit it to your teacher/editor. How much you revise will depend not only on how helpful your peers have been but on how many of their suggestions you decide to follow. Remember, the responsibility to accept or reject your peer editors' suggestions is always yours.

See Ben's revision, along with his teacher/editor's comments below. What changes has he made? How will his teacher/editor's comments improve his composition?

Ben's Revision and His Teacher/Editor's Comments

Racquetball Mania — *Good title*

Racquetball is an easily learned game that provides exercise and fun. A game of racquetball maybe exactly what the doctor ordered for those who feel out of sorts or depressed. Racquetball is faster than handball and slower than squash, but it is easier than both to learn. If you have never played, no more then one lesson will be necessary. From then on players will be able to play, exercise, and have fun perfecting their technique. After only a few games, most players find themselves starting to play the corners, take a ball off the back wall, and slam one from the back wall to the front; in fact, there's nothing they won't try. Enthusiasts say that racquetball takes minutes to learn but a lifetime to perfect. Why not try it?

Teacher's margin comments:
- Should you indicate how racquetball helps depression?
- You have shifted your point of view from 3rd person to 2nd and then back to 3rd.
- how?
- Try putting this into direct quotation.
- Reword and start sentence with "Faster" to avoid overuse of "is."
- use active voice instead of passive voice.
- Try "will not"
- *Good ending.* Why not start your paragraph with a question too?

I think your audience will be interested in trying a game of racquetball

Sometimes your teacher may ask you to revise again. This can be frustrating, especially if you have already rewritten your paper several times. But for all good writers, *writing means rewriting*. If your editors are willing to take the time to edit your work, be thankful and consider their comments.

Now, prepare your final draft, making it a polished product. When you make your final revision, the decision of whether to accept or reject your editors' suggestions rests with you. But remember, their comments were offered so that your intended reader will understand and have a positive reaction to your writing.

Read Ben's final draft below that he posted on his classroom bulletin board. (This is one way to publish your work—to present it to a final reader.) After you have completed the final draft of your own paper, think about how you would answer the questions that follow Ben's final draft (on page 17). Then give your final draft to your intended audience.

Ben's Final Product

Racquetball Mania

Who says exercise can't be fun? Racquetball is an easily learned game that provides exercise and fun. A game of racquetball every three or four days may be exactly what you need if you feel out of sorts or depressed. Faster than handball, slower than squash, racquetball is easier to learn than both. Most beginning players need no more than one lesson. From then on, you'll be able to play, exercise, and have fun perfecting your technique. After only a few games, you will find yourself hitting the ball into the corners, taking a ricocheting ball off the back wall, and slamming one from the back wall to the front. In fact, there's nothing you will not try. Enthusiasts say, "Racquetball takes minutes to learn, but a lifetime to perfect." Why not try it?

For Discussion

1. If you have never played racquetball, you could be the intended reader for Ben's paragraph. After reading it, would you want to learn how to play? Explain.
2. If you already know how to play racquetball, what else do you think Ben should have included in his paragraph? What do you think he should have deleted? Why?
3. What help has Ben received from his peer editors and teacher/editor? As a result of this help, how have his thesis statement and his supporting details changed?
4. How did your peers help you revise your paper? How did your teacher help you?
5. Now that you have completed your assignment, do you feel you are developing your own writing process so that you can approach future writing assignments with greater confidence? Explain.

"What release to write so that one forgets oneself, forgets one's companion, forgets where one is. . . ."

ANNE MORROW LINDBERG

Assignments

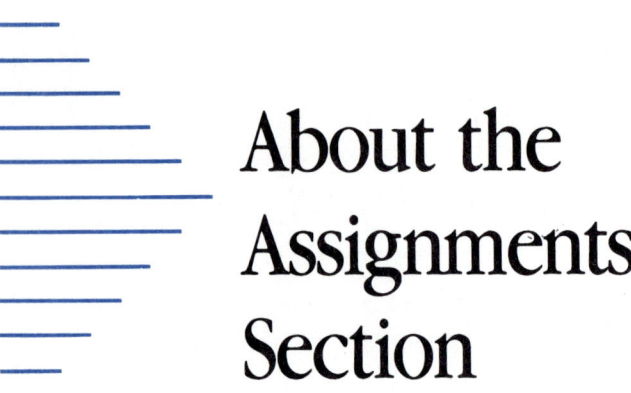

About the Assignments Section

The assignments in this section are designed to meet a variety of needs. You and your teacher can select those that are useful to you.

Each assignment chapter contains suggestions for the steps of the writing process—prewriting, drafting, and editing and revising. Each chapter also contains products—compositions written by students, teachers, and professional writers. You are encouraged to study these products—before, during, and after you do your own piece of writing. Each assignment

- a) stresses prewriting, drafting, and revising
- b) promotes peer editor and teacher/editor feedback
- c) encourages you to think about your writing variables *before* you write
- d) encourages you to write honestly, thoroughly, and emphatically

Use the following suggestions when you give your work to your peer editors or teacher/editor.

- a) On a separate piece of paper, include your list of writing variables to assist your editors in their feedback sessions.
- b) Leave enough room on your composition for your editors to write any additions, instructions, or suggestions for a further rewrite.
- c) The final piece of writing should be a polished copy that you can give to your intended reader.

1 Narrative Paragraph

There are many times when you will want to tell a story. Narration is, therefore, a form of writing you will use frequently. A narrative may be based on a real or an imaginary experience. In both cases, it is an account of events, told so that the reader shares the experience.

ASSIGNMENT ▶ In a narrative paragraph of not more than 200 words, tell about an incident that happened to you.

Prewriting Process

1. For your first narrative paragraph, choose an amusing, an exciting, a frightening, or a significant experience that you remember well. Good narrative writing brings an incident to life for your readers through the use of convincing detail. For this reason, it is usually easier to write a successful narrative about something that you have experienced.

2. Do not choose a long, involved incident. Remember: You are limited to 200 words.

3. You may want to choose an incident that involves **conflict**, a physical or mental struggle against something or someone. Conflict can be a physical struggle, a battle of wits with another person, a struggle with nature or society, or even a struggle within yourself. It is possible for a narrative to have more than one conflict. For example, your narrative might involve an argument with a relative (conflict with another person), may take place during a snowstorm (conflict with nature), and

may also involve your attempt to control feelings of anger (conflict within yourself).

4. If you have difficulty thinking of a topic, consider one of the following:

your proudest, happiest, or saddest moment
a triumph or failure
your most embarrassing mistake
a "first," such as your first date, first dance, or first job interview
a "last," such as your last date with someone, a final farewell, or the last day of school
a disaster, such as a fire, an accident, a flood, or a storm
an argument with someone
a difficult decision

5. After choosing a broad topic, narrow it to a workable limited topic. Establish your other writing variables: purpose, audience, and so on. (For more about these variables, see pages 5–8.) If your narration is to be part of a larger work, such as a letter, specify the larger format.

6. While listing your writing variables, spend time on a few brainstorming sessions, by yourself or with your peers in order to generate worthwhile ideas and appropriate supporting details. The following brainstorming techniques from Chapter 23 are particularly useful for narratives: Experience/Write, Senses Cluster, Positive/Negative/Neutral Pigeonholes, Positive Cluster, Negative Cluster, Pentad, and possibly the Cause-and-Effect Flowchart.

7. Move to the drafting process only when you are confident that you have produced sufficient material during your prewriting process.

Drafting Process

1. Your paragraph should have a **beginning**, a **middle**, and an **end**. Your beginning should capture your reader's interest. Which of these opening sentences encourage you to continue reading a narrative? Why?

I was sure the customs officer could hear my heart pounding in my chest as she opened my suitcase.

The band started to play, and then I saw her coming toward me from across the room.

"He's dead!" she kept screaming. "Your pet frog is dead!"

Your middle should relate events in a clear order—usually chronological (the order in which they happened). Vivid details should bring these events to life for your reader.

Your end should satisfy your reader by fitting well with the rest of your narrative. Your audience must not feel that your narrative has been a waste of time. Do you find any of the following endings unsatisfactory? Explain why or why not.

I counted my cash. I had enough.

. . . cautiously I placed one foot in front of the other. A stone fell, plummeting to the base of the canyon far below. My foot slipped. I fell. Down, down I plunged. Suddenly I awoke, safe and sound in my bed.

I waited impatiently for my mother's answer. Finally it came: "Yes."

2. Most narratives contain a **climax.** Climax has been defined as the decisive moment and the turning point of a narrative. Create suspense by delaying the turning point. You can do this through description and dialogue (the words the characters in your narrative speak). Make sure your description and dialogue contribute to the narrative's story line, or you may lose the story line—and your reader.

3. Use action, reaction, and dialogue to help your reader experience the incident. Describe facial expressions to capture emotional reactions. (If possible, use some of the actual words that were spoken during the incident.)

Showing what happened is much more effective than simply telling. Notice the difference between showing and telling in the following two versions of the same incident.

Telling

The coach had a bumpy trip over the stones on the rocky beach. Then it forded the river to the opposite shore.

Showing

In the late afternoon we came to the edge of a river and turned to follow its course on a wide rocky beach. The crunching of the wheels over the stones and the lurching of the coach gave us the worst shaking of the trip. When the driver found the ford, he reined the mules into it, and they began to pull slowly through the smooth shallow water. Feeling their way, they breasted the current until it reached above the hubs of the wheels, as I could see by craning my neck out of the window. When it lapped the floor of the compartment, the lady whispered, "Ave Maria Purisima." With the deepest part of the ford behind us, we drove toward the opposite shore until the mules began to pull up the slope on the other side.

Ernesto Galarza, Barrio Boy

4. Some writers "stretch" the truth to improve their narratives, a quite acceptable practice. You may want to invent part of your narrative instead of simply sticking to what really happened. If so, choose convincing details that will make what you invent believable. You do not want to lose your reader's belief—and attention.

5. When you have completed your draft, self-edit your narrative by using the four checklists on pages 271–274. If you need to write another draft, do so. Then you will be ready to have your paper edited by others.

Editing and Revising Process

When your peers edit your narrative, they can apply the four checklists on pages 271–274 as well as the following specific questions.

1. Is there anything in the narrative that you think should be altered, bearing in mind the writer's audience, purpose, format, voice, and situation?

2. Is the story interesting? Is there conflict? Is there a climax? Does the first sentence capture the reader's interest? Is the final sentence satisfying to the reader?

3. Is the story believable? If not, would dialogue and description help the story?

4. Is the sequence of events clear? Are there details that do not contribute to the narrative and should be eliminated? Are all important details included?

5. Are the point of view and verb tense clear and consistent? For example, writers who tell narratives in the first person (I) should not switch to the second person (you) or the third person (he or she). Writers using past-tense verbs should not suddenly switch to present- or future-tense verbs.

6. Do the writer's verbs give a strong sense of action? Active verbs give a much stronger sense of action than passive verbs do. For example, *My car crashed into the lamppost* is stronger than *The lamppost was crashed into by my car.*

When your peers have edited your paper, and you have taken their suggestions into consideration, revise it. Present a clean copy to your teacher for a final editing session.

Write the final version of your narrative. Proofread it for spelling, grammar, word usage, and punctuation. Then publish your narrative by giving it to its intended audience.

Products

A New Life
by Anne Baxter

What luxury, I thought, kneading my bare shoulder blades into the sandy bank. The bank slanted sharply to the smooth, silent river, and I lay on my back upside down, like a cat in the sun. Better watch it, you'll burn, you're white as a grub. The blood began to pound in my head. I kicked my legs and sat up, brushing the sand off my back and out of my hair, and swiveled on my bikini briefs to face the river. It flowed by like cooling molten glass. No wider than Wilshire Boulevard, but still Australia's largest river. I listened to birds high in the eucalyptus trees and realized how much Australia smelled and looked like parts of California. Among other things, they shared eucalyptus trees. Only here they were called gum trees. I stood up groggily and stretched. What time was it? Edwina said they'd come back and pick me up at half-past four. I remembered their amazement at my wanting to be alone on the banks of the Murray River. Like too many people, they thought making a movie was a kind of game. They certainly had no idea what a sweat this one had been. Reaching high, I plucked a frosty blue, sickle-shaped leaf and crushed it. It turned green and sticky. I sniffed it deeply and felt a shocking bite of pungence up my nostrils. I threw it in the river, grabbed my nose in pain, and sneezed. Stickybeak, I thought, smiling at a marvelous Australian word for someone nosy, and walked back to my patch of sand and sun.

The Sudden End of My Brief Career
by Ben Warshawski, student

My career as a rock star began and ended in two weeks. Three of us called ourselves the BDBs, after the initials of our first names. We rehearsed in my family's garage. I was lead guitar and singer, Dick Banks was second guitar, and Barbi Sanchez handled the drums. We were not popular with the neighbors. One evening at dinner, my father told me there had been complaints about the noise. I asked, "Do you want to stand in the way of my career?" He looked as if I had put rotten meat on his plate but said nothing. Then, on a rainy Saturday afternoon, the police came. They told us someone had called in to report a cat being tortured. (I suspect that "someone" was my dad, but I can't prove it.) Barbi gave me a thoughtful look. She said slowly, "You know, Ben, you do kinda sound like a cat in pain. . . ." Dick avoided meeting my eyes. That was the end of the BDBs. Barbi and Dick are now part of a new band. As for me, I still have my guitar—and my memories of show business.

The Weekend Chore
by Keith W. Wagner, student

I bounced down the grassy slope of our lawn toward the sun-bleached dock where our red canoe rested. Putting my towel down, I heaved the canoe into the murky water. I grabbed my checkerboard towel, and the paddles, and cautiously stepped into the bow. The morning wind was bitter as I started my journey across the lake to the club. Digging harder with the paddle, I moved out quickly. About twenty yards out I stopped to rest, but by the time I started again I had lost a good five feet of headway. Resolutely I sunk the paddle deeper to get a better pull against the miserable east wind. "Almost there," I said to myself as the bow entered the small country club cove. I expertly maneuvered the canoe next to a sixteen-foot brown and white Cobalt inboard that would have made this trip a breeze. That was how, when I was ten years old, I began my real chore: swimming class and another day in that frigid pool.

Queen of the Mountain
by Janelle McGrath, student

The sun was just peeking around the clouds, and it cast its first rays through our window in my first-period class. It had just stopped raining, and the leaves held droplets of water; the air was fresh and tingly, and the mudholes next to the walkways were in their prime. Mrs. Masterjohn, my teacher, gave the signal and we rushed excitedly to our hats and coats, ran outside, and lined up at the door of the shack where all of our bikes, Tonka toys, shovels and pails, and other outside toys were kept. When Mrs. Masterjohn opened the shack door, we rushed in and scrambled for our favorite toys. I chose a shiny red tricycle. Laboriously I pulled it out of the shack and passed the crowd of my classmates onto the wet grass. After pedaling over the bumps and holes I became bored and looked around for a bigger thrill. I eyed the smooth cement path that flowed down the hill, hopped off my tricycle and then painstakingly pushed it up. At the top I was "Queen of the Mountain." I gave myself a shove and off I sped down the hill, really flying now! My hair flipped with the wind around my face. Faster and faster the wheels spun, spitting the water that lay on the pavement out like a rooster's tail. Splat! The front wheel smacked the water in a small hole in the cement. The tricycle was thrown out of control and it sent me sailing through the air into a soft, squishy mud puddle! The cool mud oozed between my fingers and started crawling up the leg of my pants. With panic in her eyes, Mrs. Masterjohn rushed over to me and said, "Oh, Janelle, are you all right?" I told her that I was just fine, but she made me lie as still as a statue to see if I had broken anything. I tried to convince her that I was fine and that I actually enjoyed sitting in the mud. After she was sure that I would live, she insisted that I go and put on the clean clothes that she always kept for emergencies. Then I was ready to go outside and tackle that hill again.

Shopping
by Shirley Friesen, student

Only five years old, I am fascinated by this place. The ceilings are as high as the sky, and the aisles are wider than the street near my house. I cling to mommy's coattails so that she won't get lost as I walk along, admiring all the packages that line the shelves. When she stops for a moment, I let go of her to pick up a particularly intriguing cereal box. When I look up, to my horror, she is lost! I race up and down the aisles, screaming her name at the top of my lungs: "Mommy!" Out of breath, I stop running, and a smiling lady with snowy white shoes approaches me. Then gently taking my hand, she guides me to a room at the back of the store. The friendly lady sets me down, gives me some candy, and assures me that someone will find my mother in no time. After polishing off the last candy, I start thinking about mother again. It seems like hours now since we've been apart! No sooner have I finished that thought than the door swings open and there she is. I am so relieved I cry all the way home. You can be sure it will be a long time before I take my mother to the supermarket again!

For Discussion

A New Life

1. Anne Baxter was a Hollywood film star who went to live on a sheep ranch in Australia. "A New Life" is the first paragraph of her book *Intermission*, about her experiences in Australia. What details in the paragraph indicate that this is the beginning of a longer piece of writing?
2. What sentences compare or contrast Anne Baxter's old life with her new one?
3. Does this paragraph make you want to read the rest of the book? Explain.

The Sudden End of My Brief Career

1. Does this narrative have a beginning, a middle, and an end? If so, what are they? Do you think the beginning and end are effective? Why or why not?
2. What conflict is involved? Is there more than one? If so, explain.
3. What is the climax of this story?

4. Voice reveals what kind of person the writer is. What do you find out about the writer of "The Sudden End of My Brief Career"? Find sentences to support your answer.
5. Provide a set of writer's variables for this narrative. (See page 2.) Then compare your set with the sets of other students to see who has composed the best one.

The Weekend Chore

1. What mood does this paragraph create? What details help create the mood?
2. What details help make this narrative paragraph a vivid experience?
3. Is the ending expected or unexpected? Explain. Why do you think Keith Wagner did not reveal the real weekend chore until the end of the paragraph?

Queen of the Mountain

1. Do you think this narrative paragraph has a good beginning and ending? Defend your answer.
2. In your opinion, what words and details are especially vivid?

Shopping

1. The writer of "Shopping" does not write in her own voice. She assumes a persona, herself when she was five years old. (For more about voice and persona, see pages 6–7.) Part of the fun of this narrative lies in the difference between what a five-year-old girl perceives and thinks and what the audience perceives. Such a difference is called **irony**. Find at least two examples of irony in the narrative.
2. Are there any words that do not fit the five-year-old persona? If so, what are they?
3. Most narratives are in the past tense. Why do you think this writer has decided to use the present tense? Is it effective? Give reasons to support your answer.

2 Descriptive Paragraph

Description has been called a picture in words. In writing description, you re-create a scene or person by putting in words what you have experienced through your senses. Even though you may not often write purely descriptive compositions, there will be many opportunities to include descriptive elements in all other types of writing.

ASSIGNMENT ▶ In a descriptive paragraph of no more than 150 words, create a word picture of a person, place, or thing.

Prewriting Process

1. Make a list of people, places, and things that you remember vividly. Your list may include everything from a single small object to a vast scene—for example:

> the face of a friend or relative
> your face
> something you would like to own
> your room at home
> a classroom
> a building you find interesting
> the main street in your city or town
> a crowd scene at a football game
> a waterfall or other natural object

DESCRIPTIVE PARAGRAPH **31**

2. Choose one possibility from your list and explore it, using some of the following techniques.

a) Think about what you associate with your topic. List words and phrases that describe what you see, hear, smell, touch, and/or taste.

b) Assume an artist is painting a picture of the person, place, or thing you have chosen. What feature would the artist highlight? Why? How can you highlight that feature in your writing?

c) Use comparisons, even farfetched ones. How is the topic of your description like a watermelon, a sharp knife, a cushion, or some other object?

d) Determine where you are in relation to the person, place, or thing. Are you on the same level? Are you above or below it? Are you moving through a scene as a television camera does? Are you viewing it through binoculars?

3. While you select your descriptive details, make sure you consider all your writing variables. Consider your audience, for example. You would not describe a girlfriend or boyfriend to your parents in the same way you would describe that person to a friend. Consider format. Will your description be a separate paragraph or part of a longer piece of writing, such as a biology report, a friendly letter, or an autobiography?

4. Once you have collected enough supporting details, limit your topic and write your thesis statement. Then you will be ready to draft your descriptive paragraph.

Drafting Process

1. Consider the **overall impression** you wish to create, and select your details accordingly. Do you want your reader to like the subject of your description? Dislike? Be frightened? Amused? Good writers select details to get a certain reaction from the reader. They also choose words with **connotations**, or associations, that create a single overall impression. The word *slender*, for example, creates a different impression than the word *scrawny* does, even though both words mean "thin."

2. To organize a description of a scene, start at one point and proceed in an orderly direction. You might go from top to bottom or from near to far. Do not jump from one point to another without any reason.

3. Choose words that will appeal to your reader's senses. What words in these sentences enable the reader to see, hear, or smell the subject?

The red-faced infant howled for attention.

The odors of perspiration and perfume mingled in the theater.

4. A simile or a metaphor (a stated or an implied comparison of unlike things) can breathe new life into even the stalest subject. What comparisons do the following sentences make?

Raking furiously, the gardener raised the cherry blossom petals in miniature snow flurries.

Like a hawk, the salesperson swooped down upon the little man who had just come into the store.

5. Self-edit your descriptive paragraph using the four checklists in Chapter 28. Then give it to your peers to edit.

Editing and Revising Process

To make use of peer-editing, use one of the methods suggested in Chapter 28. In addition, consider the following to help you revise.

1. Does the paragraph fulfill the writing variables? For example, is the description appropriate for its intended purpose and audience?

2. What overall mood or impression does the paragraph try to create? Do the words create the picture you want your reader to see?

3. To how many senses does the paragraph appeal? Which ones does it appeal to most effectively? To which other senses could the paragraph appeal?

4. Does the choice of words add to the total effect? Should you add, delete, or substitute any words? Should you, for example, substitute more precise words? (Words such as *actually*, *really*, or *quite* can often be cut to make the writing more effective.)

5. Do the sentences have variety and emphasis?

6. After you have revised your description using your peer editors' suggestions, give it to your teacher/editor.

7. When you have revised again and just before your intended reader sees your description, read it and close your eyes. Do the words paint the exact picture you want your audience to see? Do they also bring to mind the sounds, smells, tastes, and tactile sensations you want your audience to imagine? If they do not, revise as necessary.

Products

A *Revolucionario*
by Ernesto Galarza

By the light of the candle I saw a tall figure in a jacket with metal buttons, riding pants, and leather puttees. He wore a neck scarf with a ring above the knot, and around the waist two belts, one for his pants and the other for the holster and pistol. His hair was black and rumpled, as black as the droopy mustache over his lips. In one hand he held the bridle of his horse, standing behind him in the shadows; in the other, a heavy peaked hat. In the dim light and dusty uniform he was a tired, slouching *revolucionario*.

The Little Black Box
by Raymond Schow, student

As I walked into my room, something caught my eye. It was a little black box on the floor by my dresser. It wasn't there before. It was black and about nine inches long, six inches wide, and five inches high. It was made entirely of black shiny plastic except for its bottom. That was a grayish metal plate attached to the plastic. From the box ran a black cord with a white sticker on it saying "WARNING." The cord ended in a little square plug. Wanting to see what the box would do, I picked up the cord and plugged it into an outlet. From the box came a humming noise, and a little red light lit up on its side. A loud sound at first, it changed to a steady low hummmmm—barely noticeable. I wondered what it was. Finally, I remembered. It was a pest killer. It sent out sound waves that killed 'em dead.

This Is All I Need
by Young-Mi Song, student

The five Loverboy members are at the head of my bed, smiling their blank "Hurry up and take the picture" smile. Next to that wall is Def Leppard [a rock band] on stage. Joe Elliot wears a sneer on his face, and the other members are picking away on their guitars. Then I see shelves full of my dear childhood friends and special mementos. They smile back at me, reminding me of the times we've shared. Underneath my friends are paperback books all neatly lined up from largest to smallest. Below, my usual mess: notebook papers and school books strewn across the desk top. Across the room from my desk is my dresser. Silly pictures of my best friend and me taken at the Woolworth picture booth are sticking out of the mirror. Little bottles of perfume are arranged in my special way—that is, in the order that I received them. (My record collection is also arranged in that way.) My socks are littered across the top. And I, lying in my bed, underneath the pink rose spread, listen to the radio on top of the bed stand. This is all I need.

Moving In
by Chris Moffat, student

Finally, the packing boxes are empty. Worn and beaten by the long, hard journey, they sit in a corner of the porch, waiting for a garbage truck to arrive and put them out of their misery. The belongings that lived inside those boxes are now unpacked and strewn across the floor of the room that is to be mine. Plain and square, it does not feel like my room. Its four walls, painted white, have no character, just cold emptiness. Familiar bits of junk gladly liberated from the boxes seem so out of place, so foreign to this bland room. Nothing lives here; not even ants creep along the floor. Even plants are absent from the windowsill, so how can I be expected to survive? The absence of color haunts me. How can I even try to sleep, knowing those four blank walls loom above, staring down at me, waiting for me to claim them? Tomorrow morning I have a huge task before me—to make this place my home!

Watson

by Babs Eddie, student

May 6

Dear Jim,

    I suddenly realized that two years ago today you gave me Watson. He must also know that today is a special day.

    With head and tail saluting the sun, Watson is off on his morning stroll. His rich, sable brown coat glistens with each controlled movement. Everyone takes notice. Throughout the tour of his domain Watson is well aware of his audience, for nothing escapes his alert, golden eyes. As I watch him strutting homeward, his inspection complete, I can't help but think that from the tip of his nose to the tip of his tail, Watson is an aristocrat.

    Thank you for Watson.

Babs

For Discussion

A *Revolucionario*

1. This description is a paragraph from *Barrio Boy*, Ernesto Galarza's book about his boyhood days. In it he explains that a *revolucionario* was a soldier in Mexico's revolutionary army. What details help you see the soldier?
2. What words and phrases in the paragraph do you think are particularly effective in creating word pictures?
3. Does this paragraph create an overall impression? If so, what is it?

The Little Black Box

1. Before reading the last two sentences of this paragraph, were you able to figure out what the black box was? What details provide clues about the box?
2. If you were to write a description of something ordinary so as to make it seem unusual, how would you go about it? What information would you reveal and not reveal? What kinds of details might you include?
3. Do you think that Raymond Schow, the writer of "The Little Black Box," has succeeded in making something ordinary seem unusual? If so, how?

This Is All I Need

1. What mood does this description create? How is it created?
2. In what order are the details of the description arranged? (For a discussion of different kinds of order, see pages 252–256.)

Moving In

1. What impression of the room do you get from this description?
2. To what senses does the writer appeal?
3. What implied comparisons does the writer make? What do they add to the description?
4. Besides describing a room, what does the paragraph express?

Watson

1. The second paragraph of this letter to a friend is a description. Does the description fit in with the writer's larger format? Why or why not?
2. What kind of animal is Watson? How do you know?
3. What one word would you use to describe Watson? What details in the description support your answer?
4. What is the purpose of the letter? What is the purpose of the descriptive paragraph?

3 Expository Paragraph

Exposition involves the presentation of information, ideas, and opinions. As a student, you will probably be using exposition more than any other kind of writing. You will often find yourself having to explain something, whether it is a chemistry experiment, the causes of a historical event, an insight into a short story or poem, or your opinion on an issue that concerns you.

So that you will not confuse exposition with narration or description, remember that narration tells a story and description is a picture in words. Exposition informs or presents an opinion. Notice the difference.

Narration:	Last night I got lost in the snow.
Description:	Under a microscope, a snowflake looks like a glittering gem.
Exposition:	When the temperature is lower than zero Celsius, water vapor in the air turns to snow.
Exposition:	Snowball fights on school grounds can lead to injuries and should be banned.

ASSIGNMENT ▶ In an expository paragraph of not more than 200 words, either explain something you know well or explain your opinion about an issue you think is important.

Prewriting Process

1. Choose a topic that is within your range of experience or that you can easily research. Good exposition relies on supporting material derived

from personal experience or from knowledge (your own or knowledge you can readily locate).

 2. Narrow your broad topic to a limited topic. Then develop a thesis statement. (For more about thesis statements, see page 10.) Here is how one broad topic was narrowed.

education
↓
high school
↓
graduation
↓
Every high-school student should graduate.

Here are some broad topics to consider. What limited topics and thesis statements do they suggest to you? (If you have difficulty in limiting these topics, see Chapter 24.)

| American history | weather | transportation |
| sports | travel | communication |

 As you narrow your own topic, you may come up with several possible thesis statements. Here are two thesis statements derived from the broad topic of education. Can you think of others?

No one should be compelled to go to school.

A high-school diploma increases your choices when you leave school.

 3. Here are three suggestions to consider when you limit your topic and write a thesis statement for this assignment:

> **a)** *Choose a limited topic that is suitable for the paragraph.* A topic that interests you might fill several books, or it might be so limited that you can say everything about it in a single sentence. Make sure that your limited topic is appropriate for a single paragraph of not more than 200 words. In your opinion, which of the following thesis statements would be most suitable for a single paragraph? Why?

Throughout the ages, actors have been given great respect by some but have been regarded as the lowest form of humanity by others.

Acting on stage is quite different from acting before a camera.

There are many fine actors performing on the stage and in films.

> **b)** *Choose a limited topic about which you can write with accuracy.* If you write about a topic you do not know well or about which you

are unable to gather accurate information, your reader will soon discover your ignorance. Which one of the following thesis statements sounds as if it came from a personal experience? Why?

Wild animals are hostile to human intruders.

You should not camp in a secluded part of a national park where grizzlies roam freely.

Grizzly bears are quite different from polar bears.

c) *Choose a limited topic that is important to you.* If you care about your limited topic, you will have a much better chance of arousing your reader's interest. Also, you will find that you have a great deal to say. Your problem will be what to leave out, not what to include—a very comfortable position for a writer. Which of the following thesis statements will probably lead to specific writing? Why?

Students should have a voice in determining the content of a course.

High schools today are very different from high schools fifty years ago.

All students should read every day.

4. If you are having difficulty finding a topic, think about the following statements. Choose one with which you agree or disagree. Consider whether the statement would lead to a good topic for an expository paragraph that presents an opinion.

No one under eighteen should be allowed a driver's license.

Teenagers should not hitchhike.

Spanish should be taught from kindergarten through grade 12.

An untidy room indicates an untidy mind.

All high-school sports teams should include both girls and boys.

All high-school graduates should know how to type.

Smoking should be banned from all public places.

All Americans should be compelled to serve in the armed forces.

5. Once you have settled on a limited topic, consider your other writing variables. If you write for a real *purpose* to a real *audience,* your writing process will no longer be simply an exercise to keep you busy. Write for members of a club to which you belong, for the purpose of convincing them to take a particular action. Write for the readers of a local newspaper to inform them about the history of a local landmark. Present an opinion on an issue about which you have strong feelings to any reader (or group of readers) you choose.

Decide also what your *format* will be. (Your paragraph can be part of a larger piece of writing, a letter or an essay, or it can be self-contained.) Decide what *voice* you will use. (If you write a letter to a newspaper about a local landmark, for example, you can use your own voice or adopt the persona of a citizen who has lived near the landmark for fifty years.)

6. Complete your prewriting process by going through two or three of the brainstorming techniques presented in Chapter 23. The following techniques are especially useful for expository paragraphs presenting information: Classification/Division Flowcharts, Aristotle's Topics, and Newspaper Reporter's Questions. If your topic involves an opinion, you will find the following brainstorming techniques useful: Positive/Negative/Neutral Pigeonholes, Positive Cluster, Negative Cluster, Pro/Con Ladders, and Newspaper Reporter's Questions.

Drafting Process

1. As you write, keep in mind your purpose in writing. Be aware of exactly what you are trying to do and why.

2. Keep your audience in mind. You would not write in exactly the same way to an old family friend, the other students in your class, or the readers of a newspaper.

3. For your first expository paragraph, it may be useful for you to adopt the following structure: **introduction, development, conclusion**.

Introduction. The first few sentences of your expository paragraph should capture your reader's attention, announce your limited topic, and indicate your attitude toward it. In some cases, you can do all three in one sentence, composing a thesis statement that arouses interest, states the topic, and asserts or suggests an opinion. In other cases you might have to write more than one sentence, perhaps one to arouse interest and another to serve as a thesis statement. (Ways to begin a piece of writing are discussed in detail in Chapter 25.)

Is each of the following a good introduction? Explain.

Is grade 12 worth it? What is the use of spending another year in classrooms with teachers and books when I could be making my way in the world? What is it about a high-school diploma that would make me do all that work?

There are probably half a dozen ways to bring Lake Erie back to life. To me, the most important one is to stop the dumping of chemicals now.

I am going to explain what I think would eliminate wars.

Development. You must back up your thesis statement with supporting evidence. Decide which kinds of support you should use; **facts**, **examples**, and **reasons** are three common types of support. Notice how the following paragraphs-in-progress use different kinds of support.

Facts

Racquetball is one of the United States' fastest growing sports. In 1970, there were only 50,000 players. By 1978, there were more than 6,000,000.

Reasons

Racquetball is one of the United States' fastest growing sports. There are good reasons for its popularity. It's fun, easy to learn, and one of the best ways to achieve all-round fitness.

There are several methods of organizing your supporting evidence: for example, chronological order, cause and effect, and comparison and contrast. Writers sometimes use a combination of methods. To help you decide how to organize your paragraph, study the products at the end of this chapter and the examples in Chapter 26.

Whatever method you use, your evidence must solidly support your thesis statement. If you have not provided enough supporting detail, you will fail to satisfy your reader. If your examples do not relate to your thesis statement, you may confuse the reader. If you have a feeling that your paragraph does not meet your purpose, try putting it away for a few days. Then come back to it with a fresh outlook. You may see gaps, inconsistencies, or contradictions that you missed before.

Conclusion. You should summarize what you said in your thesis statement in a memorable way. In addition to your summation, you might conclude your paragraph with a question. This encourages your reader to have an active response to what you have written.

4. As you draft your paragraph, you may find yourself substituting a word, phrase, or sentence for another and perhaps even changing the order of your sentences. You may decide to revise your paragraph one or more times before giving it to your peer editors. The process of revising is a continuous one and goes on even during the drafting process.

Editing and Revising Process

When you and your peers edit your expository paragraph, apply the checklists from Chapter 28. In addition, consider the following questions.

1. Does the thesis statement clearly express the limited topic?
2. Is it clear whether the paragraph seeks to inform, express an opinion, or does both?
3. Is there sufficient evidence to support the thesis statement?
4. Is the evidence well organized?
5. Is there anything that should be omitted because it does not support the thesis statement? Is there anything that should be added?
6. Is any sentence in the paragraph unclear?
7. Do the sentences flow smoothly and logically?
8. Are there confusing shifts in point of view? For example, the paragraph might begin with "she should" and then shift to "you should."
9. Do you see any errors in spelling, grammar, punctuation, and sentence structure?

After your peer-editing session, prepare a clean draft of your paragraph and give it to your teacher for a final editing session.

What follows is an example of the results of a peer-editing session. First, read the shortened list of the writer's variables. Then read the paragraph titled "Graduation." Consider the peer editor's comments. Would you add further comments if you were the peer editor? If so, what are they?

Writing Variables

Broad topic:	education
Limited topic:	importance of graduating
Audience:	students thinking of dropping out
Purpose:	to convince them to stay in school
Voice:	my own
Format:	self-contained expository paragraph
Situation:	I thought I might drop out of school, but my counselor convinced me to graduate. I see many students who think school is a waste of time.
Thesis statement:	One of the most important things you can learn in grade twelve is how education can help you.

First Draft and Peer Editor Comments

lowercase Graduation *title is too general*

Is ~~G~~rade ~~T~~welve worth it? What is the use of spending another year in classrooms with teachers and books when ~~one~~ *you*① could be making ~~one's~~ *your* way in the world? What is it about a high-school diploma that would make ~~me do~~ *you*② all that work? One of the most important things you can learn in grade twelve is how much a higher education can help you② If you finish getting there, you can take a long look at the choices you can make: to go to a university, to go to a community college, to go to a trade school, to get a job, or just bum around for a while before making up my mind.④ If you decide that high school is as far in the academic world as you want to go, you will at least be able to answer all those job ads that say, "Only high-school graduates need apply." *"High School diploma required."*

vague (next to "the choices you can make" line)
slang (next to "bum around" line)

① Point of view shifts from "one" to "you."
② Questions are a good introduction. Should you answer?
③ Thesis statement not clear.
④ Couldn't you "bum around" without graduating? How is this a choice graduating offers?
⑤ Paragraph seems incomplete. Could you summarize your idea to conclude?

After you have studied the first draft, read the revised paragraph on page 44. Note the changes the student made as the result of a peer-editing session. Note particularly: (a) The thesis statement—"One of the most important advantages of earning a high-school diploma is the choices it makes available to you"—is now clearly stated. (b) The problems with shifting point of view (*one, me, you*) have now been corrected. (c) Irrelevant material has been eliminated. (d) The conclusion of the paragraph restates the writer's idea by introducing a comparison with a birthday party and then ends with a strong, challenging sentence.

Do you think the paragraph is ready for its intended audience? If not, what further changes would you make?

Final Draft

Why Graduate?

Is grade twelve worth it? Is there any point in spending another year in the classroom when you could be making your way in the world? The answer to both questions is *yes*. One of the most important advantages of earning a high-school diploma is the choices it makes available to you. You can go to a university. You can go to a community college or trade school. You can find a job. If you decide that high school is as far as you want to go in the academic world, you will at least be able to answer all those job ads that say, "High-school diploma required." Leaving high school in your last year is like leaving your own birthday party before you open your presents. Give yourself the best chance to succeed in later life. Stay in high school and graduate.

Products

The Problem of Acid Rain
by Frank Brown, student

Acid rain, produced by factories spouting pollution, is contaminating the lakes and killing the forests of the northeastern United States and southeastern Canada. Smoke from petroleum and chemical refineries that contains heavy concentrations of deadly microscopic particles is falling, in the form of rain, on several thousand acres of this area. This causes severe damage to the environment as well as ruining local industries. The tourist industry has suffered heavy losses. Government agencies on both sides of the border warn vacationers to stay away from many of the more popular sites around lakes and streams found to contain high levels of noxious pollutants. Campers who have been coming to this area to enjoy the natural beauty for several seasons are staying away in droves. The hardest hit industry is, of course, the lumber industry. Trees saturated with toxins are rotting and are useless for wood products. Technology has proven to be a boon to people, but if it also proves to be a bane to our natural environment, perhaps it is time to apply technology more sensibly and become more aware of ecology.

Caring for Your New Aquarium
by Marc Attinasi, student

Many people purchase aquariums with the misconception that their relationship with their fish will be simple and carefree. This, however, is not at all the case. Aquariums require a great deal of time and attention to maintain; a neglected fish tank will quickly become a poisonous graveyard. Of primary importance is the initial setup. Never place the tank near a window or heating duct; changes in temperature can be fatal to your fish. Always follow all directions on pumps and filters, and always use at least one and one-half inches of gravel. If using an undergravel filter, use it in conjunction with a cotton/charcoal filter to eliminate wastes that cannot be broken down by the biological action of the undergravel filter. No filter can re-oxygenate water, so the tank water should be partially changed bi-weekly or monthly, depending upon the size of the tank and the number of fish. Never forget to dechlorinate the new water. While draining the water, stir the gravel around to loosen debris and allow for its removal with the foul water. Also, never overfeed your fish; the excess food sinks to the bottom and rots, discoloring the gravel and further fouling the water. Being disciplined with tank maintenance will allow for long-lived fish and a happy aquatic experience.

Daydreams
by Wun Yue Au, student

Do you ever get frustrated? And have you ever wondered what to do when work piles up at a greater rate than you can manage or when successive failures weary your body and soul? Here is an easy answer—daydream. Take a short rest and allow your oppressed mind to wander freely. In stretching itself, the mind can fly to a comforting asylum, to cure its wounds by relaxation and flights of fancy. Then, with renewed energy and confidence, all the pressure of everyday work or unpleasant experiences will seem small in comparison to the profound meanings of your fantasies. After daydreaming, you are once again your optimistic, delighted, happy self. Besides, daydreams can help you enrich yourself. With your mind traveling freely, new ideas take shape which carry you beyond your limited scope of experience—you become brighter and more flexible. Under sensible control, then, daydreaming can contribute to your mental and physical health. To be certain, daydreaming, if handled carefully and deftly, will waste no time at all.

Smokers Beware
by Tracey Rockwell, student

To the Editor:

I want to let my fellow students know about how bad a habit smoking is.

Smoking is possibly the most disgusting habit a person could engage in. Not only is it dangerous to the smoker's health, but it is just as bad for the affected nonsmoker. According to some scientists, the second-hand smoke that enters the air from the burning end of a cigarette is more damaging than the smoke being inhaled. Often a smoker will ignore the fact that he or she is polluting the air with this deadly substance simply because smoking is accepted as normal behavior. Rather, it is an inconsiderate invasion of the right that everyone has to breathe air without fear of being damaged. Fortunately, the population of smokers is gradually decreasing. Some day, with any luck, they will be of such a minority as not to do unnecessary damage to nonsmokers.

I would like to suggest that the students urge their parents to have smoking banned in all public places.

Sincerely,
Tracey Rockwell

For Discussion

The Problem of Acid Rain

1. What is the purpose of this paragraph?
2. What is the thesis statement? What details support it?
3. Do you think other details should have been added? Should some have been left out? Explain.

Caring for Your New Aquarium

1. Who might Marc Attinasi's audience be?
2. What is the paragraph's thesis statement? What details support it?

Daydreams

1. The student writer of this paragraph supports her thesis statement with reasons. What are they? Does she convince you? Why or why not?

2. Are there other reasons she should have mentioned? If so, what are they?
3. What is the conclusion of the paragraph? Is it effective, or would you change it? If so, how?

Smokers Beware

1. The expository paragraph of "Smokers Beware" is part of a larger piece of writing, a letter to a school newspaper. Although the letter is addressed to the editor, is the editor the intended audience? Explain.
2. How does Tracey Rockwell support her thesis statement? Do you think she should provide more support? Why or why not?

4 Informative Essay

The ability to inform clearly and at the same time to hold your reader's interest is one of the most important writing skills you can master. In your schoolwork, and probably after you leave school, you will be asked to do more informative writing than any other kind. Many teachers require informative essays as part of social studies and science courses. Many jobs require some kind of informative writing. In both cases, you must be able to state what you know or have found out so that your reader can understand both your facts and ideas.

ASSIGNMENT ▸ Write an informative essay of at least 400 words. You may decide to do this essay for both this writing course and another course. In this case, a teacher may assign you a topic. If the choice is up to you, choose a topic that interests you and that you know well.

Prewriting Process

1. If you have already written a short exposition (such as the expository paragraph for Chapter 3), you can make it longer by filling it out—that is, by adding more facts, examples, and/or reasons. This extra development is often the very thing your reader needs for a full understanding of your topic and ideas. Look over some of your short expository pieces, especially those about which you have strong feelings. You may

find that you have already arrived at a suitable topic for this assignment. What you need to do now is flesh it out, give it sharper focus, and structure it as a longer essay.

2. If you have no short exposition you want to flesh out, use the prewriting suggestions in Chapter 3 (pages 37–40) to find a broad topic and then a limited topic for this assignment. This time you have a wider range of choices because you do not have to restrict yourself to a topic that is limited enough for only one paragraph.

3. If you still cannot think of a topic and one is not assigned to you, think about your hobbies, the clubs and associations to which you belong, or sports and other activities in which you are regularly involved.

4. Use two or three of the brainstorming methods in Chapter 23 to probe your topic for supporting details. One of the following methods will be useful: a detailed list of responses to the Newspaper Reporter's Questions; a nonstop, half-hour Freewriting journal entry (see page 204); or Aristotle's Topics.

5. An important part of the prewriting process of an informative essay involves research. You may need to take time either to research your topic more thoroughly or to choose another topic about which you know more. Caution: If you use someone else's words to present your information, put those words in quotation marks and identify that person. Trying to pass off the words as your own is **plagiarism**, a serious offense for a writer.

6. If you are using this assignment for a paper in a social studies or a science course, use the suggestions in this chapter together with those your social studies or science teacher may make.

7. Just before you begin to draft your essay, bring everything together by writing a sentence or two showing how your other **writing variables** relate to your **purpose** in writing. This **statement of purpose** will help you compose your **thesis statement**. In the following statements of purpose, notice how writing variables are expressed.

> Because I feel strongly about the poor showing of our football team (situation), I intend to write a comparison/contrast essay (format) for our coach (audience) to let him know (purpose) why Johnson High has won every one of their last twenty games while we have won only three of ours (topic).

> In a history paper (format) for my history teacher (audience), I intend to explain the rise and activities of Hispanic movements in the United States (topic) as though I am an observer from Latin America (voice).

This essay should show why some Hispanics feel that they do not have full citizenship rights (purpose and situation).

I am writing a letter (format) to my boyfriend (audience) informing him what I think a good relationship should be. I am going to point out to him the possible consequence of his behavior on our friendship (situation and topic). I want to keep his friendship (purpose).

Drafting Process

1. After you have gathered all your supporting evidence, decide on an overall method of organization: for example, cause and effect, comparison/contrast, familiar to unfamiliar, or chronological order. For a discussion of kinds of organization, see Chapter 26. Spend a few minutes picturing your essay as one or more of the forms presented in Chapter 23: mandala, ladders, flowchart, pigeonholes, and so forth. The few minutes you spend on this activity will make your drafting process much easier.

2. Whichever method you use, follow **basic essay structure**—introduction, development, conclusion—for your first informative essay. As you write other informative essays, you can experiment with other structures. For example, you may decide to write your thesis statement at the end of your essay rather than at the beginning. But for your first paper, basic essay structure is easiest to follow: an introductory paragraph that states your thesis and arouses your reader's interest, a development of several paragraphs that present supporting evidence, and a conclusion that sums up your basic idea. (See pages 57–58.)

3. You may decide to use one or more narrative illustrations as part of your development. A **narrative illustration** is a brief story that serves as an example of your thesis statement. Sometimes it is the most effective kind of supporting evidence.

4. You may also decide to use one or more **descriptions** as part of your development. In certain kinds of papers—for example, a paper about a particular organism for a science class—description helps your reader understand your topic.

5. Before you draft, decide what style you are going to use. Will you use a straightforward style? Or will you use irony, poking fun at your topic by saying the opposite of what you mean? To discover the range of styles you might use, see the Second Workshop, especially Chapters 30 and 31.

6. Include a topic sentence for each of your paragraphs (see Chapter 24) and develop each paragraph in an orderly fashion.

7. Give yourself plenty of time to do a good job. Do not think you are going to write a coherent informative essay the night before it is due. Even an experienced writer might not be able to do it.

Editing and Revising Process

1. In editing, your peer editors should use the suggestions in Chapter 28 and on page 42 of Chapter 3. In self-editing and revising, you should also use these suggestions. In addition, the following questions will help you and your peers edit your work.

   a) Is the thesis statement clearly stated? Is there a topic sentence for each paragraph?
   b) What part of the essay is clearest? most effective? What part is not clear? Why? What can be done to make it clearer?
   c) Are important points emphasized? If not, which points need to be emphasized more?
   d) Is anything overemphasized or stated at too great a length? If so, what should be shortened or omitted?
   e) Is the organization easy to follow?
   f) Are the sentences too crammed with information? Are they poorly coordinated? If so, what can be done to make them easier to read?
   g) Are the verbs well chosen? A strong, precise verb is more effective than a vague verb bolstered by adverbs.

2. Are there any statements with which your peer editors disagree? Such disagreements may arise from serious weaknesses in your paper. You, the writer, will have to decide whether the disagreements merely reflect a difference of opinion about your topic or whether they indicate you should do some serious revision. The prospect of such revision may be unsettling, but sometimes it is the only way you can produce an effective essay.

3. Before you present your essay to your teacher/editor, check to make sure that your facts and use of writing conventions are correct.

4. When your teacher/editor hands back your essay, you are at a point that many professional writers find most satisfying. The essay is nearly ready for its final audience. Make the essay distinctly yours by testing each sentence, each word, to be sure it does precisely what you

want it to do. You might want to put the essay away for a few days, come back to it with a fresh, open mind, and then give it a final polish.

Products

Bacterium
by Dora Anyfantis, student

Allow me to introduce myself; I am a microscopic bacterium, one of the thousand bacteria that surround you in your everyday life. You try to avoid me; however, no matter where you go, you will not get away from me. I will always be near you, inside you, everywhere.

I may be microscopic in size, but I can do more damage than all wars and natural disasters put together. I can start from anywhere, entering your organism from the air you breathe, the food you eat, and the water you drink. My favorite victim is a weak organism; I can conquer one of these easily. When I enter a weak organism, I multiply extremely rapidly. I become two bacteria, which become four, the four eight, and in only a few hours we become millions. Then, unfortunately for the organism, it is doomed. On the other hand, I find a lot of resistance in a strong organism. There things are not so great for me because when I enter it, a deadly battle starts. Both I, with my toxin, and the organism, with its antitoxin, try to win the battle. Unfortunately, the strong organism always wins. Every time I fail to conquer a body, it brings disaster; I die, you see.

In spite of the damage that I cause, do not think that your life would have been as great without my presence. Fermentation is one of the effects of my work. Without me, you would have to do without foods like bread and yogurt.

Even though the damages that I bring are many, I also offer you some vital services. Therefore, I am indispensable in your life. This is my story, a story full of death but also full of life.

Before the Audition
by Rita Ringle, student

You might think it easy and a lot of fun to perform in a musical play production. You are right, but before you can perform in any production, you must do one thing: audition.

To be in a musical production you must possess many talents. You must have some knowledge of music reading, a good singing voice, good dancing skills, the ability to memorize quickly, and finally, the ability to perform in front of a large group of people without falling apart. During an audition you must demonstrate all these talents in only a few minutes.

You must prepare yourself for the audition in the same way you would prepare for a job interview. First, you should have a résumé. Your résumé should contain relevant information about yourself: for example, your personal data (height, weight, age, etc.) and information about all technical experience on and off stage, such as music lessons, voice lessons, dance experience, and prior play performances. You should also include the names of your instructors, years studied, and locations where you learned or performed in each field.

Next, you must sell yourself. In order to do this, you should familiarize yourself with the musical for which you are planning to audition. You should choose a good song and a monologue from the actual production and memorize it until it becomes second nature to you. Purchasing a record from the musical can acquaint you with the material so that you can introduce your own personality and showcase your talents.

Your monologue should be no shorter than one minute. Memorizing the monologue is easy, but how well can you make your character come alive? You should take into consideration the personality of the character you are portraying and his or her situation. Become your character and know everything about him or her.

Now you are almost ready. Before you go to your audition you should do a few things at home. First, eat a good meal. You should never perform on an empty stomach. Eating will prevent your having hunger pangs and losing your concentration. Next, you should exercise your voice so you will not strain your vocal cords during your song. You should do a few stretching exercises so you don't pull any muscles when you are asked to dance. Finally, you should make sure you have a very neat appearance. Allow enough time to get ready at a fairly relaxed pace. Rushing will only serve to make you tense. Wear something nice but very loose fitting. Tight clothes only prevent you from doing your best when asked to dance. Remember, looks can tell a person much about you.

You are now ready for the audition. Don't be discouraged by the number of people auditioning for the same role. Do your very best and don't let others change the way you do things. Never make any last minute changes in your character; they will only serve to confuse you.

In conclusion, be patient. The director knows exactly what he or she is looking for. Even if you don't get the part you wanted or don't get a part at all, don't be discouraged. There is always next time!

For Discussion Bacterium

1. To give information about bacteria, Dora Anyfantis has adopted the persona of a "microscopic bacterium." In your opinion, does the persona make the essay more or less interesting than a straightforward explanation would be? Why? What do you think a scientist would think of this use of persona?
2. The last sentence of the essay could serve as its thesis statement. Since thesis statements usually occur at or near the beginning of an essay, why do you think this writer put hers at the end?
3. What details support the thesis statement?

Before the Audition

1. Who might Rita Ringle's audience be?
2. Does this piece give the impression that she is writing from experience? Why or why not?
3. Should she have included anything else or left anything out? If so, what and why?
4. Which suggestions would be most useful to her audience?

5 Argumentative Essay

You spend much of your life absorbing and giving out information. You read and listen to become informed, and you talk and write to inform others. Many times your purpose changes. You begin by trying to inform and then find yourself trying to persuade. In such cases, the need to persuade grows out of the need to inform. You want your audience to understand your information as you understand it. To persuade your audience to your way of thinking, you argue.

When you argue in writing, remember that your audience cannot argue back. You must, if possible, anticipate objections to your argument and answer them. In order to win your audience to your side, you must argue thoroughly, logically, and convincingly. An effective argument is perhaps the most difficult kind of writing to do, but sometimes it is the most useful.

ASSIGNMENT ▶ Write an argumentative essay of at least 400 words on a topic about which you feel strongly and want your reader to adopt, or at least appreciate, your opinion.

Prewriting Process

1. You can use the prewriting suggestions in Chapter 3 (pages 37–40) to find a topic for this assignment. An expository paragraph presenting an opinion can often be turned into an argumentative essay by using more supporting details, such as facts, examples, and reasons. You may wish to look over some of your shorter expository compositions to see if any of them contains a basis for a good argument.

2. You can think about a real-life problem important to you and list a number of reasons (arguments) for and against taking a particular action. Here is a small sampling of problems you might consider.

Should I go steady?
Should I lend my best friend money?
Should I take four years of mathematics (or science) in high school?
Should I continue with my schooling?
Should I try out for a team?

3. If you cannot easily think of a personal situation on which to build an argument, choose a broad topic and narrow it down until you can write a statement about it. Answering your own question might help you narrow your topic. (For more on narrowing a topic, see Chapter 23.)

4. If you are having difficulty generating an idea, complete the brainstorming technique on Cause and Effect in Chapter 23 (page 229). Using this technique may give you several problem-solving ideas.

5. If you are using this chapter to help you write a paper for a social studies or science course, use the advice here together with any advice or material you receive from your teacher.

6. If you have not already done so, limit your topic. For example, the question "Should I take four years of mathematics?" can be limited to "Four years of high school mathematics is essential to anyone who plans to major in science at college."

7. Draft a statement in which you specify your purpose, your audience, and your attitude toward your topic. The form of your statement should be similar to this one:

I want to convince (purpose) other students who plan to major in science (audience) that a thorough grounding in mathematics is essential to their college education (attitude toward topic).

Note that such a statement includes a phrase such as "to convince" or "to persuade" rather than a phrase such as "to inform" or "to explain."

8. Write a thesis statement. (For a discussion of thesis statements, see page 234.)

9. Check to see if you need more evidence to support your thesis statement. There are a number of information sources, among them:

your own experience and observation
interviews
audiovisual materials
magazine articles
books about your topic
reference books

Nothing can be more frustrating than to start drafting and realize you do not have enough supporting evidence to build a good argument. Take plenty of time during your prewriting process to gather and record evidence for your essay.

If you think that you now have enough material for a strong argument, move on to the drafting process.

Drafting Process

Your job in writing this essay is to convince your audience that your opinion is right or at least reasonable. Remember, though, that many people are stubborn about changing their minds. You may not completely convince your intended reader and may have to be satisfied with that person conceding, "You may be right. I never thought about it quite that way." The following suggestions will help you make a strong, convincing case.

1. Respect your audience. Any reader who disagrees with you may be as convinced of the value of his or her opinion as you are of yours. Avoid name-calling, insults, and any other underhanded tactics that weaken your argument. Argue fairly.

2. Use specific evidence to support your case rather than unsupported generalizations such as, "Few teenagers are emotionally mature until they reach their eighteenth birthday." Such statements can be entirely false or only partly true, and they can seriously weaken your argument. Assume that those disagreeing with you have good reasons for their disagreement. This will encourage you to provide solid evidence to back up your opinion.

3. The more supporting evidence you produce, the more convincing your argument. Since you are not writing a book, however, you will have to be selective. Again, do not overlook the opposing side. Although you do not need to build a good opposing argument, one may exist. Weigh both sides of the argument carefully when you decide what to include and exclude.

4. You can use both narrations and descriptions as supporting examples in your essay.

5. If this is your first argumentative essay, you may wish to use **basic essay structure**: introduction, development, conclusion. Not all writers use this structure, of course, but it is a useful one for you to follow. You can organize later essays in other ways. Before you start drafting, examine the essay "The High Price of Soft Sell" and the comments that accompany it (pages 59–60) to see how one writer has used basic essay structure.

6. The **introduction** of your essay should both arouse interest and present your thesis statement. Keep both purpose and audience in mind as you draft your introduction.

7. In the **development**, you must convince your audience that you are right or, at least, that you have a good case. To accomplish this, you need sufficient supporting evidence (which you should have if you have given enough time and attention to brainstorming and research). To help your reader follow your argument, provide a topic sentence for each paragraph of your development. If you like, you can use several kinds of supporting evidence (such as facts, reasons, and examples). You can also use a variety of methods to organize your paragraphs, each paragraph with its own kind of organization. (For a discussion of kinds of organization, such as cause and effect, chronological order, and comparison, see Chapter 26.)

8. The **conclusion** may either have its own paragraph or occur at the end of the last developmental paragraph. When you draft your conclusion, consider: What is the best, effective way to clinch your argument?

Editing and Revising Process

When you self-edit and your peers edit your essay, use both the following questions and the guidelines in Chapter 28.

1. Is the thesis clearly stated?

2. Is the thesis statement adequately supported by facts, incidents, reasons, examples, or other specific evidence?

3. Is the organization logical and easy to follow? Are the topic sentences for paragraphs easy to find and understand? Does one paragraph lead smoothly and logically to another? Is the overall organization of the essay clear?

4. Is any part of the essay not clear? What can be done to make it clear?

5. If the essay tries to disprove the arguments an opponent may have, are the opponent's opinions treated fairly?

6. Will the intended audience be convinced? If not, why not? (Even if the peer editors are not part of the intended audience, they can indicate whether or not they found the essay convincing and give reasons for their opinion.)

When you are satisfied with the content and organization of your essay, proofread it for spelling, grammar, usage, and punctuation. Read it again to make sure it is an honest statement of your opinion. Make sure, as well, that you have given enough consideration to the situation of your intended audience. Now present the essay to your teacher/editor for additional editing. When your teacher gives it back to you again, consider what further revisions you need to make. Then polish the essay before giving it to its intended reader.

Products

The High Price of Soft Sell
by Ken MacMillan

The essay follows Basic Essay Structure. The **introduction** captures the reader's attention immediately because everyone has an opinion about TV advertising. The final question provides the writer's thesis statement and intrigues the reader as well.

The **development** contains three paragraphs. In this paragraph, the writer hooks the reader with a question, then provides three detailed examples. The paragraph's final sentence suitably sums up the paragraph.

The first sentence of the third paragraph is not only linked to the previous paragraph, but it also hooks

We've all been told many times that television advertising is bad, that it is mindless and repetitive, that it appeals to the materialism in our nature, and that it uses half-truths and clever distortions to sell us products and services we don't need. Each of us, moreover, has personally been irritated and offended by commercials of the mindless "ring around the collar" variety, which grate on our nerves and offend our intelligence. Everyone joins in condemning the "word from our sponsor." But how do we reconcile this general attitude with the fact that we see commercials every day which are witty and entertaining?

Isn't it true that there are commercials which far surpass in quality the programs they interrupt? Think, for instance, of the Bell Telephone commercials with their superbly photographed scenes of people enjoying simple pleasures together while the sound track carries a nostalgic song like "Heart of my Heart" or "You'll Never Know." The actual message, that we should use long distance more to get in touch with old friends far away, is very quietly stated at the end. Or again, remember the aftershave commercial which makes fun of the old movie cliché, "Thanks, I needed that," to suggest how fresh and awake we will feel after using the product. In both these cases, the commercial message is largely implied rather than stated. A different type is the "Coke has life" commercial with its lively scenes of people working and playing hard and quenching their thirst with icy bottles of Coke. Sentiment, humor, excitement are used effectively in these three examples of advertising at its most attractive.

Commercials like this, however, present a particular kind of danger to us all. It is easy to dismiss a commercial of some local car dealer reading strained witticisms from the aptly named idiot cards. They

the reader again by pointing out the "danger to us all." After presenting examples of bad commercials (in a series of questions), the writer ends with an effective rhetorical fragment which points up the idea of this paragraph: all commercials are dangerous.

The first sentence of the fourth paragraph states the topic of the paragraph in a general way. The next sentence restates it in a way that applies to the writer's audience: "We have a tendency. . . ." The third sentence provides an example of the tendency, while the remainder of the paragraph relates the tendency to the writer's main concern, commercials that are witty and entertaining.

The **conclusion** sums up the main point of the essay: resist well-made commercials. Notice how the first sentence of this paragraph answers the question posed in the last sentence of the introductory paragraph.

affront our intelligence so flagrantly that we are in no danger of being persuaded by their pleadings. But how do we react when the commercial message is presented with such wit that it is entertaining? Do we even think of the implications behind the messages? Do we think that in these inflationary days Bell should perhaps not be encouraging us to spend even more money on useless long distance calls? Do we really believe that a slap in the face with a handful of scented alcohol really makes us feel fresh? Or do we consider what a bottle of sugared soft drink does to our diets, not to mention our teeth? Probably not.

Advertising confronts us with the contemporary discrepancy between morality and proficiency. We have the tendency today to praise anything well done even if the thing is not worth doing. Our heroes are quarterbacks who have the ultimately useless skill of throwing a football further than anyone else. So our advertising agencies pay large sums of money to imaginative men and women to make art subservient to commerce. It is not surprising that commercials are skillful when more money is spent on creating a thirty-second commercial than on making the thirty-minute program it interrupts; we have to ask if we are not suffering from a confusion of values here. Perhaps we should ask if human virtues are any longer virtues when applied to a bad end. Is intelligence, in the mad scientist or the mad ad man, something to be praised when its effect is destructive or corrupting?

What is disturbing about TV advertising, then, is not that it is so bad; rather, what should worry us is that it is so good. Its glossy, polished competence presents us with a false beauty. We need to be able to make a clear distinction between what is said and how it is being said. We need to resist the lure of "good" advertising.

Smoking in Public Places
by Meldon Ellis, student

The issue of smoking in public has become of increasing concern to nonsmokers. Living in a free country, we as citizens have individual rights. On this issue, the nonsmoker unequivocally deserves the right to be free from the annoyance of cigarette smoke in public places. The smoker, of course, has the right to decide whether or not he or she smokes. However, this right should definitely not extend to the point of causing irritation to others. When smoking in public infringes upon a nonsmoker's right to inhale clean air, when it causes the nonsmoker to cough or suffer adverse physiological effects, then we have reached a point when it must be regulated by law.

Generally, when we think of the potential health hazards surrounding smoking, we think in terms of dangers for the smoker as opposed to dangers for the nonsmoking public. Indeed, most of the information we receive on the topic tends to reinforce our thinking. Recently, however, the public health authorities have directed their concern towards the detrimental effects of tobacco smoke to nonsmokers. The Medical Association announced that at least thirteen percent of our population is sensitive to cigarette smoke. Though this figure includes persons with emphysema, asthma, bronchitis, hay fever, and heart disease, the average nonsmoker is also subject to reactions from cigarette smoke. These reactions range from eye irritation, coughing, and nasal symptoms, to headaches and even dizziness. According to the Lung Association, sidestream smoke, the smoke that is exhaled, contains twice as much nicotine as the mainstream smoke inhaled by the smoker. Conclusive evidence to date suggests that sidestream smoke contains three times as much benzopyrene (a cancer-causing agent), and up to fifty times more ammonia than mainstream smoke.

The question about enacting legislation to govern nonsmokers' rights has become a civil rights issue. On one side of the argument we have the smokers, who champion that regulating this area of personal choice threatens the individual freedom this country was built upon. Unsurprisingly, this side receives support from the cigarette company executives, who maintain that in opening ourselves to this type of legislation, we are in effect leaving ourselves wide open to increased government restriction in every area of our lives. The nonsmokers, diametrically opposed to this view, simply feel that when in public places they should be afforded the right to inhale clean air without the hindrance of tobacco smoke.

If this issue could be resolved effectively through mutual respect and common courtesy, I could see no reason for government legislation. But, in concluding, I must state that an individual's right to smoke ends when the smoke of his cigarette reaches the nose of another person in a public place, who might suffer irritating or distressful consequences.

For Discussion

The High Price of Soft Sell

1. What does the title tell you about the topic of the essay and the writer's attitude toward it? Does the title make you want to read the essay? Explain.
2. What is the topic of the second paragraph? Do you think the supporting examples are well chosen? Why or why not? What other examples might you add?
3. Do you agree with the main point of the fourth paragraph? If you do, what examples, other than making heroes of football players, might you add?
4. Do you think the essay's conclusion is effective? Defend your answer.

Smoking in Public Places

1. What sentence in the first paragraph contains the thesis statement?
2. What facts does the writer present to support his thesis? How does he incorporate the facts into the essay? Do you think he should have been more precise about giving sources? That is, should he have named books, pamphlets, and/or articles and given dates of publication and page numbers? Why or why not?
3. What precisely is the writer trying to persuade his audience to do?

6 Narrative Essay

If you have already written a narrative paragraph (the assignment for Chapter 1), you know that a narrative is an account of one or more events. A narrative that is longer than a paragraph can tell about a series of connected events.

ASSIGNMENT ▶ Write a narrative essay that is at least 300 words long.

Prewriting Process

1. If you have not done the assignment for Chapter 1, or if you have forgotten the suggestions presented in that chapter, go over the prewriting suggestions on pages 21–22. Many are useful for this assignment.

2. An interesting narrative usually involves **conflict**, a struggle against something or someone. A conflict is not necessarily a physical struggle. It can be a disagreement with another person. It can be a struggle with nature, with society, or even within yourself.

3. Narratives can be written in the **first person** (I) or in the **third person** (she or he).

Here is a prewriting activity that can lead to a topic for a first-person narrative. On a piece of paper, jot down answers to these questions.

    a) When did I really want something?
    b) What prevented me from having it?

    c) What was the nature of the conflict?
    d) Who or what did it involve?
    e) How long did it take me to get what I wanted?

4. Here is a prewriting activity that can lead to a topic for a third-person narrative. On a piece of paper, jot down answers to the following questions.

    a) Do I know someone who always seems to be involved in some kind of conflict? If so, who is that person?
    b) Which conflict involving that person most intrigued me?
    c) What was the nature of the conflict?
    d) How was it resolved?
    e) What obstacles nearly prevented it from being resolved?

5. After choosing a topic, you should gather supporting evidence. To help produce worthwhile details, you should engage in two or three brainstorming sessions by yourself or with your peers. The following activities from Chapter 23 are particularly useful for narratives: Experience/Write, Senses Cluster, Positive/Negative/Neutral Pigeonholes, Positive Cluster, Negative Cluster, and possibly Cause-and-Effect Flowchart.

6. Before you draft your narrative, work out your writing variables and write them down.

Drafting Process

1. Use **dialogue**, the words people speak, to help you tell your story. The important rule about dialogue is to make sure it sounds real: fit the talk to the person. Dialogue is where you can legitimately use slang and colloquialisms in writing.

But practice artistic economy. Do not be repetitive by including everything your character said or would say. Select only what you think necessary to suggest a particular character trait or to further the development of your narrative.

Also, avoid repeating speech tags, such as "she said," too often. Some writers try to avoid such repetition by using exaggerated tags such as "she cooed" and "he squealed." This solution is often worse than the problem. Constantly using synonyms such as *cooed* and *squealed* for the simple word *said* makes the writing sound strained. Once you have established the speakers of the dialogue and made their speech distinctive, you can occasionally present their dialogue without speech tags. Make sure the dialogue contributes to the development of your narrative.

2. **Description** can also help tell a story. Use description for the same reason you use dialogue, to make the situation seem real. But make sure your description contributes to the development of your narrative.

3. Longer narratives often build up to a **climax**. Using very short paragraphs just before the climax can create the same suspenseful effect that short sentences do in a narrative paragraph. However, using several short sentences in a longer paragraph may work better. Experiment and see what works best for you.

4. Divide your narrative into paragraphs to make it easier to read. There is no hard and fast rule about paragraphing any piece of writing. (One writer wrote a story that was one long paragraph!) Even so, these suggestions may help you decide the number and length of your paragraphs.

- a) Narrative essay paragraphs are generally shorter than those of an expository essay. But unless you can justify their use, avoid a long series of paragraphs with only one or two sentences.
- b) Paragraphs that are too long may be filled with too many details that do not allow the reader time to reflect. Correct this problem by removing nonessential details. Overly long paragraphs might also include more than one idea. The solution to this problem is simple: divide the paragraph into shorter paragraphs.
- c) When you use dialogue, start a new paragraph for each speaker.

5. Work for **sentence variety**. Sentences should not all be of the same length or structure. (For a discussion of sentence variety, see page 305.) Good writers work to create the same movement in their sentences that is in the action they are relating. For example, in telling about a runaway car on a canyon highway, one long, sweeping sentence is probably more effective than several jerky ones.

6. Use vivid **imagery**, word pictures that appeal to the senses. Your job is to make your reader see, hear, and feel what happens in your narrative. Notice how the following sentences make the reader see and hear what happened through the use of a comparison, expressive verbs, and exact nouns.

> Pepe's wrist *flicked like the head of a snake*. The [knife] blade seemed to *fly open* in mid air, and with a *thump* the point *dug* into the redwood post, and the black handle *quivered*.
> John Steinbeck, "Flight"

7. Make sure your point of view is consistent. If you begin telling your narrative in the first person, do not switch halfway through to the third person.

Editing and Revising Process

To help you self-edit and revise your narrative, use the suggestions in Chapter 28. Your peer editors should also use these suggestions. In addition, both you and your peer editors should consider the following questions.

  1. What do the peer editors like most about the narrative? Which paragraph is best? Which sentences are particularly effective?
  2. Does the narrative encourage the reader to see, hear, and feel what happened? If not, which sentences might be improved by the use of comparisons, expressive verbs, and exact nouns?
  3. Do the sentences have variety, or do they seem monotonous? If monotonous, how might they be changed?
  4. Is there anything that does not move the story forward? If so, should it be deleted? (The ability to select is a major asset to a good writer.)
  5. Is anything confusing because it needs more explaining? Does the narrative need more details to be clear and understandable?
  6. Are transitional devices needed to keep the narrative from sounding abrupt? (For suggestions, see pages 264–268).
  7. Consider purpose and audience. Is it clear why the narrative was written? Are sentence structure, word choice, and style appropriate for the intended audience?

When your peer editors give you back your narrative, make what revisions you think are necessary. Then submit a clean copy to your teacher/editor. Revise again, if necessary, to make your narrative publishable. (Remember that *publishable* means your narrative is ready to present to your final audience.)

Products

Winter Morning
by Mira Mignon, student

"Have a good day now!"

"Okay. See you tonight, Dad."

"Regular time?"

"Yes, six-thirty. Bye!" I shut the car door and heaved the massive bag up over my shoulder. I trudged into the brightly lit lobby of the arena, glancing up at the clock only to remind myself of how little sleep I'd had. My bag hit the floor with a thud and I plopped myself down on the bench. I was not awake enough to speak to anyone intelligibly, but I managed a faint smile to my coach, who was sipping hot coffee from a styrofoam cup in the corner.

"You're always so vivacious at this time of day!"

"Mmm . . ."

I unzipped my bag and pulled out a wad of sweaters. I layered them on until I felt like I couldn't move and thought to myself how pointless it was. I could never manage to keep myself warm for the full hour. I wondered if I was even in my right mind for doing this; normal kids were still asleep.

With the laces all tied up now, I grabbed the scribe I used to etch my circles in the ice and headed out into the bitter cold. Down the side I glided to patch number seven. I was quite sure to be on time today, having yesterday's lecture still fresh in my memory.

Round and round the circles I slowly traced, trying to position myself correctly so as to perform the turns without error. For an hour everything was non-existent except for me and my little strip of ice.

When six o'clock rolled around I folded up the giant compass, which had frozen together at the joints and was difficult to move. Up the steps and into the lobby I plodded, slightly awakened by the cold air. My now numb hands and feet were so grateful for just those few minutes of warm air.

"Hurry it up, Mira, you've got first lesson."

Oh lucky me! I changed my skates and removed the outermost layer of clothing, grabbed my cassette and was back out into the cold. My body felt stiff and achy in the frigid air, yet I forced myself to get moving.

Slowly my muscles began to loosen and I could feel my body shift gears into a more alert mode. My body temperature rose and my senses came to life. Soon I was gliding, spinning, and jumping about, following the commands of my coach—whose voice resounded in the open air—and pausing only to remove another sweater now and then.

"All right, you'd better go on in and get changed or you'll be late for school. Oh! and I wanted you to leave the patch skates for sharpening. I'll have them done by this afternoon."

I rounded up all my paraphernalia and went inside. I changed for school, dropped off the one pair of skates at the counter and was gone, at least for a few hours. As I walked to school in the darkness of the winter morning, I thought about the lesson and my coach's apparent disapproval. He barked and growled and criticized, but deep in my heart I knew he was pleased. I came to realize I wasn't out of my mind, just incredibly lucky.

The Fight
by Bill Rasmussen, student

The first fight I ever had is the one I remember best. I was nine years old and easily the smallest kid in our cul-de-sac. Although not much of a fighter, that day I wasn't going to back down to anyone. Why I was so bold, I really don't know; I'm glad I was, though, for I gained many things from that fight: a fat lip, a bloody nose, and a valuable lesson I will remember for life.

It all started when Kevin Taber rode his bike through a puddle and splashed water on my pants. It was raining out anyway, so I don't know why I got so upset; I was just in a fierce mood, I guess. Well, to get back at Kevin, I picked up some mud and hit him in the back with it. Kevin, one year older and a great deal bigger than I, came over and told me I shouldn't have thrown mud at him. To keep from backing down, I responded with "Big deal," much to Kevin's anger. He was on the spot; if he didn't do something back at me, the name Chicken would be his for life. I stood up readying myself for his next move; Kevin gave me a firm push. The neighborhood kids gathered around us waiting for my next move. I gave them what they wanted by punching Kevin; that punch began round one.

In fact, not only did that punch start round one, it ended it as well. For as soon as Kevin realized what I had done to him, he lost his courage and ran into his house. However, just as I thought our fight was over, Kevin came back outside, his father watching out the window, both of them waiting for round two.

This round began by Kevin coming at me and taking a wild swing at my nose. Luckily it missed and I answered with another punch. The crowd, sensing more action, began to yell, but Kevin disappointed them by running back into his house again. That was the end of round two.

After this I was sure I had won the fight, but to my amazement, round three began with both Kevin and his father coming outside. Mr. Taber yelled at Kevin to come and get me and for him to stop being such a baby. Kevin had no choice but to fight me, so he made the best of it. He hit me with a right to the jaw, then a left to the head. I staggered and he connected with a blow cutting my lower lip. The fight lasted for about a minute when I noticed Mr. Taber was giving Kevin instructions on how to fight. So, like all good neighbors, the crowd began to cheer for me to even things out. As the advantage swung into my favor again, Mr. Taber yelled at my supporters to shut up. This made me mad, so I wound up and hit Kevin with a roundhouse hook, knocking him to the ground. Then all Kevin could do was cry; he just sat there on the ground and cried. Mr. Taber, sensing defeat, ran over and picked Kevin up off the ground, then shoved him back into battle.

We fought for a few more minutes with Mr. Taber continually giving Kevin instructions. Then while backing up to escape a punch, I slipped and fell down. In all interests of unfair play Mr. Taber told Kevin to come and get me. Kevin obeyed by grabbing me around the neck with his arm, choking the life out of my every breath. He was in full control, so he asked, "Do ya give, ha, do ya give?" I said, "No" with almost no breath, so Mr. Taber yelled, "Choke him harder then." Kevin did, and I had no choice but to surrender.

Then Mr. Taber yelled out, "Atta boy, Kevin, I knew you could do it," his voice hoarse from the prior yelling. He walked over and put his arm around Kevin. Then they walked away, arm in arm, as if they had won the heavyweight championship.

That fight was almost seven years ago, and the fat lip and bloody nose have long since healed. Yet the lesson I learned will be with me forever. I learned that not only do adults act like kids sometimes, but some of them never grow up.

For Discussion

Winter Morning

1. What is the conflict in this narrative? How is it resolved?
2. What details help make this a vivid narrative?
3. Do you think this narrative essay would suffer if the dialogue were eliminated? Why or why not?

The Fight

1. How is the conflict in this piece different from the one in "Winter Morning"? How is it resolved?
2. What details does the writer use to convince the reader that the fight was a real one? Are they effective? Defend your answer.
3. If you were to rewrite this narrative from Kevin's or Mr. Taber's point of view, what changes might you make?

7 Autobiographical Essay

Movie stars, diplomats, generals, musicians, and scientists write autobiographies because they want others to know what they are like and what they have accomplished. And, as the sales of many autobiographies show, a large audience is eager to learn more about such people. Sometimes writers of autobiographies have so much to tell that they cannot do it all in one book. Shirley MacLaine and John Houseman have each written three books about themselves—and, probably, there are more to come!

You do not have to write three books for this assignment. A short autobiographical essay will do.

ASSIGNMENT ▶ Write a 300-to-500-word autobiographical essay to enable your reader to get acquainted with you.

Prewriting Process

1. Jot down your **writing variables**. Decide to whom you want to tell something about yourself, what you want to tell, and why you want to tell it.

2. In a short essay, you cannot tell everything about yourself from your birth to the present. You must select information. Use what you have jotted down about **purpose**, **situation**, and **audience** as a guide in selection.

3. Decide what **voice** you want to use. Most autobiographers tell about themselves in their own voice. But it is also possible to tell about yourself through a **persona**, as Gino Nasato (page 76) has done. Read the examples at the end of this chapter before you decide what voice you want to use.

4. Try to find a thread that unifies your essay. The thread may be a generalization about your life, or a quality or characteristic you want to emphasize.

Read the following autobiographical excerpts. Find the thread that unifies each one. Explain how the thread enables each writer to tell something important about herself.

> I was born in Fort Macleod, Alberta, in the foothills of the Canadian Rockies—an area of extreme temperatures and mirages. . . . When I was two feet off the ground, I collected broken glass and cats. When I was three feet off the ground, I made drawings of animals and forest fires. When I was four feet off the ground, I discovered boys and bicycles. When I was five feet, I began to dance to rock n' roll and sing the top ten . . . songs around campfires, and someone turned me on to Lambert, Hendricks, and Ross and Miles Davis and later Bob Dylan.
>
> Joni Mitchell

> In our house on North Congress Street in Jackson, Mississippi, where I was born, the oldest of three children, in 1909, we grew up to the striking of clocks. There was a mission-style oak grandfather clock standing in the hall, which sent its gong-like strokes through the living room, dining room, kitchen, and pantry, and up the sounding board of the stairwell. Through the night, it could find its way into our ears; sometimes, even on the sleeping porch, midnight could wake us up. My parents' bedroom had a smaller striking clock that answered it. Though the kitchen clock did nothing but show the time, the dining room clock was a cuckoo clock with weights on long chains, on one of which my baby brother, after climbing on a chair to the top of the china closet, once succeeded in suspending the cat for a moment. I don't know whether or not my father's Ohio family, in having been Swiss back in the 1700s before the first three Welty brothers came to America, had anything to do with this; but all of us have been time-minded all our lives. This was good at least for a future fiction writer, being able to learn so penetratingly, and almost first of all, about chronology. It was one of a good many things I learned almost without knowing it; it would be there when I needed it.
>
> <div align="right"><i>Eudora Welty, from</i> One Writer's Beginnings</div>

To find your thread, you can think about your life to date. Make up a list of questions such as the following to discover a pattern in your life that might serve to unify your essay.

- **a)** What are my three best characteristics? My three worst?
- **b)** What people played a significant role in my life? Why?
- **c)** What events have been significant in my life? Why?
- **d)** Of what accomplishments am I proud? Of what actions am I ashamed?
- **e)** What are my goals and ambitions?

5. List events that illustrate the generalization or characteristic you want to emphasize. For example:

I am outspoken

gets me into trouble	*gets me out of trouble*
embarrassed Mom's guests	saved the family from a fire
sent to principal	chosen Class President
got a black eye	won a case in Student Court

Notice that this list is organized by comparing and contrasting events, in this case the good results and the bad results of being outspoken. Comparison and contrast might be a good way to organize your list.

6. To get more information, do two or three of the brainstorming techniques in Chapter 23. The following might be especially useful: Positive/Negative/Neutral Pigeonholes, Pro/Con Ladders, Cause/Effect Flow Chart.

7. To get even more information, write and develop a few Absurd Analogies. These can loosen up your thinking and uncover facts and ideas you didn't realize you knew. If you have trouble thinking of your own analogies, you can develop the following: "I am like a leaky faucet." "People think of me as a lion." "I'm a stew." "I'm marble." "I'm a deep pool that no one has explored."

Drafting Process

1. Plan exactly how you are going to organize your autobiographical essay. If you need to, consult the methods of organization presented in Chapter 26 and use one of them. Two methods that might be appropriate are chronological and climactic.

2. Maintain a consistent style in your writing. Work on a few practice drafts until you find the style that suits you and the events you have decided to include.

Notice the different ways of saying the same thing:

Straightforward style: I was born in Montgomery, Alabama, on July 15, 1970.

Colloquial style: I showed up in Montgomery on July 15, 1970.

Ironic style (saying the opposite of what you mean): From the hour of my birth on July 15, 1970, I was a model child; my behavior was screamingly perfect.

Humorous style: It was absolutely marvelous the way so many people turned out for my birthday on July 15, 1970. Even my mother was there.

Even before you start a draft of your essay, you may want to write a few sentences in each of these styles to find out which one suits you best.

Editing and Revising Process

When your peers edit your essay, they can use the suggestions in Chapter 28. In addition, both they and you (when you revise) should consider the following questions.

1. What part of the autobiography reveals the most about the writer? What is the most important thing the audience learns (or should learn)? Is it clearly presented?

2. Is there a thread that runs through the autobiography? Does it clearly unify the essay?

3. In what style is the essay written? Is it appropriate to the topic, purpose, and audience?

4. How does the writer organize the essay? Is the method of organization appropriate to the content and style?

5. Should any words, sentences, or paragraphs be omitted? If so, why?

6. Should anything be added? Why?

7. Should anything be changed? Why?

8. Is the autobiography as a whole appropriate to its purpose and audience? If not, why not?

When you have revised your autobiography on the basis of your peer editors' comments, present a clean copy to your teacher/editor. After you have completed a final revision, present your essay to your intended audience.

Products

Memories
by John Parker

I was born during the Depression to poor but loving Manitoba farmers who specialized in growing rocks. Piles of white rocks towering amid our spindly wheatfields are one of my most vivid memories of growing up in the thirties.

Since the nearest school was seventeen miles from our farm and the only way there was by horse and buggy, I spent my time on more important jobs—raiding crows' nests and trapping gophers for their precious tails. Think of the thrill that comes to a seven-year-old when he hands in fifty-three gophers' tails to a government agent and receives $1.06 in cash: my first paycheck.

With the outbreak of World War II, my world changed; I thought it crashed. My father joined the army and was sent to Europe; my mother, my young sister, and I moved to Arden, a small Manitoba town; and I started school. I sometimes wonder that it took a war to get me educated. At any rate, my mother decided that education and I should become acquainted, so at eight years of age, my carefree days ended. During my next few years, as my family moved around Manitoba and then to Vancouver, I attended fourteen different schools, ranging from a tiny country school with eight grades in one room to a large, city high school. Always a little behind everyone else, I remember my early education as both frightening and downright difficult.

At the end of grade nine, just when I was beginning to get the hang of school and actually enjoying it, I was forced to leave and help support my family. I spent a frustrating year as a printer getting my hands stuck between print rollers and cutting the tops off my fingernails with a paper cutter. My boss and I discovered I was not mechanically inclined. As I despaired, a friend told me about night school and how it could change my life. So at the end of each day, I scrubbed off the ink, bandaged my fingers, and attended night school. I took grades 10, 11, and 12, managing by some miracle to graduate in one year.

After a year at a teachers' college, I became a teacher. I'll never forget my first day. Nineteen, nervous, and totally dehydrated, I needed a drink of water before I walked into my grade-six class. Never be the first to drink from a drinking fountain after the summer holidays. I'm sure my delightful group of twelve-year-olds wondered why their teacher was drenched from his head to his shoes. But from that day I knew I had found my niche. I can't think of a single unhappy day that I have had in a classroom. I moved up the teaching ladder to college level, while at the same time obtaining a Bachelor of Arts in English and Drama at the University of British Columbia and a Master's Degree in Drama at the University of Washington.

Besides teaching, I've always been a dabbler in theater—first as an amateur, then as a professional. After seven years as an artistic director of two Vancouver theater companies, I moved to London, England, so that I could work as a professional actor in films and television as well as on stage. In 1977 my wife, daughter, and three sons all agreed to join me there.

After nearly three years in the world of British theater, I returned to education with good memories, no regrets, and lots of enthusiasm for a new venture: writing textbooks. You are now reading from my fourth book.

Foot Loose
by Gino Nasato, student

I am a foot. I was pulled kicking from warm security on August 16, 1957. It was not so much the cold that startled me that fateful morning, as my realization that I was forever attached to a stumbling lout named Gino Nasato. Still, life was grand during the early months; Gino simply lay on his back and played baby. At the age of eight months, though, our peaceful co-existence was shattered when the lout started to walk. Oh, to describe the pain of those early years brings back horrid memories. I was kicked, I was bumped, I was stubbed, and I was stomped. Self-preservation in mind, I fought back with a vengeance. For the first ten years I tripped him as often as possible. The knees and the elbows hated me for the pain I inflicted, and his poor mother despised me for the clothes she was always mending. Through the high-school years I was continually abused. If I wasn't being butted painfully against a soccer ball, I was risking toes and heels with daring slides into second base. My only hope was that Gino would get a soft desk job after graduating. I hoped in vain.

First it was logging and those terrible spiked boots. Tired of logging, Gino went to sea, where hard, slippery, cold steel decks awaited me. I still lose my footing when I think of how that ship rolled. In his twenty-first year Gino decided to go to Europe. The dreams I had— visions of French music and Gino sitting in cafes, resting me on stools.

Oh, the naivete of a foot! That beggar shuffled me through Paris subways, blistered me in Athens midday heat, and hobbled me on cobbled streets in Amsterdam. My only respite came when we hit the beaches of Greece. For two glorious months I was in Dr. Scholl's heaven: cool wet sand to leave my autograph in and sparkling surf to soak my calluses. But, alas, it wasn't to last; chasing a pretty face who had cold feet, Gino wound up in Vancouver.

It was about this time that I felt my toes had been stepped on long enough. I formulated a plan with the ankle, and during one of Gino's efforts to kick up his heels, we twisted severely. I was tickled pink when the doctor prescribed one month of total rest, with me kept in an elevated position. Finally, after twenty-three years, I was put on the pedestal I rightfully deserved. With some guidance from me, Gino has finally recognized the prominent role I play in his life. He's now back studying at school, which gives me plenty of time to relax. In fact, things have been going so well lately, I'm thinking of passing on my secrets to other downtrodden feet. I might even start a revolution. After all, just think of all the foot soldiers I could recruit!

For Discussion

Memories

1. You, the reader of *Writing: Process to Product*, are the intended audience for this autobiographical essay. What is your feeling about learning something about the person who is trying to help you improve your writing process? Are there things left unsaid that you would like to know?
2. The essay, for the most part, uses the direct style, but it does contain humor. Find examples of both the direct style and the humorous style.
3. Does the connecting thread, the writer's involvement in education, unify the essay? Explain.

Foot Loose

1. This is a witty example of a student autobiography using a persona. Why do you think the writer chose to use this persona instead of writing in his own voice? If you were to use a persona in your essay, what would it be? Why?
2. How did Gino Nasato's persona influence the selection of details for his essay? What kinds of details might he have left out? Why?
3. Find examples of an ironic style in this essay.

8 Biographical Essay

A biographical essay has the same relationship to a full-length biography that an autobiographical essay has to an autobiography. An essay is much shorter, and its writer must be much more selective in choosing details.

For some people, writing a biographical essay is easier than writing an autobiographical essay. Often it takes less effort to write about others than to reveal ourselves.

ASSIGNMENT ▶ Write a biographical essay of at least 300 words. Your subject should be (a) someone you know well or (b) someone about whom you know a great deal.

Prewriting Process

1. Decide who will be your subject. It could be someone you know well, such as your mother, father, grandparent, boyfriend, or girlfriend. It could be a celebrity whose career you have followed, such as a movie or television star or an athlete. At any rate, it should be someone about whom you already know a great deal.

2. Before you begin, decide on a purpose for writing the biography. (Sorry: "Because I have to write it" is not a good enough purpose.) Write a statement of purpose that includes both your topic and your audience. Notice how the following statements of purpose take both topic and audience into account.

BIOGRAPHICAL ESSAY 79

© 1972 United Feature Syndicate, Inc.

I intend to write an article for our school paper to introduce a friend who is running for the school council.

I must write and then present an introduction of a speaker at a student assembly so that students and teachers will know a little about her before she speaks.

I have been invited to a "roast" for a friend of mine. I have to deliver a speech giving a humorous account of his life.

3. Keep purpose and audience in mind as you gather information. In some cases your audience will be most interested in factual details. In other cases, they may be more interested in finding out what kind of person your subject is.

4. Like an autobiographical essay, a biographical essay needs a thread running through it to unify it. One good way to unify your essay is to choose a major characteristic of your subject and base your essay on that particular quality. If you cannot think of a major characteristic (such as likeability, honesty, or special talent), perhaps you do not know enough

about your subject to write a good biography. In that case, choose another subject for your essay.

If you have difficulty determining a major characteristic, interview your subject (if the subject is someone you personally know). Here are some examples of questions you can ask.

- a) What do you think is your best characteristic? Your worst?
- b) What makes you happiest? Saddest?
- c) What do you think your friends think of you? Your enemies (if any)?
- d) What places away from home have you visited?
- e) How many times have you moved? Where?
- f) What events were most important in your life?
- g) Of what achievement are you proudest?
- h) (If your subject is running for office) What would you do if elected?

5. To gather more information, you may want to do more reading about your subject if that person is well known. If the subject is someone you know personally, you may want to talk to others who know that person (with your subject's permission, of course).

6. To help shape your material, you can do the brainstorming technique called Newspaper Reporter's Questions (page 222).

Drafting Process

1. Plan how you are going to organize your essay. Most biographies are told in chronological order, but you may wish to use another method discussed in Chapter 26. Two possibilities are Comparison/Contrast and Cause and Effect. Your statement of purpose, as well as the unifying thread you choose, can help you decide which kind of organization is most appropriate.

2. You can write about your subject directly by telling your readers what kind of person she or he is. You can simply relate things your subject has said and done and allow your reader to infer that person's qualities. You can also quote what others have said about your subject. Often a combination of these methods is most effective.

3. As with an autobiographical essay, you should maintain a consistent style. To help you decide which style to choose, see the examples of straightforward, colloquial, ironic, and humorous styles on page 74. Then write a paragraph or so of your essay in each style to see which one best suits your subject and purpose.

Editing and Revising Process

Both you and your peer editors can use the suggestions in Chapter 28 to help them edit and you revise your essay. In addition, they and you should consider the following questions.

1. Does the information in the biography satisfy the needs of the intended audience?
2. Are the subject's qualities easily recognized?
3. Are the subject's accomplishments clearly told?
4. What kind of organization does the essay follow? Is the method of organization appropriate to the essay? Is there a unifying thread?
5. Does the essay's subject seem a real, living, breathing person? If not, would it help to include more information?
6. In what style is the biography written? Is the style appropriate to the topic, purpose, and audience?
7. Does the essay avoid the use of overworked adjectives, such as *nice*, in describing the subject?
8. Should any words, sentences, or paragraphs be omitted? Why?
9. Should anything be added? Why?
10. Should anything be changed? Why?

After you have revised your biography on the basis of your peer editors' comments, prepare a clean copy and give it to your teacher/editor. Revise again if necessary. Then publish your biographical essay by giving it to your intended reader.

Products

Fernando Valenzuela: The Titan of Pitching
by Katharine A. Diaz

For a while he was the pride of the barrio, the talk of the baseball season. The Dodger stadium organist was opening with tunes like "Quizas, quizas" [Maybe, maybe]. Dan Rather once even closed the "CBS Evening News" with "hasta la vista, buenas noches" [until tomorrow, good evening] after airing a news segment on him.

We're of course talking about Dodger super pitcher Fernando Valenzuela, who charmed his way into millions of hearts across the country. The baseball strike took him out of the news for a time, and although there was no doubt in our minds that Fernando had only just begun, what a relief it is to know that with the strike over, he will once again star on the mound.

Fernando was born on November 1, 1960 in the small village of Fundicion near Navajoa in the state of Sonora. For all practical purposes he was born into baseball. His father and six of his brothers (Fernando has 11 brothers and sisters) played ball. Being the youngest in the family, Fernando found plenty of time to play. His eldest brother, Rafael, knew he was a natural for the game. By 16 he was playing in the Mexican League. Eventually he was picked up by the AAA Puebla Angels and loaned to Yucatan. There he acquired a 10-12 record, a 2.43 ERA, 141 strikeouts and gave up only 70 bases in 157 innings pitched.

It didn't take long before he was noticed by scouts from U.S. major league teams. Indeed, the Yankees, Pirates, Mariners, Mets and Cubs were all interested in Fernando. In the end, to the good fortune of the Dodgers, he signed with them. Fernando first trained in Lodi, then went to the Dodgers' camp in Vero Beach. It was here that Fernando was to pick up the pitch that would add the kick to his arsenal of pitches. It was here that teammate and relief pitcher Bobby Castillo taught him to throw the screwball.

Since then Fernando has amazed baseball experts with his mastery of the screwball. The comment most often heard is how one so young could have mastered it so completely. And mastered it he has, to the chagrin of many a player.

If, however, Fernando had to base his baseball career on his screwball, his career might be shortlived. But when Fernando takes the mound he comes equipped with a variety of pitches, including a fastball that has been clocked at 88 m.p.h. Fernando also knows his batters, watches his signs and keeps the batters guessing. Fernando has also been called the thinking man's baseball player, fielding hits, tagging runners out. His batting average, too, is not bad.

So now we know the hard facts about Fernando, but obviously there's more to it than being a fantastic ball player. There is.

His story has fairy tale qualities to it. His humbleness, his age, his coolness and his rise to fame have enchanted us all. Fernando is a super hero and he is one of us. His success has given us a lot of pride and a sense of responsibility. And the inspiration he has been to youth makes him a national treasure.

Fernando, we are glad you are here.

Who Is Whoopi Goldberg, and What Is She Doing on Broadway?

by Pamela Noel

The empty stage of the Lyceum Theater gives no clue to what is coming—or who. In the audience sit black and white people, young and old, some in furs, others in sweat suits or jeans. They're there to see Whoopi Goldberg and, in her inimitable way, she shows up.

"Aaahround the woorlld in eightty . . . days." A scratchy singing voice wafts over the empty stage, setting off giggles from the audience. A figure struts onstage wearing dark shades, dressed in black with a bright blue scarf tied around a mass of braids. "My name is Fontaine . . . ," he says. . . .

"He" actually is Whoopi Goldberg, 34, live on stage and in many characters. In the next 90 minutes, she becomes not only the hip-walking, slick-talking Fontaine (who in the end proves even he has a heart) but a white surfer girl . . . ; a handicapped woman who talks about being in love; a Jamaican woman who inherits a fortune; an aging black tap dancer who hasn't lost his timing, and a little black girl who wants to . . . go on the *Love Boat*. . . . These are just a few of the seventeen characters in Whoopi Goldberg's repertoire and it is these characters she has brought to Broadway and used to earn praise as one of today's rising young stars.

But just who is Whoopi Goldberg, and what is she doing on Broadway?

First of all, Whoopi Goldberg isn't her real name. Whoopi says her real name is nobody's business. "It amazes me that there's been such a fervor about it," she says. "I've been Whoopi Goldberg for eight years. No one has ever questioned me about it before."

She says her mother, Emma (Whoopi also won't tell her mother's last name), divined the name Goldberg out of her head one day after convincing Whoopi that nobody would take her work seriously if she kept calling herself Whoopi Cushion (a name that came up in a discussion of what not to name a child). But why Goldberg? "I've asked her 'Why Goldberg?'," Whoopi says. "She's more private than I am. She just said 'Because it's ours.' " In some ways, Whoopi says, her name gives her an edge with audiences. "Once they get past the fact that I'm Whoopi Goldberg, then they realize anything is possible."

Whoopi is not a comedian. "I'm an actor," she says. "I've always been an actor. That is what I do."

There are other things she is willing to tell. For instance, that her mother works for Head Start in New York and raised Whoopi and her older brother, Clyde, by herself. She grew up in New York's Chelsea area, started acting in children's theater at age eight and graduated from the New York High School of Performing Arts. . . .

Whoopi first moved to the West Coast in 1974. A licensed beautician, she styled hair at a mortuary for a while. She was a bank teller, a bricklayer and a welfare recipient. But mostly she was on the road, doing her solo act, . . . working with repertory companies and with the Blake Street Hawkeyes, an avant-garde theater troupe in Berkeley. She was trained in theater at the Lee Strasberg Actors Workshop and in the early 1970s, appeared in *Pippin, Jesus Christ Superstar,* and *Hair.* She also co-wrote and performed a one woman show in which she played the late comedienne Moms Mabley.

Her big break, Whoopi says, came two years ago when someone from New York's Dance Theater Workshop, an off-Broadway theater, called to invite her to perform there the following year. It was there that stage and film director Mike Nichols first spotted her and later offered to present her on Broadway.

Since her show opened in the fall, Whoopi has continued to battle the label of comedienne. "I could never be a stand-up [comic]. It's hard work," she says, "much harder than anything I do." She also shrugs off comparisons of her offbeat characters to the work of Richard Pryor. "One style of what I do has comedic elements along the lines of Richard Pryor's 'This is the way it is folks' kind of stuff," she says. "But Richard does his thing as himself and I do *nothing* as myself."

From the moment she comes on stage Whoopi constantly becomes somebody else. "Her discipline as an actress is considerable," says veteran actor Roscoe Lee Browne. "She's very quick with her material and when she switches from one character into another, you go right with her. You believe her instantly."

Often, her characters present lessons-in-life to the audience.

"I just want people to think," Whoopi says. "I don't want people to take things at face value." It can take from ten minutes to a year for a character to fully develop in Whoopi's mind, she says. "Those people who inhabit my body actually are full-blooded people. I just kind of sit back and watch what they're up to. I become part of the audience."

But who is Whoopi Goldberg? She is, she says, a humanitarian. . . . She jogs when the feeling hits her, enjoys reading, old movies and quick trips to museums. Her constant companion these days is a Scottish terrier named Otis ("After the elevator, you know").

Even with the current success she is having (including an album of her show) she maintains a simple lifestyle at her home on the West Coast. Her one extravagance has been the purchase of a 1960 "bright, blood red" Porsche, she says.

Whoopi is looking forward, past the Broadway stage, to stardom in films—a lifelong ambition. She is fielding ideas, including a possible major role in the film version of Pulitzer Prize-winning novelist Alice Walker's *The Color Purple*. Whoopi also plans to write scripts.

"I'm fighting the label of 'black' actress," she says, "simply because it's very limiting in people's eyes, especially people who are making movies. I don't want them to say, 'Oh, she's a black actor, we can't use her.' I want them to say, 'Oh here's a great role. Call Meryl Streep. Call Diane Keaton. Call Whoopi Goldberg.' "

Personality Salesman
by Kristin Nelson, student

My stepuncle has got to be the most dynamic person I have ever known. He's constantly on the go, impatient to get on with life.

He knows more people than the average person could ever hope to meet. A good example of this was when my family took him to Lake Chelan on his first summer in Seattle. We stopped in the tiny town of Winthrop and went into an old-fashioned grocery store for ice cream. He turned around and saw a friend he had known ten years earlier!

If he doesn't already know someone, it doesn't take long. He has a way about him that makes people feel he really cares about what they say. One time we were standing in line for concert tickets, and he started talking to an elderly lady in front of us. Half an hour later, she was in a restaurant eating lunch with us!

His idea of Hell would be a place with no people. He has to have an audience, or a group of people around him at all times. He's a people-person and quickly grows bored if he's alone.

A successful real estate corporate owner, he began his career as a salesman when he was still in high school. As a teenager, he was named top salesman, selling teflon-coated pans for a local company. He owned an expensive car and had $18,000.00 in the bank to show for all his hard work. When kids at school teased him about driving "Daddy's car," his anger flared. He was proud of what he worked hard to earn, and he wanted some recognition for his achievements.

His hunger for success is typical of many "rags to riches" stories. His family was very poor when he was young, and he vowed to himself not ever to have to live in poverty again.

The key to his personality is his ability to communicate with people. He sells his personality.

For Discussion

Fernando Valenzuela: The Titan of Pitching

1. Does Katharine A. Diaz convince her readers that Valenzuela is a true titan? If so, how?
2. Is there other information you think should have been included in this essay? If so, what?
3. This biographical essay appeared in *Caminos*, a magazine for Hispanic readers. What phrases and details indicate that Diaz is writing for this audience?

Who Is Whoopi Goldberg, and What Is She Doing on Broadway?

1. Who might be the audience for this biographical essay?
2. Why do you think the essay begins with Whoopi Goldberg on the stage? What do you learn about her performance and talents?
3. Why does she stress that she is an actor rather than a comic? Do you think the details in the essay support this claim? Explain.

Personality Salesman

1. What is Kristin Nelson's attitude toward her stepuncle? What words, phrases, and details show her attitude?
2. This biography contains only a little specific information. Why do you think Kristin did not tell more about her stepuncle?
3. What might be the purpose of this biography?

9 Review

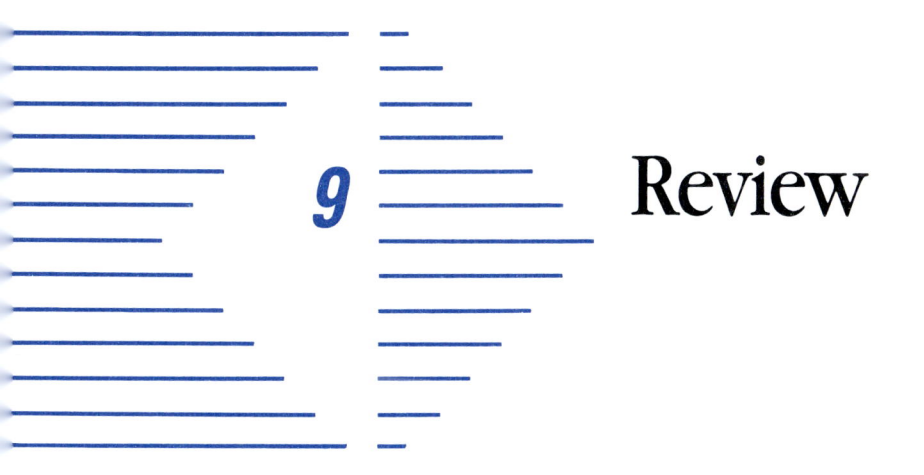

A review is a kind of argumentative essay in which a writer presents an opinion, with reasons to back it up, about a particular work of art. But a good review includes more than a well-presented opinion. Review writers cannot assume that their readers know anything about the work under review. They must present information as well as an opinion about the work. Therefore, a good review is usually a combination of information and opinion.

ASSIGNMENT ▶ In about 500 words, write a review of a book, a film, a play, a television show, a record, or other work of art.

Prewriting Process

1. Before you begin, you might like to look up back copies of newspapers and magazines to read reviews of books, plays, movies, and other works. But read cautiously. Professional critics often thrive on controversy, especially that which follows unfavorable reviews. Some critics like to show off their own cleverness with remarks such as the following.

This play is the worst thing that happened to the United States since World War II.

The actress ran the gamut of emotions from A to B.

This is Mr. Smith's first novel. Let us hope it is his last.

Avoid such statements unless they truly express your opinion of the work you are reviewing.

2. Before you gather evidence for your own review, you should read the examples at the end of this chapter to see how other reviewers present both information and opinions about works of art.

3. The main reason for writing a review is to present your opinion. Hence, you are expected to be critical. Criticizing a work of art, however, does not mean that you must be unfair or destructive. You should discuss what you think works well and what does not work well. To help you form an opinion, you might find it useful to jot down what you like about the work and what you do not like. Notice how the following reviewer jotted down good and bad points about a novel.

Good	*Bad*
interesting major characters (you care what happens to them)	poor minor characters (you never really get to know them)
convincing dialogue	long descriptions hold up the action
exciting scenes	confusing plot
well written	poor ending (nothing resolved)

At this point, you may also want to jot down evidence to support your opinion of the work's good and bad points. Such evidence can include facts, examples, and quotations—for example, a vague minor character, a confusing plot development, a reference to an exciting scene, a quotation that shows good (or bad) writing.

4. To find additional supporting evidence, complete one or two of the following brainstorming techniques from Chapter 23: Newspaper Reporter's Questions, Pro/Con Ladders, Positive Cluster, Negative Cluster.

5. To make this assignment more interesting for you, assume that your review will be published in your local or school newspaper. Assume also that your audience consists mostly of people your own age who share your interest in films, television, mystery novels, or whatever.

6. Complete a set of writing variables.

Drafting Process

1. At the beginning of the review, identify what you are reviewing. (What is the title? Is it a book, a play, a film, a television show?) Give other information appropriate to the kind of work it is: for example, author and publisher (if a book); theater (if a play); director (if a play or

film); network, date, and time (if a television show); musicians and record label (if a record).

2. If reviewing a novel, film, or television play, give enough of the plot to let your readers decide whether or not they wish to read or see the work. Do not tell the whole story; a review is not a summary. In fact, identifying the murderer in a mystery is almost as bad as committing the murder yourself. Tell enough to whet your reader's interest. (If you are reviewing a nonfiction book, you should give some idea of the information it covers.)

3. Consider the kind of work you are reviewing and its purpose. Ultimately a work of art should be judged according to purpose. Did the work succeed in entertaining you? Involving you? Informing you? Convincing you?

4. Make sure you back up your opinion with specific references to the work under review.

5. If you are reviewing a book, including a few quotations can enliven your review. Be sure the quotations you choose illustrate specific points you are making. If you do include quotations, fit them into your own prose so that the review flows smoothly. For some examples of mixing quotations with a writer's own prose, see Chapter 11, page 115.

6. A review is an expression of one writer's opinion. As you write your review, make sure your reader knows exactly where you stand. Be opinionated. (But back up your opinions!) Be emphatic. Indeed, try to include something memorable—a pun, perhaps, or a witty quotation—that sticks with the reader so that your opinion will be remembered.

7. Because a review is an argumentative essay, you may find it useful to read or review the drafting suggestions in Chapter 5 (page 57). If you have difficulty organizing your review, you may wish to follow the basic essay structure discussed in that chapter: introduction, development, conclusion.

Editing and Revising Process

Before giving your review to your peer editors, you should first judge it yourself according to the set of standards in Chapter 28 (page 271) and make what changes you think necessary. Your peer editors can decide which method presented in Chapter 28 to follow when they go over your writing. Both they and you can also use the following questions to help edit and revise.

1. Does the review give enough information to let the reader know what the work under review is about?

2. Is the reviewer's opinion of the work clearly expressed? Does the reviewer provide reasons to back up the opinion?

3. Is the review convincing? That is, would its readers do as the reviewer suggests—either read or not read, see or not see the work being reviewed?

4. Is the organization of the review logical and easy to follow?

5. Is any part of the review not clear? If so, what can be done to make it clear?

6. Does the review include appropriate quotations? Are the quotations used to illustrate particular points?

Once your peers have edited your review, make whatever changes you think necessary and prepare a clean copy for your teacher/editor. After your teacher/editor edits your writing, prepare a final version for your intended audience.

Products

Review of *Watership Down*
by Alexander Targ, student

The movie *Watership Down*, set in the English countryside some time during the early 1900s, has an exciting plot as well as a number of other features that make it a most enjoyable film. The movie, directed by Martin Rosen, is an animated version of Richard Adams's book of the same title. *Watership Down* follows the adventures of a small group of rabbits, who learn from a clairvoyant member of the group that their warren is doomed to destruction and that they must migrate to a new location to save themselves. In their migration, the rabbits have many hair-raising adventures.

Watership Down creates a world of fantasy which is believable enough to permit viewers to lose themselves in it. The fairy-tale-like setting of *Watership Down* is made believable partly because the rabbits never do anything, aside from using language to communicate among themselves, which is outside the realm of a normal rabbit's capabilities. The viewers' easy identification with the rabbit characters helps them to immerse themselves in the world created by the movie. A factor strengthening the identification is the similarity between the rabbits' motivations and those of ourselves. They are leaving a doomed yet deceptively friendly home on a hazardous trip, not only to escape the menace at home but also with the purpose of bettering their social positions. Similarly, most people have had to face temporary insecurity to bring about a change for the better.

The animation of *Watership Down* is extremely beautiful and changes with the moods of the film. Part of the animation is done with watercolor paints, which achieve a remarkable effect. The background abounds with a wealth of detail, all contributing to the believability of the settings. The film opens with a mythological interpretation of rabbit history, which is animated in the style of prehistoric art. Later, during a death sequence involving bounding symbolic red and blue rabbits, the style of drawing becomes reminiscent of Egyptian tomb paintings. The animation and watercolors are skillfully combined to produce a unique and versatile filmmaking style, which is the highlight of the film.

Through its stunning artwork and skillful portrayal of the characters, *Watership Down* presents a strong ecological message to its viewers. The rabbits must find a new home because of the destruction of their original warren by humans in preparation for a housing development. What the movie emphasizes through its characterizations of the rabbits is the humanity and degree of civilization and compassion of the rabbit way of life, as opposed to the seeming selfishness of people. By forcing one to realize that undeveloped land can be beautiful and valuable as a place where wild animals can live, the film makes one want to preserve the unspoiled lands remaining in the country.

Because of its animation, its unreal yet believable world, and its important social message, *Watership Down* is a potentially inspiring movie. The film definitely is entertaining, but the mark of a truly fine film is its ability to change the opinion of viewers or to lastingly move them in some way after they have left the theater. Though many emotions are called forth during *Watership Down*, it fails to change one viewer's outlook on life in any way. It is a charming film, but it lacks ultimate seriousness. When the beautiful watercolor prints are gone and the rabbits stop flitting across the screen, the spell is broken and the viewer is left with little to take home. While the movie is definitely beautiful and engaging, it left me feeling merely entertained.

John F. Kennedy Reexamined
by Heather Hamill, student

Who was the true man behind the famous name—John Fitzgerald Kennedy? Was he the knight in shining armor many Americans perceived, or was that just a cover to a book people didn't care to open?

In his biography, *J.F.K.: The Presidency of John F. Kennedy* (New York: Dial Press, 1983), Herbert S. Parmet attempts to distinguish the man from the myth.

Searching for the truth, Parmet delves into Kennedy's professional as well as personal life. He deals with the period from Kennedy's pursuit of the Presidential nomination until his death after only 1037 days as the nation's thirty-fifth President. He evaluates Kennedy's role in the civil rights movement, the Bay of Pigs invasion, the Cuban missile crisis and the controversy over the impending Vietnam War. This complex biography depicts a man who lived within what Parmet believed was "an artificial world that posed as a modern Camelot" (353).

A professor of history at the City University of New York, Herbert S. Parmet has written and lectured extensively on recent American history. His preoccupation with the subject, as well as his dislike of previous Kennedy biographies, prompted him to write one that struck "a balance between the romance of the early Kennedy biographies and the revisionism of later ones" (410).

In discovering the essence of the man and relating that to a deep understanding of the times, Herbert Parmet interprets Kennedy and his administration in contrast to the views of most other authors. By subtracting the charm and glamour that mark those years and by drawing upon newly declassified documents and momentous interviews, Parmet concludes that "Jack Kennedy, to whom the torch had been passed, became the orphan of failure. At best he was an 'interim' President who had promised but not performed" (354). Parmet feels that during this era "glamour overshadowed quality" (101), and he bluntly states that Kennedy's "thousand days led to the nightmare years that followed" (258).

Although he emphasizes the misgivings and the failures of the 1960s, Parmet does not deny the good that also resulted. Briefly summarizing Kennedy's accomplishments, he states, "At his death he was involved in sounding out a new, saner relationship with Cuba. The face that he put on the national purpose through such programs as the Peace Corps and the Alliance for Progress, whatever their limitations, was at least consistent with the idealism much of the world preferred to associate with America" (208). Parmet understands that what the general public wanted and needed was someone whom they could hope with, dream with and believe. That is what they saw in J.F.K.—that is all they wanted to see. Herbert Parmet states his basic theme most clearly in the Epilogue when he says, "During his brief period in the White House he established a new style and tone for the presidency, one that evoked national pride and hope. That made his limitations all the more painful" (365).

J.F.K.: The Presidency of John F. Kennedy is illuminating but disappointing. It explains the pain, struggles and failures and very few of the successes of a man who has always been a hero to me. Parmet interprets the truth in a sometimes painfully blunt fashion. Although establishing basic facts and reality, he says very little about the human qualities of the man himself and the hope he brought to many Americans. It was as if I were reading a critical review of a play which everyone but the critic seemed to enjoy.

I caution against the reading of this book to anyone who, for whatever reason, thinks of Kennedy with hope and admiration and holds in his or her heart a deep respect and love for him. This biography may shatter those dreams! Recognizing the danger of idealism when it clouds reality, I still believe that in the ever-increasing tensions of today's world, people need assurance that people in high office still hold high ideals. Kennedy brought these ideals to office with him. They are what I remember when I think of him. Perhaps if more people remembered them from past eras, we would discover them more often in our society today.

Review of *Brave New World*
by Linda Brown, student

Have you ever read a novel with several literary flaws that was still a good book? If not, here's one for you! First published in 1932, Aldous Huxley's *Brave New World* contains a couple of literary problems, but it remains interesting and worthwhile reading. Set in London sometime in the future, Huxley's novel, reminiscent of George Orwell's *1984,* presents a critical view of the result of technological advancements in the future.

As mentioned, the novel has several literary flaws. The main flaw is that two-thirds of the way through the story, Huxley drops his major character, Bernard Marx. Bernard begins to question the leaders and policies of his world and is sent away to prevent instability in the society. John Savage soon takes over as the main character, and he has to make a decision to live either "an insane life in Utopia, or the life of a primitive in an Indian village." Perhaps John is an extension of Bernard, but by the time the reader gets over Bernard and interested in John, he or she does not really care.

Several other problems exist in the novel. The first chapter reads like a science textbook. Huxley uses his scientific knowledge a bit too much, and this makes the chapter extremely verbose and confusing. If this chapter were an indication of the book as a whole, it would never have been published. Furthermore, some characters need more development. The reader knows hardly anything about Lenina, Helmholtz, or Mustapha Monde. They are there to add strength to the theme, but they leave before contributing to the story in any real way. A final problem that this reviewer found is that the conclusion is unsatisfying. John makes his choice, but the reader does not follow his reasoning.

In spite of these flaws, the novel is interesting. According to Huxley, "The theme of *Brave New World* is not the advancement of science as such; it is the advancement of science as it affects human individuals." For the time period in which the novel was written, Huxley showed startling creativity and a bountiful imagination. Babies are made in test tubes, and helicopter-like vehicles are the only form of transportation.

The novel presents us with a critical view of what the world could be like in the future. It opened this reviewer's eyes to the fact that the future is in our hands today and that what happens in it is our choice. Although the author doesn't actually come out and state his opinion, there is an underlying hint of his true feelings incorporated in the story through the use of satire.

The novel has flaws, as do most works of art, but it is interesting and worthy of our attention. It has a serious message flavored with humor that results in, according to one critic, "Mr. Huxley's most enduring masterpiece."

For Discussion

Review of *Watership Down*

1. This student review follows basic essay structure. What is the thesis of the review? Identify the topic sentences of the second, third, and fourth paragraphs.
2. What does the reviewer like about the film? What evidence does he present to support his general points?
3. What is the reviewer's final opinion of the film? What reason does he give to support his opinion? Do you think he presents enough evidence in the essay to support his opinion? Explain why or why not.

John F. Kennedy Reexamined

1. What, according to Heather Hamill, is Herbert Parmet's attitude toward Kennedy? What is her own attitude?
2. What sentence in this review best states Heather Hamill's reaction to Parmet's book?

3. Do you think Heather Hamill presents a fair statement of Parmet's case against Kennedy, even though she disagrees with it? Explain.
4. The review ends with four sentences presenting Heather Hamill's own opinion of Kennedy. Do you think the review would be better or worse if the sentences were cut? Give reasons for your answer.

Review of *Brave New World*

1. What is the thesis statement of this review? What evidence does Linda Brown present to support her thesis statement?
2. Linda Brown states that *"Brave New World* is interesting and worthy of our attention." Does her review convince you of her opinion? Explain.

10 Literary Essay

If you want to judge the effectiveness of a literary work, you write a review. In a literary essay, you interpret what the work, or a part of it, means. When you write a literary essay about a novel, short story, poem, or play, you need to go beneath the surface to explore the work's deeper meaning. Your reader should acquire a better appreciation and understanding of the work from your essay. This chapter suggests a number of approaches to interpretation, but simply retelling the story is not one of them. Keep in mind that a summary is not an interpretation. What summarizing you do should be used to support what you say.

ASSIGNMENT ▶ Write a literary essay giving your interpretation of one of the literary works on pages 367–387 (or another work chosen by you or your teacher).

Close Reading

Before you can write a good literary essay, you must be able to read a work closely—that is, to achieve a deep understanding of the work and how all its parts fit together. The following suggestions will help you develop a close-reading process.

   1. Reading a good work of literature can be like meeting a new friend; it can change your life. When you read, open yourself to the possibility of experiencing something new or of being reminded of something you

had forgotten. Good writers can engage your emotions as well as your mind, so allow yourself to feel sad, happy, angry, contented, afraid, or whatever emotion the work awakens in you.

The first time you read a work, do so without stopping to analyze it; just let it sweep you along. When you have finished, sit for a while and think about the work as a whole and what it means to you. Ask yourself what you have learned or what you have experienced in a new way. For example, you may have gained a deeper understanding of some aspect of the human condition, such as trust, honesty, people's inhumanity to other people, aging, or death.

2. Reread the work. If it is a story or a play, go beyond the plot this time. Reading for the plot alone limits you. Reading for deeper meanings allows you to think about the theme, or underlying idea, that the writer wants to convey. Good writers provide clues to help you understand their work. As you reread, focus particularly on sections or aspects that moved you, intrigued you, or even confused you during your first reading. How and why did these parts affect you? Answering this question will not only help you appreciate some aspect of the work but could also provide a topic for your literary essay.

3. We all have a tendency to put something of ourselves into what we read; a personal response makes interpretation possible. But you must be careful not to interpret the work in a way that the author never intended. Do not let your feelings or biases mislead you. Concentrate on **textual evidence**, what is actually there on the printed page. Read carefully what the author has written to discover what is implied.

Thinking about the following literary elements should help you arrive at what the author is saying.

Fiction

Tone. Very early in reading a short story or novel, you should determine the author's tone—that is, the author's attitude toward the plot and characters as revealed through her or his words. Ask yourself: Is the author being direct or ironic? (Should you take the words at their face value or understand that the author means the opposite of what he or she seems to be saying?) In order to help you decide, you should determine who the narrator is and from what point of view the story or novel is being told.

Narrator and point of view. The narrator of a story or novel may be one of the characters telling the story from a first-person point of view (I). If the story is told in the first person, ask yourself: Who is the narrator?

Is he or she to be trusted? (Not all narrators in stories or novels are trustworthy. Some may be biased, and others may be dishonest.)

Fiction can also be told from a third-person point of view (she or he). Sometimes the narrator is an all-knowing observer, who tells not only what the characters say and do but also what they think and feel. Some all-knowing narrators even speak directly to the reader, commenting on the characters and what they do. A novel or story can also be told in the third person but reveal what only one character—usually the hero or heroine—thinks and feels. In such a case, the work is essentially told from that character's point of view.

Conflict. In nearly every work of fiction, there is at least one conflict; there may be several. Conflicts can be external—with other people, with nature—or they can be internal—within the opposing sides or desires of one character. Sometimes a conflict in a story or novel is like one that you have experienced in real life. Focus on the fictional conflict to see how the hero or heroine deals with it. You will then be able to reflect on how you would deal with a similar conflict.

Often the conflicts in stories and novels represent more general conflicts that many people in many different countries and centuries have experienced. For example, many people have struggled with nature or with their own weaknesses. Such general conflicts are called **archetypal conflicts**. Stories and novels that have lasted through the ages often examine archetypal conflicts and through such examination explore what it means to be a human being. Several examples of archetypal conflict are the conflict between generations, the "lovers' steeplechase" (boy meets girl, boy loses girl, boy gets girl), and the internal struggle to become a better person. You may think that your own joy or pain is unique, but when you read fine literature, you come to realize that many situations involving pain and joy are universal and archetypal.

When you closely read a work of fiction, you should first determine the specific conflict (or conflicts) and then think of it (or them) in archetypal terms.

Character. You can arrive at an understanding of fictional characters by thinking about what they say and do, how other characters react to them, and (in some cases) what the author says about them. Just as there may be archetypal conflicts in fiction, so also an author may create **archetypal characters**—that is, characters representing general, universal types. Think about the characters you have encountered in fiction (as well as people you know). How many of them resemble or represent the following archetypal characters: the struggling student, the whiz kid, the frustrated lover, the artist, the trickster, the wise old man, Cinderella, the apprentice, the innocent, the victim, Mother Earth, the magician, the healer, the leader, the follower? (Remember that characters do not have to be the same age or sex as the archetypal character to resemble that character. The boy Piggy in William Golding's novel *Lord of the Flies* is an archetypal wise old man. The hero of Charles Dickens's *Oliver Twist* is an archetypal Cinderella.)

Symbols. A symbol stands for something else, usually a quality or idea. For example, a rose usually symbolizes beauty, and a skull can be used to symbolize death. A symbol often suggests several related ideas; thus a rose can stand not only for beauty but also for the fragility of beauty. Such related ideas can provide a clue to the work's underlying meaning, its theme.

Theme. In concluding your close reading of a work of fiction, you should study the other literary elements to determine the work's **theme**, the idea behind all the events and characters in the work. You can sometimes express the theme as a generalization about life, such as "Beauty is fleeting," or "Basic values endure." When you explore a work of fiction for its theme, think also about how the theme relates to your own experiences.

Poetry

A good poem is inexhaustible. Like good music, it will bring enjoyment no matter how frequently you read and reread it.

Poems are meant to be heard as well as read. To appreciate a poem fully, you should read it aloud. Many poems have been set to music. The same students who say that they never read poetry, or even that they hate poetry, often spend hours listening to their favorite records—all poems set to music. One exercise that will help you to appreciate poetry is to share your favorite song with your peers and explain why it is your favorite. (Is it because of the words, the images, the sounds, the rhythm, the meaning?)

In your first reading of a poem, you should concentrate on how it affects you. Allow the sounds and the meaning to work within you so that you will be left with an overall impression, a combination of emotion and idea. Then reread the poem to see how its elements work together to produce the emotion and idea.

The following questions and suggestions will help you think about a poem's elements and their effect on you.

1. What is your immediate response to the poem? Does it make you feel happy, sad, confused, concerned, hopeful, or some other emotion?

2. How has the effect been accomplished? Consider the poem's **language** (its specific use of words), its **sound**, its **imagery** (word pictures), its **rhythm**, its use of **rhyme** (words that end in the same sound, such as "take" and "make"), and its **symbols**. Many poems use two kinds of comparisons, similes and metaphors, to suggest ideas and to arouse emotion. **Similes** contain a word of comparison ("His voice is like a foghorn"); **metaphors** imply the comparison ("His voice is a foghorn"). Does the poem you are reading use similes and/or metaphors? If so, what emotions and ideas do the comparisons arouse in you?

3. Some poems rely as much on their look on the printed page as on their sound to create an effect. When you reread a poem, consider how it looks: its shape, its division into lines and stanzas (parts of a poem set off by extra space) and (in the case of a few poems) its visual resemblance to its subject.

4. Many of the critical strategies dealing with fiction apply to poetry as well. Many poems deal with conflict. All poems have at least one character, the speaker of the poem. Consider what the poem's words tell you about that character. Also, consider the poem's theme and whether it is stated directly or implied.

Drama

Plays are written to be performed rather than studied in a classroom. As you read a play, you should imagine its being performed on a stage or being shown in a movie theater or on a television screen. Even better, you and your peers can assign parts and do an oral reading of the play. Through an oral reading, you can decide how particular lines in a play should be read and what words and phrases should be emphasized to carry out the playwright's intention. After you have given the play a first reading, reread it, keeping in mind the elements presented in the discussion of fiction (page 98). Almost all these elements apply as much to drama as to novels and stories. In addition, the following strategies will help the play come alive for you.

1. As you read the play and talk about it with your peers, imagine yourself having to act in it or direct it. Actors and directors must find deeper meanings within plays.

2. Playwrights have specific reasons for including each event that takes place in a play and each character and the actions he or she performs. To help you arrive at the play's deeper meaning, think about what these reasons might be.

3. Analyzing the characters in a play is usually more difficult than analyzing the characters in a short story or novel. The reason is that a play often gives only the characters' dialogue with no indication of how the dialogue should be delivered. The following suggestions should help you analyze a play's characters.

a) Pay attention to what the playwright says about the character. A playwright might provide clues to character in a foreword to the play, in a comment included within the play, or in a stage direction.

b) Study what the characters say, but be careful not to take everything they say at face value. A character could be deliberately lying to deceive another character.

c) Note particularly what a character does. Actions are usually the best clue to character.

d) Note what other characters say about the character, but, again, do not necessarily accept their comments at face value.

e) Imagine the various ways in which an actor portraying the character might perform that character's lines. Decide which is the best way.

f) Make up a list of questions like the following about each principal character in a play and find evidence in the play to support each answer: How old is the character? Is he or she basically honest or dishonest? Is he or she basically considerate of others or self-centered? Is he or she ambitious or lazy? A bully? Cruel or kind? Mentally sound?

4. Find a line in the play that is difficult for you to interpret. Think about why the playwright might want the character to say that line.

5. Imagine you are a producer with a lot of money and want to put on a performance of the play. Visualize what an ideal, full-scale production of the play would be. Consider your choice of actors, set, lighting, and costume designs, and be prepared to give reasons for your choices.

Finally, as you give a short story, novel, poem, or play a close reading, consider **unity**—what it all adds up to as a unified work of art. Imagine that you are working on a jigsaw puzzle, with the pieces ready to be assembled. Your analysis of the work should be like the completed puzzle in which all the pieces fit together and are recognizable as a unified picture.

Prewriting Process

Often, when you are assigned a literary essay, you are also assigned a specific literary work to analyze as well as a specific topic. At other times, you are required to choose both the work and the topic. The following suggestions will help you choose and develop a topic.

   1. If you are confused about how to discuss the characters, setting, and conflict in a literary work, try one or two of the following activities before you begin work on your literary essay. When you finish each activity, read the results to your peers and ask them whether or not your writing was successful.

- a) Write a short character sketch of a member of your family or a friend so that, if that person were to walk into the room, your peers would recognize her or him.
- b) Write a short description of one of your favorite places so that your peers will be able to recognize the setting.
- c) Write a short account of a conflict in which you were involved so that your peers can know exactly with whom or what you were in conflict. Tell the results of the conflict.

You will find there is little difference between the way you discuss characters, setting, and conflict in real life and the way you discuss them in literature.

   2. If the choice of selection and topic is up to you, choose a selection that had a marked influence on you and which you think will have a similar influence on other readers. Think about why the selection is important to you and may be important to others. Consider also the reasons why you chose to write about this work and on this topic. In other words, choose a work and topic you think are important to most people and will help you and your readers reach a better understanding of what it is to be human.

   3. Consider your audience. How well does it know the work about which you choose to write? Think about how the content and approach would change if you were writing to (a) an informed reader, such as a literature teacher who has been teaching that selection for many years and (b) one of your peers who has read the selection only once. Decide how much you have to tell about a work before you interpret it. (Remember, though, that a summary is not an interpretation. Tell only as much as you have to in order to support your interpretation.)

4. Once you have chosen your selection and found a suitable topic, you should jot down information about your writing variables to guide you when you draft your essay. When you write your thesis statement, remember that the evidence from your reading should support it.

Drafting Process

A literary essay is essentially an argumentative essay in which you attempt to convince your reader that your interpretation of a literary work is right or at least valid. Before you begin to write your essay, you might wish to review the drafting suggestions in Chapter 5 (page 57). In addition, keep the following suggestions in mind when you write your essay.

1. Early in the essay, give the title and author of the work you are discussing. State the thesis of your essay clearly and early.

2. As you give evidence to support your thesis, ask yourself: Does this evidence prove what I want it to prove? If you decide it does not, you may want to look for stronger evidence or work out a new thesis statement.

3. Be selective in using quotations, events in the plot, and character descriptions. Use only those that work to support your argument. If you are writing about fiction or drama, never retell the entire plot. Assume your reader has read the work and will read your essay to gain some new understanding of the selection. (You can use a brief summary, especially one giving those details that support your argument, to lead up to your interpretation.)

4. You must support every claim you make with **textual evidence**—that is, evidence from the work itself, such as quotations, details from the plot, and the recurrent use of symbols. When you quote from the work, you must use quotation marks. If the work is a long one, such as a novel or full-length play, you may be expected to give page references in parentheses after the quotations. Try to integrate any quotations with your own writing, so that your essay reads smoothly without any abrupt jumps or shifts. For examples of how to do this, see the models on pages 106–108.

5. As a rule, you should write your essay in the third person, rather than the first, and in the present tense, rather than the past. Using the

third person helps give your essay a ring of authority, and using the present tense helps make the literary work seem alive. Compare the following two sentences.

> I think that Romeo and Juliet died needlessly. (first person and past tense.)

> Romeo and Juliet die needlessly. (third person and present tense)

Many readers would agree that the second sentence is more appropriate to a literary essay. But before you write, find out which style your intended reader prefers, especially if you are writing about an assigned work and topic and your intended reader is a teacher or a grader of essay tests. (Many literary essays are written as answers to questions in essay tests.) Whatever person and tense you decide to use, make sure you are consistent.

Editing and Revising Process

To help you revise your essay, consult pages 58–59 in Chapter 5. Your peer editors should use one of the editing methods presented in Chapter 28. In addition, the following questions can guide your peers in editing and you in revising your literary essay.

1. Are the title and author of the work clearly stated early in the essay?
2. Is the thesis statement clear and backed up by textual evidence? Is the evidence convincing?
3. Is the essay clearly written for either an informed or an uninformed audience? Should anything be changed to suit that particular audience?
4. Are quotations smoothly integrated with the rest of the essay? If not, what should be done to gain smoothness?
5. Is any textual evidence unnecessary or irrelevant? Is there any summary of the plot simply for the sake of summarizing?
6. Are there confusing shifts in tense or person? (For example, is there an abrupt and unjustified change from third person to first person?)
7. Will the essay's reader gain a new or deeper understanding of the work being interpreted? If not, what might be the problem?

After your peers have edited your essay, make what changes you decide are necessary and prepare a clean copy for your teacher/editor.

On the basis of your teacher/editor's comments, prepare a final version for your intended reader.

Products

The Theme of Temptation in "Their Mother's Purse" and "Kong at the Seaside"
by Anna Deliganis, student

(Note: The stories this essay discusses are on pages 367–371 and 373–378.)

Temptation, a force that characters in many short stories must deal with, is also a theme that often propels the main action of the story. In both Morley Callaghan's "Their Mother's Purse" and Arnold Zweig's "Kong at the Seaside," the theme of temptation is evident. Both authors use temptation to show the development of characters and move the plot. Economic temptation, the desire or need for money, is an obvious motivation but, as Arnold Zweig shows, after resisting temptation, a character becomes a stronger person. Morley Callaghan uses temptation to break a bond between two characters. By comparing the two authors' uses of the theme of temptation, a reader may better understand its meaning and role in the stories.

A common need is the need for money, and both authors present this need as a lure for their characters. In "Their Mother's Purse," Mary succumbs to this temptation by stealing from her mother. Joe observes his sister's weakness: ". . . he saw Mary standing in front of the dresser with their mother's purse in her hands. He saw at once that she had just taken out a bill and was slipping it into her own purse. . . ."

Later in the story, Mary reveals the motive behind her theft—her secret marriage to Paul Farrel, who is in a sanitarium and needs money. Thus the act is not entirely selfish. The money is necessary to Mary's emotional well-being. She would rather steal from her mother than reject her husband and so falls for the easy temptation of her mother's open purse.

In "Kong at the Seaside," young Willie is tempted to sell his dog for selfish reasons. As the man who offers him the money tells him, ". . . a hundred pounds safely invested will within ten years assure you of a university education. Or, if you prefer you can buy a small car to ride to school in. . . . a hundred pounds for nothing but a dog." Here temptation encourages the boy's selfish needs and desires. Groll, Willie's father, realizes the impact the money could have on his son and the whole family, but allows the boy to deal with the problem himself in order to strengthen Willie's character.

This example shows another use of temptation as a theme. After resisting temptation, a character's personality and convictions become more clearly defined. In "Kong at the Seaside," Groll is aware of the growth in his son's character because of Willie's choice of the dog over the money he is offered. In this case, temptation acts as a subtle force that inspires an emotional response. As the author shows, "Willie breathed more freely and, pretending to blow his nose, wiped away two furtive tears. He threw himself down in the sand next to Kong, happily piled the dog on top of himself, and began to wrestle with him. . . ." As this passage implies, Willie and his dog enjoy a more loving relationship because of Willie's resistance to temptation.

A negative effect of temptation is clearly shown by what happens to the relationship between Joe and his sister Mary in "Their Mother's Purse." Even at the beginning of the story, Joe is resentful of Mary's "easy smile, her assurance that she would not be refused." By the end of the story, Joe realizes how little he knows his sister and how far apart they have grown. He thinks that only "his father and mother had kept on going the one way. They alone were still close together." From now on, Joe and Mary will go their separate ways. In "Their Mother's Purse," Callaghan uses temptation as a catalyst that changes the relationship between Joe and Mary.

Both Callaghan and Zweig use temptation to create conflict and to bring out the human qualities of their characters. They show that temptation can help shape characters' personalities, inspire powerful emotions, and even destroy relationships.

Coping
by Martin Jones, student

(Note: The poems this essay discusses are on pages 380–383 of the Appendix.)

Remember the movie *Saturday Night Fever?* The only bright times in Tony Manero's life were when he was on the disco floor, showing what a great dancer he was. When he danced, he felt he was really somebody important.

Watching a TV talk show, I learned that psychologists call what Tony Manero did a "coping strategy." Most people have some kind of coping strategy to help them get through unpleasant times. Some people use work; others use prayer. Some people dream; others eat. My coping strategy is reading. I like science fiction by Isaac Asimov, Samuel Delaney, and Ursula Le Guin. I also like books by James Baldwin and Toni Morrison.

When I read three poems for an assignment, I learned about other coping strategies. In "Ruth" by Pauli Murray the strategy is pride—a black woman's pride. Pauli Murray tells Ruth to

Walk like a strong down-East wind blowing,
Walk with the majesty of the First Woman.

Pauli Murray tells Ruth, "Surrender to none the fire of your soul." It's obvious why Ruth needs this pride because the writer calls her "Queen of the Ghetto." Anybody in a ghetto needs pride to survive.

"Small Wire" by Anne Sexton shows another way to cope—through faith. Anne Sexton compares her faith to a wire that connects her to God. She says you need "only a thin wire" and "some love." I can only guess why she needs this coping strategy, but after reading this poem, I would say her need is great.

Through Al Young's poem, I learned about a third strategy. The title says this poem is "For Poets." The way I read it, it's for anybody with soul and imagination. You may feel you're buried underground, but don't stay there too long. "Come out into the sunlight." Walk and swim. And most of all, "Dont forget to fly."

No matter how much you need your escape world, you have to come out sooner or later. Think big. You can master the real world if you don't let it overpower you. The real power is inside you. All you have to do is use it.

I read these poems because they were part of an assignment, but I wound up really relating to them. They remind me of what I already know but forget sometimes. You can cope if you're true to what is inside you.

For Discussion

The Theme of Temptation

1. How does Anna Deliganis organize her paper? (For a discussion of different methods of organization, see pages 248–263.) Does her method help you understand the points she makes? Explain.
2. Do you understand the two stories better after reading this analysis? Why or why not?
3. Does Anna Deliganis choose her quotations well? Do they illustrate the points she makes in her analysis? Are they well integrated in the paper?
4. In your opinion, has anything important about the two stories been left out? If so, what?

Coping

1. This essay ignores one recommendation in the chapter. It uses the first person rather than the third. Do you think Martin Jones's use of the first person and his references to his own experience are justified? Why or why not? (Try rewriting the essay in the third person.)
2. Has Martin Jones made effective use of quotations to support his interpretation? Explain.
3. The writer has discovered a particular relationship among three poems in the Appendix. After reading all the poems on pages 379–383, can you relate some of them in another way, based on your own experience?

11 Short Research Paper

Finding information and then communicating what you have found in a research paper is one of the most common assignments you will get in school or in business. The research paper requires a careful and diligent search for facts, but you must show that you have mastered this information by presenting it in your own words. In many cases, however, you will find it useful to support what you say by including quotations from authorities.

Writing a short research paper will enable you to practice your research techniques as a preparation for the long research report assigned in the next chapter.

ASSIGNMENT ▶ Write a short research paper (about 250 words) about a nursery rhyme, a national holiday, the origin of an interesting or picturesque word, or an invention or discovery. Include at least two quotations in your paper.

Prewriting Process

1. The first step in writing a research paper is selecting a topic and limiting it. Several general topics are suggested for this assignment. Ask yourself what you and your intended reader might want to know about one of them and draw up a list of questions that will help you focus on the information you want to find.

Nursery rhymes. How did a nursery rhyme begin? Why? (Many nursery rhymes began as a way of criticizing British monarchs and politicians.) In order to help you focus on a specific nursery rhyme and find information about it, ask yourself such questions as: Who was "Little Jack Horner"? Why was "Mary, Mary quite contrary"? Why was it that "Jack Sprat could eat no fat"? Why was "Old King Cole" so merry?

National holidays. When and why did a national holiday come into existence? (For example, did Congress and/or the President proclaim a particular day to be a national holiday?) Has the name of the holiday ever been changed? What are people expected to do on this holiday? Here are a few holidays to consider: Martin Luther King Day, Memorial Day, Labor Day, Veterans Day, Thanksgiving Day.

Interesting and picturesque words. What is the derivation of a word? (For example, did it come from Latin? French? German?) When did it come into use? (Consulting the *Oxford English Dictionary* will help you find information about a word's use.) Has the meaning changed through the ages? If so, how? Here are some words to research, if you cannot think of one yourself: *bluestocking, laconic, taciturn, sooner, gerrymander, serendipity*. (Hint: Dictionaries present a great deal of information about words. Consulting the category *etymology*—the study of word origins—in a library's card catalog will lead you to some fascinating books about words and phrases.)

Inventions and discoveries. When, by whom, why, and how was something invented or discovered? Here are some topics to research if you cannot think of one yourself: the thumbtack, the umbrella, the lightning rod, penicillin, the video cassette recorder, Florida, gravity.

 2. The next step in writing a research paper is locating sources of information. You can probably find most of the information you need in your school library and local public library. Visit your libraries to find out what sources of information they provide. Learn where your libraries keep fiction and nonfiction books, reference books, magazines, and newspapers. Get in the habit of using the card catalog, a guide to the information found in your library's books. Learn to use the *Readers' Guide to Periodical Literature*, a guide to information in magazine articles. Find out what encyclopedias your library has and familiarize yourself with them. Do not hesitate to consult your library's most important and often most helpful resource, the librarian.

 To help you explore your school and local public libraries, read the introduction to Chapter 36 and do the exercises on pages 343–353.

3. Once you have located your sources of information, record the facts and quotations you need in the form of notes. Write your notes on index cards, which are easy to use, carry, and organize. You can almost certainly divide your general topic into subtopics. On each index card, list the topic, subtopic, and a fact relevant to that subtopic. You can also write quotations by authorities on index cards. Double check your facts and your quotations to make sure that they are absolutely accurate. At the bottom of each index card, list your source. If the source is a book, list the author, title, publisher, year of publication, and page number. If your fact or quotation comes from a magazine or newspaper, list the author, title of the article, name of the magazine or newspaper, date of publication, and page number. Notice how one student writer has recorded facts on an index card.

> Laurence Wright
> Clean and Decent
> New York: Viking Press, 1960, p. 245.
>
> Toothbrush commissioned by Queen Elizabeth I of England "whose teeth, once yellow, were in her old age, jet black."

One advantage of using index cards for recording facts and quotations is that you can easily arrange (and rearrange) the cards into what strikes you as a useful way to organize the information. (Any gaps in the organization may indicate a need for further research.) Once you have organized your cards, use them as the basis for a working outline. The outline can indicate the subtopics of your report and the facts supporting each subtopic. The following working outline organized the information presented in "Under the Eaves" (page 115).

Origin of Eavesdrop

I. First use
   A. *Eaves*: from Old English *efes*
   B. Overhanging edge of a roof
   C. *Eavesdrop*: place where water drips from eaves

II. Origin of verb
   A. 1606: first use of *eavesdrop* as verb
   B. To eavesdrop: to stand within eavesdrop of a house to overhear secrets
   C. Eaves an excellent place for listening
   D. Snoopers called "eavesdroppers"
III. Today's meaning
   A. Similar to 1606 meaning
   B. Expanded to include other ways of listening in on a private conversation

4. Draw up a list of variables to guide you in drafting your paper. Your purpose, remember, is to inform your reader; therefore, you should be thorough and absolutely accurate in presenting your information.

5. Before you write, decide whether your paper will be serious or humorous. (Yes, a research paper can be humorous; see "The Dynamic Duo" on page 116.) If you decide to write a serious report, you should probably use a direct style. Before you decide, you may wish to review the discussion of style on page 294.

Drafting Process

If you have done a thorough job of research, note-taking, and outlining, you have actually done most of the work of writing your paper. That is, you have found the information you need, recorded it for your own use, and organized it. What you need to do now is communicate what you have learned in a clear and interesting way. The following suggestions will help you draft your paper.

1. In a short research paper, you should probably state your thesis at or near the beginning. Do not settle for a dull beginning such as, "This research paper is about. . . ." For more interesting beginnings and more interesting ways of stating a thesis, see the first paragraphs of the reports on pages 115 and 116.

2. Using well-chosen quotations adds authority to your research paper. Remember that for this assignment you are asked to include at least two quotations.

3. You must indicate the sources of all your information. The traditional way of indicating sources is through footnotes. However, the papers at the end of this chapter and Chapter 12 use a method recommended in 1984 by the Modern Language Association. Sources are indicated by **parenthetical citations**. After a fact or quotation, its source is given by citing the last name of the source's author and the number of the page on which the fact or quotation appears. This information is enclosed within parentheses.

Suppose you were writing a research paper in which you decided to quote the first sentence of this suggestion. You would indicate the source of your quotation as follows:

> "You must indicate the sources of all your information in your paper" (Parker 113).

Notice that no mark of punctuation separates the author's name from the page reference, and that the period ending the sentence appears after the parenthetical citation. If the book or article has no author, or if your information is taken from a well-known reference work, use a short form of the title as part of the parenthetical citation. For example, the *Shorter Oxford English Dictionary* can be cited as *SOED*.

For this paper, try using parenthetical citations instead of footnotes. Once you get used to them, you will find that they are much easier to compose. In addition, you will be using the form recommended by the Modern Language Association, a leading and respected scholarly organization. Before you write your paper, study the way the reports at the end of this chapter indicate sources of information, and read the longer discussion of parenthetical citations on pages 355–357 of Chapter 36.

(Note: Keep in mind, however, that a research paper is written for a particular audience, most often a teacher. The teacher for whom you are writing this paper may prefer that you document with footnotes rather than parenthetical citations. If so, consult a handbook published before 1984 as a guide for proper footnote forms.)

4. Parenthetical citations depend on a list of sources, or bibliography, to make clear what is being cited. Include such a list, labeled "Works Cited," at the end of your research report. Before you compose your list, read the discussion on pages 357–360 of Chapter 36 and do Exercise 8.

5. Before you begin to draft your paper, study the research papers at the end of this chapter. Notice particularly the quotations, parenthetical citations, and bibliographies.

Editing and Revising Process

When your peers edit and you revise your short research paper, they and you can use the checklists in Chapter 28 as a guide. In addition, use the following questions.

1. Does the paper achieve its purpose? That is, does it inform the intended reader of important facts about the topic? (If some important questions are not answered, perhaps more research is needed.)

2. Is the topic of the paper clear? Is the thesis introduced in an interesting way?

3. Do all the facts relate to the topic? Are they organized in a logical way? Are there irrelevant facts that should be eliminated?

4. Should any part of the paper be rewritten to eliminate abrupt jumps from quotations to the writer's prose?

5. Are the quotations punctuated correctly? Are the parenthetical citations presented correctly? Are the sources listed in the bibliography presented correctly? (You and your peer editors should check the listings in your bibliography against the examples on pages 357–360.

Products

Under the Eaves
by Judy Chapelsky, student

In researching the origins of words, I came upon a particularly interesting account of the verb *eavesdrop*.

Derived from the Old English word *efes*, the noun *eaves* refers to the overhanging edge of a roof of a house (SOED). The noun *eavesdrop* (or *eavesdrip*) can refer to either "the dripping of water from the eaves" or "the space of ground on which such water falls" (SOED).

But around 1606, *eavesdrop* began to be used as a verb, meaning to "stand within the 'eavesdrop' of a house in order to overhear secrets; hence, to listen secretly to private conversation" (SOED). This meaning is based on the fact that there was about two feet of space between the edge of the eaves and the wall of the house, an area that turned out to be an excellent place for snoopers to crouch and listen to conversations. These snoopers were defined by law as "Such that listen under windows or the eaves of a house to hearken after discourse, and thereon to frame slanderous and mischievous tales" (Evans 137). The snoopers were called "eavesdroppers" and were said to be "eavesdropping."

Today's dictionary meaning of *eavesdrop* is strikingly similar to the 1606 use of the verb, but the everyday meaning has expanded to include more than just snooping by standing under the eaves of a house. We now speak of eavesdropping on the telephone and through closed doors, and use the verb casually to refer to the many other ways people can secretly overhear private conversations.

Works Cited

"Eaves." <u>The Shorter Oxford English Dictionary</u>, Third Edition.
"Eavesdrip, -drop." <u>The Shorter Oxford English Dictionary</u>, Third Edition.
"Eavesdrop." <u>The Shorter Oxford English Dictionary</u>, Third Edition.
Evans, Bergen. <u>Comfortable Words</u>. New York: Random House, 1959.

The Dynamic Duo
by Steven Greenaway, student

Most of us use them, one on top of the other, at least twice a day. Some spend hours polishing with them while others just use the pair for a quick rinse. Yet have any of us ever bothered to look into the history of our beloved bathroom buddies—the faithful toothbrush and its underrated partner, toothpaste?

Toothbrushes are of uncertain origin. While the Romans are said to have used them in hopes of preserving their teeth, judging from the skeletal remains that have been found, the practice seems to have had little success.

Laurence Wright, a noted authority on the subject of toothbrushes, believes the first recorded toothbrush in England was one commissioned in 1561 by Queen Elizabeth I, "whose teeth, once yellow, were in her old age, jet black" (Wright 245).

Along with the toothbrush, the aristocracy of England often used tepid water to clean their pearly whites every morning. For a majority of the working class, however, soot was popular. Other formulas for homemade "tooth soap" included ashes mixed with honey, charcoal, areca nuts, and cuttlefish bone (Wright 246).

Perhaps the next time we squeeze a cylinder of breath-freshening Aim or Colgate (with MFP)) onto our specially tapered Squibb or Reach, we should pay tribute to the wonders of modern technology!

Work Cited

Wright, Laurence. <u>Clean and Decent</u>. New York: Viking Press, 1960.

For Discussion

Under the Eaves

1. This research paper explains the origin of the verb *eavesdrop*. Is there anything further you want to know about the writer's information or her sources? If so, what?
2. What does the parenthetical citation SOED stand for? How do you know? Why is no page reference given for this citation?
3. Does this paper move smoothly from the writer's prose to quotations? If so, give examples and explain them.

The Dynamic Duo

1. This student's research paper tells about an aspect of our daily hygiene many of us take for granted. How does the writer's first paragraph work to engage the reader's attention?
2. The writer has included some humor in his report. Find examples. Is any part of the report serious? If so, what? Why do you think the writer chose to include humor?
3. Find an example of a direct quotation in the paper. Find an example of information, taken from the same source as the quotation, which the writer has put in his own words.

12 Long Research Paper

If you have done the assignment for Chapter 11, you are now ready to write a longer, more extensive research paper. The assignment in this chapter is the kind you will often be given in other courses—in high-school history and science, for example, and in many college courses.

Before you begin this assignment, carefully review the prewriting and drafting suggestions on pages 110–114 of Chapter 11. Most of the suggestions apply to this assignment as well.

ASSIGNMENT ▶ Write a research paper at least 1,000 words long on a topic of your choice. Your paper must use at least five sources of information, such as books, magazine articles, and newspaper articles.

Prewriting Process

1. A research paper topic must be limited enough so that you can do a thorough job and not just skim the surface of your topic. But it must not be so limited that you can find little information to communicate. More students make the mistake of choosing too broad rather than too narrow a topic. (Imagine covering the history of the world in a thousand words!) One good way of arriving at a topic is to start with a broad subject area and then narrow it. For example, you might start with the broad subject of United States history, narrow it to nineteenth-century

American history, and narrow it again to the Civil War. But this topic is still too broad; too much happened in the Civil War to cover adequately in one research paper. To get a sufficiently limited topic, you might narrow it to an important event, such as the First Battle of Bull Run, or a significant aspect of the war, such as the economics of the Union and the Confederacy.

To give you practice in narrowing a topic, do the following exercise. In two or more stages, narrow five of the following subject areas to a topic that you can cover in a research paper.

> Example: aviation
> jet planes
> jet airliners
>
> the development of the supersonic transport (SST)

a) baseball
b) the women's rights movement
c) American literature
d) food
e) Latin America
f) women in sports
g) space exploration
h) black history
i) Chinese Americans
j) atomic energy

2. If you have been assigned a research paper for another course, such as modern history, you may wish to write this paper to fulfill both assignments. This way you can get the benefit of your peer editors' and your teacher/editor's comments before you write your final draft and submit it to your other teacher. Make sure, however, that you have your teachers' permission to submit the paper in both courses.

3. To write this paper, you must be able to locate information about your topic. Chapter 36 tells you where and how to look for information, especially information that you can find in libraries. If you have not already done so, read pages 343–355 and do exercises 1–6.

4. As with a short research paper, the most useful way to take notes about information—both facts and quotations—is on index cards. Arranging and, if necessary, rearranging the cards can suggest a good way to organize your paper.

Remember, however, that absolute accuracy is essential to any research paper. Check and double check your facts and quotations. Make sure you have correctly recorded the sources of your information. Indicating that a quotation appears on page 128 of a book when it really appears on page 182 suggests you are a careless researcher and raises doubts about all your research.

5. You will find it useful to record the information you need for the list of sources appearing at the end of your paper on separate cards or a sheet of paper. Make sure you have all the information you need. For books, you need information about the author's name, the title of the book, the publisher, the place of publication, and the date of publication. For magazine and newspaper articles, you need information about the author's name, the title of the article, the name of the magazine or newspaper, the date of the issue, and the page or pages on which the article appears. (Nothing can be more frustrating than sitting down to compose your list of sources, only to find that you have not written down all the details and must return to the library to find a particular book.

6. To help you think about the kind of information you need, you should do one or more of the brainstorming sessions in Chapter 23. For example, if you want to contrast items, do the Pro/Con Ladders. If you want to show relationships between items, do the Cause-and-Effect Flowchart.

7. There are a number of ways to organize the facts in a research paper—for example, chronological order, sequential order, order of importance, and comparison and contrast. You may wish to read or review the discussion of organization in Chapter 26 (pages 248–259). Thinking about how to arrange your note cards will probably suggest a good way to organize your paper. Then make an outline of your topics, subtopics, and important information.

8. Before you begin to draft your essay, think about your writing variables and jot them down. Your purpose, of course, is to inform, but consider who your intended audience is. You would not write the same paper for one of your peers as you would for a history teacher.

Drafting Process

1. The drafting suggestions in Chapter 11 (pages 113–114) also apply to the longer research paper. Be guided by them, as well as by the three following needs:

the need to be clear
the need to be well organized
the need to be accurate

2. Be sure to give the source of each fact and each quotation. This book recommends you use parenthetical citations to identify your sources within the body of your paper. Parenthetical citations are explained briefly on page 113 of Chapter 11 and more thoroughly on pages 355–357 of Chapter 36. You may wish to read and review this explanation before drafting your paper. (If your teacher prefers that you use footnotes rather than citations, consult a handbook written before 1984 for proper footnote forms.)

3. Long research papers can consist of several parts. Whether you should include some of these parts depends on the topic you choose and what your teacher requires.

   a. *Title page.* The information on the title page usually includes your name, the title of your paper, the title of your course, and the name of your teacher. Find out exactly what your teacher requires before composing your title page.
   b. *Outline.* Many teachers require a formal outline to accompany a research paper. You can use the rough outline you did when organizing your facts as a basis for a more formal outline. For a discussion of outlines, see pages 282–283.
   c. *Appendix.* If your paper includes such material as charts, graphs, or long lists of items such as names or dates, you may decide to include them in an appendix at the end of your paper just before your bibliography.
   d. *Bibliography.* A bibliography listing the sources of your facts and quotations is required in all research papers. Label your bibliography "Works Cited" as the Modern Language Association recommends. See pages 357–361 of Chapter 36 for an explanation of how to set up a bibliography.

4. Before you begin to draft your paper, study the example of a research paper at the end of this chapter. Notice particularly the paper's organization, use of quotations, parenthetical citations, and bibliography.

Editing and Revising Process

The questions for editing and revising in Chapter 11 (page 114) also apply to the long research paper. You and your peer editors can use those questions, as well as the checklists in Chapter 28.

In addition, peer editors should test the accuracy of each paper they edit by checking at least two parenthetical citations, including one fact and one quotation. Editors should make sure that (1) the page references are correct, (2) the information is accurate, and (3) the quotation is reproduced without error.

Product

Acupuncture
by Lynn Stefonovich, student

Outline

I. Explanation of acupuncture
   A. Insertion of fine needles into skin
   B. Absence of pain and drawn blood
II. Chinese theory of acupuncture
   A. Meridians
      1. Relation to cause and cure of disease
      2. Basis of all theory and treatment
   B. Opposing forces: Yin and Yang
      1. Feminine and masculine principles
      2. Use of acupuncture to restore balance between forces
III. Western theory of acupuncture
   A. Reliever of pain but not a cure
   B. Effect of needles' insertion
      1. Impulses sent to brain
      2. Natural chemicals secreted
      3. "Analgesia rather than anesthesia"
IV. Acupuncturists' procedures
   A. Complete examination before treatment
   B. Methods of diagnosis
      1. Acupuncture points
      2. Pulses
      3. Changes in body openings and in skin
      4. Body odors
      5. Changes in voice
   C. Use of needles to stimulate affected organs
      1. Slow insertion and rapid withdrawal of needles
      2. Hot needles for Yang treatment and cold needles for Yin
      3. Clockwise twist for Yang and counterclockwise for Yin
   D. Response to treatment
V. Status of acupuncture in the West
   A. Researchers' attitudes
   B. Possible acceptance by Western doctors as a valid technique

Acupuncture, the ancient Chinese art of healing, is the practice by which a needle is inserted a few millimeters into the skin, left for a predetermined amount of time, and then withdrawn. Fine, flexible, and sharp, the needles may be made of various substances, but silver and stainless steel needles seem to be the most popular. Insertion of the needles should not cause pain or draw blood ("Curious" 38). Though the Western scientific theory about acupuncture differs considerably from the Chinese theory, this art of healing is apparently effective.

According to traditional Chinese theory, as set forth by Ling Shu, the human body is divided into twelve passages or meridians. These relate to the causes and cures of diseases. The "twelve meridians are the basis of all theory and treatment" (Mann 35). Through these passages flow the vital forces of life. There are two life forces, Yin (the feminine force) and Yang (the masculine force). If a person is healthy, the life forces are considered to be in proper proportion. Acupuncturists will manipulate the forces by inserting needles at critical points until a proper balance is achieved (Hassett 86). They are concerned with the energy behind the invisible forces of Yin and Yang.

Western theory differs considerably from the Yin/Yang theory. Scientific research performed on rats proves that acupuncture relieves pain but does not cure disease. When the needles are inserted, impulses are sent to the brain by way of the central nervous system, which acts as a conductor. The brain causes the body to secrete natural chemicals that resemble painkilling drugs such as morphine (Hassett 82). Scientists believe that "acupuncture produces analgesia rather than anesthesia; that is, the reduction of pain rather than the loss of sensation" (Hassett 89).

Before a diagnosis is made, the patient must have a complete examination from head to toe. Acupuncture points and the organs they are associated with are not usually close together. For example, the acupuncture points on the leg are associated with the liver, gall bladder, kidney, bladder, spleen, and stomach. Any points that are painful, even if no pressure is applied to them, are connected with a diseased organ. When the disease is cured, whether by acupuncture, Western medical methods, or the passage of time, there will be no pain at the acupuncture point (Mann, 27-30).

Another way to reach a diagnosis requiring the application of acupuncture is by taking the patient's pulses. There are twelve different pulses, six on each wrist within a given area. Six are taken by acupuncturists applying a light pressure on the area, and the other six by a heavier pressure on the same area. Each pulse is associated with a certain organ. Acupuncturists compare the characteristics of each pulse with those of a healthy pulse to form a decision. They believe that by feeling the pulse, they "can detect illness long before it appears as a noticeable symptom" (Duke 150). The pulses and the tender acupuncture points are the two most important factors in a diagnosis, but many minor observations also affect acupuncturists' decisions.

Since all the organs have counterparts on the body's surface, the well-trained acupuncturists observe changes in the patient's skin and body openings. They study the patient's eyes, tongue, and coloring because different colors relate to different organs. The senses of hearing and smell also assist acupuncturists. Body odors and changes in a patient's voice can mean a Yin/Yang disturbance (Duke 140). Combining all the necessary information from observing and touching, acupuncturists reach their diagnoses. Before treatment begins, they know precisely where the needles will go, how deep they will be placed, and how many times they will be used. The aim of acupuncturists is to "stimulate the affected organ through its meridian and restore the harmonious flow" (Moss 40). They will balance the Yin and Yang energy among the various organs, the nervous system, and the blood.

To stimulate the Yang, acupuncturists insert the needle slowly, withdraw it rapidly, and massage the spot after the needle is taken out. They stimulate the Yin in the same way. Hot needles are used for Yang treatment, cold ones for Yin. If the needle is twisted clockwise as it is inserted, the Yang will be influenced; a counterclockwise motion will produce a change in the Yin (Duke 162). Response to the treatment differs from patient to patient; some respond within a few seconds of the first needle's insertion, but some require as many as forty-two needles and several visits. A very small proportion of the patients who do not improve while being treated may notice a cure some months later. Following each treatment, a patient may feel an increase in energy, due to the stimulating effect of the needles, or may feel a pleasant drowsiness due to the sudden release in tension (Mann 200–201).

Although acupuncture will continue to be a subject of controversy, physiologist David Meyer may have summed up the general feeling of researchers when he stated, "I don't think any researcher in this field now doubts that acupuncture can reduce experimental pain in the laboratory" (Hassett 85).

More people are turning to acupuncture as a last resort to alleviate pain and disease. Some are concluding that it should perhaps have been their first resort. In the future, Western medical science may use acupuncture as a technique to treat certain painful conditions.

Works Cited

"A Curious Cure That Works." Changing Times. Nov. 1980: 37–39.

Duke, Mark. Acupuncture. New York: Pyramid House, 1973.

Hassett, James. "Acupuncture Is Proving Its Points." Psychology Today. Dec. 1980: 37–39.

Mann, Felix, M.D. Acupuncture: the Ancient Chinese Art of Healing and How It Works Scientifically. New York: Random House, 1971.

Moss, Louis, M.D. Acupuncture and You. Secaucus: Citadel Press, 1964.

For Discussion

1. What is the thesis statement of this research paper? What kind of evidence does the writer give to support her thesis?
2. Does this paper move smoothly from the writer's own prose to the quotations she uses? Give examples to support your answer. (To answer, you might try rewriting a passage containing a quotation to see if you can achieve a smoother transition.)
3. How and why acupuncture works is something few people understand. Has the writer explained acupuncture clearly and thoroughly? Defend your answer. Is there any information not given that you would like to know? If so, what is it?
4. Who might be the audience for this research paper?

13 Feature Article

Like a research paper, a feature article communicates information, but its approach and style are different. A research paper is like someone wearing formal clothes; a feature article can be informal, like someone in a sports jacket and blue jeans. Research papers rely mostly on printed matter—books, magazines, newspapers, pamphlets—for information. Feature articles use those sources, but they also draw from the writer's own experience and what can be learned from talking with others (often through interviews).

While a research paper is usually intended for a teacher, many feature articles are written for magazine and newspaper readers. You have probably come across articles with titles such as "Black History: Voices from the Past Speak to the Present," "Hard Rock Makes a Comeback," "Women in Top Jobs," and "When Governor Toney Anaya Talks, People Listen." When you write your feature article, think about what your readers would like to know and try to think of a title that will catch their attention.

ASSIGNMENT ▶ Write a feature article on a topic that interests you and you think will interest others. The article should be at least 1,000 words long.

Prewriting Process

1. Many feature articles are written for magazines. You may want to assume your article will appear in a particular magazine. Get to know

that publication by studying several issues. Try to determine its audience and the interests of that audience. (To whom does *Sports Illustrated* appeal? *Rolling Stone*? *Car and Driver*? *People*?) Then choose a topic you think will appeal to the magazine's readers.

2. If you have trouble thinking of a topic, here are some subject areas to explore: recent developments in education or science, fashion trends, popular dances (or dance crazes), local monuments or historic sites, medical discoveries (or controversial medical treatments), famous or interesting people.

3. Jot down your writing variables to guide you as you look for information. Consider especially your purpose and intended audience. You may want to postpone writing a thesis statement until you have gathered enough information about your topic so that you can decide what you wish to say about it.

4. Like a research paper, a feature article presents lots of interesting information, so allow plenty of time for research. Some of your information may come from watching television and listening to the radio, but much of it will probably come from reading books, magazines, and newspapers. Pages 344–353 of Chapter 36 tell you how to use the library to locate information in these sources. If you have not already done exercises 1–5 on these pages, do them now.

Part of your information may come from **firsthand sources**—your own experience and what you learn from other people. You may want to arrange interviews with people who are knowledgeable about your topic. If you do conduct interviews, think about what information you need and prepare your questions in advance. If you have a tape recorder, you may want to use it to record the interview. If not, bring a notebook and pencil or pen, and take good notes.

5. As with a research paper, you may want to record your information on index cards. (See page 112.) Later you can arrange the index cards to help organize your article.

6. When you think you have gathered enough information, you can do one or more of the brainstorming sessions in Chapter 23, especially Newspaper Reporter's Questions (page 222).

7. At this point, you may wish to write your thesis statement. Let the thesis statement and your list of writing variables guide you as you organize your information and draft your article.

Drafting Process

1. If you have done a good job of researching, you may wind up with much information that supports your thesis and some that does not relate to your thesis at all. To give your article unity, use only the information relating to your thesis. (If you come across a good deal of information that does not support, or even contradicts, your thesis, you should probably change the thesis.)

2. To make your article lively and interesting, you can present quotations, personal observations, descriptions, anecdotes, and opinions (including your own). But make sure that all of this material relates to your thesis.

3. Remember that a feature article is less formal than a long research paper. Sources of information need not be indicated through parenthetical citations and a bibliography. Instead, include your source within the sentence or paragraph presenting that particular information. To see how one student writer moves smoothly from mentioning sources to presenting information, see "The Fascinating World of Dreams" below, especially the article's sixth paragraph.

4. Remember also that a feature article can move from the objective (presenting facts) to the subjective (expressing thoughts and feelings). It can switch from the third person (*she, he, it*) to the first person (*I*) and go back again. Notice how Mike Chan, the author of "The Fascinating World of Dreams," blends third-person and first-person writing.

5. Appropriate graphs, charts, illustrations, photographs, or cartoons can add to your article's appeal.

Editing and Revising Process

For editing and revising, you and your peers can use the checklists in Chapter 28, as well as the questions in Chapter 4 (page 51), Chapter 5 (page 58), and Chapter 11 (page 114).

Remember that the appearance of your article is important. If you know how to type, then type at least the final version. If you include graphs, charts, illustrations, or photographs, make sure you label them clearly and correctly.

Product

The Fascinating World of Dreams
by Mike Chan, student

In recent years the study of dreams has become increasingly popular. Theories and conjectures about dreams abound, as they have throughout history, yet only recently has dreaming been investigated seriously on a large scale. The modern scientific techniques of dream research now provide very reliable data. However, much of the mystery of dreaming still remains; many questions on the topic remain unanswered.

According to the magazine *Psychology*, the earliest Greeks believed dreams came from the gods: several passages in The *Iliad* refer to dreams sent by Zeus. During the Middle Ages, religious authorities held demons responsible for bad dreams. According to *Psychology Today*, not until Sigmund Freud's work in the late nineteenth century were psychological states recognized as the cause of dreams.

Although my aunt insists she never dreams, psychologists have confirmed that everybody dreams every night. The reason for forgetting dreams, however, is still not clear.

Many people have wondered whether or not animals dream. Studies performed at the University of Southern California were designed to answer their question. Dr. C. Y. Vaughn conducted various experiments with monkeys, concluding that "animals also perceive visual images during sleep." Unable to communicate verbally with his subjects, Dr. Vaughn was uncertain what his monkeys dreamt about. Nevertheless, the doctor reports, "Judging from their facial expressions, the dreams were most likely hostile in nature."

Eye movement is the predominant physical activity during the dreaming process. Authorities report rapid eye movements nearly always accompany dreams.

Contrary to popular belief, dreaming of an activity takes approximately as long as carrying out the activity in waking life. According to *Psychology*, "Dreams do not occur in a split second, as many of us believe." A conversation I had with Dr. I. Olsen, my psychology teacher, confirmed this hypothesis. Dr. Olsen states, "People think dreams occur in a split second, but actually it takes equally as long to dream of an activity as it does to carry out the activity in the waking state. When we are asleep, our perception of time is lost."

Many people argue that dreams completely lack color. A constant dreamer myself, I tended to believe this claim. Much to my surprise, an investigation done by doctors Allen Kahn and Stuart Fisher at Texas State University provides evidence to prove all dreams are in color, but the color may be forgotten when the subject recalls the dream.

Interestingly enough, studies have shown that we dream an average of four times per night, each dream separated by a ninety-minute interval. The first dream usually occurs one hour after the onset of sleep; the last dream is nearly always the only one people remember.

A film entitled *Sleep,* shown to our class, claims that a major shift in body position indicates a dream has just ended. Dr. Joseph Collins, featured in the film, stresses the relationship between rapid eye movement and shifts in body position. According to Dr. Collins, "Rapid eye movement ceases after a major shift in body position, thus indicating the termination of a dream."

As reported in *Psychology,* dreams develop from four primary sources: day residue, past experience, external stimuli, and physiological states. Day residue and past experience are the dominant factors in determining our dreams, but the other two are equally as important.

External stimuli incorporated into our dreams fascinate me the most. Upon hearing my alarm clock some mornings, I have incorporated the sound into my dream. Before awakening, I have dreamt the phone was ringing; subsequently in my dream, I have gone to answer it.

Dreaming has always been associated with the mysterious, supernatural world of precognition and mental telepathy. History is filled with tales of prophetic dreams, and yields many eerie, unexplained accounts of the supernatural. Abraham Lincoln, for example, dreamed he entered the East Room of the White House and saw a coffin. When he asked who had died, the reply was, "The President." Lincoln died three days later, the victim of an assassin's bullet. Lincoln's dream and its subsequent realization have been considered coincidental. According to Dr. William Levy, a prominent psychologist in Boston, "Lincoln was preoccupied with death. He often dreamt of being assassinated, and I see no correlation between his last dream and the fate that befell him."

Dr. Levy does point out, on the other hand, that telepathic messages can be transmitted through dreams. A team of scientists at Maimonides Hospital in New York conducted systematic studies of thought transmission to sleeping subjects. Their findings were astonishing. Dr. Peter Krippner, head of the investigation, stated, "Certain people are able to perceive thoughts while dreaming. Further studies will hopefully teach us how these messages are sent and received."

Although the study of dreams has become much more widespread over the years and although greater knowledge of the subject has been gained, dreaming is still one activity that continues to amaze us. Fascinating, mysterious, elusive, the world of dreams will undoubtedly continue to fascinate people for many years to come.

For Discussion **The Fascinating World of Dreams**

1. Mike Chan has obviously done a good deal of research about dreams. What printed sources does the article indicate he used? What other sources did he use?
2. Find at least two examples of a switch from third-person to first-person writing. Did these switches make the article more interesting, or were they distracting? Explain.
3. In your opinion, should any part of this article be shortened? Should any part present more details? Explain.

14 Set of Instructions

If you think about it, you will realize how much of your time is spent giving and receiving instructions. How often have you given directions to your home or to a hard-to-find place? ("It's just beyond the shopping mall.") How often have you heard or read a step-by-step procedure for assembling a model plane, making a dress, doing a new dance, filling out an application form, or cooking a new dish? These are just a few examples of the instructions that make up a part of everyone's daily life.

Giving instructions in person is fairly easy. The person receiving them can tell you if something is unclear. Writing instructions requires more thought and care because your final reader is not there to ask you for a fuller, clearer explanation. You have to make sure your instructions do the job before you give them to your intended reader.

ASSIGNMENT ▶ In 200 to 400 words, write a set of instructions.

Prewriting Process

1. To tell others how to do something, you have to know how to do it yourself. Make sure the procedure you decide to explain is one you know well.

2. Decide on a format for this assignment. For example, you can include your set of instructions in a letter to a friend. You can write an

informative essay. Or you can assume you are a manufacturer who needs to include a list of instructions with a model kit or a piece of machinery that is going to be assembled by the purchaser.

3. Decide who your intended reader is. You would not write the same instructions for a friend your own age as you would for a seven-year-old child.

4. Decide on your other writing variables. You can use them as a guide when you draft your instructions.

5. Jot down everything you know about the procedure you need to explain. Make sure you have not omitted anything. Then organize the steps in the order they should be done.

Drafting Process

Once you have jotted down and organized your steps, you have done much of the work in drafting a set of instructions. What you need to concentrate on now is communicating these steps clearly and logically. The following suggestions will help you draft your instructions.

1. Often instructions are written in the second person, almost as commands: "Do this. Then do that." (The pronoun *you* is understood.)

2. If you decide to write your instructions as an informative essay, include an introduction and conclusion. Your introduction, including your thesis sentence, can indicate how your set of instructions is useful or necessary. Notice how the writers of "How to Throw a Frisbee" (page 135) indicate the usefulness of their instructions.

3. Write your first draft based on the steps that you already jotted down and arranged in logical order as part of your prewriting preparation.

4. If any step is complicated or otherwise difficult to explain, you may find it useful to divide it into substeps.

5. You may want to include one or more lists as part of your instructions—for example, a list of the tools needed to perform a certain operation.

6. Including diagrams or illustrations may help make your instructions clearer or more interesting. Notice how the writers of "How to Throw a Frisbee" make use of illustrations.

7. If you need to use a technical term, define it. But use it only if necessary. Your reader does not want to learn terminology but to understand what you write.

8. To help make your writing move smoothly, you may wish to use one or more of the transitional devices presented in Chapter 27 (pages 264–266).

9. Often short paragraphs produce clearer instructions than do long ones that seem to jam a great deal of information together. Short paragraphs also make your instructions seem less complicated and easier to follow.

10. You may wish to number each step of the procedure you explain.

11. Check your draft to make sure that your reader will understand exactly how the procedure should be performed. Is each step clear? Are the steps complete and in the right order? There is nothing more frustrating than discovering, after you have completed one step, that something else should have gone before it.

12. You have just read a set of instructions.

Editing and Revising Process

The true test of whether your set of instructions is well written lies with your intended reader. If that person can successfully complete the procedure that you have explained, then both you and your reader have succeeded. You should, however, test your instructions *before* presenting them to your audience. As you go through the steps, ask yourself: Have any been left out? Are they in logical order?

When your peers edit and you revise your writing, use the following questions, as well as the checklists in Chapter 28, as guides.

1. Is every part of the explanation clear? If not, what can be done to make it clear? Should more details be added? Should vague sentences be rewritten to make them more precise?

2. If illustrations or diagrams are used, do they do their job? That is, do they help make the explanations clear? Should illustrations or diagrams be added for more clarity?

3. Is each step of the procedure presented in the order that it should be performed?

4. Are transitional words—such as *first*, *next*, *then*, and *finally*—used to lead the reader from one step to the next? Should any other transitional words be added?

5. Do the instructions seem more complicated than they really are because the steps are jammed together into long paragraphs? What should be done (if necessary) to avoid making the set of instructions seem too difficult?

After you revise your instructions on the basis of your peer editors' suggestions, present a clean draft to your teacher/editor. Then revise again, if necessary.

Products

How to Throw a Frisbee
by Murray Suid and Ron Harris

Frisbee tossers use dozens of different throws and catches. These range from the simple techniques to elaborate trick shots only an expert can do. Here are the basics of throwing a Frisbee. Once you have them down pat, you can work on fancier throws.

The *basic Frisbee grip*. Hold the Frisbee comfortably in the palm of your throwing hand. Your first finger should rest along the rim of the Frisbee. The other three fingers curl underneath. Your thumb is on top of the Frisbee.

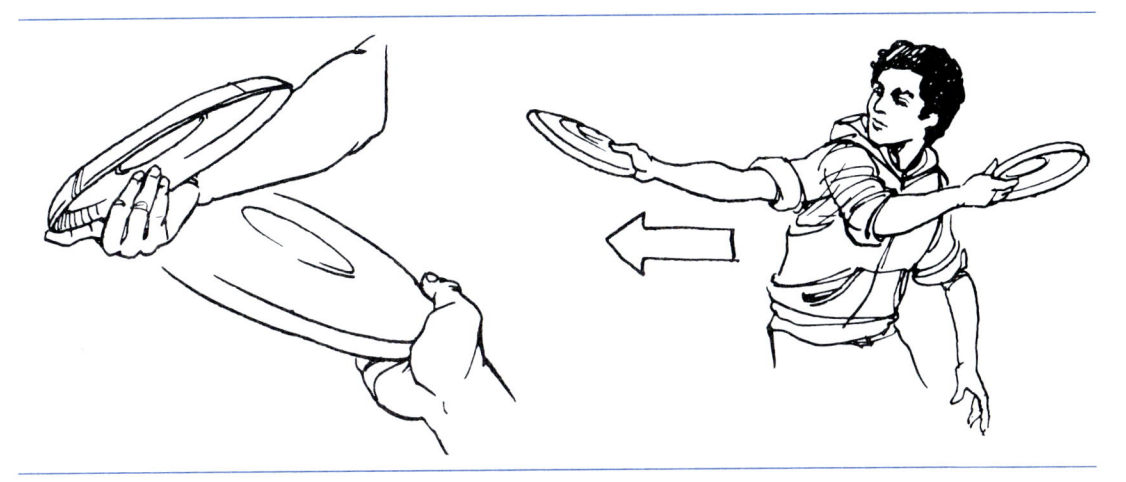

The *backhand toss* is one of the most common Frisbee throws. Turn your shoulder toward the target. Extend your arm so that your index finger points where you want the Frisbee to go. Bring your throwing arm back, bending your elbow and cocking your wrist around. Then straighten your arm. At the moment your arm is fully extended, let the Frisbee go with a snap of the wrist. At the same time take a step forward with your right foot (if you're right-handed). At the end of the throw your finger should be pointing at the target.

The key to accurate throws is to keep the Frisbee as flat as possible when you let it go. The flatter your throw, the straighter the Frisbee's path will be. When you start out, throw at a target that isn't too far away; 25 or 30 feet will do. Once you've perfected your short-range aim, begin moving the target back.

Another popular throw is the *underhand toss*. Face the target squarely, your arm pointing where you want the Frisbee to go. Use the same basic grip. But this time bring your arm behind you until it's nearly parallel to the ground. To toss the Frisbee, bring your arm forward, bending the elbow slightly as your hand comes under. Extend your arm, launching the Frisbee with a flip of the wrist. As you throw, take a step forward with the foot opposite your throwing arm (the left foot if you are right-handed). Once again, try to keep the Frisbee on a level, flat flight path.

Even if you are a beginning Frisbee thrower, you have probably learned how to throw *curves*. You simply tip the disc as it is released. To make the Frisbee's flight path curve to the right, toss the disc with the left side up and the right down. For a left-hand curve, keep the left side of the Frisbee lower than the right.

Preparation Is the Key to Success
by Terry Thilken, student

To succeed in a job interview, career advisers and interviewers suggest these steps:

1. Research the firm you are interested in joining. If possible, talk to people who already work there. Be prepared to show interest in and ask questions about the company. Include such things as company policies and future plans.
2. Find out as much as you can about the interviewer. Ask friends who work in the firm about interests, temperament, idiosyncrasies.
3. Know specifically what you want to do. Be prepared to explain how your skills relate to a specific opening.
4. Make a list of positive points about yourself. If asked about your strengths, don't be afraid to say, "I'm good with numbers" or "My human-relations skills are good."
5. Practice your responses. Ask a friend to join you in role-playing and to possibly alert you to annoying characteristics, such as distracting slang or speech patterns.
6. Be on time, or phone ahead if you are delayed.
7. Watch your appearance. You don't have to appear in "your best bib and tucker," but you should appear to be neat and professional. Some companies are more formal than others; if possible, note how people doing similar jobs to the one for which you are applying dress.
8. Give the interviewer your full attention. Employers love to hear someone wants to work for them.
9. Don't *initiate* salary discussion in the first interview, but be prepared to discuss salary so that you don't sell yourself too cheaply.
10. Be prepared to answer questions such as the following in an interview:
    a) Why should I hire you?
    b) Why do you want to work here?
    c) What interests you about this position?
    d) What are your ambitions?
    e) What are your greatest accomplishments?
    f) Why do you want to change jobs?
11. Relax. Consider the interview as a conversation.

12. Be tenacious. Don't be afraid to ask when a decision will be made. If your interviewer says he or she will call you in four days, but fails to do so, call back and ask politely if a decision has been reached yet.

For Discussion

How to Throw a Frisbee

1. The first paragraph not only introduces what is going to be explained but also suggests why readers might find this explanation useful. How do the writers justify their set of instructions? Do you think this paragraph is a good introduction? Explain.
2. The instructions about the backhand toss are divided into two paragraphs (the third and fourth). Why, in your opinion, did the writers decide not to include all this information in one paragraph? What is the topic of each paragraph?
3. Do the illustrations make the set of instructions clearer and/or more interesting? Explain.

Preparation Is the Key to Success

1. Do you think all necessary instructions are included? If not, what was left out?
2. Which instruction do you think is the most important?
3. In what way does this set of instructions differ from "How to Throw a Frisbee?" In what sense, then, can "Preparation Is the Key to Success" be considered a set of instructions?

15 Demand Essay (Answering Questions on an Essay Test)

A demand essay is a piece of writing that must be completed within a specific period of time. This essay is like the informative and argumentative essays assigned in Chapters 4 and 5, but with two important differences. The topic is one that is assigned to you, and you have only a limited amount of time to think and write. The most common kind of demand essay is the answer to a question on an essay test.

Writing to meet this kind of deadline can be an alarming experience for many students. Carrying out the assignment in this chapter will give you strategies for tackling this job and increase your confidence in undertaking it.

ASSIGNMENT ▶ Write a demand essay on an assigned topic. You must write your essay in class by a certain time.

Your writing teacher may provide a list of topics, ask you to choose one, and specify the deadline by which you must complete the demand essay. Or you might ask one of your other teachers to provide a test question in a sealed envelope. Open the envelope at the beginning of your writing class and start to plan your essay. If no other topic is available, you can use one of those below.

1. Point out how attitudes in the North and South led to the Civil War.
2. List the four major types of compounds found in living things. Describe the basic structure of each and give examples.
3. Write a critique of this book. Let the critique reflect your own experience in carrying out the assignments in the book. (For a discussion of critiques, see page 143).
4. Compare and contrast a novel and the film based on it.
5. Compare the first-person narrators (characters telling the stories) of two short stories.
6. Summarize the breakdown of a molecule of glucose during cellular respiration.
7. Relate Woodrow Wilson's personality and his treatment of Republican senators to America's decision not to join the League of Nations.
8. Analyze a poem in this book's appendix in terms of rhythm, language, and use (if any) of metaphors and similes.

Prewriting Process

1. Being well prepared is the best prewriting strategy for taking an essay test. There is nothing like the feeling of confidence that comes from knowing you can answer any question a teacher may ask about a subject.

2. To prepare yourself, predict a few questions the teacher might ask and write answers for them. This will give you experience in writing answers for this particular subject. If your predictions are correct or even partly correct, you have already done much of the work in thinking out and writing answers for the test.

3. Make sure you come into the examination room with the proper tools: pen, pencil, eraser, ruler (if needed), dictionary (if permitted), and any other tool you may need.

4. Read over the entire test. Notice all the significant words in the directions. (Don't miss the *or* in an instruction that tells you to answer parts 1, 2, *or* 3!) If the test does allow you to make a choice, choose those questions you feel most competent to answer. So that you will not run out of time, estimate how much time you will spend answering each question. Notice the point value of each question. Don't spend most of your time on a question worth twenty points only to find that you do not have enough time to answer a question worth fifty points.

5. Carefully read and reread each question before answering it. Do not write until you have a clear idea of what the question asks you to do.

6. Plan before you write. Since there is little time available for revision when answering an essay test, a little time spent in planning is a good investment.

Drafting Process

1. Rephrasing a question into a thesis statement can often guide you in organizing your answer. It can also serve as a good beginning for your answer. For example:

Question:	Explain what you would do to stop a particular company from dropping chemical wastes into the sea.
Thesis statement:	There are five things I would do to stop the XYZ Corporation from dumping chemical wastes into the sea.

2. Key terms in test questions are also good guides for organizing and developing your answers. Watch out for such terms as the following:

analyze

Analyze the structure of an onion cell.

When you are asked to analyze, you are usually required to break down what is being analyzed into parts and explain how the parts are related to the whole. If you are asked to analyze a process (such as photosynthesis), you can present the steps or phases of the process and then show their relationship.

interpret

Interpret Roosevelt's sweeping victory over Landon in the presidential election of 1936.

When you interpret, you explain a meaning. It might be the meaning of a particular line in a poem or passage in a novel, or it might be the causes or significance of (the meaning behind) a particular event.

illustrate (or *give examples*)

In *The Red Badge of Courage*, what is Stephen Crane's attitude toward heroism in battle? Give specific examples to illustrate your answer.

A question that asks you to illustrate calls for specific details to support a general point. If the question is about a novel, for example, you can support the point with specific incidents and the way the novelist presents them. If you are allowed to have a copy of the work with you when taking the exam, you may wish to quote directly from that work.

compare

Compare a monocot plant with a dicot plant.

When you compare, you look for qualities and characteristics that resemble each other. Sometimes, however, *compare* means *compare and contrast*. In this case, you might organize your answer into two parts: a discussion of similarities and a discussion of differences.

contrast

Contrast the position of women in American society today with their position one hundred years ago.

When asked to contrast, you should emphasize differences.

explain

Explain the germ theory of disease.

When asked to explain, you are expected to write an informative paragraph or essay. It is important that you write clearly and concisely.

list

List five symptoms of coronary artery disease.

The term *list* can confuse. Should you write well-developed paragraphs or simply present a list of items? If the test question calls for an essay, include the items within your paragraphs. Otherwise, present a numbered list. But indicate that you are presenting a list because that is what the question requires.

summarize

Summarize the causes of the Great Depression.

To summarize means to condense. Decide what major points to present. Then concentrate on essentials and omit minor details, no matter how interesting. Writing a summary requires not only a knowledge of the subject but also an ability to distinguish between important and less important points.

trace

Trace the route of the Lewis and Clark expedition.

Obviously, using a map or drawing a diagram would help answer this question, but if you are asked to answer in essay form, you should give a step-by-step account of what you are asked to trace.

write a critique

Write a critique of the government's policy on foreign car imports.

When you are asked to write a critique, you should not simply find fault but discuss both good and bad points. Come to a definite conclusion, but show you are taking a balanced, thoughtful view by presenting all the merits and faults of what you critique.

justify

Justify Jefferson's purchase of Louisiana although the Constitution did not specifically allow him to buy it.

To justify means to argue in favor of what you are discussing. As with any argumentative essay, you must think of as many strong arguments as possible and support them with equally strong evidence.

relate

Relate the completion of the Union Pacific Railroad to the settlement of the West.

When you relate, you should show connections between the two topics you are asked to discuss. Often the connection is one of cause and effect, one topic being a cause and the other an effect.

3. If you have trouble understanding a term, you may be able to ask your teacher what it means. Then you can answer the question with confidence.

4. Some terms may be open to interpretation. If you have misinterpreted a term but have explained in your answer exactly what you are doing and why, you may receive more credit than you would by making your reader figure out what you have tried to do.

Revising Process

When doing an essay test, obviously you will not be able to call on peer editors to help you revise. And after you answer the questions, there may not be much time left for revision. However, reserving a few minutes at the end of the test period to do the following steps may improve your answers and earn you a higher grade.

1. When you have finished writing, reread the questions, then reread your answers.

2. Make sure you have answered all the required questions.

3. Check to see you have not forgotten any important points.

4. Correct any careless errors.

5. If any of your answers are hard to read, make a clean copy of them, provided you have the time.

After your test is returned to you, study it so that you can learn from your mistakes. Determine your strengths and weaknesses. Prepare for your next exam by working to eliminate your weaknesses.

Products

Four Answers to an Exam Question

Read the four student responses to this question: "Excluding the United States, which of the other three nations studied (Spain, Russia, Great Britain) had the best claim in the Pacific Northwest because of exploration by sea? Develop a thesis paragraph, a body (using evidence), and a conclusion." As you read these essays, you might suggest a grade *before* you read their teacher's comments.

1. [Untitled]

In the 16th, 17th and 18th centuries 3 countries lay claim on the Pacific Northwest. In this essay I will discuss the claims of England, Russia, and Spain and tell who had the best claim.

Spain had the first claim on the Pacific Northwest. They came in 1542 for three main reasons: 1) to take control of any Native American civilizations; 2) seeking mineral riches, especially gold and silver; 3) to find the Northwest Passage. Spain set up forts and settlements and mapped the coastline.

England had the second claim saying it was part of their Canadian territory. They thought of trapping furs and making settlements.

Russia had the third claim on the Pacific Northwest. Their claim was it was attached to Russia which it wasn't. (They wanted it to hunt seals.)

In my opinion Spain is the nation that had the best claim on the Pacific Northwest.

2. Essay Test

I feel that due to the reasons later presented, Britain had the best claim on the Pacific Northwest. Explorers, their discoveries, and the advantage of claiming the discoveries will be presented in the following paragraphs in an effort to prove that Britain had the best claim on the Pacific Northwest.

To begin with, James Cook explored the area from Alaska to Oregon. He realized that the Pacific Northwest was rich in furs, fish, and forests. Since Britain, after the defeat of the Spanish Armada, was rising in naval power, they would be sure to make an attempt to settle the area. James Cook also found that there was no Northwest Passage. This is but one set of factors which led me to believe that Britain had the best claim in the Pacific Northwest.

Next John Meares was another prominent factor in strengthening the British claims in the Pacific Northwest. He was credited for discovering Willapa Bay, Cape Disappointment, Cape Shoalwater, Tillamook Bay, and the mouth of the Columbia River. Control of these areas could prove to be very important in claiming other parts of the Pacific Northwest. These capes and bays could develop into important ports for importing goods and military forts as defense against overzealous explorers from other countries. John Meares' claims of the Pacific Northwest are a major reason that Britain had the best claim.

A final person who made Britain's claims the best is George Vancouver. He made an extensive exploration of the Puget Sound area. Also he circled around Vancouver Island. Captain Vancouver's numerous discoveries and explorative thoroughness greatly strengthened Great Britain's claims to the region. As you can see, Captain Vancouver's discoveries gave Britain the best claim on the Pacific Northwest.

All of the areas discovered by the previously named explorers had great potential of developing into settlements. This reason lead me to believe that Britain had the best claim on the Pacific Northwest.

3. Which of the Nations Studied Had the Best Claim on the Pacific Northwest?

Three countries, Spain, Great Britain, and Russia, disagreed on the rights to ownership of the Pacific Northwest. Great Britain, though, had the best European claim on the Pacific Northwest for several reasons. (Of course, the North American Indians, being there all along, had the very best claim.)

With the defeat of the Spanish Armada in 1588, Great Britain began its rise as the world's strongest sea power. This event also triggered the beginning of the search for the Northwest Passage.

In 1776, Captain James Cook explored south from Alaska and traveled along and claimed the Washington and Oregon coasts. Cook was the first to realize the value of the resources of the Pacific Northwest. These included fish, forests, and furs. While exploring thousands of miles of the Pacific Ocean he concluded that the Northwest Passage never existed.

Next in 1786, John Meares, a British opportunist and adventurer, traveled to the Pacific Northwest. It was there that he discovered Willapa Bay, Cape Disappointment, Cape Shoalwater, Tillamook Bay, and the mouth of the Columbia River. He also sailed into the Strait of Juan de Fuca and San Juan Islands. Meares established the first lumber mill and built the first ships in the Pacific Northwest. He also conducted the first fur trade with the Orient and China. Returning from the Orient with laborers to Nootka Sound in Vancouver Island, he stirred up the so-called "Nootka Sound Controversy" because he was infringing on Spain's "exclusive rights." This nearly caused a major war between Great Britain and Spain.

Another explorer from Britain was George Vancouver, who sailed to the Pacific Northwest in 1792. He went near the mouth of the Columbia River, but instead of exploring it, he traveled north into the Strait of Juan de Fuca and Puget Sound. It was there that he met with Bodega y Quadra of Spain, to settle the Nootka Sound Controversy. Spain's exclusive rights were given up and John Meares was paid $210,000, thus weakening Spain's absolute claim on the Pacific Northwest.

Even though from 1542-1792 Spain and Great Britain both sent many explorers to the Pacific Northwest, none of them ever established any permanent settlements or developed the wealth of the area.

However, the interest that Great Britain had in the Pacific Northwest is illustrated by the building of the first lumber mill, the building of ships, and the establishment of the fur trade with the Orient.

Because of Russia's lack of interest in the Pacific Northwest, it will not even be included in this essay.

With these verifiable facts from Dale Lambert's *The Pacific Northwest: Past, Present, and Future* and other sources, Great Britain would be the logical choice for the nation with the best claim on the Pacific Northwest.

4. Spain's Claim to the Pacific Northwest

During the sixteenth to nineteenth centuries, four countries vied for the rights to the Pacific Northwest. These four countries were Spain, Russia, Great Britain, and the United States. Of these countries Spain had the best claim to the Pacific Northwest based on discovery, exploration, colonization, and the Demarcation Treaty.

Dale A. Lambert, author of *The Pacific Northwest: Past, Present, and Future,* states that Spain was the first to discover the Pacific Northwest in 1542. Spain established a few colonies along the Pacific coast, with the most significant at Nootka Sound on Vancouver Island. Strengthening Spain's claim was the fact that Great Britain did not appear until 1577. Lambert also writes that Russia arrived in 1728 and that it was more interested in the land north of the 51st parallel. The United States also had a slight claim to the Pacific Northwest but it made a major appearance much later in 1792.

Lambert also demonstrated Spain's claim to the Pacific Northwest when he listed explorers of the four countries. From the discovery of the Pacific Northwest in 1542 until 1603, 61 years later, Spain sent four sea explorers to the area. They were Bartolome Ferrelo, Michael Lok, Sebastian Viscaino, and Martin Aguilar.

In 1578 Great Britain sent one sea explorer, Sir Francis Drake. Russia didn't have a single explorer in the area. The United States also didn't commision any explorers because it wasn't in existence at that time.

In the 1490s Pope Clement established the Demarcation Line. Lambert wrote that this line divided the world for exploration purposes. Portugal was given the lands east of the line, and Spain received the lands to the west, including all of North America with the Pacific Northwest. The Demarcation Line thus strengthened Spain's claim to the Pacific Northwest.

Considering dates of discovery, exploration and colonization, combined with the significance of the Line of Demarcation, Spain had the strongest claim to the Pacific Northwest.

What makes the essays different? (To help you answer, look at the introductions, thesis statements, development, and conclusions. Examine the sentence variety, transitions, and style. Are there any writing problems? Is there anything irrelevant in any of the essays?) Make sure you assigned a grade to each paper before reading the teacher's comments and grades.

History Teacher's Comments

1. We have a long way to go this year; if you work with me, we will see much improvement by spring. Avoid using written numerals for short numbers in a formal essay. Stay away from first-person references. You should use specific names, places, and events. Order of paragraphs is good, but none of them really contain the specific information needed. Please use specific names, places and events—spell them out and explain what each means. Finally, your conclusion doesn't restate anything other than your personal opinion. Be a trial lawyer in a courtroom. Lay out the evidence before a jury, explain it, then in your final arguments sum up all the pertinent facts. The jury must vote in your favor. LOW GRADE. (D)

2. This paper has a proper focus and sticks to its task without wandering from the point. Try to avoid using first person; stay away from personal references. This paper is to be a factual argument using accumulated evidence from your study of all explorers. Your spelling is good, and you generally use strong, well-put-together sentences. Let's see you use some analysis now and then. Together we'll make much better and stronger written documents. MEDIUM GRADE (C)

3. Consider developing a stronger thesis paragraph. Perhaps name the explorers you are going to use as evidence to back up your thesis claim to Great Britain's "rights to ownership." The second paragraph should be developed with greater

detail; it lacks necessary body. The evidence is presented in a logical chronological order and provides the necessary support. Your use of specific names, places, and events shows knowledge of your subject. Again, like your thesis, your conclusion needs more than the title of the book. Perhaps a summation of evidence? For a first essay this shows promise. We will help you develop stronger written arguments during the year. HIGH GRADE (B)
4. You certainly have promise. For a first essay this paper shows research, organization, and an ability to express yourself clearly. Your thesis paragraph is well done and gives the reader a statement of things to come. The body contains good information, all of it to the point. Perhaps you might reorder the paragraphs in chronological order (by dates). You certainly make use of a goodly number of names, places, and events. On the next paper, do a rough draft, proofread it for minor errors, then do a final copy. The mechanics are good, and your paper shows considerable effort. I'm looking forward to your next paper. HIGH GRADE (A)

The above comments are presented just as George Walsh, the history teacher, wrote them. It is interesting to note that these comments emphasize the need for good writing. Did you notice that the answers in the last two essays are very different? How do you explain the fact that these two exam essays—with their opposing views—both received high grades?

16 Memo

A memorandum, or memo, is a concise message from one person to another in the same school, club, or business. You can use memos to make requests or announcements, give instructions, ask or answer questions, remind someone of (or confirm) the main points of a conversation, or summarize the results of a meeting or other event. People (especially in business) use memos because they allow for fast, easy communication and provide a record of the message and the information it contains.

ASSIGNMENT ▶ Write two memos, one in your own voice and one in the voice of a persona you adopt or create. The memos can be to members of your family or of a club to which you belong, to teachers, or (if you work) to a fellow employee of a company. The style of each memo should be appropriate to its voice and persona.

Prewriting Process

1. Decide on the topic and purpose of each memo. Remember, you can use a memo to request, announce, instruct, ask, answer, summarize, remind, or confirm. If you have difficulty thinking of a topic and purpose, use or adapt one of the following:

Request that students deposit lunch leftovers in the proper receptacles. (You may want to describe how the lunchroom looks when students don't deposit their leftovers.)

Announce a farewell party for a friend (or some other kind of party) to be held at a particular place and on a particular day, date, and time.

Summarize the arrangements for a field trip, including the place to meet and the day, date, and time.

Summarize the decisions made at a meeting of a club to which you belong.

2. Consider the situation. Ask yourself such questions as: Why should I write this memo? Why does my audience need it? The answers to these questions should not be: Because this is an assignment. If you are not writing in response to a real situation, make up a situation that provides you with a strong reason for writing.

3. Consider the needs of your audience. If you are making a request, what reasons will persuade your reader to grant it? If you are supplying information, what does your reader already know, and what does she or he need to know?

4. Consider persona. You should write one memo, of course, in your own voice. For the other, you should adopt a persona. The persona can be someone you know or a fictitious character you create. (For more about personas, see page 6.) Both memos might be on the same topic. For example, your memo might be a request for information, and the memo by your adopted persona could supply the information.

5. If you are writing a memo to instruct, request, or summarize, do one or more of the brainstorming sessions in Chapter 23. You may find that the Positive/Negative/Neutral Pigeonholes (page 217) technique is especially helpful.

6. Jot down all the facts, details, reasons, and examples you need for your memo.

7. Write a sentence that clearly states the thesis of your memo.

Drafting Process

Use these suggestions for drafting both memos. When you have completed a draft of the first memo that satisfies you, you can compose the second memo.

1. At the top left-hand corner of each memo, indicate the person or persons to whom you are sending the memo, the sender (you or your adopted persona), the date, and the subject of the memo. Use the following format:

TO:
FROM:
DATE:
SUBJECT:

Notice that each of these words is in capital letters followed by a colon. To see how this format is used in actual memos, read the examples at the end of the chapter (pages 153–154).

   2. Compose the body of your memo, using your variables and the facts, details, reasons, and examples you jotted down as a guide. Keep your message concise and to the point. (Many memos are written to busy people who do not have the time to read wordy, rambling messages.)

   3. Reread what you have written. Add, omit, or change anything that does not carry out your purpose. Make sure your message can easily be understood by your audience. Make sure you have caught your audience's attention at the very beginning. You can often catch your reader's attention with a clear statement of the memo's purpose. For other ways of catching a reader's attention, see the first sentences of Bob Horton's and Coach Reed's memos (page 153).

   4. When you have completed both memos, you can have your peers edit them.

Editing and Revising Process

When your peers edit and you revise each of your memos, they and you can use the checklists in Chapter 28, as well as the following questions.

   1. Does the opening sentence catch the reader's attention? Is the memo's purpose explained early in the memo?

   2. Has any vital information been omitted? If so, what?

   3. Is the memo too wordy? Can it be made shorter without eliminating necessary information?

   4. Does the memo's ending seem too abrupt? Should a sentence or two be added, or should the last sentence be changed to make the ending seem smoother?

   5. Will each memo meet the needs of its audience? Considering its audience, will each memo succeed in carrying out its purpose? Why or why not?

   6. Do the two memos seem to be written by two distinctly different people? (Remember, you were asked to write one memo in the voice of an adopted persona.) Or do the memos seem to be written by one person who is simply using two different names? If so, what might be changed?

When you have revised your memos on the basis of your peer editors' comments, prepare clean copies for your teacher/editor. Then revise again, if necessary. Finally, present the memos to your intended audience.

Products

TO: Members of the Basketball Team
FROM: Bob Horton, Captain
DATE: February 19, 1991
SUBJECT: The Condition of the Locker Room

That was quite a mess we made in the locker room last Friday. I know that both Coach Reed and Mr. Desmond were really upset when they saw the condition of the room.

I think the whole team should get together and apologize to both the coach and the janitor and that each member of the team should agree to clean up the locker room once a week. I don't think that's too much to ask.

TO: Members of the Basketball Team
FROM: Coach Reed
DATE: February 19, 1991
SUBJECT: Coach Reed's Tension Release Program

I would like to draw your attention to the truly successful mess you made in the locker room the other day. I think the wet towels and unrolled bandages scattered all over the floor have never been arranged more interestingly. And I'm sure the overturned benches piled on top of each other will actually improve the morale of the team.

Since you guys seem to have an overabundance of energy, I will personally try to relieve you of some of it by having early morning practices. Coach Reed's Tension Release Program will begin *tomorrow* at 7:30 a.m., under the authority of Captain Bob Horton, and will continue for two weeks.

So don't forget to tell your mommies to wake you up a little bit earlier tomorrow, or you might find yourself warming the bench for the rest of the season.

TO: Members of the History Club
FROM: Joanne Day, Acting President
DATE: March 5, 1991
SUBJECT: Next meeting

The next meeting of the History Club will be held Tuesday, March 12, after school in the meeting room beside the library.
Items on the agenda will include:

1. election of a new president (as you know, Tony Carver had to resign for personal reasons)
2. discussion of ideas for putting together a pamphlet on the school's history
3. a report on interviews with three elderly local residents
4. anything else the members want to talk about

I hope to see you there.

TO: Members of the History Club
FROM: Joanne Day, President
DATE: March 12, 1991
SUBJECT: Summary of last meeting

At the meeting of the History Club held last Tuesday afternoon, the following events took place:

1. The meeting was called to order at 3:45 p.m.
2. Joanne Day, acting president, was elected president.
3. Mike Wong proposed, and those present agreed, that the club advertise in the local newspaper for old photographs of the school.
4. Mike also suggested that students ask any parents who were also students here for a short note about their experiences.
5. Susan Delorme said that Mrs. Crane, the school's first principal, would be happy to come and talk with us about the school's beginnings. It was agreed that Joanne should ask her to attend our next meeting on Tuesday.
6. Felipe Hernandez presented a summary of his interview with three elderly ladies who were in our high school's first graduating class. It was agreed that some of the information Felipe obtained, including quotations from the three women, would be included in our pamphlet about the school's history.
7. There was no other business; the meeting adjourned at 4:30 p.m.

For Discussion

Bob Horton's Memo

1. This is an example of a request memo. What is being requested?
2. Do you think this memo will succeed in carrying out its purpose? Explain. What might be the reaction of Bob Horton's intended audience?

Coach Reed's Memo

1. Coach Reed asked Bob Horton to write this memo. What might be the purpose of this memo? For example, is the real purpose to announce the coach's "Tension Release Program"? Do you think this memo will succeed in carrying out its purpose? Explain.
2. The memo contains several examples of sarcasm, such as "the truly successful mess." Find others. Why, in your opinion, are they included in the memo?

Joanne Day's Memo Dated March 5, 1991

1. This is an example of an announcement memo. What is being announced?
2. Will this memo catch the attention of its intended audience? Explain.

Joanne Day's Memo Dated March 12, 1991

1. This is an example of a summary memo. What is being summarized?
2. If you were a member of the History Club and could not attend the meeting, would this memo provide enough information for you? Explain.

17 Proposal and Report

Sometimes, in order to get a project approved, you must write a proposal telling about the project and urging it be adopted. Once the project has been carried through, you must then write a report telling about the project's success or failure. Both proposals and reports require the skills you need for other kinds of expository and persuasive writing. You must be able to organize, give clear explanations, and present convincing details, reasons, and other kinds of supporting evidence.

ASSIGNMENT ▶ Part A: Write a proposal urging that an idea of yours become a reality or offering a solution to a problem. Part B: Write a follow-up report that tells what happened after your proposal was adopted.

Part A: Prewriting Process

1. You can write most effectively if you base your proposal on a situation you know well. Do you have a favorite project you want your school or club to adopt? Is there something wrong you know how to make right? Here are a few suggestions to start you thinking.

Propose to the principal or student council that a rock band come to your school for a lunch-hour or a school dance.

Propose to your parents that your curfew be extended to a later hour.

Propose to a friend that the two of you set up a business, such as baby sitting or mowing the neighbors' lawns.

2. Jot down a statement of your proposal and the reasons you think it should be adopted. Then jot down the kinds of information and reasons you need to persuade others to agree with you.

3. Investigate all factors involved in your proposal, such as costs, materials, time, labor, and possible results. Your research might include both information from printed sources and from persons you know (perhaps through interviews).

4. If your proposal concerns a solution to a problem, consider all possible solutions and their advantages and disadvantages before choosing the best solution.

5. Once you have all the facts and reasons you need, jot down your writing variables. Here are the writing variables Henry Ballard jotted down for the proposal on page 161.

Topic and Purpose:	to invite a rock band to give a lunch-hour concert in our high-school cafeteria
Audience:	my principal
Format:	memo
Situation:	students want a rock concert; principal may not
Voice:	my own
Thesis statement:	I propose that the student council be allowed to invite High Strung to perform at a lunch-time concert.

6. Prepare an outline for your proposal. Henry Ballard prepared the following outline.

I. Nature of proposal: to invite High Strung to give a lunch-time concert in our high-school cafeteria
II. Reasons
    A. Desire by students for a lunch-time concert
    B. Popularity of High Strung among students
    C. Possible source of funds for student council
III. Arrangements to be made
    A. Setting a date
    B. Publicity
    C. Sale of tickets
        1. Pre-concert
        2. At the door

D. Work to be done in cafeteria
   1. Setting up of band equipment and chairs
   2. Pre- and post-concert cleaning
   3. Student council responsibility for damages
   4. Faculty supervision

Part A: Drafting Process

1. Proposals are often written in memo format. If you decide to write your proposal as a memo, give the following information at the top of the memo: the person or persons to whom the memo is being sent, the sender, the date, and the subject of the memo. See page 152 and the proposal on page 161 for the correct form to follow.

2. Using your writing variables and outline, as well as the supporting facts and reasons you jotted down, write the body of your proposal. In order that your audience take your proposal seriously, you should write it in a concise, businesslike style. Make sure your word choice, sentence structure, and use of transitional devices are appropriate to your topic, situation, and audience.

3. Remember that a proposal is essentially an argument. As you write, consider what will most effectively persuade your intended audience. Make sure the advantages of your proposal outweigh any possible disadvantages.

4. Before you give your proposal to your peer editors, read it over to make sure you have provided the necessary facts and that your reasons are strong enough to convince your audience. If necessary, write another draft.

Part A: Editing and Revising Process

As your peers read the draft of your proposal, they can assume they are its final audience, the person or persons to whom the proposal is addressed. If your peers think they might turn down your proposal, they should explain why. You can consider their reasons as you revise.

For editing and revising, you and your peers can use the checklists in Chapter 28 as well as the following questions.

1. Is the proposal written clearly and concisely? Is the style businesslike and concise?

2. Is all the necessary information supplied? If not, what might be added?

3. Should anything be deleted? If so, what and why?

4. Is the information well organized? (One way to determine this point is to compare the proposal with its outline. If the outline is well organized, then the proposal should follow it closely.)

After you have revised your proposal on the basis of your peer editors' suggestions, prepare a clean copy for your teacher/editor.

Part B: Prewriting Process

Now that you have written a proposal, you can write a follow-up report explaining how and why your project did or did not succeed.

1. If the proposal you wrote for Part A of this assignment was carried out, write a real-life report about your project. If not, assume your proposal was accepted and write a fictional report in which you invent the reasons for the project's success or failure.

2. Gather (or invent) information about how your project turned out, including the time it took, what it cost, and what resulted.

3. In some cases the project may have turned out to be a mixed success—partly successful, partly not. Consider both aspects and decide whether the successful aspects outweighed the unsuccessful ones. You can use the final estimate of the project as the conclusion of your report.

4. Once you have gathered all the necessary information, jot down your writing variables. Henry Ballard wrote the following variables for his follow-up report on the lunch-time concert by High Strung. (His report is on page 161.)

Topic and Purpose:	to report the successful results of the concert and ask permission for another concert to be given
Audience:	principal
Format:	report
Situation:	success of concert may allow High Strung to return
Voice:	my own
Thesis statement:	The lunch-time concert by High Strung was very successful.

5. Prepare an outline to follow in writing your report. Organize your details in a way that is appropriate to your topic. You may decide to begin with an overall assessment of the project and then go on to such specific aspects as costs and results. Or you may decide to begin with the ways in which the project was successful and go on to the ways in which it was not. For possible ways of organizing your information, see Chapter

26. Notice that the following outline for Henry Ballard's report begins with a general assessment and then goes on to such specific aspects as student and teacher reactions and the state of the cafeteria.

    I. Student council's opinion: very successful concert
   II. Evaluation of successful and unsuccessful aspects
      A. Net profit of $315
      B. Difficulty of beginning on time
      C. Students' comments
        1. Praise for performance
        2. Reactions to fog machine, lighting, and explosions
        3. Pete Willow's comments
      D. Teachers' reactions
      E. Band's reaction
      F. State of cafeteria
        1. Relatively clean
        2. One broken chair
  III. Recommendation: that High Strung be invited back

Part B: Drafting Process

1. Using your list of writing variables and your outline as guides, compose your report.

2. You may wish to follow basic essay structure: introduction, development, conclusion. (See pages 50 and 57 for discussions of basic essay structure.) The introduction can include your thesis statement; the body can present your supporting evidence; and the conclusion might present your recommendations. (Notice that Henry Ballard's report on page 162 follows basic essay structure. His conclusion is in two parts: in the first part he presents the student council's recommendation; in the second he thanks the sponsor and the principal.)

3. As with your proposal, write your report in a businesslike style.

4. Before you give a draft of your report to your peer editors, check to see that you have included all the necessary information, explanations, and reasons. Rewrite if necessary.

Part B: Editing and Revising Process

Ask your peers to read the report as if they were its intended audience. Both they and you can use the checklists in Chapter 28 as well as the questions for editing and revising your proposal (page 158).

Products

A Proposal

TO: Mrs. Hayes, Principal of Lincoln High School
FROM: Henry Ballard
DATE: March 14, 1991
SUBJECT: High Strung concert

As a member of the student council of Lincoln High School, I would like to propose that the council be allowed to invite the popular rock band High Strung to perform at a lunch-time concert in the cafeteria.

Several students have requested that a band visit our school during a noon hour to give a concert. High Strung has played in several local clubs, as well as at a dance at Whitton High School. The band, one of whose members was a student here, is very popular among the students. Sales of tickets for a lunch-time concert by them would probably raise several hundred dollars for the student council.

If we receive your permission to invite High Strung, we will arrange with the group's manager a date when the band would be free. Members of the student council would put advertising posters supplied by the band on all school bulletin boards and would also place an advertisement about the concert in the school newspaper.

Pre-concert ticket sales would take place in the main lobby during the three lunch periods before the concert. Student council members would sell the tickets then, as well as selling tickets at the door on the day of the concert.

Volunteers chosen by the council would be responsible for arranging and cleaning up the cafeteria before and after the concert. If anything should be damaged during the concert, the student council would repair or replace it.

We would appreciate your choosing several faculty members to stay in the cafeteria during the concert, to ensure that everything goes smoothly. Mr. Smithers, our student council sponsor, has already agreed to attend.

I believe that everyone in the school would benefit if a concert by High Strung took place here.

A Report

Report on the Concert by High Strung at Lincoln High School
by Henry Ballard

The lunch-time concert by High Strung took place last Tuesday, March 26, in the Lincoln High cafeteria. In the opinion of the members of the student council, the concert was very successful.

The council's net profit on ticket sales was $315.00. Although we are very pleased with this amount, we regret that the concert did not start on time because not all members of the audience were inside the cafeteria by 12:30. Also, it was difficult to make those students still eating their lunches leave. Some of them stayed for the concert without paying.

Students commented that the band performed very well. They especially enjoyed the band's renditions of "Rock and Roll" by Led Zeppelin, "Wanna Rock" by April Wine, and "21/12" by Rush. The lighting effects and the use of the fog machine were also well received. Not everyone enjoyed the band's use of explosions, however. Some of the students were afraid that real gunpowder had been used. Pete Willows assisted High Strung's lighting man in changing the gels on the follow spot. He told us later that he may help High Strung with a few of its evening shows.

Mr. Swalloas and Ms. Williams helped Mr. Smithers supervise the concert. They had said before the concert that they did not want the band to come. But afterwards, they told members of the student council that they were pleasantly surprised at how well the band played and how well the students behaved. "In fact," Mr. Swalloas said, "we enjoyed ourselves a great deal." Ms. Williams said, "I never knew a rock concert could be so enjoyable."

The band's manager wrote us to say that the band had enjoyed playing at our high school and would be happy to play here again.

The cleanup crew had to spend only half an hour tidying and rearranging the cafeteria, even though not all the students who had volunteered for the crew stayed behind. The student council will replace one chair broken by a student, with the council and the student sharing the cost.

The council's recommendation is that Lincoln High invite High Strung to perform here again in about one month's time. We think, however, that tickets should be sold only before the day of the concert, so that students wanting to buy tickets will not have to wait in line while the concert has already begun. We also recommend that future lunch-time concerts be held in the auditorium or gymnasium, rather than in the cafeteria.

The student council wishes to thank our sponsor, Mr. Smithers, and you, Mrs. Hayes, for allowing High Strung to perform at Lincoln High.

For Discussion

Proposal

1. Is Henry Ballard's proposal well organized? Explain. How closely does the proposal follow its outline?
2. Does the proposal provide convincing reasons for inviting High Strung to give a concert? Why or why not?
3. Do you think Henry Ballard's reasons would convince the principal? Explain. Has he covered all possible objections the principal might raise? If not, what has he omitted?

Report

1. Has Henry Ballard provided a balanced report? That is, has he considered both ways in which the concert was a success and ways it was not? What evidence does he give to support his thesis statement?
2. What does he recommend? How are his recommendations supported by the evidence in previous paragraphs of his report?

18 Personal Letter

The invention of the telephone dealt a serious blow to the art of writing letters. Nowadays, people are more likely to pick up a phone and talk to a friend or relative than write.

Making a phone call is a quick, easy means of communication, of course. But when you talk on the telephone, it may be difficult to think of exactly what you wish to say or organize your ideas. Writing a letter allows you time to think over your ideas, organize them, and find the best words to express them. Furthermore, phone calls vanish the moment they end. A letter to a cherished friend can be taken out of its envelope and read again and again.

ASSIGNMENT ▶ Write a personal letter to a friend or relative. Make sure your letter follows the correct form for personal letters.

Prewriting Process

1. In preparing for this assignment, ask yourself questions like the following: Do I owe a letter to someone? Is there someone with whom I would like to begin a correspondence? If possible, make this a real-life letter to a real person.

2. Think about what you want to tell that person and what that person would like to know. Is there some news you want to relay? Has something

interesting or important happened to you or someone you know? Make a list of what you might include in your letter under the following categories:

> What you have accomplished
> What has happened to you, your family, and your friends
> What you like or do not like (for example, a film, a book, a television program, a record, the win/loss record of a school team)

Use the list as a guide when you write your letter.

   3. In the unlikely event that you cannot think of a reason to write a real person about real events, here are several suggestions you can use or adapt.

- a) Your best friend has moved to another part of the country. Write giving the latest news about yourself and your friends.
- b) A friend or relative has just won an important award (such as most valuable player, best salesperson, a literary prize, or a scholarship). Congratulate her or him and tell why you think the honor is well deserved.
- c) Assume you are on a trip around the world. Write a friend about one or more of the colorful places you visit.
- d) Adopt a persona instead of writing the letter in your own voice. (For a discussion of persona, see page 6.) For example, assume you are a detective on an important case. Write to your old friend, the retired master detective who taught you everything you know, telling about your progress on the case.
- e) Write to someone your own age in another country telling him or her what it is like to live in the United States.

   4. Jot down your writing variables, just as you would for any other writing assignment.

   5. To help you gather supporting details, work through one of the brainstorming sessions in Chapter 23.

Drafting Process

Remember that a personal letter is an extension of your personality. Be sure your letter makes a good impression.

   1. You can choose any size and color stationery for a personal letter. But be careful! Do not choose a color so dark that your audience will develop a serious case of eyestrain.

   2. Make sure you write legibly and neatly. Leave about a one-inch margin on all sides.

3. A personal letter is a kind of essay. You do have more freedom in expressing yourself than you do in an argumentative or informative essay. But avoid giving the impression that you simply dashed off the first thoughts that came into your mind. Let your letter reflect your personality but also show you thought enough of your reader to express yourself clearly and well.

4. Make sure your letter follows the correct form for personal letters. Personal letters have five parts. All the parts appear on page 168 and in the examples of personal letters on pages 169 and 170.

Heading. The heading appears in the upper right corner of a letter. The first line gives the writer's street address, and the second line the city, state, and ZIP code. (Notice on page 168 that the city and state are separated by a comma and that the ZIP code appears several spaces after the state.) The third line indicates the date on which the letter was written.

Salutation. The salutation, a way of saying hello to your reader, appears two spaces below the heading and flush with the left margin. Most salutations begin "Dear _____ ," but feel free to write any salutation you think appropriate. End the salutation of a personal letter with a comma.

Body. The body of the letter, your message to your audience, begins two spaces below the salutation. Indent the first line of the body, and indent each new paragraph.

Complimentary close. The complimentary close is a way of saying good-bye. Write the complimentary close two spaces below the body of the letter, beginning it just to the right of the center of the sheet. Capitalize only the first word of the close, and end the close with a comma.

Signature. Sign your name under the complimentary close.

5. Address an envelope for your letter, following the form shown on page 168. Notice that the sender's name and address appear in the upper right corner of the envelope: name on the first line; street address on the second; city, state, and ZIP code on the third. A comma appears between the city and state, and the ZIP code is written several spaces after the abbreviation for the state. The destination address appears in the center of the envelope.

Notice also that both abbreviations for states (NY for New York) consist of two capital letters. These abbreviations follow the recommendations of the U.S. Postal Service. Refer to the following list of recommended abbreviations for U.S. states.

Alabama	AL	Montana	MT
Alaska	AK	Nebraska	NE
Arizona	AZ	Nevada	NV
Arkansas	AR	New Hampshire	NH
California	CA	New Jersey	NJ
Colorado	CO	New Mexico	NM
Connecticut	CT	New York	NY
Delaware	DE	North Carolina	NC
District of Columbia	DC	North Dakota	ND
Florida	FL	Ohio	OH
Georgia	GA	Oklahoma	OK
Guam	GU	Oregon	OR
Hawaii	HI	Pennsylvania	PA
Idaho	ID	Puerto Rico	PR
Illinois	IL	Rhode Island	RI
Indiana	IN	South Carolina	SC
Iowa	IA	South Dakota	SD
Kansas	KS	Tennessee	TN
Kentucky	KY	Texas	TX
Louisiana	LA	Utah	UT
Maine	ME	Vermont	VT
Maryland	MD	Virginia	VA
Massachusetts	MA	Virgin Islands	VI
Michigan	MI	Washington	WA
Minnesota	MN	West Virginia	WV
Mississippi	MS	Wisconsin	WI
Missouri	MO	Wyoming	WY

Editing and Revising Process

When your peers edit and you revise your personal letter, use the checklists in Chapter 28 and the following questions.

1. Is the letter interesting? If not, why not? What might be done to make it more interesting?

2. Does the letter clearly express the personality of its writer (or of a persona the writer adopted)?

3. Is the letter's tone appropriate to the purpose and audience? (If the letter is to a close friend, its tone should be warm, and its style should be informal.)

4. Is any part of the letter not clear? If so, what and why not?

5. Does the letter follow the correct form for a personal letter? That is, does it contain all five parts? (See page 166.) Are the parts punctuated and capitalized correctly?

After you have revised your letter on the basis of your peers' comments, prepare a clean copy for your teacher/editor. Then send your letter to its intended audience.

The Five Parts of a Personal Letter

23 Bissell Way
New York, NY 10017
October 25, 1991 — Heading

Dear Jane, — Salutation

———— Body

Love always,
Ramona — Complimentary Close / Signature

Envelope Address

Ramona Suarez
23 Bissell Way
New York, NY 10017

Mary Gomberg
3117 Haymarket Boulevard
Chicago, IL 60622

Products

13 Smuffow Avenue
Chicago, IL 60625
March 6, 1991

Dear Angelina,

    So much has happened to me since I've come from Genoa to Chicago that I haven't had time to sit down and tell you about everything. Today, I have time.
    The plane was three hours late arriving in Chicago because of bad weather. In fact, we almost turned around and went back, but the pilot decided to go on instead. The customs inspector opened all my suitcases and checked everything. When I finally arrived in the area where people were waiting for arriving passengers, I could not find Uncle Giuseppe. I didn't want to start looking for him in case I got lost in that big airport. Finally I went to one of the Alitalia counters, and the lady phoned Uncle Giuseppe for me and found out he was on his way. He arrived about half an hour later and took me home, where Aunt Rita had supper ready. I was so tired I fell asleep right after supper.
    Chicago is a very big city filled with many wonderful sights, but I have never been so cold. I now know why they call it the Windy City.
    I must go to my next class now, so I can't write any more. I miss you and Carlo and Mama very much.
    Would you believe that I wrote this letter in my writing class and that I am going to get a mark for it?
    Write soon.

                        Love,

                        Lucia

> 5633 12th Ave.
> El Cajon, CA 92021
> December 12, 1991
>
> Dear Heather,
>
>   I was thrilled to hear about the new addition to your trophy collection. The regional award for best pianist is really hard to win, but I was not surprised to find out that you left the other contestants behind in a cloud of music notes.
>   Where do you play next? Are you going to the All State Music Festival? Wherever you go, I am sure that you will play your best and win whatever prize is being offered.
>   I feel congratulations are in order and am sending them along with my love and heartfelt wishes. May you succeed at whatever you try.
>   Take care of yourself. Watch those fingers!
>
>   Best wishes always,
>
>   *Ida*

To the student who is using this book:
    You have finished your first writing assignment, asked a peer to edit it for you, and received in return a piece of writing to edit yourself. Yipes! Your first editing job! What do you do? How should you go about editing this student's paper? Well, here's my advice, offered after four months of editing my fellow students' papers: Read it. Read the writing variables first.
    Read it again. Are the variables clear? Did the writer follow these variables?
    And again, read it. A lot.
    Now get your copy of *Writing: Process to Product* and turn to the charts in Chapter 28. Compare the paper you are editing with each part of the charts. The lists will help you plan what to say in your

editing comments. I know they helped me. I personally found it faster to begin with the "superior" list for each category to see where the paper fitted. Maybe the paper had a good central idea, but I didn't think there was enough supporting evidence, and so I didn't think it fitted exactly into the "superior" list. If that was the case, that's precisely what I told the writer. Continue in this way through all four charts for content, organization, style, and mechanics until you have a clear picture of where the paper stands.

Remember, you are learning how to ask questions and look for ways to improve your writing, too. Believe me, after a while, you will be able to edit a student's paper fairly quickly.

Another thing to remember when you begin to edit is that people have strengths and weaknesses not only in their writing but also in their ability to edit. In editing for others, you may learn a lot about your own writing. So, focus on the areas in which you are good and, as you continue to edit papers, begin to work on the areas in which you are weak. Student editors worry about grammar more than anything else. They think they have to correct all the grammar errors, but there is a lot more to writing than that. For example, tell the writer what you liked best about the paper and then what you liked least. Make a suggestion about how the writer could revise the paper to make it better. Before long, you'll become a very important part in your classmates' writing process, just as they will be in yours.

I have found that conscientious editing is a great shortcut in improving my writing. But peer editing can be a lot of fun, while providing students with a chance to exchange ideas. Soon you'll make a lot of good friends, too.

Good luck,

Mike Jutras

For Discussion   Lucia's Letter

1. Lucia has just emigrated from Genoa, Italy, to Chicago, Illinois, and is writing to a friend back home. What does Lucia tell that might interest her friend? If you were the friend, what else would you like to know?
2. Judging from the style and tone of this letter, what can you infer about Lucia's personality? Give evidence to support your answer. How might the letter's style and tone be different if Lucia were writing to a distant relative instead of a close friend?

Ida's Letter

1. What is the purpose of this letter? Are the style and tone appropriate to the purpose? Explain.
2. In your opinion, is the letter an appropriate length for the purpose and message? Or should it be shorter? Or longer? Defend your answer.

To the Student Who Is Using This Book

1. Consider Mike Jutras's variables. Who is his audience? What is his purpose?
2. Although this piece is different from the personal letters this chapter encourages you to write, what aspects of the letter make it personal?
3. What is your reaction in reading this letter addressed to you from someone you do not know? Has the letter supported or changed your attitude toward the peer editing process?

19 Business Letter

While a friendly letter is like one part of a conversation with a friend, a business letter is often like part of a business transaction. Such a letter is written to get a definite result. For example, you may want to have damaged goods replaced. You may want to request information about a particular subject or order something advertised in a magazine or newspaper. All these situations are occasions for business letters.

ASSIGNMENT ▶ Write one of the following kinds of business letters: a letter making a request, a letter seeking information, a letter of complaint, or a letter placing an order or enclosing payment.

Prewriting Process

1. Think of how you can make this assignment a real-life one. Let your audience be a real person or company, and write your letter to accomplish a purpose you really want to accomplish. Perhaps you can do one of the following:

Ask a former employer to be your reference for a new job.
Ask your local newspaper to provide more detailed coverage of your high-school team's football games.
Ask an elected official what her or his stand is on an issue that concerns you.

Complain to a mail order company that has not filled your order but cashed your check.

Request that an airline provide information about economy rates for several places you would like to visit.

Request a particular speaker to speak at your club's next meeting.

Write a business letter for any other reason that is important to you.

2. Think about **what** you want your letter to accomplish, **why** you want to accomplish your purpose, and **how** you plan to accomplish it.

3. As with any other assignment, draw up a list of your writing variables.

4. To gather supporting details, work through one or two of the brainstorming sessions in Chapter 23.

Drafting Process

1. While writing a friendly letter allows you a choice of stationery, plain white paper is best for a business letter.

2. If possible, type your letter. Leave a one-inch margin at the top and sides. If your letter is a long one, leave a one-inch margin at the bottom and continue on a second page.

3. Be concise; get to the point quickly. Pleasant chitchat may be welcome in a friendly letter but is usually beside the point in a business letter and often irritates the reader.

4. While business letters call for fairly formal writing, you should not write in a stilted, overly formal style. Avoid such phrases as *I am in receipt of* and *Please arrange to return*. Write *I received* and *Please return* instead.

Notice the difference between these two complaints.

Today I was in receipt of your parcel. In regards to the aforementioned parcel, there is an error in size in filling catalog item No. 332 534 567 B at $16.99 on Invoice No. 636.

On the enclosed Order No. 636, you will see that I ordered a size forty-two. I received a size thirty-two.

Which complaint do you think is more likely to get results?

5. Make sure your writing is clear and direct and gets your message across. As you write, keep asking yourself: What facts are involved?

What message do I want to convey? Am I conveying it? Compare the following two requests.

> Have you anything good for a project on Spain and how to start a project of that country? Like travel brochures, maps, posters, etc. Hopefully free.

> I am doing a project on Spain for a social studies class. I have heard that your travel agency has been very helpful to other students with similar projects. Could you recommend some useful books and articles on Spain, as well as film strips and other audio-visual material? If you have any free posters or brochures about Spain, I would appreciate receiving them.

The writer of the first request did not take the trouble to make the message clear. Eventually a reader might be able to figure out what is wanted, but such messages are more likely to be thrown away than answered.

6. Make sure your letter follows one of the accepted forms for business letters. Two common forms, which are shown on pages 176–177, have six parts.

Heading. As in a personal letter, the heading appears at the top near the right margin. It includes the sender's street address; city, state, and zip code; and the date on which the letter was written. Notice that, as in a personal letter, a comma separates the city and state and that the zip code appears several spaces after the state.

Inside Address. The inside address (not included in a friendly letter) appears about four spaces below the heading and flush with the left margin. It includes the receiver's complete name and title of address (such as *Ms.*); the name of the business firm or other organization to which the letter is being sent; the firm's street address; and the city, state, and ZIP code. If you do not know the exact person to whom you want to send the letter, you can address the letter to a person holding a particular position in the company. For example:

> Director
> Ace Travel Service
> 200 Booth Way
> Palo Alto, CA 94303

The Six Parts of a Business Letter—Semiblock Style

```
                           3251 Ragaway Lane
                           Menlo Park, CA 94025
                           December 18, 1991

Ms. Cecilia Lopez, President
Bel-Tone, Inc.
5 West Polk Avenue
Kansas City, KA 66105

Dear Ms. Lopez:
```

Heading

Inside Address

Salutation

Body

Complimentary Close

Sincerely yours,

Honor Goldstein

Honor Goldstein

Signature

Typed name

Salutation. The salutation appears two spaces below the inside address. In a business letter, the salutation is always followed by a colon. For example:

Dear Dr. Hsien:

Notice that a business letter's salutation is more formal than that of a friendly letter. A title of address—such as *Mr.*, *Mrs.*, *Ms.*, or *Dr.*—is almost always used, and a first name is hardly ever used.

Body. The body of a business letter contains your message and appears two spaces below the salutation. Business letters in block style do not indent paragraphs; letters in semiblock style do indent. (See this page and the next for examples of both styles.) If you type the letter, skip a space between paragraphs, whichever style you follow. If you write the letter in longhand, use semiblock style.

The Six Parts of a Business Letter—Block Style

> 3251 Ragaway Lane
> Menlo Park, CA 94025
> December 18, 1991
>
> Ms. Cecilia Lopez, President
> Bel-Tone, Inc.
> 5 West Polk Avenue
> Kansas City, KA 66105
>
> Dear Ms. Lopez:
>
> _____
> _____
> _____
> _____
> _____
> _____
> _____
> _____
>
> Sincerely yours,
> *Honor Goldstein*
> Honor Goldstein

Heading

Inside Address

Salutation

Body

Complimentary Close

Signature

Typed name

Complimentary close. The complimentary close appears two spaces below the body and just to the right of the center of the sheet. In a business letter, the complimentary close is usually more formal than in a friendly letter. For example:

Yours truly,

Respectfully,

Sincerely yours,

Very truly yours,

Best wishes,

Notice that the first word of the close is capitalized and that a comma ends the close.

Signature. The signature, appearing below the close, is always written in ink (not typed). If you type your business letter, type your name four spaces below the close and then write your signature above the typed name.

7. Address an envelope for your business letter, with your name and address in the upper left corner and the sender's name and address in the center of the envelope. Use the U.S. Postal Service's recommendations for state abbreviations. (See page 167.)

Editing and Revising Process

Before your peers edit your business letter, tell them about your intended reader and the circumstances that led you to write the letter. If you are writing the letter only as an assignment, tell your peers about your fictitious audience and purpose. (You might give your peer editors a copy of your writing variables.)

When your peers edit and you revise your letter, use the checklists in Chapter 28. You and your peer editors should also use the following questions as a guide in the editing and revising process.

1. Is the letter concise and to the point? Should any part of the letter be shortened or omitted? If so, why? (Is any part of the letter too brief? Why? What information would you add?)

2. Is the style formal but not stilted? Should any stilted or wordy phrases be changed? If so, what are they? What words or phrases would you use instead?

3. Does the letter get the message across? If not, what keeps it from getting across?

4. Will the letter get results? If not, what might be done to make it more effective?

5. Does the letter contain all six parts of an accepted, standard form for business letters? Are all of these parts punctuated and capitalized correctly?

After you have revised your letter on the basis of your peers' comments, prepare a clean copy for your teacher/editor. Then, after you are satisfied with the final revision of your letter, send it to your intended audience.

Products

10820 Donna Gail Drive
Austin, TX 78758
November 5, 1991

Mrs. Lesley Swain
Fashionaire, Inc.
168213 W. Fairfax Boulevard
Las Vegas, NV 89109

Dear Mrs. Swain:

    Yesterday I bought a blouse in the Fine Fashions store at Wildford Shopping Center. It was expensive. When I brought it home, I noticed that it was very poorly made and in many places the seams were not caught under, leaving raw edges.
    I was very disappointed and have returned the blouse. Your merchandise is generally satisfactory, but I feel that you should be aware of this matter.

                                       Yours truly,

                                       Kimiko Karpoff

                                       Kimiko Karpoff

658 Griffins Avenue
Seattle, WA 98101
February 4, 1991

Ms. L. Gerard, President
Vanner School for Disabled Children
1010 Charles Drive
Seattle, WA 98114

Dear Ms. Gerard:

I am writing to inform you of my desire to perform volunteer work for your organization.

Having received the list of services you need, I am requesting that I be considered for the following duties:

1. children's tutor
2. organizer of accommodations for out-of-town parents

I feel that I could be of help in these areas, having worked in my high-school library for two years, while tutoring other students in mathematics. I also have strong organizational abilities.

I will be available for work Monday through Thursday from 6:00–9:00 P.M., and on Fridays, from 1:30–3:00 P.M.

I hope that my services will be of some benefit to your organization. Please contact me at my home if you wish to interview me.

Sincerely yours,

John Leung

John Leung

For Discussion   Kimiko Karpoff's Letter

1. What circumstances led Kimiko Karpoff to write this letter? Are these circumstances clearly presented in the letter? If not, what should be added or changed?

2. Do you think this letter is effectively written to get results? What results do you think it might get?
3. Does the letter follow block or semiblock style?

John Leung's Letter

1. What is the purpose of this letter? What evidence does the writer give to help him accomplish his purpose?
2. If you were Ms. Gerard, would you interview John Leung? Why or why not?
3. Does this letter follow block or semiblock style?

20 Letter to the Editor

Have you ever read a newspaper or magazine article or editorial with which you wholeheartedly agreed or vehemently disagreed? Such agreement or disagreement shows you have your own ideas and feelings about a subject. This assignment gives you the opportunity to express them.

ASSIGNMENT ▶ Choose an article or editorial from a recent newspaper or magazine. Write a letter to the editor expressing your agreement or disagreement.

Prewriting Process

1. Find several newspaper and magazine articles and editorials that express strong opinions. Decide which one you agree or disagree with most.

(Disagreeing with an article will probably give you more to say than agreeing with it. If you choose an article or editorial with which you agree, make sure that you have enough ideas and evidence of your own to offer. Otherwise your letter may simply end up echoing what that piece says.)

2. In your journal, jot down your own ideas about the subject as a freewriting exercise. (For a discussion of keeping a journal, see Chapter 22.)

3. Do several of the brainstorming sessions in Chapter 23 to provide more supporting evidence for your letter.

4. If your journal entry and brainstorming sessions do not provide enough supporting evidence, then, despite your strong feelings, you probably do not have a great deal to say about that particular subject. If so, begin with another article or editorial.

5. You might want to engage in an informal debate about the topic of your letter with someone who disagrees with you. Such a debate will help you develop strong reasons to support your position as well as give you an idea of the arguments against it.

6. Jot down your writing variables. One writer who wished to express disagreement with a newspaper editorial jotted the following variables.

Limited topic:	the quality of education at my high school
Audience:	editor and readers of local newspaper
Purpose:	to disagree with editorial
Format:	letter to the editor
Situation:	Editorial claims high schools are doing poor job of educating America's youth; I think my high school is doing a fine job.
Voice:	my own
Thesis statement:	My high school provides me and other students with a fine education.

Drafting Process

1. A letter to the editor is essentially an argumentative essay. Before drafting your letter, you may wish to read or review the drafting suggestions in Chapter 5 (pages 57–58).

2. Write a strong opening to catch the editor's—and your final reader's—attention. (For a discussion of strong openings, see pages 243–245.)

3. Make clear to what article or editorial you are writing a reply. You may want to summarize an opposing argument very briefly before replying to it—for example:

> Your editorial of April 7, 1985, asserts that American high schools are doing a poor job of educating today's youth. My own education at Robert Frost High School makes me very suspicious of such a glittering generality.

(Such a concise summary and statement of your own position might provide the strong opening you need.)

4. State your arguments and supporting evidence clearly and concisely. Most newspapers do not provide a great deal of space for letters, and editors often cut sentences and paragraphs from reader's letters before printing them. The more concise your letter, the less chance there is that any part of it will be cut.

5. Using positive or negative slant may make your letter more effective. For a discussion of positive and negative slant see Chapter 34. Before drafting your letter, you may want to do the exercises on pages 331–335.

6. Using such rhetorical devices as climactic parallelism and balanced sentences may also increase your letter's effectiveness. For a discussion of such devices, see Chapter 32.

7. Write a strong ending, emphasizing your most important idea. You may wish to read or review the discussion of endings in Chapter 25 and do Exercise 2 (page 245) before drafting your ending.

8. Your letter should follow one of the accepted forms for a business letter discussed and shown on pages 175–179. As a salutation, write:

To the editor:

Remember to end the salutation with a colon.

Editing and Revising Process

When you submit your letter to your peers and your teacher, attach the original article or editorial to which you responded. If this is not possible, include a brief summary of the piece that provoked your response.

When your peers edit your letter, they should assume they are real newspaper editors, concerned with fitting your letter and other letters into a limited amount of space. They should consider if anything could be cut from the letter without changing the meaning or damaging its effectiveness.

Both you and your peers should use the checklists in Chapter 28 and the following questions as guides.

1. Does the letter's opening capture the reader's interest?
2. Does the letter present good reasons and evidence to support its thesis? If not, where does the letter fail?
3. Is the argument easy to follow? If not, what could be stated more clearly?
4. Is the opposing position clearly stated and treated fairly?
5. Does the letter make effective use of rhetorical devices?
6. Does the letter have a strong ending?

7. Can anything be deleted from the letter without harming its effectiveness? If so, what?

8. Does the letter follow an accepted form for business letters? Does it have all six parts of a business letter?

After you revise your letter on the basis of your peers' comments, prepare a clean copy for your teacher/editor. Then revise again if necessary. Finally, consider sending your letter to the newspaper or magazine that printed the original article. You might see your name and ideas in print.

Products

(Note: The first letter, by Roberta McFarland, appears in two versions: the first as sent to the *San Diego Herald* and the second as the *Herald* published it. As you read them, note the differences between the two.)

To the Editor:

Are we to be overwhelmed by the trauma of Olympic Games every four years? Politics and commercialism have taken over this event for the last century, and it's getting worse. The events of the '80s have shown that we are going to lose this most valuable event if we don't soon take firm action.

The original concept of the Olympic Games was to honor the athletes. Various cities would send their best athletes to Mt. Olympus. There they would compete to determine the best, the strongest, the most-skilled athlete in a particular sport. It was an individual competition: athlete against athlete. Not city against city. Not country against country. The strength or weakness of an entire nation had nothing to do with an athlete's competitive ability.

Recently both politics and commercialism have all but ruined the Olympic Games. The United States boycotted the 1980 games; in retaliation, the Soviet Union boycotts the 1984 games. The future of a 1988 world event looks bleak. Furthermore, the last three Olympic Games have cost a fortune. Which cities in the future want to be saddled with a suffocating deficit?

My suggestion is to establish one place that the Olympic Games can be held every time. A place free from politics and commercialism. A place where the money that is spent year after year on building can be put to good use. Imagine if you had the facilities from Montreal, Moscow, and Los Angeles all in one place, the hotels, stadiums, and all the other competitive areas—in one place! And what if these were all located in Greece near the original site of the games in ancient times? For the three years that the games would not be held, it could become a great vacation spot for the rest of the world! And for the year of the Olympic Games, everything would be ready. With all that vacation money coming in as well as the Olympic money from sponsors, the accommodations would be superb. And all this without suffering the political and commercial trash we have had to put up with every year. The streets of the new Olympia would practically be paved with gold.

Go for it!

Roberta McFarland

To the Editor:

Recently, both politics and commercialism have all but ruined the Olympic Games. The United States boycotted the 1980 Games; in retaliation, the Soviet Union boycotts the 1984 Games. The future of a 1988 world event looks bleak.

Furthermore, the last three Olympic Games have cost a fortune. Which cities in the future want to be saddled with a suffocating deficit?

My suggestion is to establish one place that the Olympic Games can be held every time—a place free from politics and commercialism. A place where the money that is spent year after year on building can be put to good use.

Imagine if you had the facilities of Montreal, Moscow, and Los Angeles all in one place. The hotels, stadiums, and all the other competitive areas—in one place! And what if these were all located in Greece near the original site of the Games in ancient times?

For the three years that the Games would not be held, it could become a great vacation spot for the rest of the world. And for the year of the Olympic Games, everything would be ready. With all that vacation money coming in as well as the Olympic money from sponsors, the accommodations would be superb.

And all this without suffering the political and commercial trash we have had to put up with every year.

Roberta McFarland

1922 Elm Grove Lane
Hillview, NJ 07044
October 15, 1991

Editor, Hillview *Clarion-Intelligencer*
2750 Clinton Avenue
Hillview, NJ 07042

To the Editor:

I strongly disagree with your editorial of October 13, about the Emilio Carducci Youth Center. You state the building is not safe and should be torn down. I think money should be raised to make the building safe.

I know what the Youth Center means to the teenagers of Hillview. I am sixteen years old and have spent many wonderful hours at the Center, using the Olympic-size swimming pool, playing basketball, or just hanging around with my friends in the Rec Room, listening to music. All the teens I know think of the Center as their favorite hangout.

What would happen if the Center were destroyed? Eventually another might be built, but how long would that take? Hillview would have a lot of young people with lots of time on their hands and no place to go.

Your editorial states that repairing the Center to make it safe would be expensive. But building a new center would be much more expensive and take much longer.

Mothers and fathers of Hillview, which would you prefer? A small increase in your property taxes to pay for restoring the Center? Or not knowing where your sons and daughters are in their free time?

Respectfully yours,

John Marcantonio

To the Editor:

On behalf of many students and faculty of the Shoreline district, I wish to express extreme disappointment in the (March 4) article, "Shorewood High: They've Got It Together," and its portrayal of Shorewood.

Got what together? Not much, one gathers from reading the article.

Beyond being a poor description of Shorewood life, the article did nothing more than rattle on about the honors program. The author neglected to even mention the nationally recognized Thespian troupe, the excellent DECA program, the award-winning newspaper, the band which will represent the state in Washington, D.C., this summer and the high-ranking sports program.

As a student, I am appalled at the portrayal of our student body. The "... gaudy shirt and Vuarnet sunglasses" were worn for a "Hawaiian" theme dance, a fund-raiser for the track team. Second, couples are not allowed to "squinch in the corner and neck." Shorewood's dances are well chaperoned, and such behavior is neither condoned by the school nor is it "wholesome."

And perhaps the writer meant well in labeling Jim Alderdice and Barb Schulz "master teachers," but the faculty of Shorewood is so outstanding, that singling out only two as "masters" is discriminating.

As a side note, though the photographer couldn't have known that the girl on the cover is from another school, surely the reportedly forty rolls of film produced better pictures than the ones used.

The school portrayed in the article was hardly newsworthy and certainly not Shorewood.

Karla Jackson

For Discussion

Roberta McFarland's Letters

1. What differences can you find between the original letter and the published version? Aside from making it a shorter letter, why do you think the *San Diego Herald* made the changes it did?
2. In your opinion, which version of the letter is more effective? Why?

John Marcantonio's Letter

1. What is the purpose of this letter? Who is the actual intended audience, the newspaper's editor or someone else?
2. What arguments and evidence does the writer give to support his thesis?
3. Do you think this letter has a good opening and closing? Why or why not?
4. In your opinion, is the letter fair to the opposing side? Explain.
5. What rhetorical devices does the letter use?
6. Do you think the letter will get results? Why or why not?

Karla Jackson's Letter

1. This indignant letter was written in response to an article *praising* Shorewood High School. Why do you think Karla Jackson wrote the letter? What impression of Shorewood High does the letter give?
2. What, specifically, caused the writer's disappointment in the article?
3. Do you think this letter is an effective expression of opinion? Defend your answer.

21 Résumé and Cover Letter

A résumé is a summary of a job applicant's work experience, education, and other qualifications. Often it is accompanied by a cover letter requesting an interview. Sometimes you will be able to get a job through personal contacts, but more often you will have to write a letter and enclose a résumé. Your chances of obtaining an interview may depend on how well you present yourself on paper.

ASSIGNMENT ▶ Write a résumé and cover letter.

Prewriting Process

1. You can write this assignment to apply for an imaginary job or a real one. Writing for an imaginary job will give you the opportunity to take stock of your qualifications. Writing for a real job could get you the job!

2. Find job listings to which you might want to reply. You can find such listings at employment offices, on school and community bulletin boards, and in the "Help Wanted" or "Employment Opportunities" section of a newspaper's want ad columns.

Here is a sampling of job listings that you can respond to if you are not actually applying for a real job.

(If you apply for any of these jobs, address your cover letter to the street address given and use the name and ZIP code of your own city or town.)

> **MACKENZIE'S HAMBURGER EMPORIUM**
>
> 3400 E. First St.
> Part-time counter-help applications are now being accepted. Apply in writing, please, to Juana Ruiz, Manager.

> **ACCOMPANIST**
>
> Needed to assist in auditions for musical. Must be able to sight-read music. Apply to Hal Davis, Regency Theater, 1101 Ziegfeld Boulevard.

> **ROCK BAND**
>
> Am forming a rock band. Looking for instrumentalists and singer. Apply in writing to Donna Turner, 5 Penny Lane.

> **PART-TIME**
>
> Trainee mechanic. Hours 4–6 p.m. Monday–Friday, all day Saturday. Looking for someone who likes to tinker with cars and wants to learn more about them. Apply to Andy Starkowski, Chief Mechanic, Bayshore Garage, 48611 W. Ford Street.

3. Study the job requirements of the listings you have selected. Narrow the jobs down to the one for which you would most like to apply (which is probably the one for which you feel most qualified).

4. Before writing your résumé, jot down your responses to the following items.

   a) What are the job's requirements?
   b) In what ways do you qualify for the job?
   c) What direct experience do you have? (In answering this, consider previous jobs you have had that are similar to the job you want.)
   d) What indirect experience do you have? (In answering this, consider other jobs you have had that have something in common with the job you want. Consider also interests and activities that have given you some preparation for the job. For example, raising funds for a school club or activity might qualify as sales experience.)

5. List the information you will want to present in your résumé, including:

a) educational background, including all of the schools you have attended and all of the courses you have taken that relate to the job you are seeking
b) previous jobs, including outstanding accomplishments and recognition
c) activities and interests, especially those that relate to the job you seek
d) references, both personal (people who can testify to your character and ability) and business (people who can tell about your performance on a job)

6. Jot down your writing variables before drafting your résumé and cover letter.

Drafting Process for the Résumé

1. If possible, write a one-page résumé. Busy employers do not have time to read long résumés. If your résumé turns out to be more than one page long, you may want to decide which information is most important for the employer to know and which to leave out and then rewrite the résumé.

2. The most widely used method of organization for a résumé is to present information under various categories—such as education and work experience—in reverse chronological order. That is, you can begin with your most recent schooling and most recent job and work backwards. This organization makes it easy for a prospective employer to check on your progress.

3. The résumé on page 196 uses a method of organization that you may want to follow.

a) List your name, address, and telephone number at the top of the résumé so that your prospective employer can contact you easily.
b) Next, list your education, beginning with your most recent school. (The résumé on page 196 lists the schools under "EDUCATIONAL DATA.") If any courses have prepared you for the job you seek, list those. Do not omit any kind of specialized training that relates to the job.

c) List your job experience, interests and hobbies (especially if they relate to the job), and any awards you received.

d) In presenting your employment history, specify the dates of employment, the *full* names of the companies you worked for (your prospective employer may want to contact them), and the positions you held. Give brief, but specific, descriptions of what your jobs required. A phrase such as "helped in the lunchroom" is too vague. Tell your prospective employer exactly how you helped.

e) At the end of your résumé, you can present your personal and business references or simply state, "References available upon request." Make sure you ask the people you list as references for permission. Try to get your references from a variety of sources: work, school, church, team, club, and any other organization to which you belong.

4. Phrases, rather than complete sentences, work well in a résumé.

5. Study the résumé on page 196 before you write your own.

Drafting Process for the Cover Letter

1. Because a cover letter is a business letter, you should read or review Chapter 19, especially pages 173–178, which deal with the correct forms for business letters. Make sure your cover letter contains all six parts of a business letter.

2. Make sure your letter carries out the following tasks:

a) establishing contact with the employer by indicating what job you are applying for and how you know about the job (advertisement, employment agency, personal contact, or other source)

b) arousing the interest of the employer by telling why you are interested in the position

c) convincing the employer, by briefly mentioning your qualifications, to read your résumé

d) gaining an interview by politely requesting one and indicating when you would be available for one (or that you would be willing to come for one at any time convenient to the employer)

3. If you do not have any work experience, or if the experience is not related to the job you seek, emphasize the personal qualities that would make you suitable for the position. For example:

Although I do not have any direct sales experience, my participation in many clubs shows that I have the ability to get along with others. This coupled with my competitive spirit, would, I believe, allow me to make a valuable contribution to your organization.

When deciding what qualities to mention, consider the requirements of the job. A sales position, for example, might require someone who has an attractive personality, speaks well, and is aggressive. A clerical position might require good organizational ability and attention to detail.

4. Study the cover letter on page 195 before you begin to write your own.

Editing and Revising Process

You may want to have your peer editors read the job listing to which you are responding before reading your résumé and cover letter. In addition, your peers can pretend to be the prospective employer and conduct an interview with you. During the interview, a peer may discuss some aspect of the résumé that needs more explanation. You can revise the résumé accordingly.

When your peers edit and you revise, use the following suggestions as guides.

1. Do the résumé and cover letter provide the following information?

   a) *who* the writer is
   b) *what* experience and education the writer has
   c) *where* the writer gained the experience and education
   d) *when* the writer gained the experience and education
   e) *why* the writer wants the job

2. Does the cover letter have all six parts of a business letter? Are the parts punctuated correctly?

3. Do you think the cover letter will gain the interest of the prospective employer? If not, why not?

After you revise your résumé and cover letter on the basis of your peer editors' comments, present a clean copy to your teacher/editor. Then, before you complete your final draft, make a last-minute check to be sure that your cover letter indicates why you are applying for the job and requests an interview.

If you have written your résumé and cover letter for a real job, send them in a correctly addressed envelope to your future employer.

Products

Cover Letter

1515 Awards Avenue
Chicago, IL 60200
May 3, 1991

Douglas Catering Inc.
3900 Hottens Road
Milwaukee, WI 53219

Dear Mr. Douglas:

   I am responding to your recent newspaper advertisement for an assistant chef.

   For the past few years, I have held jobs in the catering business in Chicago, Illinois. I find it an interesting and challenging area and hope to pursue a career as a chef, following graduation from high school.

   I am presently attending McNair Career Academy in Chicago, majoring in food preparation. I am planning to move to Milwaukee at the end of June and am willing to work in the evenings and on Saturdays to obtain experience in the catering field.

   I have enclosed a résumé outlining my experience and qualifications for the position you offer. If my qualifications interest you, I should be grateful if you would grant me an interview during the May 24th weekend. I will endeavor to see you any time at your convenience.

                                 Yours truly,

                                   Juan Cardozo

RÉSUMÉ

Juan Cardozo
1515 Awards Avenue
Chicago, Illinois 60200
Phone (312) 333-6767

EDUCATIONAL DATA

Sept. 1989–present McNair Career Academy, Chicago, Illinois

Specialized in food preparation and catering with grades of A in all related courses. General grade average: B+

Sept. 1981–June 1989 Nugget Elementary School, Tampa, Florida

EMPLOYMENT DATA

Jan. 1991–present Cafeteria helper, McNair Career Academy
Served lunches, prepared salads

Sept. 1991–present Busperson, Dino's Place, 6420 Number Road, Chicago

July–August 1991 Cook, Tashtego's Summer Camp, Lake Tashtego, Wisconsin

July 1990–June 1991 Counter person, McCleod's, 2620 Cedar Street, Chicago
Served the public, prepared hamburgers

May 1986–June 1990 Carrier, *Star-Phoenix*, 4310 Staves Street, Tampa

AWARDS

Most Promising Cook Award, McNair Career Academy, June 1990
Best Cook Award, 1991, Tashtego Summer Camp

References available upon request.

For Discussion: Juan Cardozo's Résumé and Cover Letter

1. Would Juan Cardozo's cover letter persuade you to read his résumé? Would the résumé persuade you to give him an interview? Explain.
2. Does the writer seem qualified for the job he seeks? If so, what are his qualifications?
3. Should anything be added or omitted from the résumé or cover letter? If so, what?

"When I write, I write because a thing has to be."
JORGE LUIS BORGES

First Workshop: Content and Organization

How to Use the First Workshop

The First Workshop helps to put you in touch with all aspects of prewriting, drafting, and editing and revising so that you can think of a topic, develop it, and, with the help of your peer editors, produce a polished product every time you write.

Before you work in this section, however, you should study "The Writing Process" (pages 2–17) and complete the Introductory Assignment (pages 4–17). Afterward, if you are still unfamiliar or uncomfortable with the steps of the writing process, you should complete particular exercises in the various chapters in this section to learn how to get the most out of your prewriting, drafting, and editing and revising processes. First, though, familiarize yourself with the contents of the First Workshop by spending a few minutes thumbing through Chapters 22 to 29.

When you work on the exercises in earnest, you should go over them with a partner (classmate, friend, or relative) so that you can talk about them in relation to your writing process. You will notice in some of the chapters that you are asked questions or given sentence or paragraph work to complete. You will need a partner to check your answers, sentences, or paragraphs.

After you become familiar and comfortable with your writing process, you can use the chapters in the First Workshop as a resource, dipping into them to check a brainstorming detail, review a point on one of the editing charts or a fact about unwriting, find a good transitional word or phrase, and so on.

22 Journal Writing and Instant Writing

As a young actor in Hollywood, Charlton Heston began to keep a journal. In 1978, he brought these experiences together to create a fascinating best seller, *The Actor's Life*.

During the last years of her short life, Anne Frank kept a journal where she recorded the impressions of the small world in which she hid while the Second World War ravaged the larger world. The result brought *The Diary of Anne Frank* into millions of homes in book form and onto stages and screens throughout the world in play and film form.

Novelist Judy Blume recently brought out a unique diary which contains no dates. Only the occasional quotation appears. Thus, she encourages the owners of her book to write down their own feelings, reactions, and sensations. She, in fact, encourages journal writing.

You may not think so at first, but once you begin to keep a journal you will discover that—like Heston, Anne Frank, and Blume—you have many interesting, valuable thoughts and experiences to record. Returning to your journal in future years will give you (and any audience with whom you choose to share it) hours of enlightening, enjoyable reading.

For at least ten minutes each day, in or out of class, write in your journal.

Some Questions and Answers about Journals

What is a journal? It is a book in which you write about your feelings, thoughts, and experiences.

Who will read my journal? Only you or anyone to whom you care to show it. Journal writing allows you to explore thoughts and ideas and to experiment with language without worrying about evaluation.

How should I organize my journal entries? So you can find a particular piece of writing quickly, you should date and label or title each journal entry.

Why should I write in a journal? To get in touch with yourself. The more you can write about your feelings, thoughts, and experiences, and the more you can experiment with paragraphs, sentences, and words, the more comfortable you should be with all of your future writing assignments. As you continue your journal entries, you should become more adventurous and should stretch your writing in untried ways so that your journal becomes more and more valuable to you. Discover your strengths; learn to recognize your own unique way with words by experimenting in your journal with different kinds of writing.

How does journal writing fit into my writing process? Journal writing has proven to be one of the best methods of brainstorming for ideas. It is an important part of the writing process.

Why should I write every day in my journal? Your goal should be to create a habit of writing. If you want to swim well, for example, you have to get into the water and practice swimming. Writing in your journal is one way to practice your writing skills every day.

May I use any of my journal writing for other assignments? Certainly. You will find that you will be able to refer to your journal for ideas, supporting details, and even a well-worded phrase.

What do I do with my journal at the end of the school term? That is up to you. If you have begun the habit of journal writing, you will probably keep it up long after your career as a student ends.

Journal Writing

Once you are in the habit of writing in your journal, it should not be difficult to identify subjects about which you want or need to write. Here are some suggestions to get you started.

1. Start with one of these openings and write about yourself. Do not be concerned about how your piece will end—just let yourself write.

People always thought I was strong (weak).
I would rather not be a lender (borrower).
I am (not) a victim of others.
I do (not) intend to get married.
I often (seldom) become embarrassed.

Or you can create your own opening.

2. Describe yourself to an imaginary reader. Tell about:

your favorite song
your favorite singer
your favorite teacher
your least favorite person
your likes and dislikes
your ambitions
other aspects of yourself

3. Recall a past event and list all the details that you can remember. For example:

an event from childhood
a highly emotional event
your last birthday
the most scary time of your life
a sad event

4. Use your senses to describe the place where you are writing. Record everything you hear, see, feel, smell, and taste. From time to time repeat this entry, from a different writing location.

5. Write about your reaction to a recent newspaper headline or news item.

6. Think about a familiar saying such as one of the following:

A bird in the hand is worth two in the bush.
You can't tell a book by its cover.
Charity begins at home.
You are what you eat.
Success is a journey, not a destination.

Explain why you agree or disagree, or tell about an incident that illustrates the saying.

7. Write a piece that concludes logically with one of the statements below, or make up your own concluding statement before you begin.

And the blind man in the pool said, "Life's been good to me."
There is no such thing as a well-adjusted slave.
No one can bring you peace but yourself.
It is impossible to go back in time.

8. Write down one of the more important aspects of the human condition, such as love, fear, hunger, greed, loneliness, or the desire for happiness. Write the word or phrase over and over until something else comes into your mind, then continue writing about that thought. Plan to write nonstop for ten minutes. If you get stuck, go back to writing the original word again until something new comes into your mind.

9. What are your ideas and feelings about some of humanity's more profound theories and beliefs? Start with a word or phrase like one of the following: belief in God, capitalism, psychiatry, the Golden Rule. Then write about it.

10. You may also use your journal to practice sentence variety and sentence combining. If you would like to master a particular method of sentence combining that you have studied, rewrite any past journal entry using that method as often as possible.

11. To develop and enrich your writing style, you might follow the suggestions in one of the Special Writing Assignments in the Second Workshop. By frequently practicing these assignments in your journal, you will soon learn a variety of ways to express your thoughts.

12. You might keep a portion of your journal to record your experiences in developing your writing process. Comment on any of the following:

> your attitude toward writing in general and how it changes throughout the term
> your feelings about using the prewriting, drafting, and editing and revising stages of the process
> your concerns about your writing style
> your improvement, as you see and feel it
> your improvement, as you watch and listen to your editors
> your improvement, as you note the reactions of your intended readers

From time to time, you can write a running commentary on an assignment. For example, after you have brainstormed a topic, make a journal commentary on your brainstorming activity. After you draft the paper, comment on your drafting process. Continue making journal entries until you give your assignment to its intended audience. If you write several different running commentaries, you will be able to look back on your entries to see how your writing process has developed.

Instant Writing

As an alternative to solitary journal writing, try instant writing—writing at a specific time for a specific number of minutes. Practicing instant writing at least once a week should not only prepare you to produce better exam essays (see Chapter 15) but also give you an additional opportunity to have a piece of writing edited.

For each of the instant-writing suggestions that follow, plan with your partner the details surrounding the writing experience. Consider the following:

what you will write about
the day and time the writing will take place
what kind of instant writing you will do
how much time to allot to each session (never more than ten minutes)
how the piece of writing will be edited
whether a rewrite would be beneficial or desirable

Until you and your partner make up your own topics for instant writing, use the following suggestions:

1. *What's the Problem?* Exchange questions with your partner. Make them as personal or imaginative as you wish—for example: What can I do to get my parents to extend my curfew hour? How can I set up a bowling alley on Mars? To the best of your ability, answer in a journal entry the question posed by your partner.

2. *What's the Answer?* Exchange questions with your partner, basing your questions on a course that your partner is studying—for example: "Point out two reasons why the German people accepted Hitler as their leader." Answer the question you are given as though it were an exam question.

3. *If I were....* Use the following beginning: "If I were _____, I'd _____." Fill in the first blank only and exchange beginnings with your partner. Use your imagination. For example: If I were *a toad* ..., *the richest person in the world* ..., *a horseshoe* ..., *my mother* .... Using your partner's beginning, write either a serious or humorous piece.

4. *The story isn't over.* Ask your partner to choose a short story, novel, play, film, television show, or radio play with which you are both familiar. Ask yourself: What will the main character in the story be doing one year after the story ends? Use your imagination to extend the story. Try to imitate the original style.

5. *Haiku.* Try your hand at writing haiku, one of the simplest verse forms. It has only three lines, the first of five syllables, the second of seven, and the third of five. The haiku is used by the Japanese for brief descriptions or to convey a mood. It can make a pleasant instant-writing session for you and can help you appreciate the importance of choosing words to create a vivid image. Read the examples of haiku on the next page, noting particularly the 5–7–5 syllabic pattern:

Crimson dragonfly,
As it lights, sways together
With a leaf of rye.

A fluttering swarm
Of cherry petals; there comes,
Driving them, the storm.

On the lake's green bank,
Living green, a quiet frog
Looks with bulging eyes.

(Note that the first and third lines of a haiku can rhyme, as in the first and second examples.)

Exchange topics for a haiku with your partner. Write a haiku and compare it with your partner's.

6. *A word.* The object of this exercise is to use a given word and all related words in the piece of writing. Exchange topics and a single word with your partner—for example: Write on the topic of mountain climbing, using the word *serene* and all related words. (You may use your dictionary if you are unfamiliar with the word or if you do not know all of the related words. Words associated with *serene* would be *serenity, serenely, sereneness.*)

7. *Almost freewriting.* Although the choice of topic is not free, the procedure of this instant-writing session is similar to that of freewriting. Exchange a single word with your partner—for example: *money, sports, clothes.* The object of this suggestion is to write about that word for a specified number of minutes. If you cannot think of anything to say, simply write that word over and over until something comes into your mind.

8. *Reacting to a quotation.* Find a quotation—for example: "Injustice anywhere is a threat to justice everywhere" (Martin Luther King, Jr.).

Exchange it with your partner. The object of this session is to write about that quotation for a number of minutes. If you cannot think of anything to write, keep returning to the quotation and simply write it down until something comes into your mind.

9. *The unknown.* You and your partner can arrange to write a story or essay the following way. One of you can write an opening sentence, then pass it on for the other to add the second sentence. When the second sentence is completed, pass on the piece of writing for the third sentence to be added. The assignment is completed when one of you writes "The End." Do not discuss the subject either before or during the writing. Afterward, you can discuss the effectiveness of the piece, the difficulties encountered, as well as any errors that you might detect.

10. *Found poetry.* Independently, you and your partner find a part of one of the models in *Writing: Process to Product* (especially a sentence or two that you may not fully understand or appreciate). Exchange and rewrite the portion on a page as a poem. Experiment by repositioning words until you find an arrangement that either makes the meaning clear or brings forth an appreciation of the setting. You may leave out parts of a sentence or combine sentences.

23 Brainstorming

Few writers are lucky enough to have an inspired, full-blown idea and supporting details spring into their minds in a beautifully complete and organized manner. In order to find an idea and generate supporting details, they use two methods: they think about it by themselves, and they talk about it with several people until their idea becomes workable enough for them to begin to write their first draft. Throughout *Writing: Process to Product* the term *brainstorming* is used to name both of these methods for generating ideas and supporting details. When you use the first method, you should imagine storming (that is, capturing) your own mind for an idea and evidence to support it. When you use the second method, you brainstorm the minds of those in your "think tank" for their ideas and supporting details. Although both methods are valuable, two or more minds working together will usually produce a larger number of ideas for you to consider. Furthermore, in a group brainstorming session, you may often be able to see flaws in your own thinking.

When you brainstorm, let your creative juices flow. During your prewriting process, record everything that you are thinking about, no matter how obvious, ridiculous, or peculiar the idea or the supporting evidence may seem. (You should engage in brainstorming sessions during your drafting and editing and revising processes as well.)

Whether you participate in a brainstorming session with an entire class led by your teacher, with a peer group, with a partner, or by yourself, you should devise a way to record your ideas. When you have recorded your brainstorming session, you will often be able to link certain items together, to recognize forceful details, to eliminate useless details, to see the need for further additions, and to start another brainstorming session. One idea inevitably leads to another, if you allow it. Everything you say or think contains endless possibilities for more ideas and more supporting details.

(Keep the records of your brainstorming sessions; they can be very useful during later drafting and revising sessions. If you detect a weakness in your completed paper, you may want to check earlier brainstorming notes and continue brainstorming for further ideas and supporting details.)

There are many techniques of brainstorming. For your first few papers, use as many techniques as possible in order to familiarize yourself with each one. Eventually you might use a combination of techniques or even devise a new one to suit your needs. But keep in mind four points: (1) there are no rules to follow, (2) there is no special order to follow, (3) record everything you think of about your topic, and (4) keep everything. After a thorough prewriting brainstorming session, you will have a great deal of material that is all related in some way to your topic.

The following exercises are designed to help you learn specific brainstorming techniques. The exercises are organized into three types:

- **a)** those to help you clarify and limit your topic
- **b)** those to help you find supporting details
- **c)** those to help you organize your ideas and supporting details

(Note: To learn how to benefit from using all of the brainstorming methods, it is best to do most of the exercises with at least one other person. By asking each other questions, you can easily clear up any points that may confuse you.)

Brainstorming Techniques to Help You Clarify or Limit Your Topic

EXERCISE 1 ▸ *Think/Write (especially useful when you are alone and know you will soon begin to write an assignment)*

Many writers do a lot of thinking before they put any words on paper. They may even compose whole sentences in their mind, memorize them, and when they begin to draft, write the sentences from memory. Other writers may carry a note pad to record their thoughts, in case they forget them before they draft. Take a few minutes for you and your partner to list some of the ideas or problems that have been concerning you. They might relate to society, the environment, politics, or something personal. Share a topic from your list with a partner. Explain why you might want to write about it and who your audience might be.

You might like to use one of the many brainstorming techniques in this chapter to develop your topic, rather than begin to draft your paper immediately.

EXERCISE 2 ▶ Talk/Write (especially useful if you like to talk through your ideas, rather than write them out)

Sometimes you can brainstorm a topic by talking with one or more people. By listening to other people voice their opinions, you are often able to clarify your own.

Choose a topic from one of those sessions, and brainstorm it by talking about it with your partner. If you cannot think of a topic, look over the list below. Find one on which the two of you have differing opinions and brainstorm it to the point where you could use it for an assignment. (Before you draft, however, you might like to brainstorm further by using one or two other techniques.)

Do teenagers have too little freedom?
Should students be allowed to have credit cards?
Do teachers give too much homework?
Should all teenagers be required to have military training?
Should service personnel (bus drivers, pilots, post office and telephone workers) be allowed to strike?

EXERCISE 3 ▶ See/Write (especially useful if you would like to write about a number of activities that you see)

Tell your partner about something that you see on a regular basis, for example, a particular sports event or a television show. Why specifically do you watch the event or show? What events or shows would you refuse to see on a regular basis? Why?

Share with your partner something you have seen recently that you would like to write about. To whom do you want to write? Why?

Afterward, you may like to participate in another brainstorming activity to find more supporting details for your ideas.

EXERCISE 4 ▶ Experience/Write (especially useful if you would like to write about a number of activities that you are involved in)

Tell your partner about some of the things that you enjoy doing. What do you particularly enjoy about these experiences? Why? What are some of the things that you do not enjoy? What do you particularly dislike about these experiences? Why?

Share with your partner an experience that you would like to write about. It may be something that you enjoyed or disliked. To whom do you want to write? Why?

Afterward, you may like to participate in another brainstorming activity to find more supporting details for your ideas.

EXERCISE 5 ▶ Read/Write (especially useful if you want to write about what you have read)

Tell your partner about your reading habits. Which newspaper do you read? What parts of the paper do you read regularly? Do you have favorite columnists? Which magazines do you read? Other than books required for courses, name the last three books you have read. Who are your favorite authors? Why are they your favorites? Is there a book, essay, or poem about which you would like to write? Why?

Afterward, you may like to participate in another brainstorming activity to flesh out your ideas.

EXERCISE 6 ▶ Assign/Write (especially useful to help you write an assignment quickly)

As a student, you can use this technique in most of your classes. If you have such an assigned essay coming up in one of your courses, ask your partner to predict an essay question for the course. Explain how you would attempt to answer it. Perhaps you might then participate in one or two other brainstorming activities in order to accumulate supporting details. (See Chapter 15 for more suggestions on how to write a demand essay.)

EXERCISE 7 ▶ Write/Write (especially useful to find out what you want to write about)

A number of writers believe that they do not know what they want to write about until they start to write. In fact, they write to *find* a topic. If you have begun to keep a daily journal, you perhaps know how it feels to sit down without preparation and write. As you write, you find that ideas do come. To carry out this exercise, decide on a possible topic even though you do not know if you will end up with a satisfactory product. Write all your thoughts about that topic as they occur to you. Do not worry about getting your thoughts well organized.

(One of the most important brainstorming sessions you can engage in, therefore, is to keep a daily journal. See Chapter 21 for more details.)

EXERCISE 8 ▶ Free Association Cluster (especially useful in gathering more ideas that can produce a limited topic to write about)

Free Association is similar to playing a word association game. In word association you say the first word that comes into your mind when you hear another word. In Free Association, you continue generating words or phrases based on your own responses. For example, to *thunder* you might add *lightning*, to *lightning* you might add *bad storm*, to *bad storm* you might add *I am afraid to be in a bad storm*, and so on until you have a great deal of material. If you get stuck along the way, go back to an earlier word and begin the process again. For example, to *lightning* you might add *streaks of electricity*, and continue the Free Association technique.

So that you do not lose any of your material, gather it by using a clustering method similar to the Free Association Cluster on page 213. Note that the cluster began with the word *thunder*. If you wish, you can add to this cluster.

When you complete a Free Association Cluster, connect various entries to see if you can come up with a suitable limited topic for a writing

BRAINSTORMING

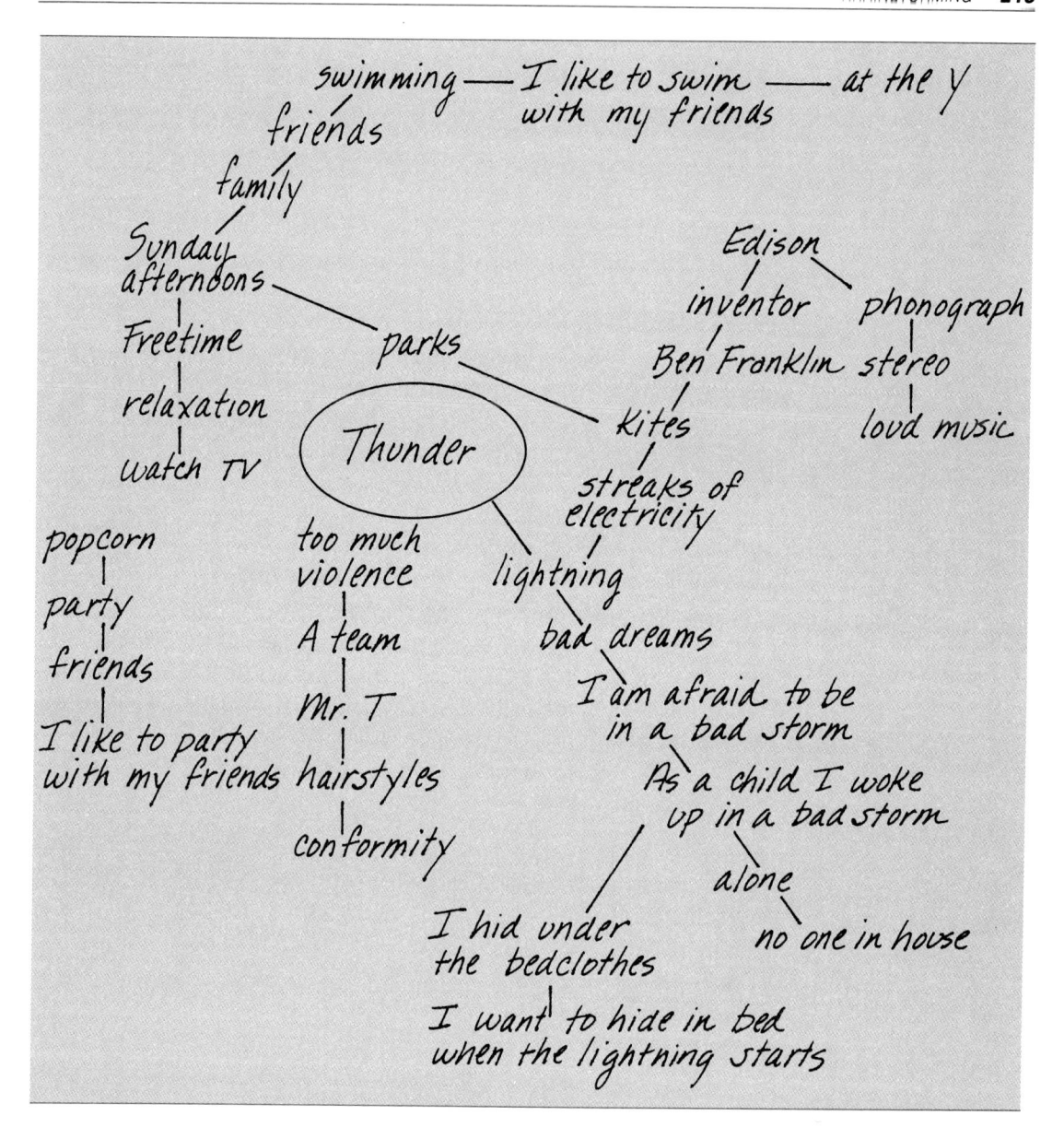

```
                swimming ——— I like to swim ——— at the Y
         friends /           with my friends
            \
           family
             \
         Sunday                              Edison
         afternoons ─.                        /
             |           parks              inventor    phonograph
         Freetime           \                 /            |
             |               \             Ben Franklin   stereo
         relaxation         ( Thunder )      /             |
             |               /     \       Kites        loud music
         watch TV           /       \        /
                      too much       streaks of
   popcorn           violence         electricity
      |                 |                /
    party            A team          lightning
      |                 |                \
   friends           Mr. T             bad dreams
      |                 |                  \
 I like to party     hairstyles         I am afraid to be
 with my friends        |                in a bad storm
                    conformity             \
                        \                As a child I woke
                         \               up in a bad storm
                          \              /      \
                           \            /       alone
                        I hid under    /          \
                        the bedclothes           no one in house
                        I want to hide in bed
                        when the lightning starts
```

assignment. When you have a limited topic, choose one or two other brainstorming techniques to gather supporting details.

When you do this exercise with a partner, choose the same word for a Free Association Cluster. Keep going until each of you comes across a topic that might become a good limited topic. Afterward, compare topics and clusters. If you cannot agree on a word, use *airplane*.

EXERCISE 9 ▶ Absurd Analogies (especially useful for creative writing projects, poetry, short stories, drama, narrations, reviews, and literary analysis)

Sometimes when you start to write a paper, you may decide to illustrate an idea, problem, or event by using an analogy. In other words, you would compare something unknown (or imprecisely known) to something known. You are encouraged to write in your journal, using Absurd Analogies as a brainstorming technique. Compare your topic to anything, literally *anything*. The purpose of this exercise is for you to stimulate your imagination and have some fun while you come up with some provocative ideas.

When you create an Absurd Analogy, list an aspect of your topic (thing, activity, problem, event) and say that it "is like" another thing, activity, problem, or event that you know. For her topic "Bag Ladies," a student tried comparing a bag lady to a chocolate chip cookie, to a theater, and to a rose. "How absurd!" you may think. "There is nothing that a chocolate chip cookie, a theater, and a rose have in common with bag ladies." Nonetheless, the student continued to think about and work on her Absurd Analogy. Eventually she wrote more specifically: "A bag lady is like a faded rose."

Then, she started to make a list to describe a faded rose. The list included the following:

> once colorful
> beautiful smell has disappeared
> smells foul
> pale
> brown around the edges
> broken, twisted, bent
> thorns hardened
> fragile, a light breeze could blow petals off stem

Here is what the student produced:

> A bag lady is like a faded rose. Once a lovely and sweet-smelling bud, she is now withered, pale, and foul-smelling. Resting in alley ways or feeding off refuse, a bag lady will often appear broken, twisted, and bent, ready to be uprooted and thrown on the dump heap. Indeed, she looks as though a light breeze will blow her apart, leaving only an

old stem. But come too close or try to interfere with this old lady and you will feel her thorns. She may be old, but a bag lady can draw blood if you don't approach with care.

Produce a few Absurd Analogies for a topic of your choice. Ask some of your peers to read them over so that you can get their reactions. If you cannot think of a topic and an Absurd Analogy, choose one from the first column and one from the second.

Possible Topics	*Absurd Analogies*
writing an essay	eating
Disneyland	peeling an onion
a crisis in a foreign land	getting a vaccination
a computer	a venetian blind
a problem you have	any musical instrument
break dancing	making a sand castle

Brainstorming Techniques To Help You Find Supporting Details

EXERCISE 10 ▶ *Random Lists (especially useful for gathering a great deal of supporting evidence)*

To ensure that you do not forget to do certain things, you perhaps already have the habit of making lists—for example, making a Christmas list, a packing list, or a list of things to take to a picnic. The random order of the list usually depends on which item you thought of first and which you thought of last. If a special order is important to the list, you will recopy the list according to a plan that serves your needs—for instance, from particular to general, chronological, climactic, or sequential. (These and other plans for organizing a piece of writing are discussed in Chapter 26.)

Making a Random List can also help you gather supporting details for a future piece of writing. Assume that you and your partner have to write paragraphs to explain how you clean your room, prepare for a party, or study for an exam. Independently, make a Random List of about twenty items. Afterward, compare your lists to see if you have thought of the same items. You might like to suggest a method of reordering the items as they would appear in the paragraph.

EXERCISE 11 ▶ Senses Cluster (especially useful for descriptions, narrations, literary analysis, reviews, poetry, and drama)

By thinking creatively about your topic and its sound, sight, taste, smell, and feel, you will often enrich an otherwise drab piece of writing. To help you gather words and phrases that link and extend your topic and senses, jot them down in the form of a Senses Cluster. How detailed your Senses Cluster will be depends on how creatively you brainstorm. Before he wrote a description of his dog, a student produced the following Senses Cluster. Can you add to it?

```
                    always aware of    clean              Tail and head
                    scent in air              fresh       salute the sun
                                                              rich sable
                          ( SMELL )                           brown coat
           soft                                                  streets - controls
   warm     ( FEEL )                       ( SIGHT )             movement
   smooth         well cared for                           alert
                            ( MY DOG )                     golden eyes
                                                              proud sounds only
                                                              - never whines
                    ( TASTE )         ( SOUND )          an even quiet pant
                he enjoys the
                taste of              bark is
                his food              challenging
```

After choosing a specific topic that you might use for a piece of writing, enrich it by using a Senses Cluster. If you cannot think of a topic, use a piece of toast, a break dancer, a villain in a movie, or a particular location in or near your home.

EXERCISE 12 ▶ Positive/Negative/Neutral Pigeonholes (especially useful in observation techniques, narrations, comparison/contrast essays, argumentative writing, and literary analysis)

When you are trying to add details to an incident or event, you might find it useful to list all the associations (events, characters, conflict, dialogue, setting, descriptions, and so on) in three columns—Positive, Negative, Neutral—with several pigeonhole boxes under them. In the Positive column include good, happy, warm, fun associations. In the Negative column include bad, sad, frightening, angry ones. In the Neutral column include the ones that do not have strong associations for you. Probe deeply.

Record the events as they occur to you. Do not worry about logical order. Examine the following partial results of a Positive/Negative/Neutral brainstorming session on the topic of a student's fear of heights:

Positive	Negative	Neutral
liked being on Father's shoulders	couldn't look down from heights	maybe I suffer from vertigo
liked tall people	suffered	Mother has fear of heights
loved to watch Ferris wheels from the ground	fell down stairs	don't mind going upstairs now
liked to swing	pushed down a slide	didn't want to go upstairs as a kid
would go upstairs with someone	afraid of dark at top of stairs as kid	thought ghosts lived upstairs

After you complete the session, try to connect some of the pigeonholes that may have a comparison/contrast or cause/effect relationship. Notice the connecting lines in the pigeonhole boxes about fear of heights. What relationship do the items indicate? Can you draw further connecting lines?

After choosing a specific topic that you might use for a piece of writing, enrich it by using Positive/Negative/Neutral Pigeonholes. When you fin-

218 WRITING: PROCESS TO PRODUCT

ish, connect some of the pigeonholes by drawing comparison/contrast or cause/effect relationship lines. If you cannot think of a topic, use one of the following: a style of dancing, an incident that recently happened to you, a holiday, a family conflict, a trip, or an event that you learned about from a friend.

EXERCISE 13 ▶ Positive Cluster (especially useful for argumentative writing)

To probe your limited topic deeply, you might select a single point of view and think only of your topic and its positive associations. Notice in the cluster below how one student decided to connect his topic, "The Rewards of Going to School," to seven positive characteristics of the human condition. Look closely at the connections made. Can you add to this partial Positive Cluster?

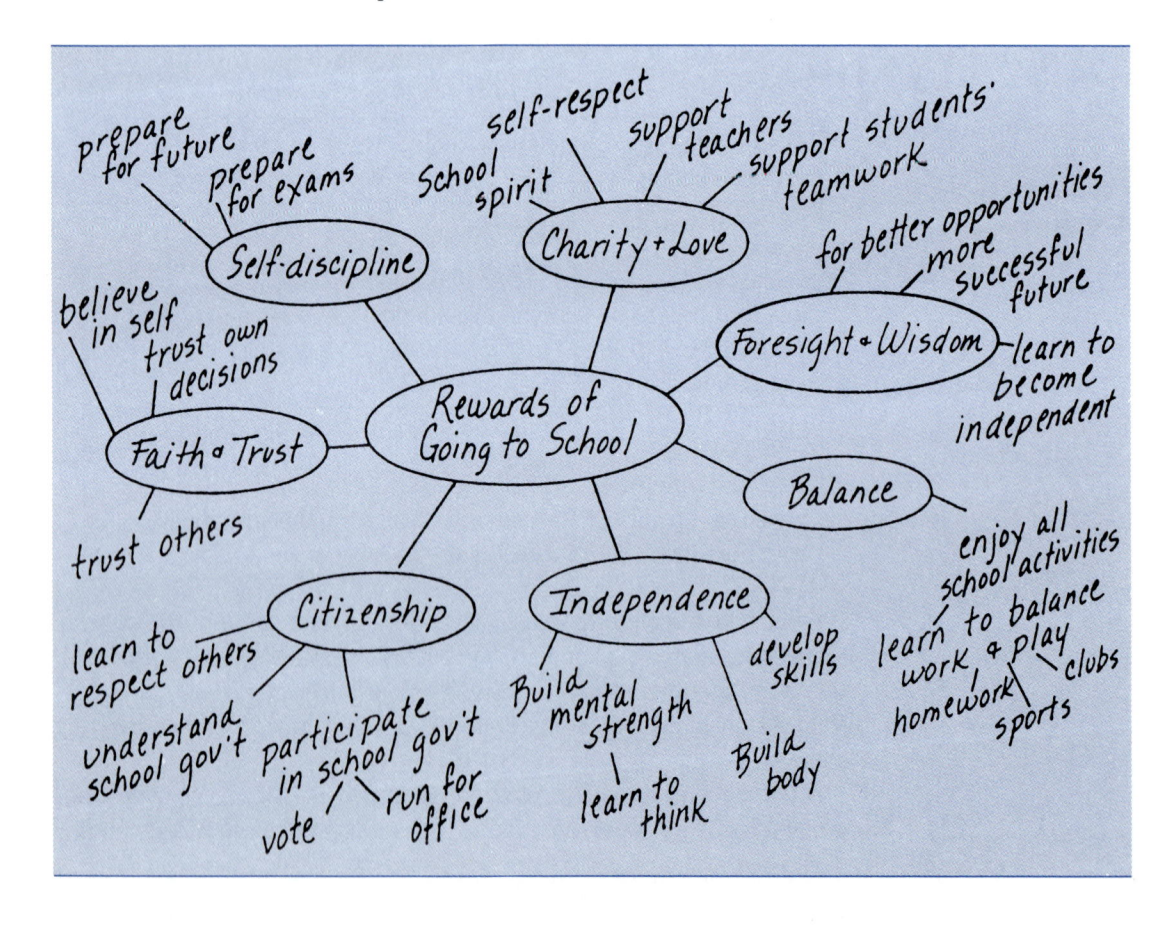

```
                    self-respect
  prepare                      support
  for future    School         teachers   support students'
      prepare   spirit                    teamwork
      for exams                                    for better opportunities
         Self-discipline    Charity + Love              more
                                                        successful
  believe                                                future
  in self    trust own                  Foresight + Wisdom  learn to
              decisions                                     become
     Faith + Trust          Rewards of                      independent
                           Going to School
                                                    Balance
  trust others
                                                              enjoy all
                                                              school activities
  learn to      Citizenship    Independence           learn to balance
  respect others                                      work & play
                                              develop              clubs
     understand                                skills  homework
     school gov't  participate   Build                        sports
                   in school gov't  mental     Build
                    vote  run for   strength   body
                          office      learn to
                                      think
```

After choosing a limited topic, enrich it by using a Positive Cluster. Use the same seven characteristics of the human condition as the above cluster or choose your own positive characteristics. If you cannot think of a topic, use one of the suggested topics in Exercise 12.

EXERCISE 14 ▶ Negative Cluster (especially useful for argumentative writing)

When you brainstorm, you can use just about any organizational device to record your ideas. By focusing only on the negative aspects of your limited topic and recording them in the form of a cluster, you will already be thinking about the organization of your piece of writing. If you were to focus on the negative aspects of the same topic you used in the previous exercise, you could collect supporting details for a good contrast paper.

If, for example, you were writing an essay on the benefits of buying a car, you might brainstorm the negative aspects as well. By making a negative cluster, you will write a much more unbiased paper. Notice how one student recorded the negative aspects of buying a car. Can you add to her partial Negative Cluster?

Negative Aspects of Buying a Car cluster diagram with branches:
- **Too much responsibility**: Need to work in order to pay for car; Need to become defensive driver; Often asked to take passengers; What do I do if someone wants to borrow my car?
- **Expensive**: gas, insurance, possible fires, possible accidents
- **More Work**: cleaning & polishing; asked to do more errands; Using car for family matters
- **Waste of Time**: spend too much time just driving around; spend more time in car & less at home; Creates laziness — less physical exercise

EXERCISE 15 ▸ Pentad Cluster (especially useful in narrations, literary analysis, short stories, and drama)

The Pentad Cluster allows you to explore five aspects of a topic.

Act: What was done?
Agent: Who did it?
Agency: By what means or with what was it done?
Scene: Where and when was it done?
Purpose: Why was it done?

In order to see how to use the Pentad, study the following partial cluster based on the topic "Going to a Summer Camp." Can you add to this Pentad Cluster?

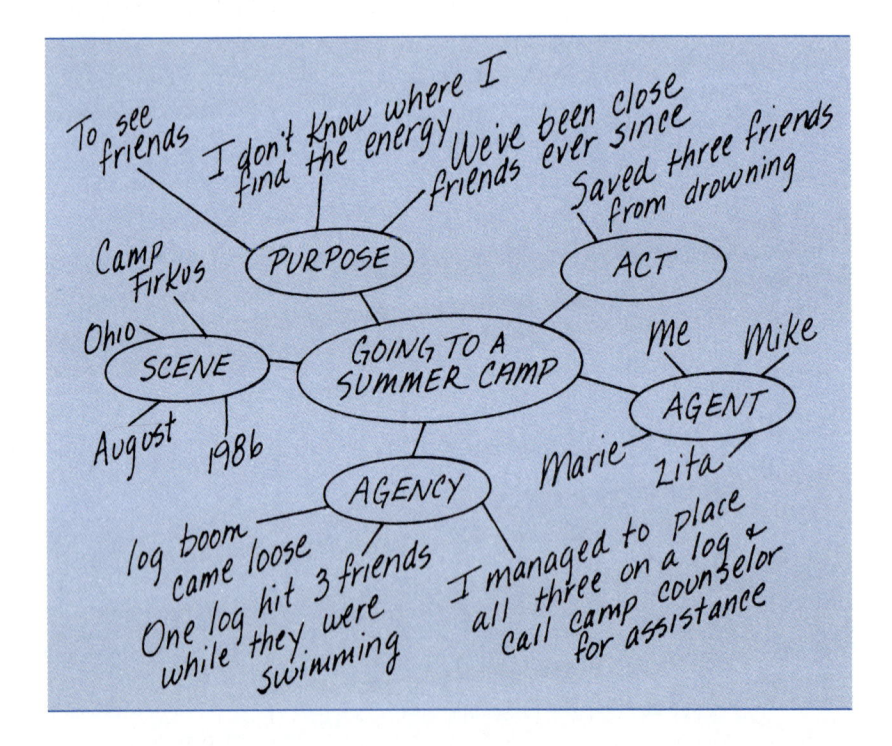

Pentad Cluster for "Going to a Summer Camp":

- **SCENE:** Camp Firkus; Ohio; August 1986
- **PURPOSE:** To see friends; I don't know where I find the energy; We've been close friends ever since
- **ACT:** Saved three friends from drowning
- **AGENT:** me, Mike, Marie, Lita
- **AGENCY:** log boom came loose; One log hit 3 friends while they were swimming; I managed to place all three on a log & call camp counselor for assistance

After choosing a topic that you might use for a piece of writing, enrich it by using a Pentad Cluster. Use the same five points as the above cluster. If you cannot think of a topic, use a conflict that you were involved in, your first day of elementary school, your last day of an important event, or a doctor's visit. You may also use a conflict that involves a character in a piece of literature.

Brainstorming Techniques to Help You Organize Your Ideas and Supporting Details

Perhaps nothing in your writing process ever fits neatly into perfect steps. You may blend two steps, repeat one, or move from drafting back to brainstorming. The following brainstorming techniques are useful in producing ideas and supporting details, but they also have a built-in bonus: if done thoroughly, they will practically organize your paper for you.

EXERCISE 16 ▶ Pro/Con Ladders (especially useful for argumentative writing)

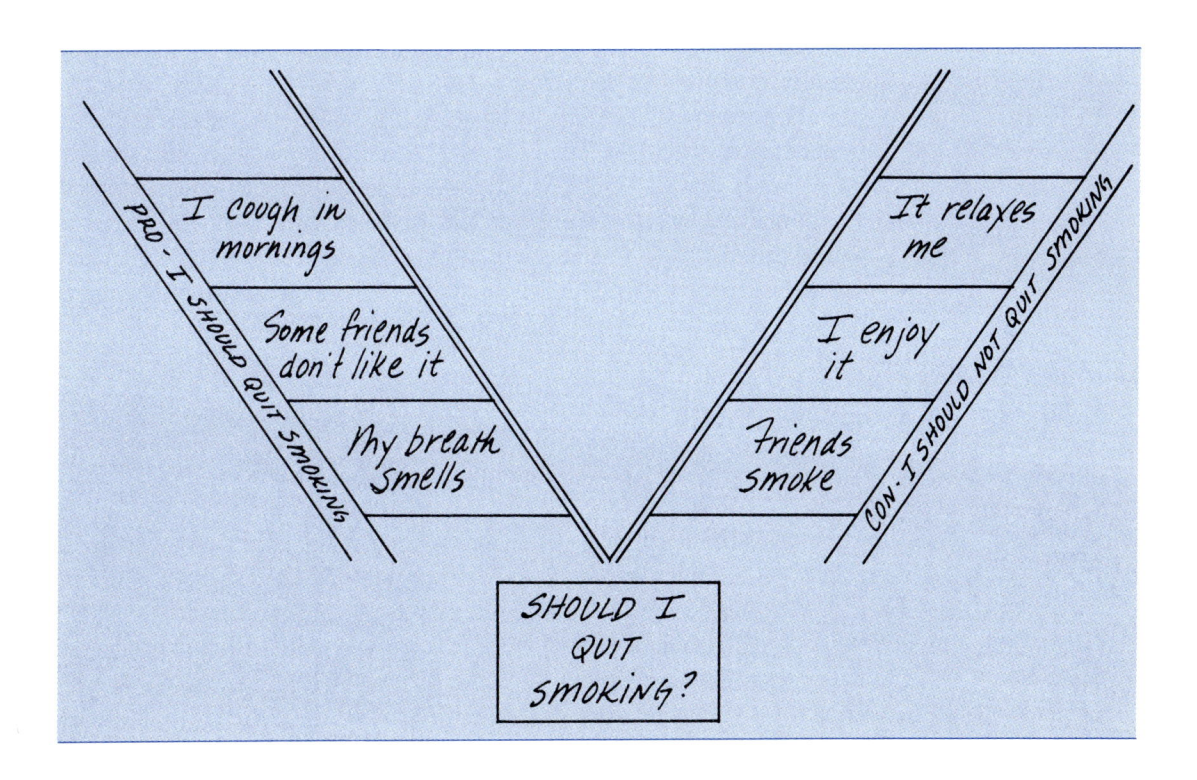

If you want to write an essay in which you argue for or against a particular action or opinion, use Pro/Con Ladders. Draw two ladders,

each with ten rungs. Label one ladder "Pro" to indicate support for your argument. Label the other "Con" to indicate support for an argument against your position. Under the ladders, draw a box in which you will write your limited topic. By filling in as many rungs as you can on *both* ladders, you will see your argument from both your vantage point and an opponent's. Thus, you will not be able to ignore your opponent's viewpoint.

Study the partial Pro/Con Ladders on page 222. Can you complete them?

After choosing a limited topic, develop it by using Pro/Con Ladders. If you cannot think of a topic, use "I should give up smoking [or some other habit]," or "My family should move."

EXERCISE 17 ▶ Aristotle's Topics (especially useful for comparison/contrast or cause/effect essays)

In his *Rhetoric* Aristotle provided instructions for public speakers in ancient Greece. Today, you can still use his suggestions to organize your ideas. Put simply, you should **define** your limited topic, **compare and contrast** it, point out its **cause-and-effect relationship**, and **provide evidence** to support your idea.

Before you work on this brainstorming technique, examine Ben's treatment of Aristotle's Topics in the Introductory Assignment (pages 8–9). Then, make a similar list on some aspect of a topic of your choice. Try to provide as many related details as you can, even though you may not use them in your final piece of writing. If you cannot think of a topic, use one of these: attending school in an urban or a rural area, watching TV or reading, or living in the United States.

EXERCISE 18 ▶ Newspaper Reporter's Questions (especially useful for informative or argumentative writing)

By using the traditional newspaper reporter's investigation techniques in relation to your topic, you could produce an extensive and useful list of supporting details. Before she started on her argumentative essay on the topic of providing homes for homeless teenagers, a student produced the following extensive list by using the Newspaper Reporter's Questions. As you examine the Who-What-When-Where-Why-How list, note its details and its usefulness. Can you add to any of the six parts?

Homeless Teenagers

WHO? "street kids" and the people who are involved with the problem

What kinds of people are involved with the problem?
- teenagers
- their parents and families
- government officials (social workers)
- police
- criminals
- concerned citizens

How do these people affect the problem?
- home problems add to number of runaways
- increased family breakups
- homes are less stable
- social workers try to intervene to reunite families
- police often regard homeless kids as potential or actual criminals
- criminals use teenagers as customers or recruit them as accomplices

How much do the involved parties mean to one another?
- breakdowns in communication cause teenagers to distrust not only their parents but also other adults, including those who want to help
- criminals find victims among homeless teenagers
- indirectly all Americans are affected by great numbers of homeless, disillusioned teenagers because, rather than contributing to society, they take from it

What is each person's relationship to the problem?
- the different parties involved with homeless teenagers have different and often incompatible solutions—for example: social workers and many parents strive to return runaways to their homes, while some kids want secure shelter *away* from their homes
- some criminals see teens as victims to be exploited
- most citizens are unaware of or unconcerned about homeless teenagers ("It's not my problem!")

Are the same people involved with the problem now as when it started?
- there have always been runaway teenagers, but a higher incidence of family breakdown and more media coverage make it seem as though it is a greater problem now

Are there more or fewer people involved?
- involvement of criminals with runaway teens has increased
- more social workers specialize in the problems of runaways
- media are more concerned

(The rest of this list is presented in abbreviated form.)

WHAT? money/many different crimes

What are the details of the problem?
> to get money to survive, homeless teens eventually come into contact with the criminal elements
> special shelters and programs for the homeless teens would reduce crime

Do all those involved agree on what the details are?

WHEN? past/present/future

Why is time important to the problem?
> the longer it goes on, the more serious it becomes
> the longer teens are away from home, the less likely they are to want to return
> the longer they are on the streets, the more likely they are to become involved in crime

How does time affect the problem?
When is a bad/good time for the problem?

WHERE? back alleys, cheap hotel rooms, flop houses, hostels, all-night restaurants and movie houses, the streets

Does the problem always occur in the same place?
Does it get better in some places?
Worse in others?
What and who determines where it occurs?
Does the place of occurrence contribute anything to the problem?

WHY?

Why does the problem exist?
Why is it a problem?
Why does it continue?
Why might it eventually end?
Why don't we end it right now?

HOW?

How does the problem happen?
How could it be prevented?
Who or what causes it? How?
Is there a sequence of events that could make a solution happen?
How are the events of the solution related?
How did it begin?
How did/will it end?

Make a similar Who-What-When-Where-Why-How list on a limited topic of your choice and answer all the questions as completely as you can. Remember: try not to be superficial, but keep asking a series of related questions similar to the above list. If you cannot think of a topic use a current social problem in your community, one of your ambitions, or a topic that you have to write about for a subject other than English.

EXERCISE 19 ▶ *Classification Flowchart (especially useful to limit topics and organize most writing)*

When you classify, you separate a topic into classes or categories. Then you can break down the class into divisions or subcategories.

As a student, you will often be asked to write an essay on a broad topic. For example: "Write a 500-word essay on communication." Such a question requires a brainstorming session in order for you to find a limited or manageable topic. For the above topic, a student produced the following Classification Flowchart:

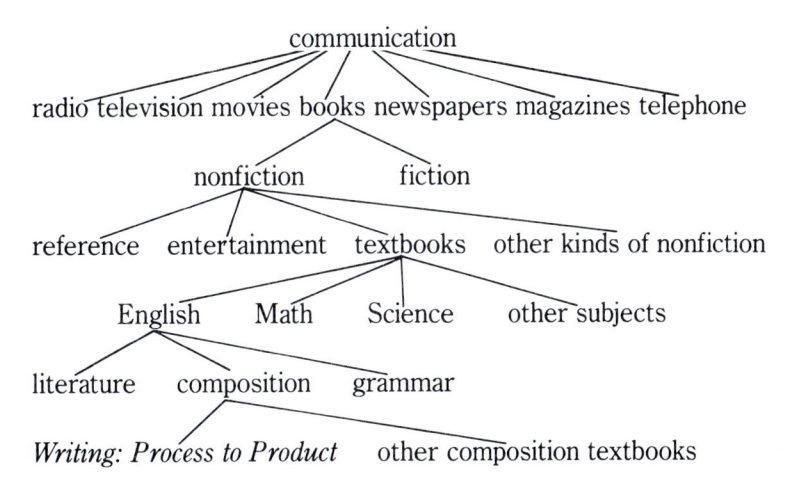

```
                        communication
      ┌──────┬──────┬──────┼──────┬──────┬──────┐
    radio television movies books newspapers magazines telephone
                          ┌───┴───┐
                      nonfiction  fiction
              ┌───────────┼───────────┬──────────────┐
          reference  entertainment textbooks  other kinds of nonfiction
                      ┌────────┬────┴──┬──────────┐
                   English    Math  Science   other subjects
                 ┌─────┼─────┐
            literature composition grammar
                       ┌──────┴──────┐
         Writing: Process to Product   other composition textbooks
```

Do you see how the above Classification Flowchart limits the topic into narrower and narrower categories until it becomes difficult to classify any more? Do you also see that as you move down the flowchart, each category becomes more manageable? "Textbooks" is a much more limited (and therefore manageable) topic than "Communication."

Make a new Classification Flowchart on communication. Use one of the other main categories from the above flowchart. When you finish, check to see that none of your categories overlap.

Think of a problem that can serve as a topic for a paper, and create a Classification Flowchart to help arrive at a solution. If you cannot think of a problem, choose one of the following: Which computer should I buy? What country is the most (least) ideal to visit? Which kind of books should I read? The following illustrates how you might begin a Classification Flowchart in response to the first question:

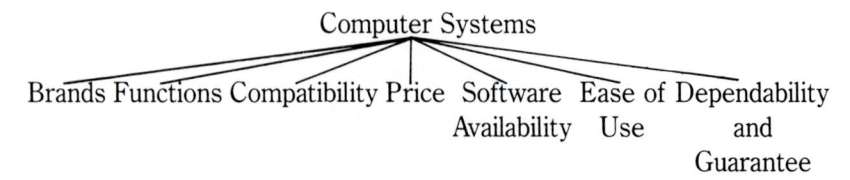

```
                        Computer Systems
    ┌──────┬──────────┬──────┬──────┬──────┬──────┐
  Brands Functions Compatibility Price Software Ease of Dependability
                                    Availability  Use    and
                                                      Guarantee
```

Notice that none of the above headings overlap. If you then continued the Classification Flowchart to concentrate on manufacturers, you might get the following:

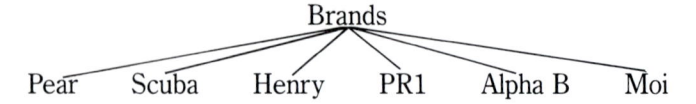

```
                      Brands
         ┌──────┬──────┬──────┬──────┬──────┐
       Pear  Scuba  Henry  PR1  Alpha B  Moi
```

(Note: For the purposes of this exercise, made-up names are used for manufacturers and computer models. If you were to carry out this exercise, you would rely on your knowledge of real manufacturers and models.)

If you continued the Classification Flowchart to concentrate on the models of the first manufacturer, you might get:

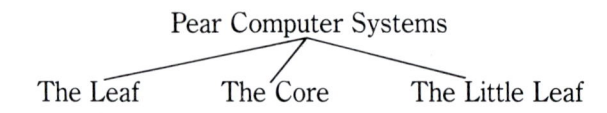

```
            Pear Computer Systems
         ┌──────────┬──────────┐
      The Leaf   The Core   The Little Leaf
```

In order to add more details to the flowchart, you would need to use the division process presented in Exercise 20. See this exercise to find out how a Division Flowchart would help you decide which computer to buy.

EXERCISE 20 ▶ Division Flowchart (especially useful to limit topics and to organize most writing)

When you divide something, you break it down into its parts. It might be helpful for you to examine the following Division Flowchart to see the parts of *Writing: Process to Product*:

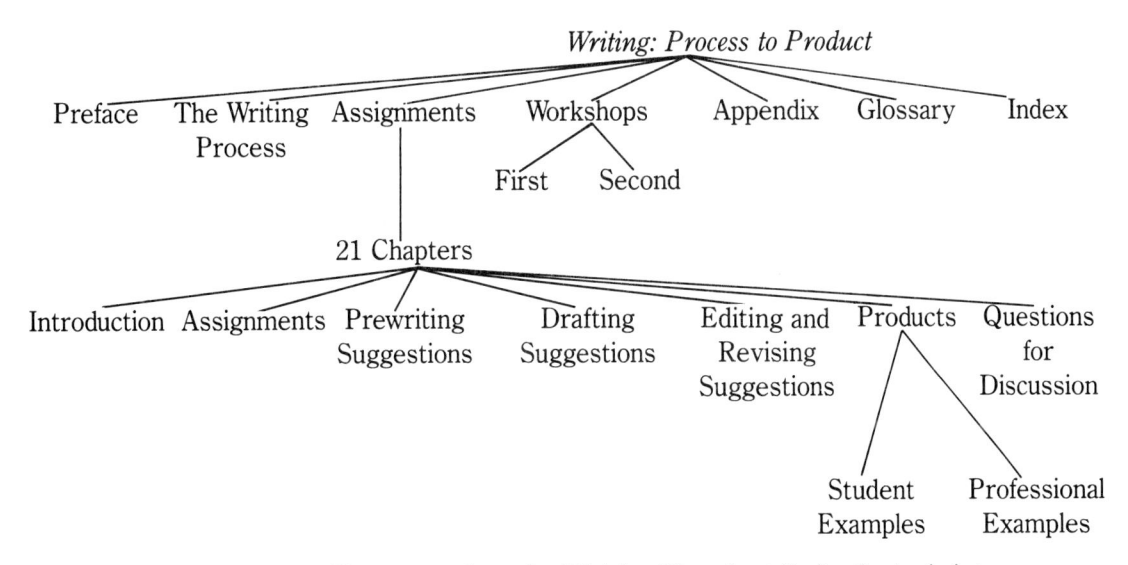

```
                          Writing: Process to Product
        ┌──────┬──────────┬────────────┬───────────┬──────────┬──────────┐
     Preface  The Writing  Assignments  Workshops   Appendix   Glossary   Index
              Process                   ┌─────┐
                                      First  Second
                            │
                       21 Chapters
    ┌──────────┬──────────┬──────────┬──────────┬──────────┬──────────┐
Introduction Assignments Prewriting  Drafting  Editing and  Products  Questions
                        Suggestions Suggestions  Revising              for
                                                Suggestions          Discussion
                                                           ┌─────┬─────┐
                                                          Student  Professional
                                                          Examples  Examples
```

Do you see how the Division Flowchart limits the topic into narrower and narrower parts until it becomes difficult to divide any more? Do you also see that as you move down the flowchart, each part becomes more manageable as a possible topic? "The products of professional writers in *Writing: Process to Product*," is a narrow, and therefore, easy topic to write on.

Make a Division Flowchart on one of your other textbooks. When you finish, check to make sure that you cannot divide any of the parts into more specific parts.

The following flowcharts illustrate how you would continue to solve a problem from Exercise 19 ("Which computer should I buy?") by using a Division Flowchart.

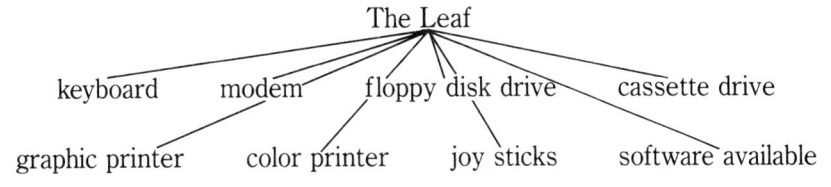

```
                        The Leaf
        ┌──────────┬──────────┬──────────────┬──────────────┐
     keyboard    modem    floppy disk drive   cassette drive
        │           │           │                │
  graphic printer  color printer  joy sticks   software available
```

(If you were to make a Division Flowchart on the Core and the Little Leaf, you would find that they have exactly the same parts as the Leaf.)

If you were to continue to compare the Leaf and the Core, you would find that they are different in two significant ways: the Leaf keyboard is two-and-a-half times more expensive than the Core keyboard, and the Leaf software is not compatible with the Core system. By continuing the division process, you could find out the difference between the two keyboards. Note the differences:

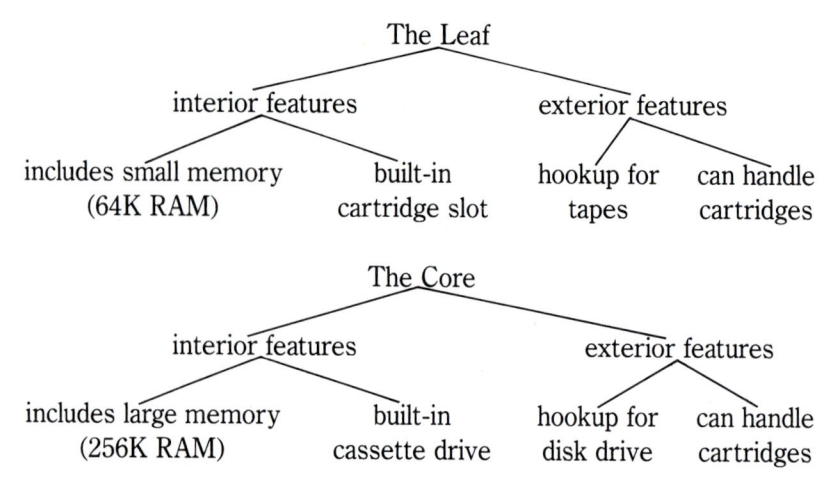

```
                            The Leaf
                 ┌─────────────┴─────────────┐
          interior features            exterior features
          ┌──────┴──────┐              ┌──────┴──────┐
   includes small memory   built-in      hookup for    can handle
        (64K RAM)       cartridge slot      tapes       cartridges
```

```
                            The Core
                 ┌─────────────┴─────────────┐
          interior features            exterior features
          ┌──────┴──────┐              ┌──────┴──────┐
   includes large memory   built-in      hookup for    can handle
        (256K RAM)       cassette drive   disk drive    cartridges
```

Before you divide your own topic, you might like to add to the above Division Flowcharts. For example, divide "software available" into several parts.

Now complete your own Division Flowchart. Make sure that you cannot divide any of the parts further.

Armed with Classification and Division Flowcharts—as well as a set of writing variables and an outline—you should be able to move to the drafting process with confidence.

EXERCISE 21 ▶ Comparison/Contrast Ladders (especially useful for all formats in which you need to point out the similarities and differences)

Similar to Pro/Con Ladders (page 221), Comparison/Contrast Ladders allow you to list similarities and differences in a useful way.

Assume that you must write a paper to compare and contrast yourself with your partner. Through discussion, attempt to find out all the similarities and differences between you. To help you organize your facts, use two ladders, one for similarities and one for differences. When you hit upon a similarity or a difference, record the detail on the rung of the appropriate ladder as shown on page 229.

Choose a broad topic, narrow it, and brainstorm it by completing Comparison/Contrast Ladders. Or choose one of the following: two rock bands, two presidents, two countries, two schools, or two film or television stars.

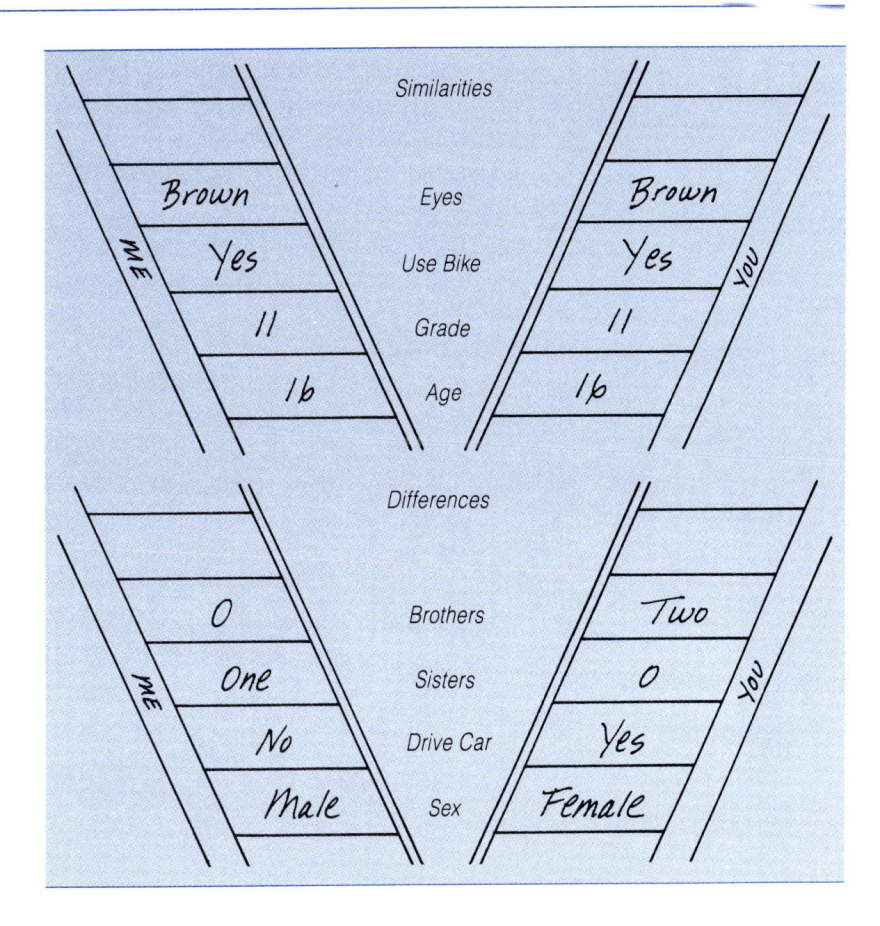

[Ladder diagram showing Similarities and Differences between ME and YOU:

Similarities — ME: Brown, Yes, 11, 16 / YOU: Brown, Yes, 11, 16 (Eyes, Use Bike, Grade, Age)

Differences — ME: 0, One, No, Male / YOU: Two, 0, Yes, Female (Brothers, Sisters, Drive Car, Sex)]

A completed pair of ladders will help you draft your paper. You can then use the AAA/BBB or ABABAB methods of comparing and contrasting discussed on pages 251–252.

EXERCISE 22 ▶ Cause-and-Effect Flowchart (especially useful for papers in which you wish to demonstrate a cause-and-effect relationship)

For want of a nail, the shoe was lost;
For want of the shoe, the horse was lost;
For want of the horse, the rider was lost;
For want of the rider, the battle was lost;
For want of the battle, the kingdom was lost, . . .

Cause and effect form a continuum, stretching from the most distant past into the most distant future. In the lines from the famous proverb on page 229, can you follow the cause-and-effect relationships that eventually resulted in the "fact" that an entire kingdom was lost because a nail was lacking?

You cannot exist without affecting people or things, and they in turn affect you. Even the air around you changes because of your presence. A cause produces an effect; an effect is produced by a cause and then itself becomes a cause. People and things are both causes and effects. In other words, literally everything about you and in you is a part of the continuous cause-and-effect process.

You can employ the cause-and-effect brainstorming technique not only to help you organize your writing, but to reveal a more precise, limited topic. You can use cause and effect in reasoning, in solving problems, in determining the significance of facts and ideas, and in predicting possible outcomes.

To find causes, you work backward in time and ask the question "Why?" To find effects, you work forward and ask "So what happened?" To find possible future effects, you ask "So what will happen?" If, for example, you had to explain to a police officer why you were speeding, you might answer "I am late getting to school." [Why?] "Because I slept late." [Why?] "Because I didn't hear the alarm." [Why?] "Because I went to bed at three o'clock this morning." [Why?] "Because I was studying." . . . Listening to you relate this later, a friend might ask what happened. "The police officer felt sorry for me." [So what happened?] "She gave me a police escort to school." [So what happened?] "With boosted self-confidence, I got an A on my exam." [So what will happen?] "I will get an A in my Law in Action class."

Take a few minutes to list two or three skills in which you excel. If you are an extremely talented piano player, tennis star, or reader, you will have an easy time making up the list. If, however, you feel you do not have any excellent skills, you will have to probe more deeply. Maybe you are an excellent listener, talker, walker, eater, sleeper, sports fan or friend.

Decide on one skill that you would like to analyze for past causes and present and future effects; for example, Juan feels that he "excels" in watching TV. Using a Cause-and-Effect Flowchart to analyze his TV watching, Juan kept asking himself questions. Try to make a similar flowchart for your skill. Start with an event, a situation, a decision, a judgment, or a question, and write about the present. Then work back into the past and forward into the possible future. Your flowchart should be similar to the following one that Juan made.

(Present event)

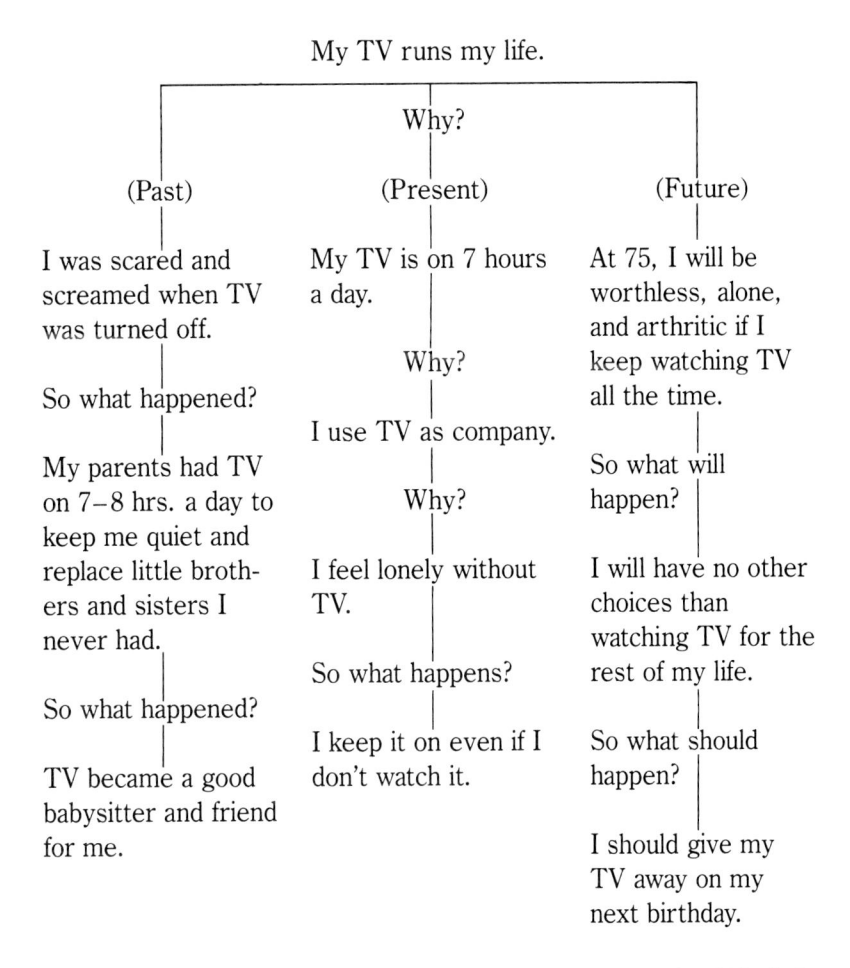

My TV runs my life.

Why?

(Past)	(Present)	(Future)
I was scared and screamed when TV was turned off.	My TV is on 7 hours a day.	At 75, I will be worthless, alone, and arthritic if I keep watching TV all the time.
So what happened?	Why?	
My parents had TV on 7–8 hrs. a day to keep me quiet and replace little brothers and sisters I never had.	I use TV as company.	So what will happen?
	Why?	I will have no other choices than watching TV for the rest of my life.
So what happened?	I feel lonely without TV.	
TV became a good babysitter and friend for me.	So what happens?	So what should happen?
	I keep it on even if I don't watch it.	I should give my TV away on my next birthday.

When you brainstorm a cause-and-effect relationship, you should include in your flowchart every cause and effect that occurs to you. But not every point will contribute directly to the development of your limited topic. Other causes and effects that Juan thought of included: "I didn't have any older brothers and sisters," "I try to watch *All My Children* every day," "My parents gave me a Betamax for Christmas," and "I'll probably have to have my eyeglass prescription changed." Why do you think he excluded each of these from his flowchart?

As he examined the causal relationships in his flowchart, Juan came to the conclusion that his "skill" of watching TV might have undesirable effects. In addition, because he thought that many Americans had become TV addicts for the same reasons he did, he decided to make "Americans watch too much TV" the limited topic of an argumentative essay.

Using the cause-and-effect technique of organization, you might solve a personal problem, which in turn could result in a worthwhile essay topic. Brainstorm with your partner a personal decision you will have to make. For example, you may be wondering whether to continue with your education, leave home, or buy a car. Describe to your partner the causes that could influence your decision. For example, all your older brothers and sisters had their own cars at age sixteen. If you do not explore the causes influencing your possible decisions and thereby understand the effects, you cannot seek solutions.

Once you have brainstormed your problem for a few minutes, draw a Cause-and-Effect Flowchart. Use specific cause-and-effect questions—for example:

(Present judgment)

I doubt that I can successfully pass mathematics.

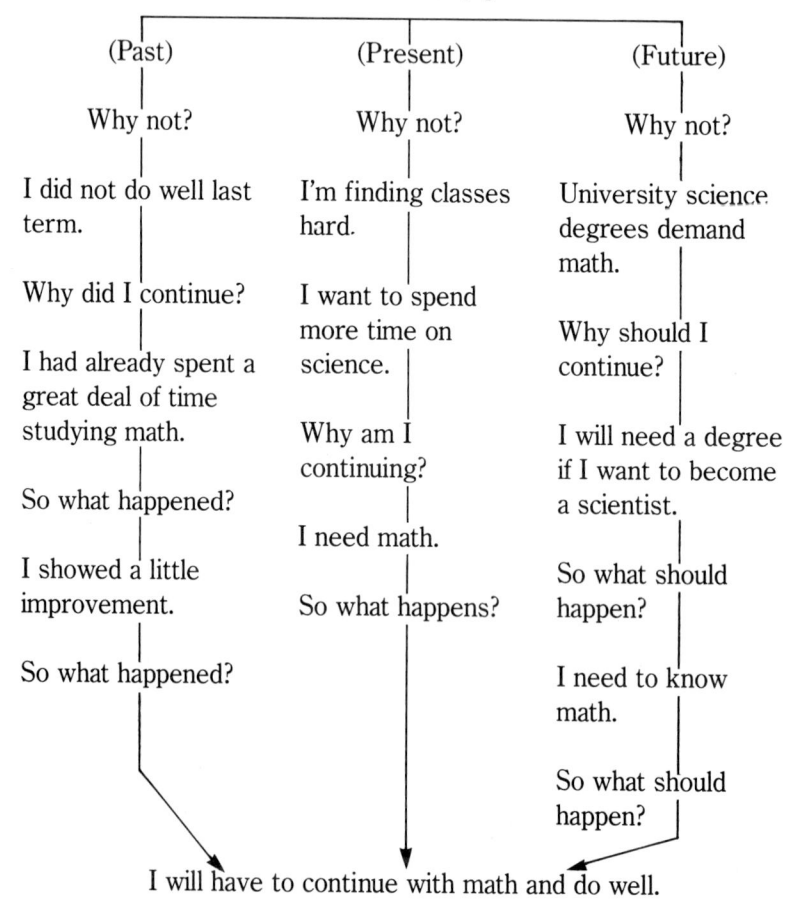

(Past)	(Present)	(Future)
Why not?	Why not?	Why not?
I did not do well last term.	I'm finding classes hard.	University science degrees demand math.
Why did I continue?	I want to spend more time on science.	Why should I continue?
I had already spent a great deal of time studying math.	Why am I continuing?	I will need a degree if I want to become a scientist.
So what happened?	I need math.	So what should happen?
I showed a little improvement.	So what happens?	I need to know math.
So what happened?		So what should happen?

I will have to continue with math and do well.

Choose one of the following questions or another question important to you. Then make up a flowchart, and compose a set of writing variables. If you are successful in brainstorming the cause-and-effect relationship of any of the following questions, you may want to use the flowchart to draft a piece of writing.

If an election is soon to take place, what would be the possible effects if a particular candidate wins? (Consider your school's elections as well as other elections.)

What were the results of the Cuban Missile Crisis, Sputnik, the invention of the computer, or the popularity of home videos?

If a nuclear power plant were built near my home, what would be the effects?

What would happen if I won a million dollars in a contest?

When you make a flowchart, make sure you precisely identify the causes and effects. Make sure you differentiate a cause from an effect. Establish whether the cause or effect is past, present, or future. Distinguish real causes and effects from possible and probable ones.

If you have taken time to go through the preceding brainstorming techniques in this chapter, you will have amassed a great deal of raw, unorganized, and (sometimes) useless material. But you will also have unearthed a number of worthwhile things you will want to say about your topic. Brainstorming sessions help you to focus your attention on your thesis statement, that part of your limited topic that you want to develop. (For more about thesis statements, see the next chapter.)

24 Thesis Statements and Topic Sentences

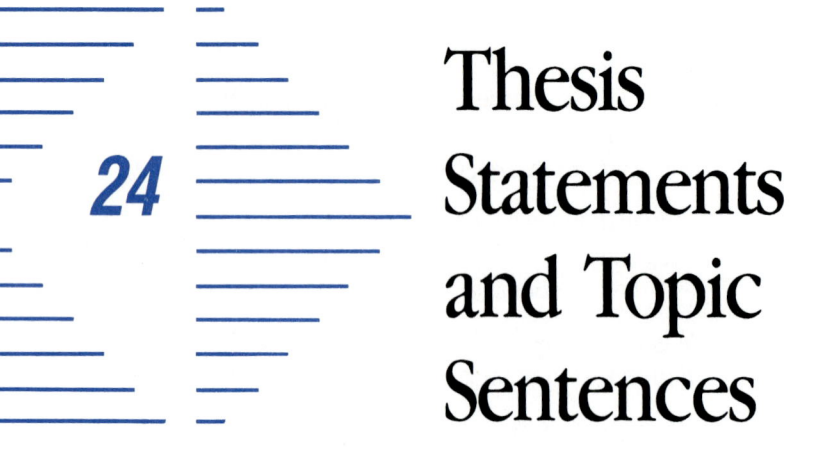

When you write, you choose a broad topic to write about and limit it by narrowing it to a workable size. After considering your other writing variables—audience, purpose, format, voice, situation, and point of view—you limit your topic, bringing it into focus. Finally, you present your limited topic in a sentence called a **thesis statement**, which controls the development of your entire piece of writing. In a longer paper, your thesis statement will probably contain several points that you want to discuss. You usually treat each point in a separate paragraph and express that point in a statement called a **topic sentence**, which controls the content of a single supporting paragraph.

When you include a clear thesis statement and topic sentences in a piece of writing, you use them not only to help you develop and structure your prose, but also to guide your readers. Thesis statements and topic sentences are like road signs. When road signs are well posted, both driver and passengers enjoy the scenery and arrive at their destination without getting lost. In the same way, when thesis statements and topic sentences are clearly expressed, both writer and readers enjoy the details and arrive at a clear understanding of the writing without losing their way.

So that you begin this workshop chapter with a clear understanding of the terms used, you and a partner (classmate, friend, or relative) should study and discuss the following two flowcharts that illustrate the development of a topic.

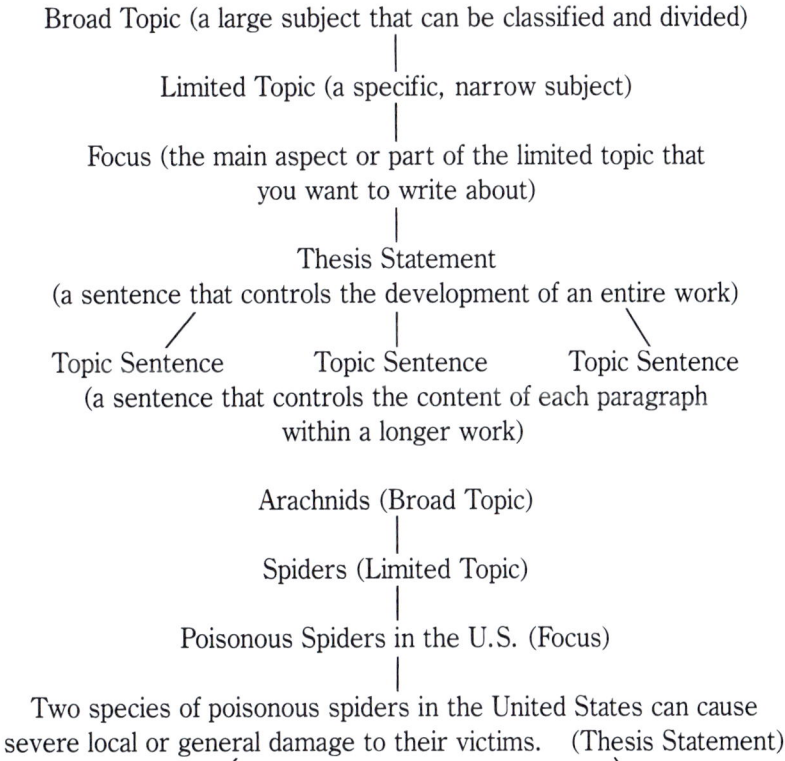

Broad Topic (a large subject that can be classified and divided)
|
Limited Topic (a specific, narrow subject)
|
Focus (the main aspect or part of the limited topic that you want to write about)
|
Thesis Statement
(a sentence that controls the development of an entire work)
/ | \
Topic Sentence   Topic Sentence   Topic Sentence
(a sentence that controls the content of each paragraph within a longer work)

Arachnids (Broad Topic)
|
Spiders (Limited Topic)
|
Poisonous Spiders in the U.S. (Focus)
|
Two species of poisonous spiders in the United States can cause severe local or general damage to their victims.   (Thesis Statement)
/   \
The black widow spider is notorious. (Topic Sentence for first supporting paragraph)   The bite of the brown recluse spider causes severe reactions. (Topic Sentence for second supporting paragraph)

If you have completed the Introductory Assignment on pages 4–17 of this textbook, you have already been introduced to the process of moving from choosing a limited topic to writing a thesis statement. In this chapter, you can reinforce your understanding of the important concepts relating to thesis statements and topic sentences.

EXERCISE 1 ▶ Why Write a Thesis Statement or Topic Sentence?

Writers need a controlling idea in the form of a sentence both to limit the ideas discussed and to order the structure of an essay or paragraph. The following paragraph demonstrates an uncontrolled piece of writing.

The ideas and details are fine, but the piece is aimless—neither the writer nor the reader really knows precisely where the paragraph is going. Either you or your partner should read it aloud and find evidence that both writer and reader are hampered because the paragraph contains no controlling sentence.

 The air is permeated with the smells of bubbling caldrons of shellfish at Fisherman's Wharf, which is in San Francisco. You also notice rows of white-tiled counters neatly stacked with clean, red cooked crabs, lobsters, and prawns. If you stand near the edge of a pier and look down, you would see all kinds of sea life—some quickly moving, some lying in wait for a bit of food, and others dead and floating. Sounds of the fiesta spirit of the tourists who crowd the streets under brightly colored awnings fill your ears. And your nostrils fill with the persistent tang of the sea: seaweed, fish, and spilled fuel from pleasure crafts. You can hear the creak of swaying fishing boats, the cries of sea gulls, and the persuasive cries of noisy barkers inveigling customers into the seafood restaurants. The crowds are always huge on Fisherman's Wharf. You can also see the parked automobiles with little trays of seafood cocktails hooked onto the open windows. People love to eat seafood when they visit this other world.

Now read the following aloud, noticing how the topic sentence limits the content of the paragraph by telling you exactly what to expect. The writer of this paragraph has obviously worked through the prewriting process.

 At Fisherman's Wharf in San Francisco you enter another world, a world filled with inviting smells, sounds, and sights. It is a world pervaded with the aroma of bubbling caldrons of shellfish, the fiesta spirit of the tourists who crowd the streets under brightly colored awnings, the persistent tang of the sea, the creak of swaying fishing boats, the cries of sea gulls, and the persuasive cries of noisy barkers inveigling customers into the seafood restaurants. The parked automobiles with little trays of seafood cocktails hooked onto the open windows and the rows of white-tiled counters neatly stacked with clean, red cooked crabs, lobsters, and prawns beckon you to eat.

1. In the second paragraph, the opening topic sentence controls the content. Find words in the rest of the paragraph that reinforce "filled with inviting smells, sounds, and sights."

2. In the first paragraph, the writer has used general to particular order to structure the content. Point out several larger, more general, details of what you would expect to smell, hear, and see at Fisherman's Wharf. Then point out several smaller, more particular, details.

3. What does the first paragraph contain that has been left out of the second? Why have those details been omitted?

(Note: These paragraphs are modified versions of one taken from *Fifth Chinese Daughter* by Jade Snow Wong. Her original will appear later in this workshop.)

EXERCISE 2 ▸ Placement of Topic Sentences

A topic sentence can be placed anywhere within a paragraph. It is up to the writer to decide where it is most effectively placed.

1. *At the beginning.* The most common place for a topic sentence is in the first sentence of the paragraph. After reading an opening statement, readers expect to see supporting details such as examples, reasons, or explanations. The following example is a version of the paragraph in Exercise 1:

> *At Fisherman's Wharf in San Francisco, Jade Snow Wong and her brother entered another world, a world filled with inviting smells, sounds, and sights.* This world was pervaded with the aroma of bubbling caldrons of shellfish, the fiesta spirit of the tourists who crowded the streets under brightly colored awnings, the persistent tang of the sea, the creak of swaying fishing boats, the cries of sea gulls, and the persuasive cries of noisy barkers inveigling customers into the seafood restaurants. The parked automobiles with little trays of seafood cocktails hooked onto the open windows and the rows of white-tiled counters neatly stacked with clean, red cooked crabs, lobsters, and prawns beckoned them to eat.

2. *At the end.* The second most common position of the topic sentence is in the last sentence of the paragraph, using the supporting details to build up to the main idea. The following paragraph (on which the other paragraphs in this exercise are based) is from *Fifth Chinese Daughter* by Jade Snow Wong.

> They entered another world, a world permeated with the aroma of bubbling caldrons of shellfish, with the fiesta spirit of the tourists who crowded the streets under gay awnings, with the persistent tang of the sea, the creak of swaying fishing boats, the cries of sea gulls, and the persuasive cries of noisy barkers inveigling customers into the

seafood restaurants. The parked automobiles with little trays of seafood cocktails hooked onto the open windows, the rows of white-tiled counters neatly stacked with clean, red cooked crabs, lobsters, and prawns—*where else would you find all these sights and sounds and smells but at Fisherman's Wharf in San Francisco?*

3. *At the beginning, with a clincher sentence at the end.* Sometimes you might use both the first and last sentences to show your complete topic. The last sentence can clinch (emphasize) a topic that you expressed in the first sentence, and can even extend that topic.

At Fisherman's Wharf in San Francisco Jade Snow Wong and her brother entered another world. This world was pervaded with the aroma of bubbling caldrons of shellfish, the fiesta spirit of the tourists who crowded the streets under brightly colored awnings, the persistent tang of the sea, the creak of swaying fishing boats, the cries of sea gulls, and the persuasive cries of noisy barkers inveigling customers into the seafood restaurants. The parked automobiles with little trays of seafood cocktails hooked onto the open windows and the rows of white-tiled counters neatly stacked with clean, red cooked crabs, lobsters, and prawns beckoned customers to eat. *Indeed, they were in a world filled with inviting smells, sounds, and sights.*

The best way for you to determine the effect of moving a topic sentence to different places in a paragraph is for you to do an exercise similar to the one you have just read. It is time consuming, but the results are rewarding.

EXERCISE 3 ▶ How to Limit Your Topic and Come Up With Your Focus

Coming up with a suitable focus and ultimately a successful piece of writing depends on your choosing a topic that interests you, limiting it to a manageable size, and considering your narrow topic in terms of the writing variables: audience, purpose, format, situation, voice, and point of view. Using each writing variable to flesh out your limited topic, you will arrive at the precise focus you want. Assume, for example, that your broad topic is *break dancing.*

1. Independent of your partner, both of you should list a possible response for each writing variable as in the examples below. In addition, you should record a specific aspect of the topic on which your writing will focus. Finally, write either a thesis statement (for a longer work) or a topic sentence (for a paragraph within a longer work).

Broad topic:	break dancing
Audience:	my cousin Pedro. Real. I intend to send it.
Purpose:	to suggest that he enter a break dancing contest
Format:	a letter
Voice:	my own
Situation:	Both Pedro and I love break dancing.
Point of view:	I will use first person (*I, we*) and second person (*you*) because this is a casual letter.
Limited topic:	the fun of break dancing
Focus:	the fun of entering a break dancing contest
Thesis statement:	I think you should enter the break dancing contest this Saturday night at the mall for several very good reasons.

Broad topic:	break dancing
Audience:	my biology teacher. Real. I will hand it to her.
Purpose:	to support her criticism that break dancing injures growing teens
Format:	scientific review paper
Voice:	my own
Situation:	I want to fulfill a required biology assignment, but also to prove from scientific research that I have read that break dancing causes permanent damage to the spinal column. I know of teens who have even broken their necks while break dancing.
Point of view:	I will use third person (*he, she, they*) because this is a formal assignment.
Limited topic:	the dangers of break dancing
Focus:	I will stress the fact that break dancers should be aware of the dangers and think before they dance.
Thesis statement:	The latest scientific research demonstrates that break dancing during the formative years can cause permanent damage to many parts of the body.

If you have trouble writing your thesis statement, return to your writing variables. Perhaps you should change one or more of them in order to focus your ideas more specifically.

2. You and your partner can compare and discuss your lists of variables. If you cannot easily predict what kind of writing will result from your variables, make the necessary changes.

EXERCISE 4 ▶ Writing Thesis Statements and Topic Sentences

Both thesis statements and topic sentences should be clear, unified, precise, and limited. A thesis statement controls the development of an entire essay (and usually is placed at or near the beginning of the work), while a topic sentence focuses on the content of a single paragraph within an essay (and can be placed anywhere within the paragraph).

1. With your partner, discuss the difference between the thesis statement and topic sentence in each of the following pairs.

Thesis statement:	In most high schools throughout the nation, students are able to choose from a variety of extracurricular activities.
Topic sentence:	The drama club consists of students with both on-stage and backstage interests.
Thesis statement:	When I go out to dinner, I go either to an Italian or to a Chinese restaurant.
Topic sentence:	My favorite Italian dish is linguine with clam sauce.

2. Look over the following list of questions. Independent of your partner, answer each question "yes" or "no." Find which one(s) you both have ideas about and, through discussion, narrow the subject to the point where you could use it as a limited topic with a specific focus for an assignment.

Should teenagers work for spending money instead of receiving allowances?
Should four years of English be required of all high-school students?
Should the voting age be lowered to sixteen?
Should drunk drivers lose their licenses?
Should girls hitchhike?
Should high-school graduates know how to type?

Each of you can compose a set of appropriate writing variables and a thesis statement for a long piece of writing. Finally, each of you can write a topic sentence for one or more of your supporting paragraphs.

3. You and your partner can compare and discuss your thesis statements and topic sentences. Can you readily see how they will become road signs for your readers so that they will easily find their way through your essay? Should they be changed to make the journey easier for your readers? If so, why?

EXERCISE 5 ▸ Recognizing and Evaluating Thesis Statements and Topic Sentences

1. Ask your partner to assign you an essay to read (for example, one of the essays that appear at the ends of chapters in the Assignments section). Your task is to find and evaluate the thesis statement. In addition, you should comment on how well the writer developed the thesis statement. Finally, find and evaluate the topic sentences for each of the paragraphs within the essay.

2. After you and your partner read a model paragraph (such as one of those at the end of Chapters 1, 2, and 3), find and evaluate the topic sentence.

EXERCISE 6 ▸ Filling in the Blanks With Thesis Statements and Topic Sentences

1. Read the following examples carefully so that you can write an appropriate thesis statement and an appropriate number of topic sentences. Remember that each should be a complete sentence that controls what is discussed.

Example:

Limited topic:	eating out
Focus:	joys and disasters of eating out
Thesis statement:	At times, eating out can be a joyous affair; other times, it can be disastrous.
First topic sentence:	Three weeks ago, when my date and I went to McCookie's, I hoped the evening would never end.

Second topic sentence: Last night, in the same restaurant with the same date, I discovered that I had forgotten my wallet.

Limited topic: vitamins and minerals
Focus: benefits of taking vitamins and minerals
Thesis statement:
First topic sentence:
Second topic sentence:
Third topic sentence:

Limited topic: swimming
Focus: comparing recreational and competitive swimming
Thesis statement:
First topic sentence:
Second topic sentence:

2. Ask your partner to present you with another limited topic and focus so that you may continue this exercise.

3. Discuss the entire exercise with your partner until you understand perfectly how a thesis statement controls the content of an entire piece of writing and a topic sentence controls the content of a paragraph within a longer piece.

25 Beginnings and Endings

Most writers find that beginning and ending their pieces of writing are their most difficult tasks. The advice of the King of Hearts in *Alice in Wonderland*—"Begin at the beginning, go on until you come to the end, and then stop"—is much harder to follow than most people think.

What do you want to accomplish at the beginning and end of your piece of writing? At the beginning, you hope to capture your reader's attention by introducing your topic and indicating your purpose for writing. At the end you want to sum up your piece in a new and interesting way so that the reader will think about what you have written.

This chapter deals with ways to write beginnings and endings for paragraphs and essays, and provides exercises to make these tasks easier. For a discussion of the "middles" of paragraphs and essays, see the next chapter.

EXERCISE 1 ▶ Beginnings

From your own experience you know how important first impressions are. Discuss with your partner some of the following first impressions.

What attracted you to your best friend?
If you saw a record album by a group you did not know or had not heard before, what would cause you to buy the album?
What makes you pick up a magazine from a magazine rack?
What kinds of opening sentences attract you to a piece of writing?

Consider also the people, clothes, music, and books that you have rejected because of your first impression of them.

Every writer strives to compose a catchy sentence or two that will grab the reader's attention. Many writers, finding themselves unable to write an attention-getting opening, will draft an entire essay before they draft the beginning. They may not even think of a title for their work until they have completed it. The following are some of the many types of beginnings that can be developed for the topic "Racquetball."

1. The **statement**, the most commonly used opening, does not exactly serve as an attention-getter, but it does indicate the subject of your piece of writing:

Racquetball has become very popular throughout North America.

2. The **generalization**, another common introduction, simply introduces your piece of writing with a broad statement:

Everyone should have some way to stay physically fit.

3. You can use an **attention-getting tactic** such as an exaggeration, but be cautious about using it:

Racquetball can save your life.

4. The **question** is another frequently used method of introduction:

Who says exercise can't be fun?

5. The **summary**, a useful introduction, tells your reader of several possible approaches, and then the one to be dealt with in the piece of writing:

All racquetball players have their reasons for taking up the game. One good reason for playing racquetball is a desire to find a sport in which both sexes can compete on equal terms.

6. The **quotation**, if it is appropriate, can give authority to your piece of writing:

A leading physical fitness expert says, "Racquetball provides one of the best ways to achieve all-round fitness."

7. The **analogy**, a comparison that can be sustained throughout the piece, can result in an effective piece of writing:

For many people today, the war against flab is waged on a rectangular, whitewashed battlefield—the racquetball court.

With your partner choose a topic about which you both know something. Then write beginnings for your topic in each of the seven ways outlined above. When you have both completed your seven beginnings, discuss the effectiveness of each one.

The next time you are engaged in revising a piece of writing, check your beginning. If you have begun with a weak opening such as "I feel . . . ," "I think . . . ," or "In this essay I am going to . . . ," return to this exercise for an idea about how to write a better beginning.

EXERCISE 2 ▶ Endings

Life is filled with beginnings and endings. With your partner discuss some of the endings you have experienced. Use these suggestions as the basis for your discussion:

How does one of your favorite songs end?
What happened during the last moments of saying farewell to a friend or acquaintance?
Which movie ending do you remember most vividly? Why?
What do you look for in the ending of a novel?

Ending a piece of writing can sometimes be a difficult task. From the time you first started to write, you were probably told that your conclusion should summarize your writing in a new and interesting way. Frankly, this suggestion can be frustrating. What kind of ending qualifies as "new and interesting"? Something new for its own sake has no place in good writing.

The best ending a piece of writing can have is one that satisfies the expectations your beginning and, of course, middle have built up in your reader. Imagine your surprise, perhaps even disappointment, on your birthday morning when you open a gift from a special person. Through suggestions and hints prior to your birthday, you are convinced that you will receive the very thing you desire—a digital wristwatch. But when you open your gift, you find an alarm clock! In the same way, if you have led your reader to expect a conclusion to a piece of writing presenting the dangers of smoking, and you end with the statement, "Drinking coffee can also be habit forming," you have let your reader down. No matter how well written your piece is, a poor conclusion may ruin it.

As you move toward your conclusion, keep thinking about your topic and your attitude toward it. Then your conclusion should satisfy you, your purpose, and your reader.

1. Working with your partner, match these endings with the seven sample beginnings given in Exercise 1.

a) Tennis is out; I have become a racquetball maniac.
b) That a sport can be so much fun and at the same time so healthful makes it a natural choice for almost anyone.
c) Why not try it?
d) Fight flab; take up racquetball.
e) If fitness is important to you, consider starting a racquetball program.
f) Any time my court and my opponent are ready, so am I.
g) These are just a few of the reasons I enjoy racquetball.

2. Write three different endings for one of the beginnings that you and your partner developed in Exercise 1. Avoid an ending that merely sums up and adds nothing of interest, such as "And these are the many things that describe a racquetball player." Discuss the appropriateness of each of your endings, and then decide on the best one.

EXERCISE 3 ▸ Titles

Many writers think of a title before they begin to write. Others use a working title, which they may or may not use for their finished piece of writing. Still others do not even think of a title until they have completed their writing. No matter when you think of it, a good title is important.

In composing a title, you should not merely put down the name of your limited topic. A title should catch readers' attention and let them know what to expect from the work.

1. Draw on your own experience and discuss the importance of titles with your partner. Use the following questions as a basis for discussion:

   a) Which musical groups do you think have the most suitable names (titles)? Why? Which ones do you think do not suit their names? Why?
   b) Think of several products that you use regularly, such as soap, deodorant, and toothpaste. What first drew you to these products? How important are their names (titles)? Try to think of new ideal names for the products.
   c) What kind of title would make you pick up a book? Why?

2. Provide two or three titles for a particular piece of writing. Discuss with your partner their effectiveness and suitability.

EXERCISE 4 ▶ Narration and Description

The previous exercises have dealt with exposition. In this exercise you can work on various ways to enliven beginnings and endings for your narrative and descriptive writing.

1. Assume that you and your partner are going to write a narrative about a car accident.

   a) Independently, each of you should write two different beginnings.
   b) Compare them and determine which would probably make the most effective openings.
   c) Then, independently, each of you should write two different endings.
   d) Compare the endings and determine which ones would probably provide the most effective conclusions.
   e) Then, independently, each of you should write two different titles.
   f) Compare them and determine which ones would probably be the most effective titles.

2. Repeat this exercise for a description of a person, place, or thing.

26 Unity

When you draft a piece of writing, you must make sure everything within it is unified. That is, everything should deal with the same limited topic and support your thesis statement and attitude toward your topic.

During brainstorming sessions, you learned how to collect the details you needed to support limited topics. In some brainstorming sessions you may have begun to organize your material while you collected it. During your drafting process, you should check over all of your brainstorming notes to see which items relate to your writing variables. To have a unified draft, you should retain all the relevant notes and use them in your work. You should also decide which notes are not relevant—and would detract from the unity of your piece of writing—and discard them.

From the mass of material you have gathered during brainstorming, you should decide what types of supporting details you will need to develop your piece of writing. Your decision will depend on which types serve your purpose best. In writing about the view from your window, you will need to use **descriptive details** (the cherry tree in the front yard, the hedge by the side of the house, the crabgrass in the lawn). If, however, you are writing an argumentative essay about the dangers of nuclear power, you will have to collect **reasons** why nuclear power might be dangerous (risk of serious accidents at power plants, problems with the storage of spent fuel, contamination of air and water). Other types of supporting details include **examples**, **facts**, **results**, **incidents**, **illustrations**, **questions**, **lists**, and **quoted material**. You will find examples of all of these types in this chapter.

EXERCISE 1 ▶ Visual Organization

If you find that your prewriting material is disorganized and that you really do not know how to begin to unify your first draft, determine how your supporting details for your limited topic would fit with one of the following techniques:

pro/con ladders (see page 221)
comparison/contrast ladders (see page 228)
flowcharts (see page 225)
pigeonholes (see page 217)

The more you write, the more ways of listing supporting details you will discover and want to try.

1. With your partner, study several of the techniques in Chapter 23. Determine which kind of supporting details has been used (descriptive details, examples, reasons, and so on). Then take a batch of your own brainstorming notes and arrange them in an appropriate way. Make sure you can identify the main kind of supporting details you are listing and the main method of organization.

2. A mandala is an ancient circular design that represents wholeness and harmony. All of the pie-shaped parts of a mandala fit together to make a whole. With your partner, study the mandala on page 250.

Notice how the supporting details are listed. On the outside of the circle are listed the names of groups involved in the American legal system, while within the divisions of the mandala are listed the specific details about each group.

3. Use one of the following thesis statements (or one of your own choice) and, independent of your partner, construct a mandala with the thesis statement in the middle. You should both use the same thesis statement so that you can compare your mandalas.

   a) Everyone should learn to swim.
   b) Maui offers magnificent underwater scenery for swimmers.
   c) Swimming is a great sport for young and old alike.
   d) My swimming holiday at Camp Tiki was filled with exciting moments.

250 WRITING: PROCESS TO PRODUCT

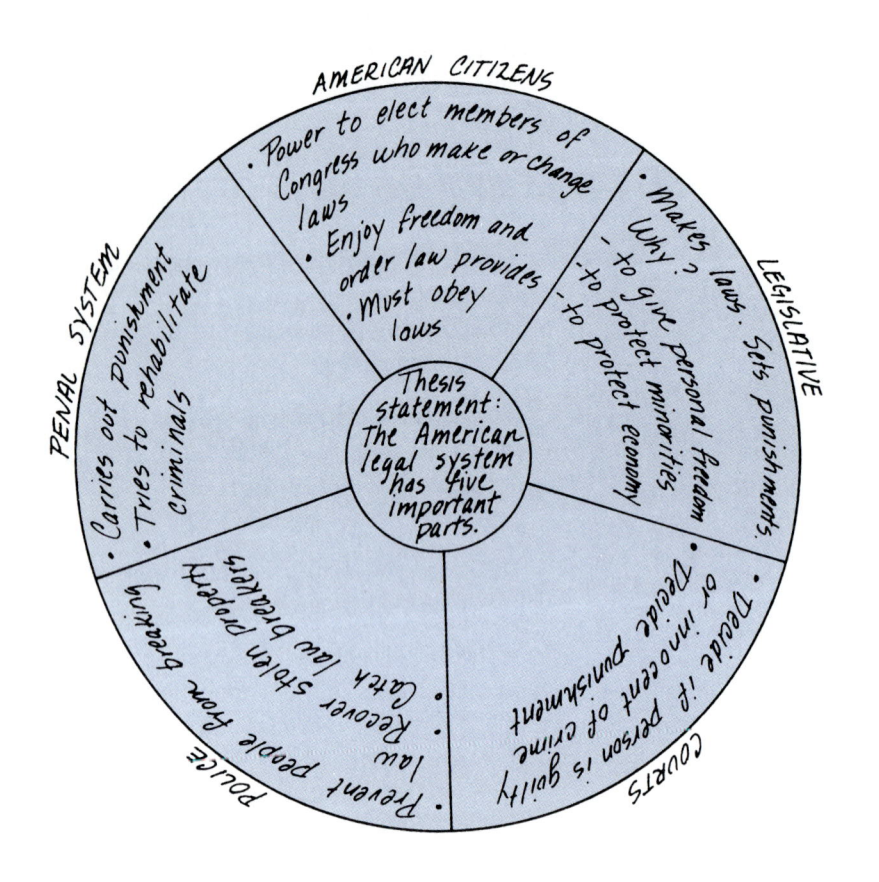

A word mandala with the thesis statement "The American legal system has five important parts" at its center, divided into five sections:

- **AMERICAN CITIZENS**: Power to elect members of Congress who make or change laws; Enjoy freedom and order law provides; Must obey laws
- **LEGISLATIVE**: Makes laws. Sets punishments. Why? — to give personal freedom, to protect minorities, to protect economy
- **COURTS**: Decide if person is guilty or innocent of crime; Decide punishment
- **POLICE**: Prevent people from breaking law; Recover stolen property; Catch law breakers
- **PENAL SYSTEM**: Carries out punishment; Tries to rehabilitate criminals

4. Compare your word mandala with your partner's. Should anything be added or deleted in either mandala? If you were to develop your mandala into an essay, would it be narrative, descriptive, or expository?

5. You might find it easy to organize a piece of writing by drawing cartoons or pictures, gathering pictures and making a collage, or drawing a line or bar graph. While you create your visual display, you will have to decide the order of your cartoons or pictures. From a completed visual display, you should be able to write your first draft.

6. Assume that you must write an essay on one of the topics mentioned below. Independent of your partner, decide in what way you would list supporting details: comparison/contrast ladders, mandala, flowchart, pigeonholes, cartoons or pictures, collage, or line or bar graph.

- a) the history of the fork as an eating utensil
- b) the ways to eat with a fork
- c) the duties of the president of a club you belong to
- d) the difference between a typical North American meal and an African Masai meal
- e) ways to study
- f) the beds of the poor and the wealthy
- g) why everyone should learn to ski

When you finish, compare your decisions and discuss the suitability of your choices.

EXERCISE 2 ▸ Comparison/Contrast

One method of organization is pointing out similarities (comparisons) and differences (contrasts) between two subjects. You might first talk about Subject A and then talk about Subject B. That would produce a paper using the AAA/BBB method. If you were to discuss one aspect of A and point out how it is similar to or different from the same aspect of B and do the same with other aspects, you would be using the ABABAB method. You can use the AAA/BBB or the ABABAB method for either comparison or contrast. Furthermore, you can write a comparison/contrast paper using either method to point out both similarities and differences.

1. Choose two subjects to compare or contrast, using one of the following suggestions:

   - a) life in the U.S. and life in a country of your choosing
   - b) life in your grandparents' time and life now
   - c) your high school and your elementary school
   - d) another topic of your choice

2. Use two columns, one for each subject. Whenever you put a detail in one column, add a corresponding detail to the other one. (Instead of using two columns, you might want to draw comparison/contrast ladders. See Chapter 23, pages 228–229.)

3. Exchange your lists. Discuss their completeness and decide on the better method for organizing each paper, the AAA/BBB or ABABAB method.

4. If you like, you can make a collage of pictures contrasting or com-

paring two things or places. Then point out the differences or similarities to your partner. A good collage will provide an excellent foundation for an essay. The following are examples of topics for collages contrasting bathing habits:

a) pictures of people bathing in beautiful bathrooms contrasted with people bathing in muddy rivers
b) different styles of bathtubs in use today
c) different customs of bathing
d) different kinds of bathtubs through the ages
e) different kinds of shower systems

EXERCISE 3 ▶ Cause and Effect

A piece of writing can be unified by presenting either the causes of a problem followed by the effects or the effects of a problem followed by the causes.

1. Find two pictures: one showing a cause of a problem and the other an effect. Give them to your partner. (If you cannot find pictures, provide word pictures.) For example, you could find one picture of a factory that dumps sewage in a river (cause) and one of a dead fish (effect).

2. Your partner's task is to find or draw pictures or write word pictures to bridge the cause-and-effect relationship. Your partner should point out how the effect came from the cause. For example, pictures of a smoke stack, rain, waste being dumped, and a river with fish swimming in it can help explain a cause-and-effect relationship.

3. Your partner should then give you a step-by-step oral explanation of the cause-and-effect relationship, with each picture representing one step. For example, your partner should explain how each picture logically leads from the cause (factory) to the effect (dead fish).

4. Then your partner can reverse the process by beginning with the effect and ending with the cause. For example, point out the effect (dead fish) first, and the cause (factory) last. Decide which order was better, cause/effect or effect/cause.

5. Choose a different topic. This time your partner can find the cause-and-effect pictures and you can bridge the relationship. You may also want to study the cause-and-effect flowcharts on pages 229–233 of Chapter 23. You may find them useful in helping you organize a cause-and-effect paper.

EXERCISE 4 ▶ *Sequential Order*

Sequential order is a useful method of organization for listing instructions or analyzing a product to see how it has been made. You will also find sequential order useful in writing a literary or scientific analysis. In arranging supporting details in sequential order, you place items in the order in which they should be (or have been) carried out.

1. Choose one of the following topics. Make up a list of instructions, writing each instruction on a *separate* piece of paper. Then have your partner organize the pieces of paper in sequential order. Repeat the exercise, reversing roles.

how to cook an omelet
how to serve a tennis ball
how to change a typewriter ribbon
how to bake a cake

2. Now choose one of the following topics. Make up a list of the steps in that process, writing each on a *separate* piece of paper. Then have your partner organize the pieces of paper in sequential order, assuming he or she were writing a process analysis. Repeat the exercise, reversing the roles.

how I write an essay
how I won a particular game

EXERCISE 5 ▶ *Spatial Order*

In arranging supporting details in spatial order, you present descriptive details in terms of how you want your reader to see them: near to far, far to near, right to left, up to down, or some other order you think appropriate.

1. Describe orally the room in which you sleep so that your partner can draw a map of it. (You are not allowed to look at your partner's map during your description.) Begin with the dimensions of the room, giving the location, number, and size of the doors and windows.

In your description you must mention at least twenty things to be included in the map. To help your partner draw the room accurately, begin with the exact position of the bed so that your partner can position everything else in relation to it. To help make your oral description clear, use transitional words such as *next to, above, opposite to,* and *behind.*

2. When your partner finishes the map, see how accurate a picture of your room it is. If there are glaring mistakes, discuss why they occurred.

3. Repeat the exercise, reversing your and your partner's roles.

4. If you were to write a description of the room, explain how you would employ spatial order. For example, decide on the order of the items in the room. Where in your description would you mention the size of the room, doors, windows, and decorations?

(Note: You can also refer to the Pigeonhole boxes on page 217 of Chapter 23 to help you organize a paper in spatial order. Many of the boxes relate to other boxes, making it easier to choose an appropriate spatial order.)

EXERCISE 6 ▶ Chronological Order

In following chronological order, you arrange events in the order in which they occur. If you introduce events out of order (flashbacks or flash forwards), you should prepare your reader for the shift in time.

1. Tell your partner a story from the first-person viewpoint (I) or the third-person viewpoint (he/she). Use a chronological order. All your partner has to do is number each new event that happens in your story. To keep your narrative coherent, you can use transitional devices, such as *although, as, in order that, then,* and *since.*

2. Discuss with your partner the order of your events. Did your story have a beginning, middle, and end? Were the events in the best order? In what other order could you have told the story?

3. Now your partner should tell his or her story while you number the events. Then discuss.

EXERCISE 7 ▶ Climactic Order

In following climactic order, you should arrange events, details, facts, or reasons in the order of their importance, with the most important one coming last.

1. Ask your partner to provide six or seven reasons, facts, and examples to support a statement. (Since this is an oral exercise, allow a few minutes for preparation.) Make up your own statement or use one of the following:

   a) Some of the rules at our school could be eliminated.
   b) There are many kitchen gadgets that are useless.
   c) Teenage clothing is conformist.

Make sure your partner takes a strong stand, either for or against something. The argument should open with a thesis statement and then have particulars to support the statement. Transition words such as *furthermore, similarly, moreover, in addition,* and *finally* will help the argument move from particular to particular.

2. When your partner finishes, challenge any piece of information that you thought was either incorrect or inappropriate. If a statement is not absolutely accurate, it should be researched and corrected or omitted.

3. Discuss the order of the items. If you start with the least important item and end with the most important, you are building to a climactic ending. Do the ideas move from least to most important? Should any item be moved? Why?

4. Now reverse the exercise so that *you* present ideas to support a statement.

EXERCISE 8 ▶ *Familiar to Unfamiliar*

In arranging supporting details in unfamiliar-to-familiar order, you should introduce the unfamiliar item, explain it in terms of something familiar, and conclude with the unfamiliar item.

1. Orally explain one of the following technically difficult subjects to your partner. Take a few minutes to decide on something familiar that you can compare your subject to. For example, a lymph node is similar to a filter.

   logarithms, bytes on a computer disk, IQ testing, hypnosis, transistors, Rubik's cube, satellite TV transmission

To help you in your explanation, use transitional expressions such as *similarly, on the one hand ... on the other hand,* or *somewhat like.* Continue your explanation until your partner says, "I understand."

2. Then your partner should explain one of the other items to you, following the same instructions. (You may have to research some of the items before you give your explanation.)

3. You and your partner might like to make up your own exercises on variations of this method of organization. For example, you might want to use an **analogy** (sustained figurative comparison). You might want to use **restatement** of the thesis statement in different words.

Identify appropriate methods of organization for the following topics:

a) Mother Teresa
b) "Love makes the world go round"
c) teaching babies to swim
d) your heritage

EXERCISE 9 ▶ Supporting Details/Methods of Organization

Each of the following pieces of writing has been developed using one main type of supporting detail and has been organized in one specific manner. The headings indicate the type of supporting detail and the method of organization. With your partner, find words, phrases, and sentences within each piece that illustrate both the type of supporting detail and the method of organization.

| **Type of Supporting Detail** | **Method of Organization** |

Descriptive Details   Spatial Order

A giraffe, the tallest animal in the world, is certainly unique. He has long legs (in order to outrun most of his enemies). His body is protectively colored with large sandy-to-chestnut angular spots, closely spaced. A giraffe's most distinctive feature is his long neck, which he uses to reach for his favorite foods, acacia and mimosa leaves. As he quickly strips a tree with his extendible tongue and mobile lips, a giraffe looks positively indifferent, especially if he lowers his long eyelashes. But, if he lifts his head to look at you, his two short hairy horns seem to crown one of the haughtiest faces in the world.

Incidents   Cause and Effect

Because there had been a lot of ice and snow on the road, Dad didn't want me to drive his car. But I had promised to meet some of my friends at the mall, so I borrowed it anyway. The road seemed all right, but it was just my luck that I hit the only patch of ice on an otherwise clear road and skidded into a telephone pole. Then, to make matters worse, I discovered that I was a little short of money, so I had to call Dad to pay the tow-truck driver for towing the car to the garage. Now I'm grounded for a month. Talk about bad luck!

Facts   Comparison

Julie and Julian are the two best-looking students in the room. Although of opposite sexes, they are similar in every other respect. Their hair is blond and curly; their eyes are blue; their complexion is smooth and healthy. They sound the same; even their laughs are indistinguishable. With their slim, athletic bodies, they wear their clothes like professional models. And no wonder—Julie and Julian are twins!

Descriptive Details   Climactic Order

When I entered her bedroom, I could not help thinking that it was the untidiest place I had ever seen. Books, clothes, and shoes almost completely covered the floor; I couldn't even tell if there was a carpet. The mahogany dresser, strewn with cosmetic bottles and lidless jars of congealing cream, was even more disorganized. But the masterpiece was the bed. Covered with clothing, books, magazines, even what looked like a bearskin rug, it seemed to offer no hope at all to anyone wanting to take a nap.

Examples   Climactic Order

Have you ever listened to our political leaders' voices during an election—not so much what they say but their vocal range? The ones in power use their middle registers, indicating their confidence in the people's ability to make the sensible choice and return them to power. Those seeking power use their lower registers, trying to persuade voters that they are even more capable than their opponents. Most noticeably, those with no hope of gaining power use their upper registers, demonstrating their distress at the trouble the country will suffer because of the voters' rejection of them.

Illustration Through Description   Climactic Order

To appreciate a zoo, you should spend time in front of each cage. If you just walk by a tarsier's cage, for example, you might miss this monkeylike little beast altogether. Because the tarsier chooses darkness as protection from its enemies, you will have to be patient to get a glimpse of it. When you do, though, you will see a round head, closely set in its shoulders, a froglike face, naked ears, and enormous eyes. Without moving its tiny body, the tarsier can turn its head to look directly to the rear—almost instantly. And if what the tarsier sees is alarming, it can jump six or seven times its length.

Descriptive Details   Familiar to Unfamiliar

Though it is often called a bear, and though its roly-poly body seems to resemble a teddy bear's, the giant panda actually belongs to a family that includes raccoons. It survives in the wild only in a small area in the high altitudes of western China and Tibet. Its diet consists largely of bamboo shoots, along with eggs and small mammals.

Illustration Through Narration   Chronological Order

I used to be fond of cats until six months ago. When a friend of mine asked me to adopt her Persian, Napoleon, because she could no longer keep him, I accepted gladly, little knowing what was in store for me. His name should have given me a clue to his habits. He would eat only what he wanted, when he wanted, and where he wanted. Food left in his dish for more than an hour was sniffed at disapprovingly and never touched again—so much for leftovers! And no matter what was in his dish, he always preferred to see what he could scrounge from nearby humans. No sooner had I discovered his finicky eating habits than I became aware that he wasn't completely housebroken. Then, as spring came, he began to shed handfuls of white fur all over my green sofa. The final straw was his incessant howling in front of the apartment of the female cat down the hall. With the pleas and threats of my fellow tenants ringing in my ears, I took Napoleon to the animal shelter. Adieu, Napoleon, and good riddance.

Questions   Particular to General

Are you awed by Westminster Abbey and St. Paul's Cathedral? Does your heart skip a beat when you think of the changing of the Guard at Buckingham Palace? Does the sight of Big Ben or a red double-decker bus in an English movie bring back happy memories? Then chances are you've fallen in love with London, a city whose great and small sights attract millions of tourists every year.

Quoted Material   Restatement

There are as many ways of describing love as there are lovers. It is "like a red, red rose" and "like sunshine after rain." It "makes the world go round." It is "a flame" or "a sickness"; it is "nature's second sun" or "the coldest of critics." It is "that orbit of the restless soul" and "the sweetest thing on earth." My favorite definition of love, though, is "that state in which the happiness of another person is essential to your own." Now that you have read how others have defined love, can you create your own definition?

Reasons   Cause and Effect

Many people believe in the existence of lake monsters, but I find the evidence unconvincing. There is no physical evidence of sightings of lake monsters except for photographs, and photographs can easily be faked. Most "sightings" turn out to be hoaxes, inspired by practical jokes and media publicity. Towns near lakes supposedly inhabited by monsters often earn a lot of money from tourists who come to see the "monsters" in person, so that circulating stories about monsters helps their economy. For these reasons, unless I see a monster myself, I will remain skeptical.

Descriptive Details   Analogy

A campfire is a thing of sensual delight, as entertaining and appealing as any ballet. Consider the flaming whirling dervishes, roaring and sighing as they perform their dance. This performance, divinely choreographed, duplicates no movements. The sparks ignite in a frantic conflagration, kindled by the caressing fingers of heat massaging away the nocturnal fears and bugaboos.

EXERCISE 10 ▸ Combination of Methods

Up to now you have been working with only one method of organization at a time. A knowledge of all of the methods, however, is extremely important before you start using combined methods of organization. Most writers use combinations of supporting details and methods of organization.

1. Find several paragraphs similar in length to the one below. Ask your partner to read and analyze them with you.

2. You should determine what methods of organization were used. In other words, say something about *each* sentence and its function in the paragraph. The following is an example of the way you should analyze the paragraphs.

> The invention for which the twentieth century will be remembered in history will not be the motion picture or the television set, or even the silicon chip. *(This introduces the paragraph and builds up to the main idea by saying what the writer believes will not be true.)* It will be the atomic bomb. *(topic sentence)* This diabolical device, though it is so simple to construct that an intelligent high-school student can build one, is capable of destroying the earth and everything on it in a matter of seconds. *(a comparison and a result)* Its main ingredient, plutonium or enriched uranium, is supposedly under strict supervision of the countries who possess a supply. *(a fact)* But enough of the stuff to make several hundred bombs the size of the one that destroyed Hiroshima has "disappeared" from storage facilities or in transit. *(a fact)* A number of films—*In Like Flint, Thunderball,* and *Superman I,* to name three—have been based on someone's building or stealing an atomic bomb and holding the world for ransom. *(examples)* With the possibility of total destruction at the whim of a small group of people becoming ever more probable, we can only hope that there will be someone around a millennium hence to remember the twentieth century. *(Conclusion links back to the beginning.)* (The overall method of organization is cause and effect.)

EXERCISE 11 ▶ Examining a Longer Piece of Writing

Read the following newspaper review to see how all the pieces fit together to make a unified whole. You and your partner should note particularly the overall method of organization and the types of supporting details. Suggestions and questions to help your analysis are given in parentheses throughout.

Two Plays as Different as Onions and Dirt
by Joe Adcock, Seattle Post-Intelligencer, Oct. 17, 1982

(After reading the title, can you determine the overall method of organization?)

Our sense of smell is usually unimportant when we go to the theater. We see, we hear, we sometimes at least imagine what things feel like and taste like. But smell? *(How has the beginning involved you?)*

Well, smell is having its day in Seattle theaters just now. During the course of *Peer Gynt* at the Bathhouse Theater, the title character pulls an onion apart. The smell is pungent, pun-gent!

And from the moment you enter Intiman Theater, where *A Dream Play* is being performed, you pick up this dry-dirt scent. And, lo, you then notice that the whole playing area is a mass of dry dirt! *(What do the two productions have in common? And what makes them different?)*

These olfactory details are probably entirely incidental to the respective directors' intentions. But they provoke a tiny insight into the contrasting natures of these two Scandinavian plays, plays that are so rarely performed that the fact they are being produced simultaneously in Seattle right now fairly demands comment of some kind. *(Do you think Adcock has a "tiny insight" or a very large insight? You may need to read more of the review to answer this question.)*

Both Ibsen's *Peer Gynt* and Strindberg's *A Dream Play* are performed rarely, with good reason. Both have large casts and a multitude of sets. The company that decides to produce either work is asking for trouble. *(This short paragraph is developed by giving a result and providing a reason. What are they?)*

But—such is life in the theater as elsewhere—rewards are commensurate with challenges and risks. Both the Bathhouse and Intiman accepted the big challenge, took the big risk, and came up with very rewarding productions. Very rewarding, and very different. As different as onions and dirt. *(Notice that the reason/result development continues, but the contrast method is reintroduced.)*

The onion is strong, coarse, homey, a bit vulgar, essential in any stew that has any hopes for piquancy. Dry dirt is slightly irritating. It's dusty. Like sand, it can take any shape, but it doesn't hold its shape for long. There's a metallic quality to its smell. *(The differences between an onion and dry dirt are clearly stated.)*

Which brings us to the essential contrast between these plays and these productions. *Peer Gynt* is organic. *A Dream Play* is inorganic. *(The thesis of the review is stated. The essential difference between the two plays is provided, and the thesis is tied to onions and dirt.)*

Anyone who sees either show will probably emerge from the theater talking to his or her companion about imaginative staging effects. The troll masks or the dark sunbursts that frame the playing areas, for example, are striking in *Peer Gynt*. The white dove, the white disembodied hands, the white costumes, the huge white cloth that indicates the firmament are all striking in *A Dream Play*. *(Note the details about the staging effects.)*

But the striking details in *Peer Gynt* are notably integral, the sorts of touches that make us think, "That's just the way it ought to look. If I were a little more creative, I'd come up with something just like that." The striking details in *A Dream Play* are brilliantly contrived, the sorts of touches that make us think, "Far out! I would never in a hundred years have thought of anything like that." *(The contrast is built more solidly. How do the contrasts of onions and dirt tie into this paragraph?)*

A Dream Play is the more extravagant production, not only in terms of imagination but also in terms of dollars. It cost about $114,000 to produce. *Peer Gynt* cost about $20,000. *(A concrete difference is stated.)*

As literary texts, leaving production values aside for the moment, the plays are similar in certain ways. Both are amply larded with neuroticism. *(Preparations for a comparison are laid.)*

The hero of *Peer Gynt* suffers from what Carl Jung called the "puer eternus," or "eternal youth," syndrome. He thinks he's ever so special, he can't commit himself to anything, and he has moments when he's just insufferably self-centered and self-absorbed.

Just about everyone in *A Dream Play* (and there are lots and lots of characters in *A Dream Play*) is into what Eric Berne in *Games People Play* calls, "Ain't It Awful." From the very first scene, we are apprised that life is wretched. Further scenes do nothing to contradict this foregone conclusion.

Both plays posit that favorite literary saying, "Love conquers all." Ibsen posits it to affirm it. Strindberg posits it to negate it. *(A comparison is set up only to point up a contrast.)*

Both plays are full of irony. But when *Peer Gynt* is mouthing off in a way that demonstrates Ibsen's satirical intent, we realize that things are not nearly so bad as Gynt, with his blinkers, makes them out to be. When someone in *A Dream Play* says something that is patently absurd, we see that they are deluded by foolish, Pollyanna hopes, and things are a good deal worse than they make them out to be. *(Do you see what makes the plays different?)*

Probably both plays were in part psychodramas for their authors. *Peer Gynt* came at a time in Ibsen's career when he really was giving up some of his injured pride and hoarded grievances. *A Dream Play* indicates Strindberg's insistence that injuries and grievances are the main and essential source of emotional and aesthetic stimulation. . . . *(In what way are the playwrights similar and different?)*

Both of these shows are highly theatrical. Theater professionals will especially want to see *A Dream Play*, if only to get a state-of-the-art update on what can be done to make a good show out of a nasty text. The director struggles with Strindberg and comes out on top. As for the director of *Peer Gynt* and Ibsen, they work as a compatible cooperative team. *(How has Adcock tied the contrast of onions—organic—and dirt— inorganic—into his last paragraph? How has he used the ABABAB method of contrast throughout his review? Has he written an insightful review? Explain.)*

Once you have learned to organize your writing, unifying it should pose no difficulty. You should be able to see which details support your thesis statement and which are irrelevant or illogical. Drafting your piece of writing is a natural, easy, logical outcome of all the work you have done in collecting, listing, organizing, and unifying your supporting details. Do you see how easy it will now be to draft a piece of writing?

27 Coherence

When your writing is coherent, your reader cannot help but understand what you are saying. Everything is tied together clearly and logically. To keep your writing flowing and to help your readers follow your ideas, concentrate on the following four points when you draft:

1. Use some logical method of organization (Chapter 26).
2. Structure your sentences in such a way that the sequence in which they are arranged links them to each other (Chapter 26).
3. Use transitional devices to connect sentences and paragraphs (dealt with in this chapter).
4. Repeat a key word or phrase to remind your reader of the important points of your piece of writing (dealt with in this chapter).

EXERCISE 1 ▶ Transitions

Transitions show relationships between thoughts and give a sense of direction and continuity to your writing. They assist your reader in moving not only from detail to detail within a single sentence, but also from sentence to sentence and paragraph to paragraph. Like signposts, transitions inform your readers that one part or stage of the discussion has ended. Transitions also give them a hint of what connection the next phase of thought has with the just-completed phase. Transitions are a vital factor in coherence.

The following list contains some useful transitional expressions and conjunctions. As you and your partner read the list, notice the specific reasons for introducing certain words into your sentences. Keep this list handy when you draft a piece of writing.

addition	in addition, besides, moreover, further, furthermore, equally important, in fact, likewise, next, too, then, and, both . . . and, not only . . . but also, first, second, in the third place (Do not use *firstly, secondly, thirdly.*)
comparison	similarly, likewise, in like manner, by comparison, compared to, just as surely, in the same way, not only . . . but also, both . . . and, either . . . or
contrast	but, however, yet, still, nevertheless, on the one hand, on the other hand, for all of that, on the contrary, notwithstanding, in contrast, in contrast to, rather, neither . . . nor, although, though, in spite of, whereas
emphasis	in fact, indeed, in truth, certainly, definitely, emphatically, unquestionably, undoubtedly, without a doubt, undeniably, without reservation, naturally, obviously
example	for example, for instance, in this case, in another case, on this occasion, in this situation, as proof, as evidence, take the case of . . . , the proof of this, the evidence of this, thus
exception	yet, still, however, nevertheless, in spite of, despite, nonetheless, though, although
place	near, beyond, opposite to, adjacent to, at the same place, here, there, from, over, in the middle, around, in front of, in the distance, farther, here and there, above, below, at the right (or left), between, in the foreground, on this side, beside
purpose	for this purpose, in order that, in this way, since, so that, on that account, in case, with a view to, for the same reason
repetition	in other words, that is to say, as I have said, again, once again

result	accordingly, thus, consequently, hence, therefore, inevitably, under these conditions, as a result, as a consequence, consequently, because, because of, so that
sequence	first, second, third, next, then, at the outset, following this, at this time, now, at this point, after, afterward, after this, subsequently, lastly, finally, consequently, before this, previously, preceding this, simultaneously
summary	in brief, on the whole, in sum, to sum up, to conclude, hence, for this reason, in short, in summary, in conclusion
time	at once, immediately, in the meantime, meanwhile, at the same time, in the end, in the interim, then, soon, not long after, at length, at last, finally, some time ago, later, afterward, from this time on, from time to time, after, before, until, at present, all of a sudden, instantly, at this instant, suddenly, now, without delay, at this point, a few minutes later, formerly, yesterday, later in the day, since then, when, whenever, next, henceforth, thereupon, sometimes, in a moment, shortly, previously

EXERCISE 2 ▶ *Experimenting with Transitions*

Examine the following sentences with your partner.

No Transition

Countries in the Middle East have an abundance of oil. The United States does not produce enough oil for its needs.

Transition Added

Countries in the Middle East have an abundance of oil; *in contrast*, the United States does not produce enough oil for its needs.

Weak Transition

Huge tankers carry imported oil thousands of miles in all kinds of weather, *and* they are vulnerable to accidental spills and sinking.

Stronger Transition

> Huge tankers carry imported oil thousands of miles in all kinds of weather; *as a consequence*, they are vulnerable to accidental spills and sinking.

No Transition

> America's energy policymakers want Americans to depend less on foreign energy sources. They think we should cut down on the amount of energy we use.

Transition Added

> America's energy policymakers want Americans to depend less on foreign energy sources; *in addition*, they think we should cut down on the amount of energy we use.

No Transition

> Nuclear power was once considered the answer to our future energy needs. No nuclear power plant has been ordered in the United States since 1978.

Transition of Contrast Added

> Nuclear power was once considered the answer to our future energy needs; *however*, no nuclear power plant has been ordered in the United States since 1978.

No Transition

> CANDU reactors use natural uranium and heavy water. They are considered safer to operate than other types of reactors. The uranium contained in them has been used by some countries to make atomic bombs.

Transitions of Result and Contrast Added

> CANDU reactors use natural uranium and heavy water. They are, *consequently*, considered safer to operate than other types of reactors. *Nevertheless*, the uranium contained in them has been used by some countries to make atomic bombs.

No Transition

The Alberta tar sands in Canada are considered an almost unlimited source of oil. Exploration in the Beaufort Sea has revealed large supplies.

Correlative Conjunctions Added for Transition

Not only are the Alberta tar sands in Canada considered an almost unlimited source of oil, *but* exploration in the Beaufort Sea has *also* revealed large supplies.

No Transition

In most parts of America, garbage is considered a nuisance and a health hazard. In some parts of the world (including some U.S. communities) it is burned to generate electricity.

Coordinate Conjunction Added for Transition

In most parts of America, garbage is considered a nuisance and a health hazard, *yet* in some parts of the world (including some U.S. communities) it is burned to generate electricity.

Subordinate Conjunction Added for Transition

Although in some parts of the world (including some U.S. communities) garbage is burned to generate electricity, it is considered a nuisance and a health hazard in most parts of America.

EXERCISE 3 ▸ Key Words

One method of achieving coherence is to repeat your subject throughout your writing. But repetition for its own sake can be boring. You might find it a good idea to use replacement nouns or pronouns instead. You might, for example, in an essay discussing President Reagan, refer to him as "Mr. President" or "the chief of state," as well as using pronouns such as *he*, *his*, and *himself*. So long as you do not overuse these nouns or pronouns, your reader should remain interested in and aware of your subject.

Prepare a one-minute talk for your partner on one of the following topics or another topic of your choice. As you talk, your partner should record your use of key words. Afterward, you might like to write a short paper on your topic, making sure that you use the transitional device of key words.

one of your parents or guardians   the oldest person you know
your best friend   a favorite movie star

EXERCISE 4 ▶ Sentence Work

1. Independently of your partner, choose a reason for joining each of the following sets of sentences. Then use an appropriate transition to join them. Compare your use of transitions with your partner's.

a) Negotiations have been successfully completed with many native Americans. Hydroelectric projects have been built on their land.
b) Churchill Falls in Labrador furnishes power to nearby Quebec. It exports excess capacity to New York State.
c) Offshore oil rigs have been built off the California coast in the Pacific Ocean, off the Atlantic coast, and in the Gulf of Mexico. Oil rigs appear in all the main bodies of water surrounding the United States.
d) Some people have attempted to harness the wind to generate energy. There are commercial wind "farms" near San Francisco.
e) Solar energy provides the cheapest source of power. The United States has made little use of the sun's energy. Other countries (notably Australia) use solar energy to a high degree.

2. The following sentences include and support the topic sentence "Nuclear power can be dangerous." Rearrange the supporting details in a logical order, making sure every sentence is relevant to the claim. Change some key words to pronouns and use a few of the transitional devices presented in this chapter. Compare your paragraph with your partner's. Have you both produced coherent paragraphs?

Nuclear power can be dangerous.
There was an accident at Three Mile Island in Pennsylvania.
You never know when there might be an accident at a power plant.
People should be concerned about such problems as the disposal of radioactive waste.
Many people from nearby Middletown were evacuated by the National Guard and the Pennsylvania state authorities.
Authorities were afraid the radioactive core of the reactor would melt.
There were no casualties at Three Mile Island.

28 Self-Editing, Peer-Editing, and Teacher-Editing

Revision is an ongoing process for every writer. For many it is standard practice to have a number of editors and several rewrites.

This textbook has gone through several drafts. Every section has been revised, reformed, refined, and reshaped because the author clarified his thoughts while developing the manuscript, and listened to comments from fellow teachers, editors, and consultants. Furthermore, the manuscript was tested by teachers (who served as advisers) and their students. The result of their interest and concern is *Writing: Process to Product*.

In this chapter you will learn a few strategies for editing not only your own writing but also that of your peers. Before you start looking at the strategies, however, you should realize that there is no precise list of questions which you can apply to everything you are asked to edit. Your task as editor will be to maintain the writer's uniqueness while at the same time making sure that the reader will comprehend the message.

Every draft of everything you write will benefit from a second pair of eyes before you present it to your intended reader. Essentially, an editor makes a draft more readable by paring down, building up, moving things around, improving grammar, quickening the pace, clarifying confusions, and correcting inaccuracies. If this paragraph sounds a little overwhelming, remember: The least you can do for a writer after reading a draft is to say, "I love it," or "I don't understand what your point is."

EXERCISE 1 ▶ *Revising Your Own Work*

This textbook suggests that when you have completed a draft, you should ask your peer editors and teacher/editor for their opinions before you submit your paper to its intended reader. But *before* you give it to your editors or intended reader, you yourself should examine your content, organization, style, and mechanics. Using the suggestions in the following four categories—content, organization, style, and usage and mechanics—judge your work as *superior*, *average*, or *unsatisfactory*. Afterward, if you are not satisfied with your paper, you should write another, improved draft.

CONTENT

Content involves the limited topic (subject, main idea, thesis) of the paper and its development.

Superior
1. The central idea is worthwhile: fresh, true, specific, and clear. The writer has expressed the central idea in a thesis statement or topic sentence accurately and interestingly.
2. The idea is suitable for the length of the paper. The writer has developed it perfectly.
3. The writer has presented all the details fully, through high-quality facts, reasons, examples, or other concrete ways.

Average
1. The central idea is apparent but unoriginal. The thesis statement or topic sentence is clear but not always interesting.
2. The development sometimes relies on predictable details.
3. The development is often incomplete or repetitious and includes unimportant, obvious, or irrelevant support.
4. There may be some inconsistencies in the logical development of the limited topic.

Unsatisfactory
1. The central idea is either nonexistent or totally unimportant and trite. The writer may or may not have expressed the central idea in a thesis statement or topic sentence.
2. If there is a good idea, the writer provides no specific support of the thesis.

> 3. The development of a reasonable idea is confused and worthless.
> 4. The thesis statement and its development are inappropriate for the length of the assignment. The idea is either underdeveloped or presented in an overly repetitious way.

How would you judge your content: *superior, average,* or *unsatisfactory?*

ORGANIZATION

Organization involves how a piece of writing is developed, how the sentences within a paragraph are linked, and how the writing progresses from one paragraph to the next. (See Chapters 26 and 27.)

> *Superior*
> 1. The writer has developed the central idea clearly and logically. It is obvious that the writer has considered the writing variables. The reader moves effortlessly from one section of the paper to the next.
> 2. The development has a specific method of organization—for example: comparison, cause and effect, spatial, chronological, climactic. The writer has given each supporting detail just the right emphasis and attention. Furthermore, the supporting details are in exactly the right places in the paper.
> 3. There is nothing irrelevant in the paper.
>
> *Average*
> 1. The paper apparently has an organizational plan, but at times it loses its focus.
> 2. There is something wrong with the emphasis or order of some of the points. The writer over- or understresses them or places them incorrectly.
> 3. Sometimes the writing is hard to follow because the needed transitional devices are missing.
>
> *Unsatisfactory*
> 1. There is no clear organization.
> 2. The supporting details are either sketchy or redundant.
> 3. The paragraphs are not unified or coherent; transitions are insufficient or confusing.
> 4. Often, a writer introduces a new idea in a paragraph before fully developing the previous one.

How would you judge your organization: *superior, average,* or *unsatisfactory?*

STYLE

Style involves not only the choice of words and sentences but also the effectiveness, the arrangement, and the appropriateness of these words and sentences for each particular piece of writing. (For a discussion of style, see Chapter 30.)

Superior
1. The readers are always kept on track because the point of view is consistent.
2. Sentence variety is apparent throughout. The mode of expression is as interesting as the thought it contains.
3. The word choice is clear and accurate, always appropriately linking the writer and the subject to the reader.
4. The level of language is consistent.
5. The writer often uses effective figurative language.
6. The beginning and ending of the piece seem just right.

Average
1. The sentence structure is correct but often lacks variety and emphasis. Some sentences may be wordy.
2. The writer often uses generalized rather than specific words; they are correct but not always appropriate.
3. Sometimes the writer mixes levels of language.
4. If the writer uses figurative comparisons, they are sometimes strained, ineffective, or inappropriate.

Unsatisfactory
1. Sentences are confusing and monotonous.
2. Sentences lack emphasis, often because the writer uses weak verbs and overuses pronouns such as *it, this,* and *which.*
3. The writer's word choice is limited and often ineffective or inappropriate.
4. The writer relies on slang and trite expressions to communicate.
5. The point of view shifts constantly.

How would you judge your own style: *superior, average,* or *unsatisfactory?*

USAGE AND MECHANICS

Usage and mechanics deal with the nitty-gritty of writing: spelling, punctuation, grammar, and so on.

Superior
1. Grammar usage, punctuation, and spelling are generally accurate.
2. The paper is usually free of small mechanical errors, such as misuse of apostrophes and hyphens, errors in citing numbers, capitalization errors, and so on.
3. The writer punctuates sentences correctly and shows an understanding of the more complex punctuation marks: the semicolon, parentheses, and dashes, as well as double and single quotation marks.
4. The writing contains no serious sentence errors, such as fragment faults, dangling modifiers, run-on sentences, lack of subject-verb agreement, and so on.

Average
1. Occasional mechanical errors creep into the writing.
2. The writing is often correct and careful, but to avoid making mechanical mistakes, uses only commas and periods for fear of misusing other punctuation marks, such as semicolons, colons and dashes.

Unsatisfactory
1. Because mechanical errors abound, a reader often makes no sense of sentences. The writer has not come to terms with writing problems, not knowing why she or he makes mistakes, and does not know how to correct them. The writer continues to shift tenses or voices in mid-sentence, to run sentences together, and to let unintentional fragments stand as complete thoughts.
2. Punctuation marks are absent or incorrect.
3. Spelling errors are frequent.
4. Many pronoun references are wrong.

How would you judge your usage and mechanics: *superior*, *average*, or *unsatisfactory*?

EXERCISE 2 ▶ Revising the Writing of Your Peers

Peer-editing is so beneficial to the revision process that you and your peers should attempt to offer each other suggestions on every assignment. Even professional writers require editors, who serve as an important part of their writing process. So, how can you, a beginning writer, possibly ignore the benefits of peer-editing? Once you and your peers become comfortable with editing each other's work, you will probably find that you will ask them for their comments before submitting anything you write to your intended reader.

The more familiar you become with the workshop sections of this textbook, the more suggestions for revision you will be able to share during peer-editing sessions. Some of the most recent research refers to this step in the writing process as "reformation," where you, as editor, should encourage the writer to "re-form" what he or she has written. In essence, a worthwhile peer-editing session should give you an idea of the effect that your writing will have on the intended audience and provide ideas and suggestions on how to sharpen that effect.

What follows are some specific guidelines and suggestions for handling peer-editing sessions.

1. Every writer appreciates praise, so begin by pointing out the things that work well. Here are a few questions you might respond to, after you have read one of your peers' papers.

Which senses were stimulated?
What part created the strongest impression?
What part was the most genuine?
What overall emotion will remain with the intended audience?

2. During a peer-editing session make sure that you and your peers comment on the writing variables. You should routinely ask questions like the following:

Is the limited topic worthwhile?
Is the limited topic narrow enough or too broad to suit the length of the paper?
Is the limited topic clearly stated in the form of a thesis statement or topic sentence?
Is the writer's attitude toward the topic clear?
Does the material fulfill its purpose?

Would the piece of writing be better in another format?
Has the writer's and audience's situation been fully realized? Does the piece of writing reflect the writer's consideration of situation?
Is the choice of the writer's voice appropriate? Should the writer have used a persona instead of writing in his or her own voice?
Is the point of view consistent and appropriate?

3. You should make suggestions about what to delete, add, substitute, or move; this applies to words, sentences, and paragraphs. In this part of the editing process, you should consider the effectiveness of each sentence. If you write directly on the author's paper, get into the habit of using the proofreading and editorial symbols on pages 364–366. Using these symbols will save you a great deal of time.

4. A successful peer-editing session requires honesty and courage. You must be truthful, and the writer must be willing to accept your criticism. Thoughtfulness and thoroughness are also essential. When something is unsatisfactory, you should tactfully say so, pointing out what is wrong and making suggestions to improve the piece of writing.

5. Peer-editing takes time. It is very easy to say that everything someone writes is wonderful. This kind of statement saves a lot of talk, prevents any anxiety, and perhaps wins an immediate friend. Such a statement, however, does not help a beginning writer. Treat your peer-editing sessions as an essential part of the writing process, and be prepared to spend time talking about a paper's thesis statement, organization, sentence variety, and word choice. If you, as a peer editor, feel something in the paper is not working, *even if you do not know exactly what is wrong or how to fix it*, you should say so. When you say "I'm having a problem with this part," a worthwhile discussion is bound to follow. Your comments and suggestions will probably be tentative at first, but as you continue, you will find the words to explain your confusion with the paper you are editing. When you are involved in a peer-editing session, you are involved in both a learning and a teaching experience. When the members of your group learn to share knowledge with each other, you will all learn to write better.

6. All of the assignments in *Writing: Process to Product* have specific suggestions for peer editing sessions. If you are involved in peer-editing with more than two people, make sure one of you takes on the duties of leader for that particular session. The leader should be responsible for keeping the discussion going and asking the questions contained in the editing and revising process for each assignment. Your first attempts at editing may not be too successful, but research has shown that you can learn from your peers.

Keep a record of your changing attitudes to peer-editing. Right now, take a few minutes and write a journal entry on your feelings about peer-editing. After you have experienced a few peer-editing sessions, make another journal entry on your feelings.

EXERCISE 3 ▶ *Help for Your Editors*

From time to time you might like to try one or both of the following suggestions during your editing sessions with your peers and your writing teacher. Both will help you produce a better product.

1. *State your writing variables:* You should provide a statement of your writing variables for your editors. Include the following:

a) who you are; whether you are writing in your own *voice* or role-playing (using a *persona*); why you chose your persona

b) who your *audience* is; what your relationship is to the audience; how familiar your audience is with your topic; any information about the audience that you think would affect your approach to the topic; whether your audience is real or imagined

c) what your *purpose* is for writing; how other variables influence your purpose; whether you are writing for a real-life or a made-up reason

d) what your *limited topic* is; what your *thesis statement* is; what kind of development you are employing to support your thesis statement

e) what the *situation* is for you (the writer) and your audience; whether the situation is real or invented for this assignment; how the situation affects the writing

f) what your *format* is; whether the piece is complete as is or is part of a larger work

g) what your *point of view* is (first-, second-, or third-person)

2. *Evaluate your own writing:* Attach to your paper a note of your own evaluation of it so that your peers can read what you think about your writing. Respond to one or more of the following questions:

a) How long did it take you to write the paper?
b) What part of the writing process did you find easiest?
c) What part of the writing process did you find most difficult?
d) What do you consider the strongest point in your paper?

e) What do you consider the weakest aspect of your paper?
f) What do you like best in your paper?
g) What do you not like in your paper?
h) What aspects of writing are you strongest in: sentence structure, diction, comparisons, and so on?
i) What part of your paper do you think needs revision?
j) What would you like your editors to help you with?

EXERCISE 4 ▶ Different Kinds of Peer-Editing Sessions

You and your peers can choose from a variety of peer-editing sessions. No matter what kind of peer-editing session you choose, you, as editor, should consider all the editing suggestions in this chapter as well as the editing suggestions for each of the assignments in the first twenty-one chapters of *Writing: Process to Product*.

When editing, get into the habit of using the proofreaders' symbols on pages 364–366.

For Pairs of Students

Silent Reading

a) Exchange papers with your partner.
b) As you read, prepare yourself to talk about what has been written, beginning with the strengths of the piece of writing, but not ignoring the weaknesses.
c) Write directly on the piece of writing or make comments on a separate paper.
d) Do not talk until both papers have been read. Then discuss one paper at a time, using any of the suggestions in this chapter.

Reading Aloud

a) Read your paper aloud. Your partner should be able to see what you are reading. This way he or she can hear your inflections while seeing your written words. Often your partner will see what you do not see. A writer often reads what she or he *thinks* is there, not what really *is* there.
b) Your partner should not interrupt your reading, but, at the end, may ask you to reread the paper so that she or he can then interrupt in order to ask questions or make a particular point.
c) After the reading, you and your partner should discuss the paper.
d) Repeat the procedure with your partner's paper.

For a Three-Member Peer Group

Numbers and Letters

   a) Exchange papers.
   b) Every time you, as editor, see something that you would like to comment on, place a number in the margin near it.
   c) Then on a separate piece of paper, place the number and your favorable or unfavorable comment. For example:

   1. opening is very good
   2. should appeal to the sense of smell
   3. grammatical mistake (I think.)

   d) Then pass the piece of writing, with the numbers on it, to the next person to read. (Do *not* pass your comments. All the next person should see is the piece of writing with a series of numbers in the margin.)
   e) The next person should repeat the same process, except she or he should use letters instead of numbers. For example:

   A. opening suspenseful
   B. a run-on sentence
   C. good image—I could really see it!

   f) When the piece of writing has been read twice, the writer should receive it with the two comment sheets.
   g) Up to now, there should have been no talking, only reading and writing numbers or letters with comments. Now is the time to talk about the writing. The writer should ask for explanations if any of the comments are confusing.

Reading Aloud

   a) The writer should read the paper to the others in the group. No one should interrupt the reading, but one person should sit so that he or she can see the paper. This way that person can get a better understanding of the purpose by being able to both hear and see what is written. The other editor should listen and take notes.
   b) A discussion should follow the reading, beginning with the notetaker's comments. Start with praise.
   c) When the group is satisfied that everything was said that should have been said, the next person should read his or her paper aloud, and the editing can continue in the same way.

Duplicating the Paper

a) The writer can give each member of the group a copy of the piece. Comments can be written directly on the paper or on a separate piece of paper.
b) It is possible, using this method, for papers to be taken home in order to have more time to prepare for extensive editing. Thus class time can be spent on discussion rather than reading. This method is ideal for longer essays and reports.
c) At home, editors should write comments on the paper. The next day they can discuss what they thought of the writing and how it might be improved.
d) The writer can incorporate into the final copy both the suggestions that were written on the draft and those that were made in discussion.

EXERCISE 5 ▶ *Follow-up to a Peer-Editing Session*

Once you have had your paper peer-edited, you should prepare to write your final draft, using or rejecting your peers' suggestions. In some cases your peers may suggest that you revise your paper completely and show them another draft at a later date.

For most of your assignments, you will show your latest revised draft to your teacher/editor, who should seldom be your final intended reader. This one-to-one session will help you polish your writing for its intended audience. Remember: You should, if possible, write for a real audience and for a real purpose. Even if both purpose and audience are imaginary, you should make them seem real to you. Writing something just for the sake of writing for a grade often produces bad results—at the least, a dull paper!

After you have had your paper edited by your teacher, you should share his or her comments and suggestions with your peer editors. Through this sharing experience, you not only will be reinforcing what your teacher has told you but also will be helping your peers improve their editing process.

Are you becoming aware that it takes time to produce good writing? If a professional writer spends hours on revision, it is almost impossible for you, as a beginning writer, to dash off a high-quality, 1000-word essay the evening before it is due.

EXERCISE 6 ▶ Publishing

Like professional writers who desire to have what they write published, you should publish your final product too. As this book uses the word, *publish* simply means presenting your paper to its intended audience. After you have spent so much time prewriting, drafting, and revising your paper, you should certainly publish it instead of shoving it into your notebook or discarding it.

In most cases, publishing will merely require your giving or sending your product directly to your reader. For example, you will give your piece of writing to your family, peers, or teachers or send it to newspapers, officials, or people who live far from you. In most cases, your writing process will be complete when your product leaves your hands. Sometimes you will get a reaction from your reader, such as thanking you for the information, agreeing or disagreeing with your ideas, or reacting in various other ways. When you receive a reader's response, you find out exactly what your reader thinks of your product. Always remember that your writing is an extension of you; it represents you. You should make sure that your product represents you favorably.

Even though your editors (both peers and teacher) may give you a great deal of help, offer you various suggestions, and even re-edit several of your drafts so that you can finally produce a perfect paper, there comes a time when you must take full responsibility for it. The ultimate choice of accepting or rejecting editors' suggestions must always rest with the writers. Just before you send your piece of writing to its audience, you should once more check for errors: misspellings, punctuation forgotten, lack of subject-verb or pronoun agreement, and so on. Final proofreading is your responsibility.

Take a few minutes to share with your peers some past reactions of your intended readers to your written products. Have they been satisfied? Dissatisfied? Why did they react in this way? How can you use these reactions to improve your future writing?

29 Unwriting—Paraphrase, Précis, and Outline

As a student, you may have had to take notes during lectures, condense essays, boil down chapters of textbooks, or rewrite complicated passages. In most cases you were the audience, and the purpose for condensing was to make reviewing the material faster and easier. In doing these tasks, you reversed the writing process. Rather than building a piece of writing from limited topic to finished product, you reduced a finished product to its main points. This process can be called "unwriting." In this chapter you will examine several forms of unwriting: the paraphrase, précis, and outline. As well, you will learn how to pick out thesis statements or topic sentences.

This chapter on unwriting, however, has another important purpose. The author has placed it after the important chapter on editing and revising to show you how to use unwriting as an editing process. If you are having difficulty self-editing or editing someone else's paper, you might try to unwrite all or a portion of the paper in the form of a paraphrase, précis, outline, or statement of the main idea. The piece of unwriting will often point out something that is missing in the original piece of writing: a step in a set of directions, a cause of an effect, or a point in an argument that was unsupported. The process of unwriting can show a writer what needs to be included in a final draft.

EXERCISE 1 ▶ Getting Familiar with Unwriting

1. Tell your partner a story, anecdote, joke, personal experience, or anything else that you can think of. Your partner should listen and enjoy without interrupting.

2. When you have finished, your partner should retell in her or his own words what you have said. This repeated story in your partner's words is a **paraphrase** of your original words.

3. Now, ask your partner to retell the story, condensing it to half its original length. He or she must decide what to include and what to omit. The main point and only the most important parts of the development should remain. This summary is a **précis** of the original.

4. Next, your partner should write an informal **outline** of your story by following these steps:

a) List about three to five important points in the order they occurred, leaving at least three lines between each point. Put a Roman numeral and a period before each point.

b) Underneath each important point, list at least two details that tell more about that particular point. Put a capital letter before each detail and a period after the letter.

The following example shows how Roman numerals and capital letters might appear in an informal outline:

I.
  A.
  B.
II.
  A.
  B.
  C.
III.
  A.
  B.
  C.
  D.

(For an example of a formal outline, see page 122.)

5. Then repeat the activity. This time your partner tells a story, and you do the unwriting.

EXERCISE 2 ▶ Paraphrasing an Essay

1. Find a piece of nonfiction writing of about 300 words from the editorial pages of a newspaper or magazine.

2. Read the article aloud to your partner. Your partner may make notes but may not interrupt you or look at what you are reading.

3. When you finish, ask your partner to tell you the subject of the article. Your partner will be paraphrasing. Remember, whether the paraphrase is shorter or longer than the original, it should be easier to understand.

4. When your partner finishes the paraphrase, discuss whether any important points were either left out or not clarified.

5. Then, together produce an outline.

6. Repeat the exercise, with your partner reading his or her article to you.

EXERCISE 3 ▶ Writing a Précis

In many colleges, students are expected to take a test to determine whether they will be admitted into the regular first-year English course. Often, as part of the test, they must write a précis. The original material is usually about 600 words long; the students are required to write a précis of approximately 300 words.

Using the following short piece of writing, imagine that you are writing for a college entrance test. Keep in mind that the college wants to find out how well you can read and write.

The following excerpt is from a *Time* magazine article by Richard Corliss about Steven Spielberg, the film director, whom *Time* calls "the Prince of Hollywood." The phenomenally successful films that Spielberg directed include *Jaws, Close Encounters of the Third Kind, E.T. the Extra-Terrestrial, Raiders of the Lost Ark,* and *The Color Purple.*

> Spielberg's memories of his childhood are as dramatic and fantastic as you might expect from a master fabulist. Could real life have been nearly so much fun? "It was creative and chaotic at our house," says Steven's father, Arnold, 68, a computer executive with twelve patents to his name. "I'd help Steven construct sets for his 8-mm [millimeter] movies, with toy trucks and papier-mâché mountains. At night I'd tell the kids cliffhanger tales about characters like Joanie Frothy Flakes and Lenny Ludhead. I see pieces of me in Steven. I see the storyteller." . . .
>
> The fateful day when this movie-mad child got close to his Hollywood dream came in the summer of 1965, when 17-year-old Steven, visiting his cousins in Canoga Park, took the studio tour of Universal Pictures. "The tram wasn't stopping at the sound stages," Steven says. "So during a bathroom break I snuck away and wandered over there, just watching. I met a man who asked what I was doing, and I

told him my story. Instead of calling the guards to throw me off the lot, he talked with me for about an hour. His name was Chuck Silvers, head of the editorial department. He said he'd like to see some of my little films, and so he gave me a pass to get on the lot the next day. I showed him about four of my 8-mm films. He was very impressed. Then he said, 'I don't have the authority to write you any more passes, but good luck to you.' "

The next day a young man wearing a business suit and carrying a briefcase strode past the gate guard, waved and heaved a silent sigh. He had made it! "It was my father's briefcase," Spielberg says. "There was nothing in it but a sandwich and two candy bars. So every day that summer I went in my suit and hung out with directors and writers and editors and dubbers. I found an office that wasn't being used and became a squatter. I went to a camera store, bought some plastic name titles and put my name in the building directory: Steven Spielberg, Room 23C."

Two years later, Spielberg enrolled at California State University, Long Beach, but it is safe to say he matriculated at Universal U. Cramming 15 1/2 units into two frenetic days of classes a week, he was able to spend three days on the studio lot, asking executives to watch his films. "They were embarrassed when I asked them to remove their pictures from the wall so I could project my little silent movies. They said, 'If you make your films in 16-mm or, even better, 35-mm, then they'll get seen.' So I immediately went to work in the college commissary to earn the money to buy 16-mm film and rent a camera. I had to get those films seen." . . .

And so, bankrolled by a young friend with hopes of being a producer, he wrote and directed, in ten days, for $10,000, a short film called *Amblin'*, about a boy and a girl hitchhiking from the desert to the Pacific Ocean. The day after Spielberg showed the film at Universal, he was called in by Sidney Jay Sheinberg, head of TV production, and offered a seven-year contract to direct Universal TV series. He was 20 years old. "I quit college," Spielberg says, "so fast I didn't even clean out my locker."

Today, after 20 summers on and off the Universal lot, the erstwhile trespasser practically owns the place. He might deserve to: *E.T.* and *Jaws* have grossed $835 million on a $19 million investment. Moreover, Sheinberg, now president and chief operating officer of Universal's parent organization, MCA, has maintained a paternal relationship with Spielberg. So, according to Sheinberg, "when Steven called me about two years ago and said, 'I want to come home,' I said, 'When?' and 'How much space do you need?' " In this fashion the man who saw a boy's film called *Amblin'* determined 15 years later to build that boy the movie industry's most sumptuous clubhouse as headquarters for Spielberg's Amblin Entertainment. The building is reputed to have cost between $4 million and $6 million to construct and furnish. Spielberg says he doesn't know, and will never ask, the price tag, and Sheinberg won't snitch. "It would be like telling how much the birthday present cost," he says.

1. *Before* you write a précis of this excerpt, you and your partner should write a paraphrase together. Follow the instructions in Exercise 2.

2. Now you and your partner each write a précis in paragraph form. Your paragraph should be one half to one third as long as the original excerpt.

3. When both you and your partner complete your précis, compare them to see how effective they are.

EXERCISE 4 ▶ Using All the Kinds of Unwriting

1. For this final unwriting exercise, write a paraphrase, précis, outline, and thesis statement for this excerpt from Owen Phillip's *The Last Chance Energy Book*.

In the search for new energy sources, the sun is an obvious candidate. It is generally believed that solar energy is surely the long-term answer, and this belief is almost certainly justified. In the United States, we have been somewhat behind other countries in developing solar power. Even a casual visitor to Western Australia would notice that many of the new houses there have solar panels built into their roofs. It is quite routine, not at all exceptional. That part of the world has always been energy poor—there is no oil, not much coal (the deposits that do exist being of indifferent quality), and little hydroelectric power. On the other hand, the climate is generally sunny with a month of cloudy weather per year so that solar panels, together with a small back-up system, provide plenty of hot water for heating and for household use. Why cannot we do the same thing in this country on a larger scale?

No doubt we shall; this is one of the personal options open to us. It takes no great foresight to anticipate that domestic solar panels will become increasingly more economical over the long run as the technology for their manufacture improves and as the prices of alternative fuels rise. They will make a great difference to our personal budgets and will help to reduce the national demand for oil and natural gas. But solar panels are not for everyone. What about all the people who live in apartment houses, hotels, and condominiums? Or in areas of the country where the sun shines only intermittently in winter, precisely the time when the heat is needed most? It is probably an overstatement of the case, but not an outrageous one, to assert that domestic solar collectors will provide for the energy problem the same kind of contribution that backyard vegetable plots provide for our food supply—sufficient for a relatively few fortunate people and a valuable supplement for others, but that's all.

Solar energy may indeed be the long-term answer, but the use of domestic collectors is not the only way to capture it. Another option could be to cover the deserts with solar collectors, using the heat to generate electric power. But there are problems. Do we really want to cover the deserts with solar collectors? New Englanders may not mind, but the people who live in Arizona may be less than enthusiastic. The ecology of the desert is a fragile thing, and the impact of large farms of solar collectors may be difficult to assess. Are we prepared for the enormous capital costs? Solar collectors work very well when the sun is shining, but they are not very useful at night. Energy would need to be stored in very large amounts to carry us through for nighttime use or during extended cloudy periods; either this or a backup system of large capacity that is used only intermittently and is consequently expensive. Solar power from the deserts may well be part of the solution, but we should not assume that it is the whole solution.

2. Compare your pieces of unwriting with those of your partner. If you do not agree on the essentials, review the directions in exercises 1–3.

EXERCISE 5 ▶ Revising by Unwriting

You can use unwriting to help you revise one of your completed drafts. Choose a partner for this exercise who is unfamiliar with your writing.

1. Read the draft to your partner.
2. When you finish, ask your partner to paraphrase, in his or her own words, what the essay is about.

3. By listening to your partner, you will hear what your intended reader will get from your paper. Are you satisfied with your partner's paraphrase? If not, who is at fault—you, because your paper does not include what you thought was in it, or your partner, because she or he did not listen to your reading of your paper with complete concentration? Discuss the results of the unwriting exercise with your partner until you know what you should include, alter, move, or perhaps eliminate in your paper.

4. You can vary this exercise by asking your partner to present a précis or an outline. If your partner has done a fine job, you should be able to note any deficiencies in your paper and, as a result, revise it with confidence.

EXERCISE 6 ▶ Unwriting and Graphics

A **graphic** shows relationships in visual form. For a variation of Exercise 5, have your partner read your essay and then draw a graphic of its organization and content. (See pages 217–232 for examples of graphics such as pigeonholes, comparison-contrast ladders, and flowcharts.) By seeing the essentials of your essay on ladders, pigeonholes, a flowchart, or a mandala (see page 249), you will readily see that you may need to include more supporting details or that your method of organization is illogical or items are out of order. By completing the graphic that your partner has drawn, you will be able to revise your paper more easily.

EXERCISE 7 ▶ The Twenty-five-Word Summary

In this exercise, you are to ask your partner for a piece of writing. Your task is to summarize the selection in twenty-five words. Whether a word is one letter or twenty letters, you should consider it as one word. (The author's name and the title of the selection, which you should include in your summary, will *not*, however, count toward the twenty-five words.)

If in your early draft, you have two or three words too many, you must eliminate them; a twenty-five word summary is not the place for repetitions, passive voice, weak verbs (*be*, *seems*, *says*, *has*, *appears*, *feels*), or ineffective adjectives and adverbs.

The benefits of writing a twenty-five-word summary are many:

practicing "unwriting,"
ensuring that you understand the meaning of a selection,
choosing exact, powerful words,
improving your vocabulary, and
using precise punctuation.

Before you write your twenty-five-word summary, read the following example. It summarizes the excerpt from *The Last Chance Energy Book* beginning on page 286.

[Owen Phillips, in *The Last Chance Energy Book,*] states that solar energy, although used in Western Australia, is probably a partial, not a complete, solution to the problem of America's future energy needs.

"Most of the basic material a writer works with is acquired before the age of fifteen."

WILLA CATHER

Second Workshop: Style

About the Second Workshop

In this section you will find exercises and special writing assignments to help you improve particular aspects of your writing. At times you may need to refer to a dictionary, thesaurus, or handbook. Perhaps your writing teacher will recommend specific reference books so that you and your classmates will be using the same authorities when you do an exercise.

You can apply each chapter to any writing you are doing. If you are writing, for example, an exposition and are worrying about your word choice, look at Chapter 30. If you are writing a letter and want to include a figurative comparison, look at Chapter 33. If you are working on a research paper and want to make sure your bibliography is correct, look at Chapter 36.

If you take some time to discover what the Second Workshop contains, you can then turn to a particular chapter or exercise and use it to help you fulfill a particular need. If you cannot decide which chapter to begin with, do the first few. Your teacher/editor or your peers may suggest that you should work on a particular chapter so that you can sharpen an aspect of your writing.

The Second Workshop is designed so that you work with one other person: a classmate at school as well as a friend or relative at home. Although you can get some benefit from working alone, you really need someone to talk to, to check with, and to ask and answer questions.

Whenever possible, talk through the exercises with your partner rather than write them out. You will be able to do many more exercises this way.

You, with the help of your teacher, should decide which chapters and exercises you need to do. Sometimes you should do an entire chapter; sometimes not. Sometimes you may start at the beginning of a chapter; sometimes in the middle. If only one partner needs to do a chapter, however, the other should act as an adviser and help her or his partner. (By teaching your partner, you will learn new things yourself.) The important thing to remember in using the Second Workshop is that it should fulfill *your* writing needs.

Each chapter ends with a writing project that you can do *for* your partner. It is possible for you to do the project for your teacher/editor as well.

30 Style

Every day you encounter things with style: clothes, music, telephones, stores, and so on. Writing also has style—qualities that distinguish the work of one writer from that of another.

Most beginning writers consider a personal writing style difficult to define and impossible to achieve. They believe only the professionals—the Shakespeares, the Hemingways, the Weltys—can create a writing style. This chapter attempts to disprove this myth and shows you how to identify your own writing style.

EXERCISE 1 ▶ Style in Comics

1. You and your partner bring to class the comics from a Sunday newspaper.

2. Determine which is the most *formal* comic strip, that is, the one that is most sophisticated or the one using above-average dialogue and cartooning techniques. Support your answers by saying two or three specific things about each of the following: the cartooning technique, the subject, the story line, the uses of color, and the dialogue of the characters.

Example

"Prince Valiant" is the most formal. The artist draws realistic pictures instead of cartoons; the use of color makes each panel seem like an oil painting; the story line is about the high deeds of knights in King Arthur's time; and the dialogue—not placed in balloons—communicates the serious thoughts of the characters.

3. When you have discussed all the specific things about each comic strip, choose an overall word to describe the style of each strip. This word should cover all the specific comments you made about the strip.

Example

The style of "Prince Valiant" is *dignified*.

EXERCISE 2 ▶ *Dialogue for Comics*

1. At home, find a comic strip from a newspaper that is a few weeks old (so your partner will not remember it). Cut out the words in all the balloons and bring the comic strip to class.

2. Give each other blank comic strips in order to supply each balloon with formal dialogue that fits the characters and the situation. When finished, discuss the appropriateness of the dialogue to the comic strip. (If the cartooning style is informal, for example, the dialogue should not be formal.)

3. Now each of you supply each balloon with the dialogue that you think the creator of the comic strip wrote. When finished, compare yours with the original. How close were you? Were yours and the creator's style close? What word would you use to describe the overall style of the original comic strip?

4. Provide appropriate dialogue for this cartoon:

EXERCISE 3 ▶ Newspaper Styles

1. Each of you bring an entire newspaper and a pair of scissors to class.
2. Cut out the photos that you think are the most serious, the most comic, and the most sensational.
3. Exchange photos. Label your partner's photos *serious*, *comic*, and *sensational*. Then each of you think of five reasons for your choices.
4. Discuss your reasons with your partner.
5. Each of you can then cut out ads that you think are the most *dignified*, the most *comic*, and the most *sensational*. Exchange ads and follow points 3 and 4 once again.
6. Each of you cut out two headlines from different newspapers: one headline that you think is sensationally misleading and one that is completely factual. Exchange headlines with their accompanying articles. After reading the article, rewrite each headline so that you change its style.

Example

You can change the sensationally misleading MILLIONS WILL STARVE to the completely factual WHEAT SHORTAGE FEARED.

7. Each of you cut out several letters to the editor. Your task is to arrange them in order from the most cautiously written to the most aggressively written. When finished, discuss your arrangement with your partner, giving specific reasons.
8. Each of you cut out articles that have the following styles: serious, comic, sensational, matter-of-fact, dull, exciting. Exchange articles and discuss your reasons for your choices.

EXERCISE 4 ▶ Topic vs. Style

1. Bring to class at least three different articles that deal with exactly the same topic. (If you like, one can be from your daily newspaper, one from a weekly newspaper, and one from a news magazine such as *Time* or *Newsweek*.)
2. Exchange your three articles with your partner.
3. Read the articles, carefully noting the similarities and differences. Jot down the differences in order to determine the style of the article. Take into account these fundamentals:

a) Vocabulary contributes to style. Words can be classified as formal, colloquial, or slang.
b) Attitude contributes to style. A writer can take a positive or negative approach to the topic. A sincere, direct piece is quite different from a comically satiric piece.
c) The length of sentences can also contribute to style. One can write entire selections with short, direct sentences (under ten words), with long involved sentences (over thirty words), or with a combination of short-, long-, and medium-length sentences.
d) A writer can develop the thesis in specific, concrete ways or in more general, abstract ways.
e) If a writer uses too many rhetorical devices too often, the style may seem contrived, rather than natural.
f) Sometimes a writer may use many figurative comparisons (even lengthy analogies); other times she or he may use no figures of speech at all.
g) Point of view affects style. Sometimes a writer uses a persona rather than his or her own voice.

4. In determining style, try to place each piece you read on a scale between very aggressive and very cautious. Then find details to support your decision.

5. Discuss each of your articles with your partner. Use the fundamentals presented in number 3 above to discuss stylistic differences. You may both want to practice on the following three articles and discuss the questions following the articles before you work on the three articles that you have found.

Example One

Ottawa—Canadian Ambassador to Iran Kenneth Taylor announced at a press conference today the details of the concealment and subsequent departure from Iran of six American diplomats.

For almost three months, the six, escapees from the besieged American Embassy in Tehran, hid in the Canadian Embassy basement and in the residence of Ambassador and Mrs. Taylor and that of an embassy staff member. Last week they were smuggled out of Iran, using forged Canadian passports, and flown to West Germany.

The six were identified as Robert G. Anders, Kathleen and Joseph Stafford, Cora and Mark Lijek, and Henry Lee Schatz.

Example Two

To Americans he has become known as the Scarlet Pimpernel, after the dashing fictional hero who helped French nobles escape the guillotine. Smiling, curly-haired Canadian Ambassador to Iran Ken Taylor outdid his fictional forebear by spiriting six American diplomats out from under the noses of Moslem terrorists and the Ayatollah Khomeini's Revolutionary Guard and on the way to safety in West Germany.

Already calls are coming from Americans throughout the United States declaring that Ken is an American hero. His picture appears on the front page of *Time*; a ticker-tape parade is held in his honor, in New York City; he has achieved celebrity status on the talk shows; and he will be the subject of a best-selling nonfiction paperback and a prime-time TV production.

Example Three

The usual battleship gray of an Ottawa day, the sort of day that makes bureaucrats glad to be alive because it matches their personality so well, turned into the first day of spring to welcome Canada's newest golden boy, Ambassador to Iran Ken Taylor.

At today's news conference, this tousle-haired, genially reluctant hero grinned modestly as he proclaimed his exploit to be "part of the job." Taylor told the full story of hiding six American diplomats under the Ayatollah's long nose and the Moslem fanatics' watchful guard. Taylor also related how he and his staff obtained forged Canadian passports for the Americans and escorted them through the heavily guarded airport to a plane bound for West Germany and freedom.

Thank you, Ken Taylor.

For Discussion

1. Which of the three articles is easiest to read? Why?
2. Which one mixes levels of vocabulary? Provide examples.
3. Which one contains the longest sentence?
4. Which is developed in the most specific, concrete way?
5. Which is developed in the most subtle, abstract way?
6. Which contains figurative language? Provide examples.
7. Which writer is closest to the reader?
8. Which is the most personal? impersonal?
9. Which is the most aggressive? cautious? Provide examples.
10. What word would you use to describe the overall style of each article? Use the list of words in Exercise 5.

EXERCISE 5 ▶ Your Style

Being able to recognize style in something you read is useful, but it is even more important to acquire your own writing style. Your background has a definite influence on your writing style: your age, education, experiences, travel, amount and kind of reading, interests, opportunities, and so on. You should not think of your writing style as better or worse than someone else's style—just different. Perhaps you never thought that you had a writing style. Well, think again.

1. To prove that you have style, you and your partner apply the points presented in Exercise 4 to your most recent assignment. As you discuss each idea, find specific details to support your statements. End the exercise by using one of these terms to describe your style:

cautious	aggressive	mixed
ironic	straightforward	colloquial
distinguished	technical	abstract
objective	informative	vigorous
easy-to-read	conversational	dignified
impressive	familiar	eloquent
moving	stiff	journalistic
down-to-earth	slangy	formal
breezy	didactic	comic
uneven	confusing	direct
serious	sincere	humorous
concrete	impersonal	consistent
subjective	informal	abstract
personal	ambiguous	rambling

2. Now, reverse the exercise by analyzing your partner's latest piece of writing.

3. Conclude this exercise by discussing whether or not you are satisfied with your writing style. If not, what must you change? Talk about how you can make the changes.

EXERCISE 6 ▶ Persona

Most of what you will write will be from your own personal point of view. It is possible for you, however, to pretend that you are someone else and write with a different personality (**persona**) in order to fulfill a different purpose for a particular piece of writing. Have you ever imitated someone else's way of talking in order to give an impression of that person? If so, you have already used a persona.

1. With your partner, read these three pieces by Mark Twain.

A proud moment for me? I should think so. Yonder was Arthur, King of Britain; yonder was Guinevere; yes, and whole tribes of little provincial kings and kinglets; and in the tented camp yonder, renowned knights from many lands; and likewise the selectest body known to chivalry, the Knights of the Table Round, the most illustrious in Christendom; and biggest fact of all, the very sun of their shining system was yonder couching his lance, the focal point of forty thousand adoring eyes; and all by myself, here was I laying for him. Across my mind flitted the dear image of a certain hello-girl of West Hartford, and I wished she could see me now. In that moment, down came the Invincible, the rush of a whirlwind—the courtly world rose to its feet and bent forward—the fateful coils went circling through the air, and before you could wink I was towing Sir Launcelot across the field on his back, and kissing my hand to the storm of waving kerchiefs and the thunder-crash of applause that greeted me!

A Connecticut Yankee in King Arthur's Court

It was a real bully circus. It was the splendidest sight that ever was when they all come riding in, two and two, and gentlemen and lady, side by side, the men just in their drawers and undershirts, and no shoes nor stirrups, and resting their hands on their thighs easy and comfortable—there must'a' been twenty of them—and every lady with a lovely complexion, and perfectly beautiful, and looking just like a gang of real sure-enough queens, and dressed in clothes that cost millions of dollars, and just littered with diamonds. It was a powerful fine sight; I never see anything so lovely. And then one by one they got up and stood, and went a-weaving around the ring so gentle and wavy and graceful, the men looking ever so tall and airy and straight, with their heads bobbing and skimming along, away up there under the tent-roof, and every lady's rose-leafy dress flapping soft and silky around her hips, and she looking like the most loveliest parasol.

The Adventures of Huckleberry Finn

First, we drew up my principal's will. I insisted upon this, and stuck to my point. I said I had never heard of a man in his right mind going out to fight a duel without first making his will. He said he had never heard of a man in his right mind doing anything of the kind. When he had finished the will, he wished to proceed to a choice of his "last words." He wanted to know how the following words, as a dying exclamation, struck me:

"I die for my God, for my country, for freedom of speech, for progress, and the universal brotherhood of man!"

I objected that this would require too lingering a death; it was a good speech for a consumptive, but not suited to the exigencies of the field of honor. We wrangled over a good many ante-mortem outbursts, but I finally got him to cut his obituary down to this, which he copied into his memorandum-book, purposing to get it by heart:

"I DIE THAT FRANCE MAY LIVE."

I said that this remark seemed to lack relevancy; but he said relevancy was a matter of no consequence in last words, what you wanted was thrill.

"The Great French Duel"

2. It may be hard for you to believe that these pieces were written by the same writer, but indeed they were. You may conclude, after reading the pieces, that Mark Twain was a most accomplished writer. Discuss the following questions until you and your partner agree on the answers:

a) What can you deduce about the identity of each persona? What sort of person is each?
b) For what purpose has Twain assumed each persona?
c) How do the differences in sentence structure and word choice reflect the purpose of each piece?
d) If you had a chance to read one of the entire selections from which these excerpts were taken, which one would it be? Why?

3. In *Gulliver's Travels*, Jonathan Swift assumes the persona of an adventurous young doctor. Harper Lee assumes the persona of Scout, a young girl, to narrate *To Kill a Mockingbird*. Can you think of other writers who have assumed a persona?

4. Tell your partner what you felt about watching a recent movie, TV show, or sports event.

5. Now assume the persona of someone who did not like the performance.

6. Now assume the persona of a visitor from another planet who is bewildered by the antics of human beings.

EXERCISE 7 ▶ Detecting Style

You and your partner say at least five specific things about the style of each of these selections. Use the items in Exercise 4 to get you thinking. Then choose one word to describe the overall style of each selection.

1. Lemons
by Mary-Lou Gazeley

Lemons were used by Elizabethans to cleanse their teeth and to lighten the skin. You can make a hair rinse from lemon juice that will remove every last trace of shampoo and add shine. Use the juice of half a lemon, strained and diluted in a glass of water, then follow with a rinse of cool, clear water.

2. Cale Yarborough's Camaro

Cale's Camaro weighs 2,531 pounds and has a 350-cubic-inch engine that's been bored out to 393 cubic inches, and it'll pound out 600 horsepower. The body sits on an "outlaw" frame; that is, a 108-inch chassis designed for small, backwoods U.S. racetracks—and that's the trick that has gotten it into Le Mans in its GTO category, right in there with the BMWs and other good stuff, all of which come up to about the door handles of Cale's car. It's a real stock car, and the only things on it that ever saw a Camaro production line are the taillights.

3. from *Pilgrim at Tinker Creek*
by Annie Dillard

Darkness appalls and light dazzles; the scrap of visible light that doesn't hurt my eyes hurts my brain. What I see sets me swaying. Size and distance and the sudden swelling of meanings confuse me, bowl me over. I straddle the sycamore log bridge over Tinker Creek in the summer. I look at the lighted creek bottom: snail tracks tunnel the mud in quavering curves. A crayfish jerks, but by the time I absorb what has happened, he's gone in a billowing smokescreen of silt. I look at the water: minnows and shiners. If I'm thinking minnows, a carp will fill my brain till I scream. I look at the water's surface: skaters, bubbles, and leaves sliding down. Suddenly, my own face, reflected, startles me witless. Those snails have been tracking my face! Finally, with a shuddering wrench of the will, I see clouds, cirrus clouds. I'm dizzy, I fall in. This looking business is risky.

4. Autobiography of a Tumbleweed
by John McLean, student

Born of the Earth, sheared from my umbilical stalk by the wind's sharp knife, I begin my journey. Gathering momentum and scraps of debris to round and fill my personality, I'm suddenly trapped by a barbed wire fence. The struggle for freedom only causes more misery from the twisted, devilish barbs. Finally, after gaining freedom, I wearily roll down the hill to spin lazily in the ditch; I cross the road only to be struck by a car, then land in the opposite ditch. Fences, roads, cars, hills—all are the obstacles of my life. Again, my courage must be found to fight and escape, my will steeled to overcome mental and physical barriers. When all goes well, open fields and good rolling are mine, but a house, fence, or rusting farm equipment may lie waiting. At worst a farmer's son can set a match to me; then, I go up in a puff of smoke. So ends my existence, my life as a tumbleweed.

5. "1 Corinthians 13"

Love is patient and kind; love is not jealous or boastful; it is not arrogant or rude. Love does not insist on its own way; it is not irritable or resentful; it does not rejoice at wrong, but rejoices in the right. Love bears all things, believes all things, hopes all things, endures all things.

Love never ends; as for prophecy, it will pass away; as for tongues, they will cease; as for knowledge, it will pass away. For our knowledge is imperfect and our prophecy is imperfect; but when the perfect comes, the imperfect will pass away. When I was a child, I spoke like a child, I thought like a child, I reasoned like a child; when I became a man, I gave up childish ways. For now we see in a mirror dimly, but then face to face. Now I know in part; then I shall understand fully, even as I have been fully understood. So faith, hope, love abide, these three; but the greatest of these is love.

Special Writing Assignment

Choose not only a limited topic but also a persona that you think will interest your partner, and write a short selection. Concentrate on unifying the content, tone, word choice, and sentence structure so that you achieve a distinctive style. Once you have chosen a persona, do not be afraid to put yourself entirely into your persona's position. Write firmly, using the style of the persona.

Make sure you have a full set of writing variables before you draft your special writing assignment. After you have written a draft, ask your partner to point out instances where you could improve your style by adding, subtracting, or substituting.

31 Sentence Variety

In this chapter you have the opportunity to study the infinite variety of sentence structures with someone else, asking questions, testing emphasis, and clearing up problems.

EXERCISE 1 ▶ Simple to Complex

Every sentence contains one basic idea, but some sentences add to the basic idea, making the sentence's idea more complex.

Simple Idea

Bobby Jones set a record.

Complex Idea

In 1930 the great golfer Bobby Jones set a record, which still stands, by winning the U.S. Open, the U.S. Amateur, the British Open, and the British Amateur tournaments.

1. Do you see the simple idea, *Bobby Jones set a record*, within the complex idea?
2. You and your partner should now work separately to convert these simple ideas into more complex ones.

   a) Babe Didrikson Zaharias played golf.
   b) Tom Watson won money.
   c) Nancy Lopez attracts fans.

d) The golfer made a hole in one.

e) The young golfer won a university scholarship.

3. Compare your sentences. Chances are that no sentence is identical to another. Already you are noticing the possibilities of sentence variety.

EXERCISE 2 ▸ Complex to Simple

The reverse process is just as easy to apply. To be able to isolate the parts of a complex idea is useful when you practice sentence combining.

Complex Idea

The gymnast earned a perfect score of 10 points while performing flawlessly in the floor exercises.

By taking every important word, you can put the parts into simple sentences.

Parts

There is a gymnast.
The gymnast earned a score.
The score was perfect.
The score was 10 points.
The gymnast performed.
The performance was flawless.
The gymnast performed in the floor exercises.

1. Working separately from your partner, break these sentences into their parts.

a) Vivacious American gymnast Mary Lou Retton won several gold medals at the 1984 Summer Olympics.

b) The People's Republic of China sent an impressive gymnastics team to the Los Angeles Olympics.

c) Cathy Rigby was the first American gymnast to win a medal in the Olympics.

d) Olga Korbut and Nadia Comaneci inspired thousands of young people throughout the world to start gymnastics training.

2. Compare your sentence parts with your partner's. They should be nearly the same.

EXERCISE 3 ▶ Sentence Combinations

Notice how you might break down the following sentence into seven parts, each a sentence with a simple idea.

The talented young skater executed a perfect triple axel and won a gold medal.

Sentences with Simple Ideas

There is a skater.
The skater is young.
The skater is talented.
The skater executed a perfect jump.
The jump was a triple axel.
The skater won a medal.
It was a gold medal.

Read over some of the different ways of combining these sentences with simple ideas.

a) After executing a perfect triple axel, the talented young skater won a gold medal.
b) The talented young skater who executed a perfect triple axel won a gold medal.
c) By executing a perfect triple axel, the talented young skater won a gold medal.
d) The talented young skater who had executed a perfect triple axel won a gold medal.
e) A gold medal was won by the talented young skater who executed a perfect triple axel.
f) The talented young skater, the one who executed a perfect triple axel, won the gold medal.
g) A perfect triple axel was executed by the talented young skater who won a gold medal.
h) Executing a perfect triple axel, the talented young skater won a gold medal.
i) With a perfectly executed triple axel, the talented young skater won a gold medal.

See how many ways you and your partner can combine the sentences on the next page.

308 WRITING: PROCESS TO PRODUCT

1. *Sentence with Two Ideas*

   Rosalynn Sumners won a silver medal at the 1984 Winter Olympics. She had won the 1983 U.S. Championship.

2. *Sentence with Three Ideas*

   In 1980 Eric Heiden set a record.
   He won five Olympic gold medals.
   He was a speed skater.

3. *Sentence with Four Ideas*

   Jayne Torvill and Christopher Dean were ice dancers.
   They were from Great Britain.
   They won Olympic gold medals.
   They retired after the 1984 world championships.

EXERCISE 4 ▶ *Rearranging*

Because there are so many ways of combining sentences, you will need to determine which combination serves your purpose. If you are dissatisfied with the way you have written one of your sentences, rearrange the most important words to achieve the greatest impact for a specific purpose and audience. Often, the best places for key words are at the beginning and end of sentences.

Example

a) In the 1981 Wimbledon tennis finals, five-time champion Bjorn Borg lost to American John McEnroe on a hot July day before a packed Centre Court.

b) Five-time champion Bjorn Borg lost to John McEnroe in the 1981 Wimbledon tennis finals on a hot July day before a packed Centre Court.

c) In the 1981 Wimbledon tennis finals on a hot July day before a packed Centre Court, five-time champion Bjorn Borg lost to American John McEnroe.

1. Which of the above sentences creates the most impact? Why? The least impact? Why?

2. You and your partner should separately rearrange the parts of the following sentences to create the greatest impact for an imagined audi-

ence and purpose. First pick out the idea you want to stress and place it in a position of importance.

- a) Over the last ten years, because of extensive television coverage, tennis has become a very popular sport in North America and around the world.
- b) Tennis has become such a popular and profitable sport that many parents send their talented children to tennis camps so that they can receive professional training.
- c) The Davis Cup, open to both amateur and professional players, is a world championship frequently won by American players.
- d) Coveted by every player is the "Grand Slam" of tennis, for which in one year a player must win the Australian Open, Wimbledon, the French Open, and the United States Open.

3. Compare and discuss the impact of your sentences.

EXERCISE 5 ▶ *Emphasizing*

1. Working separately, you and your partner should combine each group of ideas into a single sentence in what you consider the best way. Concentrate on making your sentence emphatic.

- a) Richard Petty is probably the most famous stock car racer of all time.
  His father, Lee Petty, was a champion driver.
  His son, Kyle, is also a driver.
  He holds a number of NASCAR records.
- b) She was the first woman licensed to run Top Fuel dragsters in the United States.
  Her story was told in the film *Heart Like a Wheel*.
  She is from Michigan.
  Her name is Shirley Muldowney.
- c) Most auto races take place on special tracks.
  The Brickyard at Indianapolis is the most famous auto racing track in the United States.
  Grand Prix races take place on city streets.
  A Grand Prix race is held every year in Detroit.
- d) A. J. Foyt has won 67 championship races.
  He has won the Indianapolis 500 four times.
  He has finished second at Indianapolis twice.
  He also won the Grand Prix at Le Mans in 1967.

e) Many people consider auto racing a dangerous sport.
Talented drivers have been killed during races.
Two of these drivers were Jim Clark and Gilles Villeneuve.
Auto racing is still a very popular spectator sport.

2. Compare and discuss your and your partner's sentences and decide which are more emphatic.

EXERCISE 6 ▶ Subtracting

So far you have had practice in combining and rearranging in order to create emphatic sentences. By subtracting certain unnecessary words, you can give even more emphasis and variety to your sentences.

Example

From

The team of male basketball players that represented the United States of America in the Olympic Games held in Los Angeles in the summer of 1984 won first place and was awarded a gold medal.

To

The U.S. men's Olympic basketball team won a gold medal at the 1984 Summer Olympics in Los Angeles.

Working with your partner, subtract the unnecessary words from these sentences.

a) Men whose height is greater than seven feet now appear on a regular basis in basketball as played by both professional and college teams.
b) Wilt Chamberlain, who bore the nickname of "The Stilt" because he was so tall, played professional basketball and also played professional volleyball.
c) If a professional basketball player commits more than five infractions that are considered personal fouls, the player is disqualified and forbidden to play any more in that game.
d) Bill Russell played in the position of center for the Boston Celtics basketball team, and he was also the first black person to coach a major professional team because he coached the Boston Celtics from 1965 to 1969.

e) The University of California at Los Angeles, which has a basketball team that is called the Bruins, has had more players from its team join the National Basketball Association than has any other college or university.

EXERCISE 7 ▶ *Expanding*

If you are always aware of your audience when you write, you will strive to create the best possible impact by combining, rearranging, and subtracting ideas. If there is the possibility that your reader may be confused, you should also be prepared to expand your ideas to make them clearer. By posing the questions *who, what, where, when, why,* and *how,* you may discover the effectiveness of adding something extra to a sentence.

Needs expanding for clarity:

Tom Dempsey kicked a field goal to set a record.

Key Idea: kicking a field goal

Who: Tom Dempsey of New Orleans
When: Nov. 8, 1970
Where: in a game against Detroit
Why: to set a record
How: it traveled 63 yards
What: (already indicated)

Notice the process of *combining, rearranging,* and *expanding*.

a) On Nov. 8, 1970, in a game against Detroit, Tom Dempsey of New Orleans kicked a field goal that traveled 63 yards to set a record.
b) Tom Dempsey of New Orleans set a record on Nov. 8, 1970, in a game against Detroit, when he kicked a field goal that traveled 63 yards.
c) During a game against Detroit on Nov. 8, 1970, Tom Dempsey of New Orleans set a record when he kicked a 63-yard field goal.

1. Does one sentence show the most emphasis through combining, rearranging, and expanding, or are they equally emphatic?

2. You and your partner should work separately to expand each of the following key ideas into a full sentence. Then present to each other the one sentence which you consider the most emphatic. Discuss the effectiveness of each choice.

playing high-school football
playing in the school band
seeing a Super Bowl game
becoming a cheerleader

EXERCISE 8 ▸ *Reforming*

1. Using **rearrangement** and **subtraction**, combine the following sentences into one well-formed paragraph. You and your partner should work separately, making sure your sentences are varied. Use some short sentences, some long. Put key words first in some, last in others. Make sure, though, that your whole paragraph flows logically and smoothly.

Soccer is a popular game. It is played all over the world. Few Americans watch it. Even fewer play it. Outside North America, soccer is called "football." More people watch soccer than any other sport. A soccer team consists of eleven players. One player is the goalkeeper. Only the goalkeeper can pick up the ball. The other players move the ball around the field. They can kick the ball. They can bounce the ball off their heads. The players try to score goals. The team with more goals wins the game. Soccer is not a complicated game. It is exciting and challenging.

2. When you both finish, compare the variety of your sentences and the emphasis of your paragraphs.

EXERCISE 9 ▶ Kinds of Sentences

All of the sentences used in Exercises 1 to 8 have made statements (declarations). **Declarative sentences** are the most common in English. There are three other types of sentences, however, that can add variety to your writing: **questions**, **exclamations**, and **commands**.
Notice what you can achieve without using a declaration:

Who was the greatest baseball player of all time? Stop and think a minute. Was it the fabulous Babe Ruth, probably one of the most popular sports figures of all time? "Hammerin' Hank" Aaron, who broke the Babe's home-run record? Ty Cobb, "the Georgia Peach," whose career hit record has stood for more than fifty years? Or was it perhaps a pitcher, such as Walter Johnson, who pitched an astounding 113 shutouts during his career? Don't forget more recent players such as Pete Rose and Nolan Ryan! Hard to decide, isn't it?

1. Notice the punctuation of each of the sentences. Which are questions? Exclamations? Commands?

2. Although you should not overuse these three kinds of sentences in your writing, try to write a paragraph without using a single declaration.

3. Ask your partner to check that you have not used any declarative sentences and that your paragraph holds together.

EXERCISE 10 ▶ Minor Sentences

In your early writing days, you learned that a sentence is a group of words with a subject and a verb. If you forgot the subject or the verb, you were told your sentence was incomplete. You had written a sentence fragment, and that was taboo. So through your schooling you avoided anything resembling a fragment and spent those years perfecting whole sentences. Complete thoughts.

But writers do use fragments in order to communicate. (Which sentence in the preceding paragraph is a fragment? Did you understand it? Also, did you spot the question fragments in the paragraph in Exercise 9 about the "best baseball player of all time"? You can easily supply the missing parts of these **minor sentences** from the context, so you will not misunderstand the sentences.)

1. Perhaps the following paragraph uses the rhetorical fragment excessively. But how does the style of the writing relate to its topic? Do the minor sentences communicate complete thoughts?

> Sunday afternoon. Crisp fall weather. Time for football! Off to the stadium. Pep rallies. Tailgate parties. Thousands of fans. Bands. Cheerleaders. Go team! Touchdown! We won! What greater thrill can there be than a well-played game and victory?

2. You and your partner can each write a short piece where you use at least one minor sentence.

3. Exchange your pieces of writing and discuss whether you have written a rhetorical fragment (that works) or a fragment fault (that needs revision).

Special Writing Assignment

On a topic that you think will interest your partner, write a paragraph in which you include various kinds of sentences, including minor sentences. Ask your partner to discuss the effectiveness of your sentence variety.

Before you write your paragraph, read the following one. Comment on its effectiveness in fulfilling the Special Writing Assignment.

> Has this workshop whetted your appetite? If so, you should plan to spend time learning the finer details of sentence variety. You can work alone. At your own pace. In school. At home. Anywhere. Any time. Start right away! By experimenting with sentence variety, you will have acquired the habit of good writing. And once acquired, the habit will be yours for life.

32 Rhetorical Devices

Rhetorical devices are techniques that you can use to create a certain effect on an audience. When used with discretion, rhetorical devices can help achieve your purpose—that is, to emphasize, to shock, to add humor, to draw attention to word choice, to create suspense, and so on. Some rhetorical devices mentioned in this chapter have been included in other parts of *Writing: Process to Product*. Therefore, only the ones not found elsewhere will be discussed in detail.

EXERCISE 1 ▶ Examples of Rhetorical Devices

Read through each rhetorical device with your partner and discuss what purpose it serves. Take turns thinking of a new example of each rhetorical device before you go on to the next one.

1. Use a **rhetorical question** when you want to ask a question to which the answer is already known or implied.

Can anyone deny that video tapes will revolutionize the film industry?

2. Use **abnormal word order**—a variation on the usual subject-verb sentence pattern—to give variety and emphasis to your writing.

Normal Word Order (Subject-Verb)

The inspiration for rock superstar Prince's film *Purple Rain* came from his own life.

Abnormal Word Order (Verb-Subject)

From his own life came the inspiration for rock superstar Prince's film *Purple Rain*.

3. Use a **minor sentence** or **rhetorical fragment** when a full sentence is not necessary for sense.

Who won an Oscar as Best Actress for her role in *Terms of Endearment*? Shirley MacLaine.

Lights! Camera! Action!

4. Use **repetition** for emphasis and rhythm.

Genevieve Bujold played Queen Anne Boleyn, the queen for whom Henry VIII broke with the Catholic Church, in *Anne of a Thousand Days*.

5. Use a **pun** when you want to play with words.

Michael Sarrazin was murdered twice in *The Reincarnation of Peter Proud*. Now that is overkill!

The talented Jack Nicholson, who has played a great variety of roles, could be called a "Jack-of-all-parts."

6. Use **exaggeration (hyperbole)** when you want to emphasize a fact.

Boris Karloff was so scary in the movies that no one would dare speak to him in real life for fear of having his or her blood congeal.

Bela Lugosi became so famous as Dracula that blood banks locked their doors when they saw him coming.

7. Use **understatement (litotes)** when you want to create the reverse effect (and add a touch of irony) by making the fact seem less significant.

Harrison Ford's most famous character, Indiana Jones, has occasionally found himself in a bit of a jam.

8. Use **climactic parallelism**—going from least to most important—when you wish to present several facts in order of importance.

Sally Field's roles have ranged from Gidget and the Flying Nun through companion to Burt Reynolds in *Smokey and the Bandit* to her Academy Award winning roles in *Norma Rae* and *Places in the Heart*.

9. Use a **balanced sentence** when you wish to express two or more equal and parallel ideas.

In 1946 Donna Reed was the love of James Stewart's life in *It's a Wonderful Life*, and in 1984, she was the love of J. R. Ewing's life—his mother, Miss Ellie—on *Dallas*.

10. Use **opposites** when you want to contrast two opposing ideas.

Gina Lollobrigida, a star in front of the camera, has also had a successful career behind the camera as a photographer.

11. Use **reversals (chiasmus)** when you want to make a balanced sentence even more memorable.

Many of the characters John Wayne portrayed would have agreed with the saying: "When the going gets tough, the tough get going."

12. Use a **periodic sentence** when you wish to withhold an important part of the sentence until the end. The sentence should not make complete sense until you have read the last word.

From his beginnings in film, in a supporting role in *The Woman of Dolwyn*, through Shakespeare and Edward Albee, to his last role, with his daughter Kate in the miniseries *Ellis Island*, strode one of Britain's greatest gifts to American film, Richard Burton.

13. Use a **figurative comparison** when you wish to present your audience with a strong image. (Figurative comparisons are discussed more fully in Chapter 33.)

Sylvester Stallone shines like a diamond in the rough in the *Rocky* films, but he only twinkles like a *Rhinestone* next to Dolly Parton.

14. Use an **allusion** when you want to save yourself a great number of words, and you think your audience will appreciate the reference. (Allusions are discussed more fully on pages 326–327.)

Her roles in films such as *E.T.* and *Irreconcilable Differences* have made Drew Barrymore the Shirley Temple of the 1980s.

15. Use **alliteration**—repetition of the initial sounds of words—to draw attention to a string of words.

From an Egyptian temptress in *Land of the Pharaohs* to Alexis Carrington in *Dynasty*, Joan Collins has played characters who were stunning, scheming, and slick.

16. Use **rhyme** to make two or more words memorable.

In 1984 Bill Murray was both frightened (in *Ghostbusters*) and enlightened (in *The Razor's Edge*).

17. Use **onomatopoeia**—words that imitate or suggest sounds—when you want to draw attention to the sound of a word.

Today's films are as likely to feature the beeps and buzzes of computers as the chirps of birds. Cascading waterfalls have been replaced by humming machines and whirring laser swords.

18. Use **underlining (italics)** to emphasize certain words.

Many Americans would be amazed to know that Mary Pickford, known as "America's Sweetheart," was born <u>Canadian</u> Gladys Smith.

EXERCISE 2 ▸ Publicity and Rhetorical Devices

Can you and your partner find these rhetorical devices in "The Shape of Things to Come": alliteration, climactic parallelism, exaggeration, rhetorical fragment, pun, rhyming words, rhetorical question, and opposites?

The Shape of Things to Come
by Patricia Davies, student

Hey, guys and gals! If you've been dreaming about a slim, strong, sleek physique, now is the time to *do* something about it.

If you're pining for a willowy figure, and want to whittle the excess "waste" off your trunk, there's no need to be stumped for a solution. We have numerous branches in the city ready to help you.

In our centers, there are as many different kinds of equipment as there are clients. Everyone can find facilities to suit his or her taste: an indoor track, a dance studio, an exercise room, a swimming pool, a sauna, a whirlpool, and even a licensed restaurant.

Some people visit "The Shape of Things to Come" to enlarge their bodies; others go there to shrink them. We design programs to suit each person's individual needs.

Come and have a personal talk with one of our thousands of helpful representatives. They will be pleased to provide you with full details on all our equipment and programs.

Who doesn't want to look great? A dynamic physical appearance can be a great confidence builder when looking for employment and when meeting new people.

Use your head! Think ahead! The time to start doing something is *now*. Satisfaction guaranteed or money refunded.

Special Writing Assignment

In the future, consider using a few of these tricks of a writer's trade. An effective rhetorical device can often enliven a dull patch of prose. Use these devices with discretion, however; overuse of rhetorical devices can result in an unnatural, or even unintentionally humorous, effect.

Write an advertisement in which you include at least five of the rhetorical devices discussed in this chapter. Your task in this assignment is to attract your partner's attention so that he or she will come, go, buy, sell, or do whatever you want. When you finish, list the rhetorical devices that you used so your partner knows which ones to evaluate.

33 Figurative Language and Allusions

Figurative language relies on comparison, either stated (she runs *like the wind*) or implied (she *breezed* through the exam). By using a figurative comparison, a writer can help his or her readers see something or someone in a new way.

EXERCISE 1 ▶ Literal and Figurative Comparisons

A comparison can be either literal or figurative. *She runs like an Olympic champion* is a literal, or factual, comparison. *She runs like the wind* is a figurative comparison. If taken literally, the latter expression does not make much sense!

1. Provide three literal (factual) comparisons on the appearance of a friend. You should use someone or something who actually looks like your friend. For example,

   a) Bob looks like (Henry).
   b) Bob looks like (his father looked at the same age).
   c) Bob looks a little like (Michael J. Fox).

2. Now provide three figurative comparisons. (In choosing your comparisons, you should think of at least one aspect of your friend's appearance, so that you can compare it with a similar aspect of something or someone else.)

a) Bob looks like (a young prince).
b) Bob looks like (a Greek god).
c) Bob looks like (death warmed over).

3. Check your responses with your partner to see that you have made literal and figurative comparisons.

EXERCISE 2 ▶ Original Figurative Comparisons

Working with your partner, try to complete some of these sentences with an original figurative comparison. Discuss the effectiveness of each comparison.

Getting married is like *traveling to a strange country*.
Going to sleep is like *blowing out a candle*.
Going to school is like . . .
Falling in love is like . . .
Driving a car is like . . .
Playing football (or another sport) is like . . .
Watching TV is like . . .
Going on a date is like . . .
Getting up in the morning is like . . .
Going on stage is like . . .

EXERCISE 3 ▶ Kinds of Figurative Comparisons

There are several different kinds of figurative comparisons. Read each term and example below. Then, make up a sentence about your friend, using that type of figurative comparison.

1. A **simile** is a figurative comparison that uses a word of comparison, such as *like* or *as*.

Valerie runs like a gazelle.
Valerie's temper is as hot as boiling tar.

2. A **metaphor** is a figurative comparison stating or implying that one thing is something else.

Valerie is a gazelle.
Valerie burns everyone with her temper. (This implies that she has a hot temper.)

3. **Personification** gives inanimate objects life.

The branches wrapped themselves around Valerie's arms.

4. An **allusion** makes a comparison by reference to a character from literature, mythology, history, or legend.

Valerie thinks she is Olive Oyl, but she is actually more like Princess Leia.

5. An **analogy** keeps up a figurative comparison for a certain length: sometimes a paragraph, sometimes an entire essay, or even an entire book.

> Auntie Muriel is both the spider and the fly, the sucker-out of life juice and the empty husk. Once she was just the spider and Uncle Teddy was the fly, but ever since Uncle Teddy's death Auntie Muriel has taken over both roles. Elizabeth isn't even all that sure Uncle Teddy is really dead. Auntie Muriel probably has him in a trunk somewhere in the attic, webbed in old ecru lace tablecloths, paralyzed but still alive. . . . Auntie Muriel, so palpably not an auntie. Nothing diminutive about Auntie Muriel.
>
> from *Life Before Man* by Margaret Atwood

After you have written your simile, metaphor, personification, allusion, and analogy, discuss your sentences with your partner.

EXERCISE 4 ▸ Rules for Figurative Comparisons

Once you begin to think figuratively, your writing can improve tremendously. But there are a few pitfalls to avoid when writing figurative comparisons.

Read these rules and study the examples. Then, with your partner, follow the suggestions after each rule to write a sentence with a figurative comparison.

1. *Rule One:* In a figurative comparison the two things compared are usually not alike in every respect. In order for the comparison to work, however, they must have at least one thing in common.

My aunt's sapphire eyes frightened me more than all her harsh words.

(The aunt's eyes are being compared to sapphires. Both sapphires and her eyes are blue and hard.)

Subject: a relative's eating habits.

Comparison: the way a bird eats.

2. *Rule Two:* In a figurative comparison, the object you compare your subject to should be able to do in reality what you want it to do figuratively. If your comparison does not make complete sense, your metaphor will be strained. Why does this metaphor not work?

Jim's fists stabbed his opponent like rocks.

(Generally, rocks *smash*; they do not *stab*. If the writer wanted to keep *stabbed*, to what could *rocks* be changed?)

Subject: your report card.

Comparison: a battlefield (Make sure that whatever happens in, on, or to your report card also happens on a battlefield.)

3. *Rule Three:* In a figurative comparison you should not begin with one comparison and end with another. Why would a mixed metaphor such as this be confusing?

After Susan's campaign caught fire, she snowballed her way into the presidency of the student council.

(A snowball cannot catch fire any more than a fire can snowball. What would you change *caught fire* to, if you wanted to keep *snowballed*?)

Subject: the weather

Comparison: an animal (Do not mention anything that is inconsistent with either the animal or the weather.)

EXERCISE 5 ▶ Dead Metaphors

1. When using figurative comparisons you must avoid dead metaphors, that is, metaphors that have been used too often and are now clichés. You and your partner should each study these three examples:

When she got the job at the supermarket, Nancy was *as happy as a lark*.

The principal *hit the nail on the head* when he declared that students from other schools were responsible for spray-painting our school walls.

When our houseboat sank, all our possessions went to *Davy Jones's locker*.

2. Now, you and your partner work separately, each trying to substitute new figurative comparisons for the italicized clichés. As you both do so, test each one according to the three rules in Exercise 4.

You would not use *happy* as a *swan, hit the log on the head,* or *Davy Brown's locker* because they have nothing in common with anything in the comparison (Rule One).

You would not change *happy as a lark* to *happy as a frog* because in reality a frog is not known for its cheerful noise (Rule Two).

If you changed *hit the nail on the head* to *hit the nail in the belly,* you would be mixing metaphors (Rule Three).

3. After you have compared your answers with your partner's, discuss both sets of answers in relation to the following. Are yours more original? Why?

When she got the job at the supermarket, Nancy was *as happy as a newlywed.*

The principal was *right on the mark* when he declared that students from other schools were responsible for spray-painting our school walls.

When our houseboat sank, all our possessions went *the way of the Titanic.*

4. Now, you and your partner write three sentences with dead metaphors. Give them to each other. Each must substitute three original figurative comparisons for the clichés. Evaluate your responses by applying the three rules.

EXERCISE 6 ▶ Analogy

An analogy is an extended comparison of two things that have one or more features in common. Using an effective analogy in your writing will not only catch your reader's interest but also clarify a particular idea. (The purpose for including analogies is to illustrate or make something clear. If you use an analogy to try to prove a point logically, you may produce a shaky argument.)

1. To learn how to write an analogy, work with your partner on the following activity. Assume that the subject is a friend and that you are going to compare her/him to a whirlwind. You should bring your friend to life by describing her/him in terms of the figurative comparison. As a

prewriting exercise, fill in the right column with at least ten words or phrases that you would use to describe a whirlwind. For example:

My Friend	Whirlwind
	powerful
	uncontrollable
	made up of air
	carries all before it
	can't be stopped
	must run its course

In writing your analogy, choose words from the right column to describe your subject. Because not all of the words will apply to your subject, you will not be able to use all of them. For example, a person is not made entirely of air. Also, remember when you write an analogy that you cannot use any words that describe only your subject. For example, you cannot mention a person's long, unruly hair because a whirlwind does not have hair.

Begin your piece of writing with "My friend is like _____," and use details of similarity to sustain it. When you finish, test your analogy to see that you have brought your subject to life. For example:

Effective Analogy

My friend is like a whirlwind. She is a powerful force who, once she has decided to do something, carries everyone along with her.

False Analogy

My friend is a whirlwind. She moves at eighty miles an hour, smashing windows and tearing the leaves from trees as she goes.

2. Choose either a topic of your own or one of these epigrams (short pithy sayings) and write about it, continuing the analogy until you can no longer sustain the figurative comparison.

All the world's a stage. (William Shakespeare)

Illusions are like umbrellas; you no sooner get them than you lose them. (Oscar Wilde)

Memory is the diary that we all carry about with us. (Oscar Wilde)

I am a camera with its shutter open, quite passive, not thinking. (Christopher Isherwood)

It is with rivers as it is with people: the greatest are not always the most agreeable nor the best to live with. (Henry Van Dyke)

3. Have your partner check your analogy, keeping in mind the three rules in Exercise 4.

EXERCISE 7 ▶ Allusions

An allusion is a reference (often to a work of literature) that a writer expects readers to recognize. Writers who use allusions can save themselves dozens of words. When they see a similarity between their subject and something else that they know well and expect their readers to understand, they will unhesitatingly link them together.

Readers will not fully appreciate a particular allusion unless they are familiar with the specific reference. Let us hope that as you work through this exercise, you will not find yourself like Saint Paul on the road to Damascus, blind and uncomprehending. (Do you understand this allusion?)

1. Look in recent newspapers and magazines and find five titles containing allusions. Bring them to class to share with your partner. See if she or he recognizes each reference.

Example

"The Night Stuff" refers to Tom Wolfe's *The Right Stuff*.

2. Explain the allusions in these titles:

"Tail of Two Cities"
"Oliver Twit"
"Their Town"
"Twenty Thousand Slugs Under the Leaf"
"Huckleberry Fun"

3. Find five allusions in local newspaper or magazine articles and bring them to class to share with your partner. See if he or she recognizes each reference.

4. As you examine each of the following, note the allusion (in italics). Make a record of those you definitely understand, those you could make a reasonable guess at, and those that elude you. Discuss with your partner the significance of each allusion that you recognize. (Since these were written by magazine correspondents who wanted the general public to understand what they had written, you can see that they expected their readers to have a wide general knowledge.)

a) Like *Sisyphus*, Ronald Reagan is pushing uphill.

b) The outcome would be uncertain—but even a victory would not be much sweeter than it was for the defenders of *Masada*.

c) It seems that dentistry is about to adopt the *Ronald McDonald* system for the future.

d) The industry-administration coalition that has opposed a strong Superfund bill all along is now shedding *crocodile tears* over the bill's threatened expiration.

e) We'd rather be accused of *crying wolf* than . . . of not doing the proper thing at the proper time.

f) It [*New York Times*] is a great paper, but they're *Luddites* when it comes to television.

g) However *West 57th* [a news program] fares, the reports of *the death of news programs have been greatly exaggerated.*

EXERCISE 8 ▶ Figurative Language in Cartoons

1. Find five cartoons with figurative comparisons in your local newspaper or in magazines you have around the house. (Many cartoonists use figurative comparisons, especially allusions.)

2. Bring them to school to share with your partner and see if he or she recognizes the two things that are being compared.

3. What two things are being compared in this cartoon?

HERMAN

"Listen...if we get this right, we'll be famous."

Herman by Jim Unger. Copyright, 1979, Universal Press Syndicate. Reprinted with permission. All Rights Reserved.

Special Writing Assignment

The true test of mastering figurative comparisons is recognizing them in your reading and using them in your writing.

1. For your partner, write a short paragraph in which you create an analogy by sustaining a figurative comparison. You can use similes, metaphors, personifications, and allusions.

2. Ask your partner to evaluate the paragraph according to the rules in Exercise 4.

3. Read the student models below. Test the figurative comparisons and discuss their effectiveness with your partner. Study how the student writers created successful analogies by sustaining certain images: waves on a beach compared to a sea battle, a talker's words compared to waves drowning the listener, a girl's death compared to the plucking of a rose, and trees on a cliff compared to tired soldiers.

Sea Battle
by Margaret O'Connell, student

The waves attack the shore like soldiers in battle—charging the beach in frenzy, dying in foamy agony. And as each wave slowly falls, then retreats into the sea, the next one comes in its place. It, too, seems eager to make its hopeless assault; it, too, is doomed, as sure of defeat as its predecessor. On and on the battle goes, an incessant and futile struggle against the impregnable defenses of the shore.

Drowning
by Gordon Bookey, student

Whenever he talked to me I felt as if I were drowning. His words poured out in torrents, hitting me like sweeping waves determined to pull me under. I would struggle onward, and with my head bobbing to and fro try to concentrate on his speech. At times, he would grow calm, and I'd feel my ordeal was at an end. But then, with all the hidden energies of the deep, the onslaught would continue until, drained and overcome, I'd helplessly go under.

Why?
by M. A. Clarkson, student

My neighbor, Mrs. Frances, has a lovely family that she has nurtured and cared for like a garden. Her four children, like beautiful flowers, blossomed around her. But she had one special rose, Zoe, her first-born, who came into this world a very frail child. No one expected her to live. For seventeen years, Mrs. Frances, like a devoted gardener, nursed and watched over Zoe in a special way. She admired her daily as Zoe matured into a strong, beautiful rose, bringing joy to everyone. Suddenly, on a Sunday morning, Mrs. Frances' rose was plucked from her garden, and her every heartbeat asks why. . . .

The March
by Mike Hawkins, student

Marching up the jagged cliff like tired soldiers, the young pines drop their heavy arms toward the ground. At first, they march in rigid formation, only occasionally interrupted by one or two (perhaps gunned down by a shot of lightning) lying at the feet of their fellows, or another leaning on his neighbors for strength. Closer to the top, all semblance of order disappears; the trees, virtually unprotected, tremble and shiver in the biting wind. Some sway with fright, others surge forward, determined to overcome the merciless enemy. At the top stands their leader, a tall pine, strong and immortal, who surveys the disorderly troops as they struggle up the jagged steps to join the leader in their eternal battle.

34 Slant

The term **slant** is used to describe the way in which a writer may, consciously or unconsciously, convey attitudes or feelings to the reader. As a result of the writer's purpose or attitude, his or her material may have a **positive slant** or **negative slant**.

EXERCISE 1 ▶ *A Talk*

We are often unaware of the slant in our own material. This exercise will help you to appreciate how your presentation changes, depending on your audience and situation.

1. Recall the last time you were out with someone. Think about what kind of a time you had. Write down several key words that honestly describe your experience—for example, *choice, great, foolish, terrific, okay*, and so on. These words are for your eyes only.
2. Now, imagine telling the person you were out with about the time you had. Write down the words you would use. Compare the original list with the new list. Which of the original words would you not use? What words would you use instead? (For example, if you had used *terrible* to describe the occasion, you might not want to use that word to your companion. You might use *not bad* instead.) What thoughts might you leave unsaid?

3. Next, imagine telling one of your parents (new audience) about the time you had. Which words in the previous lists would you not use? Which words would you use instead? Which details about the experience would you leave out of your account?

4. Now, in the classroom (new situation) tell your partner (new audience) about the time you had. How many of the original key words did you not use?

EXERCISE 2 ▶ Description

Your presentation is also affected by your attitude toward your subject.

1. With your partner, choose a subject (for example, an activity, a person, or a location) that one of you likes and one dislikes.

2. Each of you write a description of your subject. Do not state how you feel about your subject, but merely describe it.

3. Compare your descriptions. Discuss the differences in word choices, facts, and so on.

EXERCISE 3 ▶ Ways to Slant

There are three ways that writing may be slanted in either a positive or negative manner:

Words: Words with positive connotations will cause your reader to feel good about your subject and possibly about you; words with negative connotations will cause your reader to react against your subject and possibly against you as well. Which of the following sentences use words with positive connotations? negative connotations? Which sentences merely state the facts?

> The team members ran into position on the court.
> The so-called team members stumbled to their spots.
> The team quickly took their positions on the gym floor.

> The man laughs a lot with his friends.
> The dope giggles his head off with his buddies.
> The fellow chuckles a great deal with his pals.

Comparisons: If you compare your subject with something pleasant, your reader will know you approve of your subject; if you use unpleasant comparisons, your reader will know you disapprove of it. With your partner, discuss which of the following common comparisons are positive and which are negative.

> He eats like a bird.
> He eats like a pig.
> She has a voice like a nightingale.
> She has a voice like a crow.

Now, make up three positive comparisons and three negative comparisons.

Details: You can influence your reader by the specific details that you choose to report about your subject. If you choose only favorable details and ignore unfavorable ones, you are slanting your material in a positive manner. If you choose only unfavorable details, you are slanting negatively. Discuss which of the following statements have positive or negative slant.

> Wars give an economy a much-needed boost.
> Microcomputers are simply a modern form of home entertainment; everyone who owns one has a stack of video games.
> Cars are a menace; they kill people all the time.
> Joggers can suffer shin damage and shin splints.
> The benefits of jogging include improved cardiovascular fitness.

EXERCISE 4 ▶ Degrees of Slant

Words can have no slant, positive slant, or negative slant. For example:

Positive	*No Slant*	*Negative*
physician	doctor	pill pusher
mansion	house	shack

1. Draw a chart similar to the one above. Choose five of the words from the list below (or five words of your own) and write them in the *No Slant* column, then write words for the positive and negative columns that mean almost the same thing as your original word.

police officer, child, muscular, sleeps, eats, small, large, round, money, prison, party, angry, language

Remember that within the positive and negative categories, there will be degrees of slant. For each term, you could have several words, each one a little more positive or negative than another. This fact makes your search for "just that right word" a challenge.

2. When you have completed this activity, go over your lists with your partner. It might be an interesting exercise for you both to choose at least one word that is the same, work on it separately, and then compare your responses.

EXERCISE 5 ▶ Slant in Advertising

Advertising overwhelms us with examples of slant—television and radio commercials, newspaper and magazine ads, direct-mail circulars, and billboards.

1. Choose ten advertisements from the print media that illustrate either positive or negative slant. Consider the names of the products. Also discuss words that are used to describe the product. (Most advertisements will have positive slant. Why? In what ways might they use negative slant?)

2. Exchange advertisements with your partner to see if you both can find the negative and positive slant in each other's collection. Discuss your findings.

EXERCISE 6 ▶ Propaganda

Propaganda also provides examples of slant. Notice the use of negative and positive slant in the following sentences:

> The Americans are storing weapons to be able to protect the democratic system of government from total destruction, while the Commies are stockpiling them in order to enslave the rest of the world.

> The Union of Soviet Socialist Republics, with its impressive increase of weapons, is enlarging its sphere of socialist influence on other countries in order to save them from the Yanks and their imperialist bombs.

1. Can you pick out examples of each kind of slant? The language has been carefully chosen to appeal to the reader's emotions. An intelligent reader soon realizes that propaganda arouses the emotions but does not satisfy the intellect, for it provides little information.

The sentence below is a rewrite of the propaganda piece. Notice that it contains information with no emotional slant:

> The main difference between the American and Soviet arms buildup is that the American purpose is defensive, while the Soviet purpose is offensive.

2. Write a short piece of propaganda telling why your school is better or worse than another. Then, rewrite your piece so that it is objective, without negative or positive slant.

3. Discuss your pieces with your partner.

EXERCISE 7 ▶ Slant in Writing

Read the following selection; then, using the questions that follow the selection, discuss it with your partner.

Harvesting Misery

Farm life is not always the idyllic existence many city dwellers fantasize. On the farm where I grew up during the Depression, summers were insect-ridden and winters snowbound.

In spring and summer, our sparse grain fields were always at the mercy of unpredictable weather. If sneaking late frosts didn't nip the heads off seedlings, or scorching winds didn't burn weak stems, ruthless hailstones would crush the grain just before we could harvest it. If by some stroke of luck the capricious weather took a year off to devastate another unsuspecting farmer's crop, hungry grasshoppers munched their way across our fields, while gophers, mice, and crows devoured the remaining kernels.

Summers like these do not see families through bitter winters. Every winter, searching for work far from home, my father left my mother, sister, and me to fend for ourselves. Blizzards smothered our two-room tar-papered shack with impenetrable snowdrifts. We had to dig tunnels to feed the starving livestock in their barns. I remember one three-month stint when we never did see the sky. That year when the thaws finally came, starving wolves ravaged the countryside. Scrawny though we were, we must have smelled like tender tidbits. Many an April night we were huddled around our potbelly stove with shotguns aimed at our front door while we listened to them snarling and clawing on the other side. When spring finally did come, my father returned and the whole rigmarole started all over again.

No wonder, when World War II erupted, my father and many of his neighbors gave up the farm life to fight the Axis while we traded our farm for bustling Chicago. Anything looked better than our barren homestead—Il Duce's chin, the Fuhrer's moustache, even living in a crowded city.

For Discussion

1. In general, would you say that this selection has positive or negative slant?
2. What words or expressions contribute to the emotional impact of the selection?
3. What details has the writer included about the topic? What other details might have been included to give an opposite slant to the material?
4. Discuss the meaning of the allusions: "Il Duce's chin," and "the Fuhrer's moustache." How do these contribute to the slant of the selection?

Special Writing Assignment

Before you use slant in what you write, ask yourself: Do I want positive or negative slant in my writing? Or do I want a mixture of positive and negative slant because I want to support one thing and reject another? Always consider your writing variables when you are making these decisions.

1. Find a piece you have already written but would like to rewrite in order to give it a stronger slant. If you do not have such a piece available, you will have to write one, using words, comparisons, and details to give your selection positive or negative slant.
2. Ask your partner to discuss the effectiveness of your slant. Does it help to achieve your purpose, or does it leave him or her unconvinced and mistrustful?

35 Satire

To **satirize** is to ridicule a social ill, condition, or tradition; an aspect of the human condition; or even a specific person. Of all the types of writing, you will perhaps find satire the most difficult, even though it is easy to talk about and usually easy to see in other people's writing. Before you use satire in any format (from a serious expository essay to a humorous personal letter), you should decide whether the purpose and topic warrant a satiric treatment and whether your audience would appreciate it.

EXERCISE 1 ▶ Selecting Topics

1. You and your partner can make a list of ten things that are wrong with today's society.

Example

There are too many regulations to follow and forms to fill out.

Which item from your list would you find easiest to satirize? How would you satirize it?

Example

In the future there will be so many forms to fill out that people will have to fill out an application simply to get permission to fill out an application.

2. You and your partner can make a list of ten things that are part of the human condition. Try to think of some of those silly, human things you do that seem serious at the time, but you laugh about afterwards.

Example

    When you discover a blemish on your face, you think everyone notices.

Which item from your list would you find easiest to satirize? How would you satirize it?

Example

    When I noticed my first . . . oh, I can't say the word . . . but when I noticed It, I knew I would have to go into hiding until my face cleared up.

EXERCISE 2 ▸ Satire in Cartoons

    You can see satire at work in newspapers. Almost every editorial page has a political cartoon depicting the latest actions of civic, federal, or world leaders. No one is safe from the cartoonist's mocking eye.

1. Bring two satiric cartoons to class. Exchange them with your partner. Discuss what is being satirized. Study each cartoon carefully to

Chuck Ayers © 1983 Akron-Beacon Journal
Courtesy, Akron-Beacon Journal

see the overall effect as well as the details. Point out to each other the reason why it is or is not effective satire.

2. Write new satiric dialogue or captions for your two cartoons even if they already have a dialogue or captions. Discuss with your partner the effect of what you wrote.

EXERCISE 3 ▶ Sardonic Satire

Many daily, weekly, and monthly columnists satirize society's ills. Of the many specific kinds of satire they could use, they seem to delight in airing their insults in **sardonic** (biting, contemptuous, sometimes hilarious) ways.

1. Find a column that uses sardonic satire and exchange it with your partner. Then each of you answer these questions:

   a) What exactly does the columnist want changed?
   b) In what ways is the satire sardonic?

Example

The television, surely the most misused invention in the history of humanity, dispenses violence as regularly as deodorant commercials. Slayings are fed to us as we eat our TV dinners. We have gotten to the point where we can tune out the violence in our society as easily as we tune out the sponsor's message.

Analysis

   a) The writer does not want violence on TV.
   b) The viewers become accustomed to violence.
   c) By comparing the regular appearance of violence to the constant advertising of deodorants, he shows sardonic satire.

2. Working together with your partner, write an example of sardonic satire.

EXERCISE 4 ▶ Invective

Reviewers and critics are sometimes unkind. They will often pour out satirical **invective** (a verbal attack often using insults) as they write a critique of a book, play, movie, or event.

1. Find an example of a critic's satire and exchange it with your partner.

   a) What has displeased the critic?
   b) Do you think the critic is justified in using invective?

Example

   The orchestra . . . was, of course, out of sight in the pit, but the curious sounds that wafted forth from the bunker-like refuge gave the impression that much of the score was being played on jugs and bottles, combs and toilet tissue, and, possibly, kazoos.

   Christopher Dafoe

Analysis

   a) Dafoe was displeased with the quality of the music.
   b) Simply saying "The orchestra did not play well" would not create the impact of this review. Nor would it be suggestive of how badly the critic feels the orchestra actually played. If the music was truly bad and people wasted their money by buying tickets, the invective may be justified.

2. Now you and your partner can write your own examples of invective. Compare and decide which example is more effective.

EXERCISE 5 ▸ Parody

On television and stage you often see an impressionist who satirizes well-known celebrities, politicians, or movie stars. The impressionist obviously has studied the subjects very well in order to **parody** them (make fun of them through exaggeration).

1. Talk about parodists with your partner. Do you have a favorite? Rich Little and Debbie Reynolds are popular impressionists who are international stars. What techniques does a parodist use to bring the subject to the stage so that the audience recognizes who is being parodied?

2. If you imitate another writer to poke fun, you are parodying. You can do this by imitating the writer's style and tone or by using words from the original piece.

Many school songs are parodies. You and your partner can write a new song for your school. Use many of the original words as well as the original rhythm and tune. To make this task easier, write out the original and see which words you need to change to fit your school. Although a parody can contain invective, keep yours good-natured.

3. Here are three famous and often-parodied quotations from Shakespeare. You and your partner, working separately, can write a parody of each. (In the speech from *Hamlet*, key words have been italicized, and the first line of a parody has been started to help you.)

a) from *Hamlet*:

> To *be*, or not to *be*, that is *the question*:
> Whether 'tis *nobler* in the *mind* to suffer
> The *slings* and *arrows* of outrageous *fortune*,
> Or to take *arms* against a sea of troubles,
> And by *opposing, end them*.

Sample first line of parody:

To pass, or not to pass, that is my problem.

b) from *Romeo and Juliet*:

> O Romeo, Romeo, wherefore art thou Romeo?
> Deny thy father and refuse thy name;
> Or, if thou wilt not, be but sworn my love,
> And I'll no longer be a Capulet.

c) from *Macbeth*:

> Tomorrow, and tomorrow, and tomorrow,
> Creeps in this petty pace from day to day,
> To the last syllable of recorded time;
> And all our yesterdays have lighted fools
> The way to dusty death.

EXERCISE 6 ▶ Irony

Irony may be used to achieve satire. Irony is a figure of speech in which the words express a meaning that is often the direct opposite of the intended meaning. For example, if someone says to you, "Lovely weather, eh?" when there is a sub-zero blizzard, that person would be either grossly out of touch with reality or would be ironically satirizing the weather.

Although you can often use irony effectively, avoid using sarcasm, a form of irony used to wound a hearer or reader. Sarcasm is usually found in speech, where tone of voice can make a biting taunt even more biting.

1. Working separately, you and your partner can each write a piece of irony satirizing a social problem or an aspect of the human condition.

Many writers of irony adopt a persona, making sure that readers will know that what the persona thinks is not what the writer really thinks. In Jonathan Swift's *Gulliver's Travels*, for example, Lemuel Gulliver praises humans' ability to wage war. But the reader knows that Swift really condemns the bloodthirsty practices his persona praises.

Some writers adopt personas—perhaps philosophers, scientists, professors, or politicians—who spout pretentious and absurd ideas. Other writers use personas who plead ignorance and in their innocent but shrewd way expose the silliness of commonly accepted practices or attitudes. If you decide to use a persona as a vehicle for irony, what kind you use is up to you.

2. After each of you writes your piece of irony, compare them and discuss how well each of you has succeeded.

EXERCISE 7 ▶ Recognizing Satire

Read the following examples of satire with your partner. What is being satirized in each?

> Many years ago, I revealed the secret of the New York subway system: the secret of finding your way around in it is actually a secret. That's right. There are things about the subways that you are not meant to know. One of the things is how to get from the Bronx to midtown. You don't believe me? Ask yourself why the New York subway system, alone among the mass transit systems of the world, has maps inside rather than outside the trains. It's to force you to get on the wrong train in order to find out where you're going. Then you have to shove your way through a lot of people who look irritable and maybe dangerous to find a map upon which no one has spray-painted "Rico-179." Then, assuming that you are a graduate of the Royal Institute of Cartography, you decipher the map to discover that the first step in reaching your destination is to get off the wrong train at the next stop.
>
> *Calvin Trillin*

> Each year millions of people attempt to shed excess pounds by dint of strenuous diet and exercise. They nibble carrot sticks, avoid starches, give up drinking, run around reservoirs, lift weights, swing from trapezes and otherwise behave in a manner that suggests an unhappy penchant for undue fanfare. All of this is, of course, completely unnec-

essary, for it is entirely possible—indeed, easy—to lose weight and tone up without the slightest effort of will. One has merely to conduct one's life in such a way that pounds and inches will disappear as of their own volition.

Magic, you say? Fantasy? Pie in the sky? Longing of the basest sort? Not at all, I assure you, not at all. No magic, no fantasy, no dreamy hopes of any kind. But a secret, ah yes, there is a secret. The secret of exploiting an element present in everyone's daily life, and using to its fullest advantage the almost inexhaustible resources available within.

That element? Stress. Yes, stress; plain, ordinary, everyday stress. The same type of stress that everyone has handy at any time of the day or night. Call it what you will: annoyance, work, pressure, art, love, it is stress nevertheless, and it is stress that will be your secret weapon as you embark on my foolproof program. . . .

Fran Lebowitz,
"The Fran Lebowitz High-Stress Diet and Exercise Program"

It was a crisp and spicy New England morning in early October. The lilacs and laburnums, lit with the glory fires of autumn, hung burning and flashing in the brilliant air, a bridge provided by kind Nature for the wingless wild things that have their home in the tree-tops and would visit together. The larch and the pomegranate flung their purple and yellow flames in broad splashes along the slanted westward sweep of the woodland; and the sensuous fragrance of innumerable deciduous flowers rose upon the atmosphere in a swoon of incense. Far in the empty sky, a solitary pharynx slept among the empyrean on motionless wing. And everywhere brooded stillness, serenity, and the peace of God.

Mark Twain

Special Writing Assignment

To write a piece of satire is not easy, but if you investigate your present surroundings, you will probably see something you can satirize for your partner. A word of caution about satire: You cannot suddenly drop a single example of irony, parody, and so on, into your straightforward, logical prose. Your *entire* piece of writing must have a satiric tone.

When your partner has finished reading your piece, discuss the method of satire you used and any satirical points that your partner missed.

36 Research Skills and Documentation

The English writer Samuel Johnson observed, "Knowledge is of two kinds. We know a subject ourselves, or we know where we can find information upon it." Much of this chapter deals with the second kind—knowledge of how and where to find information. This kind, essential if you are preparing to write a research paper, is also very useful for other kinds of informative writing.

The rest of the chapter deals with documentation: the currently accepted forms—both in scholarly writing and student research papers—for showing where you got your information.

EXERCISE 1 ▶ A Library Tour

Before you and your partner work with the card catalog and specific reference works, you should take a library tour to find out what your school or local library has to offer and where different kinds of material are located. In particular, note the following:

The card catalog. Most libraries keep a record of the books they have on catalog cards. The cabinets containing these cards are often located near the center of the library.

The reference area. This area contains important research books, such as dictionaries, encyclopedias, indexes, atlases, and almanacs. These reference books are not usually allowed out of the library. If you use the reference area a good deal, you will soon get to know where specific reference works are kept.

The periodical area. Most well-stocked libraries subscribe to current magazines and newspapers. Back issues are often bound in hard covers, year by year, or kept on microfilm. To find out how to get back issues, you should ask the reference librarian.

The media area. Many libraries contain collections of tapes, records, slides, films, microfilms, and microfiches (microfilm on plastic cards). You should familiarize yourself with this area and plan to spend some time there. Your media area may have tapes and slides on grammar, biology, or chemistry, which you can use to help clear up a problem. As well, you may be able to borrow a film or set of slides to help you with a special presentation you have to make for a class.

The vertical file. Many libraries maintain files that contain pamphlets and clippings on various subjects.

The stacks. The stacks, usually the largest part of a library, contain the library's books. Books are usually divided into fiction and nonfiction, with fiction arranged alphabetically according to author, and nonfiction arranged according to one of two systems, the Dewey decimal system or the Library of Congress system. These systems are discussed on pages 347–349.

    1. After you and your partner tour your school or community library, draw a chart that shows where the following kinds of material are located: (a) fiction books, (b) nonfiction books, (c) an unabridged dictionary, (d) the card catalog, (e) encyclopedias, (f) magazines, (g) newspapers, (h) the media area, and (i) the vertical file. Indicate as well any special features of your library.

    2. Find out the answers to the following. If you are not sure about an answer, consult the librarian. Unquestionably, librarians are a library's most important resource. Most librarians have a knowledge of and love for their collections and are only too glad to encourage you to get to know their library. So if you have not already done so, make yourself known to your local librarian.

    a) Are the nonfiction books in your library organized according to the Dewey decimal or Library of Congress system?
    b) What is the smallest dictionary in your library? the largest?

c) Which encyclopedia seems to be the most comprehensive? How can you tell?
d) Give the title of one world atlas in your library.
e) What almanacs does your library's reference section contain?
f) Name two current magazines and one newspaper available in your library.
g) If your library has a media area, what does it offer?
h) If your library does not have a book you want, can it help you get that book? If so, how?

EXERCISE 2 ▶ *The Card Catalog*

If you want to find a book about a particular subject, you can use the slow way—browsing along the shelves—or the fast way—consulting the card catalog.

Almost all libraries keep a record of all their books on catalog cards, which are arranged alphabetically in a card catalog, a cabinet or set of cabinets with small drawers. There are at least two cards for each fiction book: an author card and a title card. There are at least three cards for each nonfiction book: author, title, subject. Some books can be classified under more than one subject, and so there is more than one subject card for them. Notice the following example.

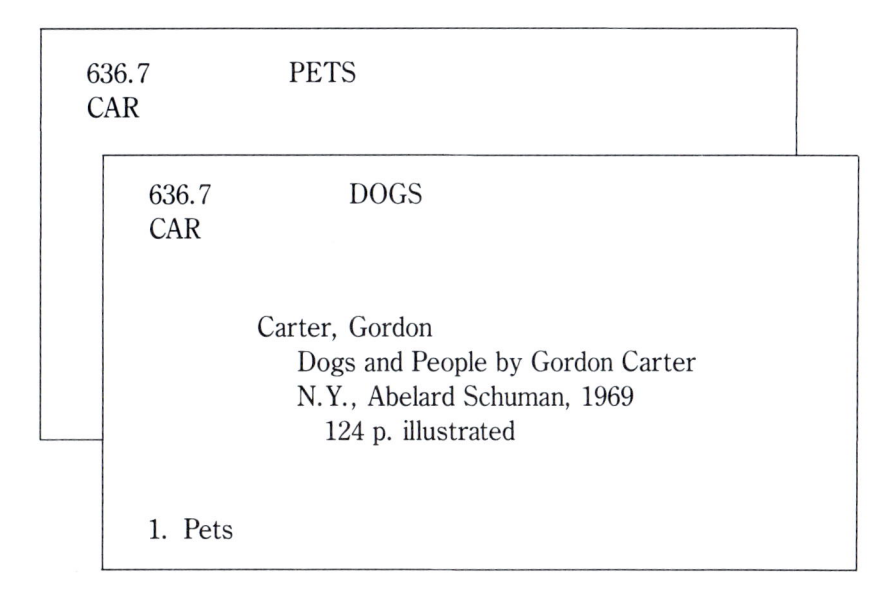

```
636.7           PETS
CAR
          636.7           DOGS
          CAR

                 Carter, Gordon
                     Dogs and People by Gordon Carter
                     N.Y., Abelard Schuman, 1969
                       124 p. illustrated



              1. Pets
```

In addition to author, title, and subject, a catalog card provides other information.

The call number. The book's call number, appearing in the upper-left corner of a catalog card, is based on either the Dewey decimal or Library of Congress system, and helps you find that book in the stacks. If you were looking for a book about dogs and came across *Dogs and People* in the card catalog, you would copy the call number $\frac{636.7}{CAR}$ and go to the nonfiction shelves until you came to 636.7. Then you would look for a book that has the call number $\frac{636.7}{CAR}$ on its spine.

Other useful information. A catalog card indicates who published the book, the year it was published, how many pages it has, and what special features it has, if any. The publication date suggests how up-to-date the information is. Sometimes you may want the very latest information. If you wanted the most recent information about dogs, would you consult *Dogs and People*?

The publisher's name is sometimes useful. Certain publishers have a reputation for publishing especially fine books in such fields as medicine, engineering, or art history. Who published *Dogs and People*?

The indication of special features is useful when you are looking for one or more of these features. If you need a book about the Spanish exploration of the New World, you may want to be sure the book contains maps tracing the explorers' routes. If you need information about dogs, you may want a book that has photographs or illustrations of different breeds. Does *Dogs and People* provide illustrations?

Some catalog cards also indicate other categories under which a book can be found. If you are trying to think of a related subject to look up, this information can be useful. Under what category other than "Dogs" can a subject card for *Dogs and People* be found? Where is this information given on the card?

1. You and your partner can each do research in the card catalog about five of the following subjects. Each of you should list the author, title, call number, publication date, publisher, and special features of a book about each subject.

nuclear energy	Latin American poets
sports	African folklore
car racing	breeds of cats
scientists	the plays of William Shakespeare
ancient Mayan civilization	famous suffragists

2. On the basis of what you have discovered (including publication date and special features about each book), discuss which of these books would be most useful to consult if you were preparing to do a paper on these subjects.

EXERCISE 3 ▸ How Libraries Organize Books—the Dewey Decimal and Library of Congress Systems

Libraries organize their nonfiction books according to the Library of Congress or Dewey decimal systems. Many university libraries and large research libraries (and, of course, the Library of Congress) use the Library of Congress system, which classifies books by letter. The letter *A*, for example, indicates general works; *J* indicates books about political science; *N*, books about the fine arts; and *P*, books about language and literature. Most other libraries—including, probably, your school and local libraries—use the Dewey decimal system.

Melvil Dewey was a student library assistant at Amherst College when, in 1872, he began to develop a system for organizing the library's books. Since then, many libraries have adopted this system, which uses the numbers 0 to 999 to classify books.

Major Categories of the Dewey Decimal System

000–099	General works (including encyclopedias, yearbooks, guides, and almanacs and books about journalism and library science)
100–199	Philosophy (including logic; ethics; and ancient, medieval, and modern philosophy)
200–299	Religion (including the Bible, the history of religions, and devotional and practical religion)
300–399	Social sciences (including political science, economics, public administration, and education)
400–499	Language (including the study of language and dictionaries and grammars of various languages)
500–599	Pure science (including mathematics, astronomy, physics, chemistry, earth sciences, and biology)
600–699	Technology (including medicine, engineering, agriculture, and chemical technology)
700–799	The arts (including architecture, sculpture, painting, photography, music, theater, films, recreation, and sports)

800–899 Literature (including fiction, poetry, drama, and the literatures of nations)
900–999 History and related subjects (including geography, travel, biography, American history, and the histories of other nations)

Just like decimal numbers, Dewey decimal categories can be divided and subdivided. For example, the category 600–699 (Technology) divides into the following less general categories:

600–609 General
610–619 Medical science
620–629 Engineering
630–639 Agriculture
640–649 Home economics
650–659 Business
660–669 Chemical technology
670–679 Manufacture
680–689 Other manufacture
690–699 Building construction

These categories can, in turn, divide into even more specific categories. For example, 630–639 (Agriculture) includes 633 (Field crops), 635 (Garden crops), and 636 (Animals), and each of these has further subdivisions. Gordon Carter's book *Dogs and People* comes under the Dewey number 636.7 (the category for dogs).

1. Even though you will probably be relying more on the call numbers of catalog cards to find books about a particular subject, a general knowledge of the Dewey decimal categories is useful when you do research. Sometimes it helps, when you know the Dewey number of a subject you want to research, simply to walk up to those shelves and see what books your library has.

Under which general categories would you be likely to find the following books? (A history of British drama, for example, would be found under the general category 800–899—Literature.)

a) a Spanish dictionary
b) a book about raising cattle
c) a book about the Super Bowl
d) a book about French Impressionist painting
e) a book about recent discoveries in physics
f) a book about the Early Christian Church

g) a history of French settlements in North America
h) a book about the economics of running a small business
i) a book about encyclopedias
j) a collection of modern American poetry

2. After you and your partner have separately jotted down answers to these questions, compare what you have written.

EXERCISE 4 ▶ *Information About Information*—The Readers' Guide to Periodical Literature *and Other Indexes*

Indexes are guides to where information can be found—in magazines, newspapers, books, and other sources. Probably the most widely used index, and the one you will use most, is *The Readers' Guide to Periodical Literature*, a guide to information in magazines.

The Readers' Guide lists all the articles published within a certain period of time in a variety of magazines, from *American Artist* to *The Writer*. This guide comes in several forms: as a paperbound booklet published twenty-two times a year; as a thicker booklet covering three months of publication; and as a hardbound book, serving as a guide to articles published within a year. When using *The Readers' Guide*, be sure to check the period it covers. If you want the very latest information, consult the latest *Readers' Guide* you can find. If you are looking for information about an event that took place during a certain year, look first in *The Readers' Guide* for that year.

Like a card catalog, *The Readers' Guide* organizes its information alphabetically under both author's name and subject. Information is presented in a compact form, almost in a kind of code. But you can crack the code with very little effort.

Suppose you wanted to find articles about Stevie Wonder, and you looked in *The Readers' Guide* for May, 1985. You would find:

Wonder, Stevie
about
Prince, Stevie Wonder spice up Oscar Awards as top music winners. il pors *Jet* 68:14-15 Ap 15 '85
Stevie Wonder welcomes S. African ban on music. por *Jet* 68:56 Ap 15 '85

This entry indicates that in April, 1985, two articles about Stevie Wonder appear in the April 15, 1985, issue of *Jet* magazine. The first article—"Prince, Stevie Wonder spice up. . . ." —appears on pages 14–15. (The notation "68:14–15" indicates first the volume number of the magazine and, after the colon, the page numbers.) This article contains both illustrations ("il") and portraits ("pors") of Stevie Wonder and Prince. The second article appears on page 56 and offers a portrait of its subject. As you can see, *The Readers' Guide* makes extensive use of abbreviations. If you are puzzled by an abbreviation, consult the key to abbreviations at the front of the *Guide*.

You can use *The Readers' Guide* as you would a card catalog. If you are looking for articles by a particular writer, look for entries under that writer's name. If you are looking for articles about a particular subject, look for that subject heading. Like many card catalogs, *The Readers' Guide* indicates other related headings under which articles may be found. For example:

Women musicians
  See also
    Women rock musicians
Women opera characters *See* Women in opera
Women photographers
  See also
    Schwartz, Madalena
Women poets
  See also
    Gallagher, Tess

Other useful indexes include:

Biography Index
Book Review Digest (guide to reviews of books published in a particular year; also includes excerpts from reviews)
Essay and General Literature Index
Humanities Index
Granger's Index to Poetry
Index to Plays
Index to Short Stories
New York Times Index (guide to all articles published in the *New York Times*; especially useful for information on current events and events occurring in a particular year)
Social Science Index

   1. Find out which of these indexes your school and community library have and where the indexes are located.

   2. You and your partner can each find an entry for an article in *The Readers' Guide to Periodical Literature*. First copy the entry as it appears in the *Guide*. Then, in a sentence or two, restate the information. For example, the entry for the second article about Stevie Wonder on page 349 can be restated: An article about Stevie Wonder, titled "Stevie Wonder Welcomes South African Ban on Music," appears on page 56 of the April, 15, 1985 (Volume 68) issue of *Jet* magazine. The article is accompanied by a portrait.

Compare your restatements and discuss which best sums up the information given in *The Readers' Guide*.

3. You and your partner can assign each other at least three subjects to research in *The Readers' Guide* and other indexes your library has. Each of you must find at least one article about each assigned subject. The subjects might relate to rock music, films, television, recent scientific discoveries, teen fashions and trends, nuclear power, and events in the news.

EXERCISE 5 ▶ Encyclopedias and Other Useful Reference Works

In addition to indexes, libraries have many other reference works, including encyclopedias, atlases, almanacs, and biographical works. Since you may find several of these kinds of books useful when you gather information for a research paper, you should take some time to familiarize yourself with them.

Encyclopedias. Encyclopedias are essentially collections of articles about a wealth of subjects, from *Abyssinia* to *Zwingli, Huldreich* (a Swiss religious thinker). Most encyclopedias consist of many volumes and organize their articles alphabetically. The latest edition of the *Encyclopaedia Britannica*, the most scholarly and comprehensive of encyclopedias, is an exception to this rule.

If you wish to consult the *Britannica*, you should know that it is organized into a one-volume *Propaedia*, a nineteen-volume *Macropaedia*, and a ten-volume *Micropaedia*. The *Propaedia*, which aims to be an outline of all knowledge, also functions as a topical guide to the *Macropaedia*, which contains over 4,000 long comprehensive articles on a great variety of subjects. The *Micropaedia* contains over 100,000 much shorter articles.

(Many libraries have an earlier, as well as the latest, edition of the *Encyclopaedia Britannica*. Earlier editions of this work do, like other encyclopedias, organize their articles alphabetically.)

Other useful encyclopedias include:

Collier's Encyclopedia
Encyclopedia Americana
World Book Encyclopedia (This encyclopedia, intended for younger
  readers, provides useful introductions to many subjects that
  the *Britannica, Americana,* and *Collier's* cover more
  comprehensively.)

In addition, the following one- and two-volume encyclopedias provide useful introductions to many subjects:

Columbia Encyclopedia
Random House Encyclopedia
Lincoln Library of Essential Information

Almanacs. Almanacs are collections of facts and statistics, many of them in the form of lists. If you look in an almanac, you might find the following:

a list of baseball players that played in World Series games
actors and directors who won Academy Awards
major rivers of North America
places in the United States with a population of 5,000 or more
Pulitzer Prize winners
Nobel Prize winners

Useful almanacs include:

World Almanac
New York Times Encyclopedic Almanac
Information Please Almanac

Atlases and Gazetteers. An atlas is a collection of maps. Many atlases also provide statistics and other information about particular places. A gazetteer is a geographical dictionary that organizes its information alphabetically under the names of places. If you want information about a particular place, you might consult a gazetteer.

Useful atlases and gazetteers include:

Hammond Contemporary World Atlas
National Geographic Atlas of the World
Rand McNally Cosmopolitan World Atlas
Columbia-Lippincott Gazetteer of the World
Webster's New Geographical Dictionary

Biographical reference works. In addition to individual biographies, libraries carry books that provide information about many noted persons. Useful biographical reference works include:

Current Biography (contains articles about newsworthy persons)
Who's Who (provides information about notable living British persons)
Who's Who in America
International Who's Who

Dictionary of National Biography (provides biographies of British notables)
Dictionary of American Biography

Biographical works useful for literary research:

American Authors 1600–1900
British Authors Before 1900
Twentieth Century Authors and *Twentieth Century Authors: First Supplement*
World Authors: 1950–1970 (takes up where *Twentieth Century Authors* leaves off)

Find out what reference works your school or community library provides, if necessary by consulting with the librarian. Then you and your partner can make a list of the library's encyclopedias, almanacs, atlases, gazetteers, and biographical reference works.

EXERCISE 6 ▶ Researching

When you must write a research paper, you most probably will need to spend a few hours in the library, gathering facts. The following suggestions should make your research easier:

1. Purchase a set of index cards on which to write your notes. Write one note per card so that you can organize them as you wish.

2. If you plan to use any portion of a book, first make up a bibliography card. It should look something like this:

Call number

Author's name

Title

Facts of publication

```
817 [Dewey decimal system]
Masters, Edgar Lee
Mark Twain: A Portrait
New York, Biblio and Tannen,
1966
```

3. At the top of the next card write a subject heading to help you organize and find the card quickly. Identify the source of your quotation by listing the author's last name and the page number on which you found the quotation. When you quote an author's exact words, use quotation marks around them; in this way you will help yourself avoid unintentional plagiarism. Your card should look like this:

> Masters p.7   Twain's Life & Halley's Comet
>
> "... born on Nov. 30, 1835. Halley's Comet was at its perihelion on Nov. 16 of that year. Among Mark Twain's many superstitions, he accepted the comet as somehow pacing his life and influencing it. In fact, it reached its perihelion again on Nov. 16, 1910, a few days before Mark Twain's death."

4. Wherever possible, summarize what you read. This way you can select and extract what is important to your purpose. Too many quotations in a research essay or report give your reader the feeling that you have not written it but have merely strung together statements made by others. When you do summarize long portions, you should still identify the source and provide a subject heading:

> Masters pp 8-9   Twain's Birthplace
>
> Mark Twain was born in a very humble log cabin, which housed his large family in Florida, Missouri. His beginnings have been compared with Lincoln's meager start in life.

5. For practice, you and your partner can make up a research paper topic for each other. Go to the appropriate area in your library to do the following things:

   a) Write on an index card one direct quote that you would like to use if you were to write an essay on your partner's topic.
   b) On another index card write out the bibliographical information on the book you used.
   c) Find another book on your topic and write on an index card a summary of something that you would like to use if you were to write the essay. If your summary takes up two cards, indicate at the top of each card: 1st of 2 and 2nd of 2. This will help keep your cards organized.
   d) On a fourth index card write out the bibliographical information on the book you used for (c).
   e) Give all cards to your partner so that she or he can check the entries against the suggestions in steps 1 to 4 above.
   f) Here are some general topics if you cannot think of one:

   foreign aid
   cross-country skiing
   medieval mystery plays
   baseball
   lumber industry
   amnesia

EXERCISE 7 ▶ Parenthetical Citations—Documenting Your Sources Within a Research Paper

Documenting means backing up all the quotations and information you use by showing where you got them. For a research paper, you document in two ways. You include a bibliography listing all your sources at the end of the paper. (Bibliographies are discussed in Exercise 8.) And, within the paper, you indicate a source each time you present information, a quotation, or someone else's idea or opinion.

The traditional way of indicating sources in a research paper is through footnotes. However, in 1984 the Modern Language Association (MLA), an organization of scholars, recommended a new method now used in colleges. The advantages of the new method are that it is easier to use and makes your research paper easier to read.

As recommended by the MLA, a writer shows a source by using a **parenthetical citation**, a brief reference in parentheses. Such a reference is enclosed *within* the sentence presenting the information, quotation, or idea. The most common parenthetical citation includes the name of the author of the book or article from which the information came, together with the page number on which the information can be found. For example, Steven Greenaway's research paper about toothpaste (page 116) uses a quotation from a book by Laurence Wright:

> Laurence Wright, a noted authority on the subject of toothbrushes, believes the first recorded toothbrush in England was one commissioned by Queen Elizabeth I, "whose teeth, once yellow, were in her old age jet black" (Wright 245).

The parenthetical citation after the quotation refers to Laurence Wright's book *Clean and Decent*, which is listed in the paper's bibliography (page 116). Notice that no mark of punctuation separates the author's name from the page reference, and that the period ending the sentence appears *after* the parenthetical citation.

In the next paragraph of this research paper, Steven Greenaway presents information from the same book without quoting it. Nevertheless, he does cite the source of his information.

> Other formulas for homemade "tooth soap" included ashes mixed with honey, charcoal, areca nuts, and cuttlefish bone (Wright 246).

If you are using two books or articles by the same author, you should include a shortened but easily understood form of the title. In this case, a comma should separate the author and title, but no punctuation should separate the title and page number. For example, assume you include two books by Justin Kaplan in your bibliography, and you quote from one of them, *Mr. Clemens and Mark Twain*.

> "Mark Twain's disgust with his times was partly the index of his involvement with them, and his disgust grew more bitter through the 1870s" (Kaplan, *Mr. Clemens* 158).

If you quote or give information from a book or article by two authors, use both their last names in the parenthetical citation. If no author is mentioned, use a shortened version of the title. You may have to do this when you cite from magazines, newspapers, dictionaries, encyclopedias, and handbooks. Notice that Lynn Stefonovich's paper on acupuncture (page 122) presents information from an article titled "A Curious Cure

That Works," which appears in the November, 1980, issue of *Changing Times*. Her parenthetical citation includes a short form of the article's title:

> Fine, flexible and sharp, the needles may be made of various substances, but silver and stainless steel needles seem to be the most popular. Insertion of the needles should not cause pain or draw blood ("Curious" 38).

The short version of the article's title is enclosed by quotation marks; the title of a book would be underlined or put in italics.

(Note: Although this book recommends that you use parenthetical citations to document sources, remember that a research paper is written for a specific audience. Usually that audience is the teacher who has assigned the paper. If your teacher prefers that you use footnotes rather than citations, refer to a handbook published before 1984 as a guide to proper footnote forms.)

EXERCISE 8 ▶ Bibliography

Readers expect that a research paper include a bibliography, a list of all the sources of the information you use in your paper. If you use parenthetical citations within your paper, it is especially important that you also present a bibliography at the end, since the bibliography makes clear what are the works you cited within parentheses.

According to the MLA guidelines, a bibliography titled "Works Cited" should include all the sources of your facts, quotations, opinions, and ideas (if they are borrowed from someone else). The list should be alphabetical, according to the author's last name. If no author is given for the book or article, then it should be alphabetized according to the first word of the title, other than *a*, *an*, or *the*.

A typical entry for a book:
Author's last name, first name. Underlined Title. City of Publication:
    Publisher, Year of Publication.

(Notice how the entry is punctuated. A comma divides the author's last and first names. Periods follow the author's first name, the title, and the year of publication. Two spaces follow each period. A colon follows the city of publication, and a comma follows the publisher's name. The second line of the entry is set in five spaces.)

A typical entry for a magazine article:
Author's last name, First name. "Title of Article in Quotation Marks." <u>Underlined Title of Periodical</u>. Date of publication: page number(s).

(Again, notice the punctuation. Periods follow the author's name, the title of the article, and the page number. A colon follows the date of publication.)

The best way of understanding how to record the various bibliographic entries is to look at a few examples. When you and your partner examine each of the following, note the information given, the order in which it is given, and the use of capitalization and punctuation. In addition, the MLA suggests that you shorten the publisher's name—for example, Harcourt for Harcourt Brace Jovanovich.

One author:
Newby, Elizabeth Loza. <u>A Migrant With Hope</u>. Nashville, Tennessee: Broadman Press, 1977.

Two authors:
Millet, Nancy C. and Helen J. Throckmorton. <u>How to Read a Short Story</u>. Boston: Ginn, 1969.

Three authors:
Young, Richard E., Alton L. Becker, and Kenneth L. Pike. <u>Rhetoric: Discovery and Change</u>. New York: Harcourt, 1970.

More than three authors:
Chester, Lewis, et al. <u>An American Melodrama</u>. New York: Viking, 1969.

(*Et al.* means "and others.")

Two works by the same author:
Kaplan, Justin. <u>Mark Twain and His World</u>. New York: Crown, 1983.
———. <u>Mr. Clemens and Mark Twain: a Biography</u>. New York: Simon and Schuster, 1966.

(Notice that, in the second entry, three hyphens followed by a period are substituted for the author's name.)

Editor as author:
De Bell, Garret, ed. <u>The Environmental Handbook</u>. New York: Ballantine, 1970.

Book with no author:
The Chicago Manual of Style. 13th ed. Chicago: University of Chicago, 1984.

Article in a book edited by someone else:
Trilling, Diana. "The Image of Women in Contemporary Literature." The Woman in America. Ed. Robert J. Lifton. Boston: Houghton, 1965.

Corporate author or public document:
American Red Cross. Standard First Aid and Personal Safety. 2nd ed. Garden City: Doubleday, 1979.

Signed magazine article:
Bradlee, Benjamin. "He Had That Special Grace." Newsweek 2 Dec. 1963: 38.

Unsigned magazine article:
"A Whale of a Failure." Time 13 July 1970: 44–45.

Signed newspaper article:
Sperling, Godfrey. "Campus Warning for Nixon." The Christian Science Monitor 1 July 1970: 1.

Unsigned newspaper article:
"Kansas City Will Sell Its Old Parking Meters." Los Angeles Times 23 Apr. 1975, sec. IV: 1.

Signed encyclopedia article:
Ryther, John H. "Marine Biology." World Book Encyclopedia, 1976 ed.

Unsigned encyclopedia article or dictionary entry:
"Country Music." Encyclopedia Americana. 1975 ed.

Motion picture:
Indiana Jones and the Temple of Doom. Dir. Steven Spielberg. Paramount. 1984.

Television or radio program:
White, Jim. At Your Service. KMOX. St. Louis. 13 Mar. 1981.

"Nancy Astor" part 7. *Masterpiece Theatre*. PBS. WNET, New York. 27 May 1984.

Recording:
Newhart, Bob. "Merchandising the Wright Brothers." *The Button-Down Mind of Bob Newhart*. Warner Bros. WS 137, 1960.

Computer software:
Oogle, Boris. *Fun with Numbers*. Computer software. Krell Software, 1985.

Personal Interview:
Nought, John. *Personal Interview*. 12 May 1985.

1. Assume that you are going to do a research paper on "The Mysteries of the Brain," and that you have cited information, quotations, and opinions from the following sources.

   a) A book by David Attenborough titled *Life on Earth*, published by Collins (a London publisher) in 1979.
   b) A book by Wayne W. Dyer titled *Pulling Your Own Strings*, published by Harper and Row (a New York publisher) in 1978.
   c) Another book by Wayne Dyer titled *The Sky's the Limit*, published by Pocket Books (a New York publisher) in 1980.
   d) A book by Durk Pearson and Sandy Shaw titled *Life Extension: A Practical Scientific Approach Adding Years to Your Life and Life to Your Years*, published by Warner Books (a New York publisher) in 1982.
   e) An episode from a television series called *The Brain*, produced by PBS (Public Broadcasting System) and broadcast on October 10, 1984, by station WGBH in Boston. The episode is called "The Enlightened Machine."
   f) An encyclopedia article "Brain" in the 1983 edition of *Funk & Wagnalls New Encyclopedia*.
   g) An article by Otto Friedrich titled "What Do Babies Know?" in the August 15, 1983, issue of *Time* magazine. The article appeared on pages 52–59.

Write a bibliography for these sources. Make sure you punctuate and alphabetize your entries correctly. If in doubt, study the examples on pages 116 and 125. Title your bibliography "Works Cited," as the MLA suggests.

2. Trade papers with your partner and check each other's bibliography for correctness. If there are any disagreements about how an entry should be listed, consult your teacher/editor.

Special Writing Assignment

Ask your partner to give you a question to which he or she does not know the answer. The question should start with *what, who, where,* or *when* and be one that can have a short answer. Research the question, and write the answer in no more than fifty words. Include at least one direct quotation and one piece of information in your own words, each from a different source. Make sure that your parenthetical citations and the bibliography at the end of your paper are accurate and written correctly.

Your question can be something like one of the following:

What is vitamin B-12?
Who is the pole-vaulting champion of the world and when did that athlete make a record jump?
For whom was the Sam Browne belt named and why?
Who invented the phonograph and in what year?
What are the Elgin Marbles and where can they be found?

When you have completed your very short research paper, ask your partner to edit it by considering the following questions.

a) Is the research thorough? Has any part of the question been left unanswered?
b) Are there any signs of plagiarism? That is, has the writer presented information or an idea taken from another source and not given credit for it? If so, where? How might this part of the paper be rewritten?
c) Are the quoted material and the writer's own words blended smoothly together?
d) Are the quotations punctuated correctly? Are the parenthetical citations and the bibliography presented correctly?

Appendix

A. Proofreaders' Marks and Other Symbols for Editing

After you are satisfied with the overall content and organization of a piece of writing, you and your editors should take the time to read it for errors. You should be able to answer "yes" to questions such as these:

Are my sentences clear?
Are they grammatically correct?
Did I use the right words?
Is my punctuation correct?
Is my spelling correct?

Following are some proofreaders' marks and other symbols that you and your editors can use at the editing and revising stage of the writing process.

Symbol	Meaning	Example	Correction
⌐	delete, take out	Take out out.	Take out.
∧	insert	This my best writing.	This is my best writing.
#	insert space	pictureframe	picture frame
︿	insert a comma	A polished publishable	A polished, publishable
˅	insert an apostrophe	teachers guide	teacher's guide
˅˅	insert a quotation mark	"Out! he shouted.	"Out!" he shouted.
⊙	insert period	Washington, D C	Washington, D.C.
∼	transpose letter or word	Trasnpose word this.	Transpose this word.
≡	use a capital letter	arizona	Arizona
/	use a lowercase letter	Northern Minnesota	northern Minnesota
¶	begin a new paragraph	¶ Even though an . . .	Even though an . . .

PROOFREADERS' MARKS

Symbol	Meaning	Example	Correction
⌒	do not begin a new paragraph	. . . often. Once we started . . .	. . . often. Once we started . . .
◡	join	He was out spoken.	He was outspoken.
sp	spelling error	sp misteak	mistake
t	tense	t I have went.	I have gone.
U	usage	U I did good.	I did well.
RO	run-on sentence	It was my first day even I was happy.	It was my first day; even I was happy.
cs	comma splice	It was my last day, I was sad.	It was my last day; I was sad.
F	fragment	F Because I wanted to go to the concert.	I went because I wanted to go to the concert.
MM	misplaced modifier	MM She had only swum two laps.	She had swum only two laps.
DM	dangling modifier	DM Running down the street, the burning house came into view.	Running down the street, I saw the burning house.
agr	agreement of subject and verb	Every person in the stands are dressed warmly.	Every person in the stands is dressed warmly.
P	pronoun reference	Henry and Bill P gave me his drink.	Henry and Bill gave me their drinks.
?	unclear	? This is a problem.	Your spelling is a problem.
SS	subject shift	SS One should do his best.	He should do his best.
TS	tense shift	He gives while I TS took.	He gives while I take.

Symbol	Meaning	Example	Correction
vs	voice shift (active to passive or passive to active)	I gave it to him and suddenly it vs was eaten.	I gave it to him and suddenly he ate it.
R	repetitive (redundant)	R She rushed R quickly.	She rushed.
T	transition needed	He refused to come out for practice. T The coach dropped him from the team.	He refused to come out for practice. Consequently, the coach dropped him from the team.
//	lacks parallelism	He was strong // and of a tall stature.	He was strong and tall.

B. Literature Selections

Fiction

Their Mother's Purse
by Morley Callaghan

Joe went around to see his mother and father, and while he was talking with them and wondering if he could ask for the loan of a dollar, his sister Mary, who was dressed to go out for the evening, came into the room and said, "Can you let me have fifty cents tonight, Mother?"

She was borrowing money all the time now, and there was no excuse for her, because she was a stenographer and made pretty good pay. It was not the same with her as it was with their older brother, Stephen, who had three children, and could hardly live on his salary.

"If you could possibly spare it, I'd take a dollar," Mary was saying in her low and pleasant voice as she pulled on her gloves. Her easy smile, her assurance that she would not be refused, made Joe feel resentful. He knew that if he had asked for money, he would have shown that he was uneasy and a little ashamed, and that his father would have put down his paper and stared at him and his mother would have sighed and looked dreadfully worried, as though he were the worst kind of spendthrift.

Getting up to find her purse, their mother said, "I don't mind lending it to you, Mary, though I can't figure out what you do with your money."

"I don't seem to be doing anything with it I didn't use to do," Mary said.

"And I seem to do nothing these days but hand out money to the lot of you. I can't think how you'll get along when I'm dead."

"I don't know what you'd all do if it weren't for your mother's purse," their father said, but when he spoke he nodded his head at Joe, because he would rather make it appear that he was angry with Joe than risk offending Mary by speaking directly to her.

"If anybody wants money, they'll have to find my purse for me," the mother said. "Try and find it, Mary, and bring it to me."

Joe had always thought of Mary as his young sister, but the inscrutable expression he saw on her face as she moved around the room picking up newspapers and looking on chairs made him realize how much more self-reliant, how much apart from them, she had grown in the last few years. He saw that she had become a handsome woman. In her tailored suit and felt hat, she looked almost beautiful, and he was suddenly glad she was his sister.

By this time his mother had got up and was trying to remember where she had put the purse when she came in from the store. In the way of a big woman, she moved around slowly, with a far-away expression in her eyes. The purse was a large, black, flat leather purse, but there never had been a time when his mother had been able to get up and know exactly where her purse was, though she used to pretend she was going directly to the spot where she had placed it.

Now she had got to the point where her eyes were anxious as she tried to remember. Her husband, making loud clucking noises with his tongue, took off his glasses and said solemnly, "I warn you, Mrs. McArthur, you'll lose that purse some day, and then there'll be trouble, and you'll be satisfied."

She looked at him impatiently, as she had hunted in all the likely corners and cupboards. "See if you can find my purse, will you, son?" she begged Joe, and he got up and began to help, as he used to do when he was a little boy.

Because he remembered that his mother sometimes used to put her purse under the pillow on her bed, he went to look in the bedroom. When he got to the door, which was half closed, and looked in, he saw Mary standing in front of the dresser with their mother's purse in her hands. He saw at once that she had just taken out a bill and was slipping it into her own purse—he even saw that it was a two-dollar bill. He ducked back into the hall before she could catch sight of him. He felt helpless and knew only that he couldn't bear that she should see him.

Mary, coming out of the bedroom, called, "I found it. Here it is, Mother."

"Where did you find it, darling?"

"Under your pillow."

"Ah, that's right. Now I remember," she said, and looked at her husband triumphantly, for she never failed to enjoy finding the purse just when it seemed to be lost forever.

As Mary handed the purse to her mother, she was smiling, cool, and unperturbed, yet Joe knew she had put the two dollars into her own purse. It seemed terrible that she was able to smile and hide her thoughts like that when they had all been so close together for so many years.

"I never have the slightest fear that it's really lost," the mother said, beaming. Then they watched her, as they had watched her for years after she had found her purse; she was counting the little roll of bills. Her hand went up to her mouth, she looked thoughtful, she looked down into the depths of the purse again, and they waited almost eagerly, as if expecting her to cry out suddenly that the money was not all there. Then, sighing, she took out fifty cents, handed it to Mary, and it was over, and they never knew what she thought.

"Good night, Mother. Good night, Dad," Mary said.

"Good night, and don't be late. I worry when you're late."

"So long, Joe."

"Just a minute," Joe called, and he followed Mary out to the hall. The groping, wondering expression on his mother's face as she counted her money had made him feel savage.

He grabbed Mary by the arm just as she was opening the door. "Wait a minute," he whispered.

"What's the matter, Joe? You're hurting my arm."

"Give that bill back to them. I saw you take it."

"Joe, I needed it." She grew terribly ashamed and couldn't look at him. "I wouldn't take it if I didn't need it pretty bad," she whispered.

They could hear their father making some provoking remark, and they could hear the easy, triumphant answer of their mother. Without looking up, Mary began to cry a little; then she raised her head and begged in a frightened whisper, "Don't tell them, Joe. Please don't tell them."

"If you needed the money, why didn't you ask them for it?"

"I've been asking for a little nearly every day."

"You only look after yourself, and you get plenty for that."

"Joe, let me keep it. Don't tell them, Joe."

Her hand tightened on his arm as she pleaded with him. Her face was now close against his, but he was so disgusted with her he tried to push her away. When she saw that he was treating her as though she were a cheap crook, she looked helpless and whispered, "I've got to do something. I've been sending money to Paul Farrel."

"Where is he?"

"He's gone to a sanitarium, and he had no money," she said.

In the moment while they stared at each other, he was thinking of the few times she had brought Paul Farrel to their place, and of the one night when they had found out that his lung was bad. They had made her promise not to see him any more, thinking it was a good thing to do before she went any further with him.

"You promised them you'd forget about him," he said.

"I married him before he went away," she said. "It takes a lot to look after him. I try to keep enough out of my pay every week to pay for my lunches and my board here, but I never seem to have enough left for Paul, and then I don't know what to do."

"You're crazy. He'll die on your hands," he whispered. "Or you'll have to go on keeping him."

"He'll get better," she said. "He'll be back in maybe a year." There was such an ardent fierceness in her words, and her eyes shone with such eagerness, that he didn't know what to say to her. With a shy, timid smile, she said, "Don't tell them, Joe."

"O.K.," he said, and he watched her open the door and go out.

He went back to the living-room, where his mother was saying grandly to his father, "Now you'll have to wait till next year to cry blue ruin."

His father grinned and ducked his head behind his paper. "Don't worry. There'll soon be a next time," he said.

"What did you want to say to Mary?" his mother asked.

"I just wanted to know if she was going my way, and she wasn't," Joe said.

And when Joe heard their familiar voices and remembered Mary's frightened, eager face, he knew he would keep his promise and say nothing to them. He was thinking how far apart he had grown from them; they knew very little about Mary, but he never told them anything about himself, either. Only his father and mother had kept on going the one way. They alone were still close together.

The Censors
by Luisa Valenzuela

Poor Juan! One day they caught him with his guard down before he could even realize that what he had taken as a stroke of luck was really one of fate's dirty tricks. These things happen the minute you're careless and you let down your guard, as one often does. Juancito let happiness—a feeling you can't trust—get the better of him when he received from a confidential source Mariana's new address in Paris and he knew that she hadn't forgotten him. Without thinking twice, he sat down at his table and wrote her a letter. *The* letter that keeps his mind off his job during the day and won't let him sleep at night (what had he scrawled, what had he put on the sheet of paper he sent to Mariana?).

Juan knows there won't be a problem with the letter's contents, that it's irreproachable, harmless. But what about the rest? He knows that they examine, sniff, feel, and read between the lines of each and every letter, and check its tiniest comma and most accidental stain. He knows that all letters pass from hand to hand and go through all sorts of tests in the huge censorship offices and that, in the end, very few continue on their way. Usually it takes months, even years, if there aren't any snags; all this time the freedom, maybe even the life, of both sender and receiver is in jeopardy. And that's why Juan's so down in the dumps: thinking that something might happen to Mariana because of his letters. Of all people, Mariana, who must finally feel safe there where she always dreamed she'd live. But he knows that the *Censor's Secret Command* operates all over the world and cashes in on the discount in air rates; there's nothing to stop them from going as far as that hidden Paris neighborhood, kidnapping Mariana, and returning to their cozy homes, certain of having fulfilled their noble mission.

Well, you've got to beat them to the punch, do what everyone tries to do: sabotage the machinery, throw sand in its gears, get to the bottom of the problem so as to stop it.

This was Juan's sound plan when he, like many others, applied for a censor's job—not because he had a calling or needed a job: no, he applied simply to intercept his own letter, a consoling but unoriginal idea. He was hired immediately, for each day more and more censors are needed and no one would bother to check on his references.

Ulterior motives couldn't be overlooked by the *Censorship Division*, but they needn't be too strict with those who applied. They knew how hard it would be for those poor guys to find the letter they wanted and even if they did, what's a letter or two when the new censor would snap up so many others? That's how Juan managed to join the *Post Office's Censorship Division*, with a certain goal in mind.

The building had a festive air on the outside which contrasted with its inner staidness. Little by little, Juan was absorbed by his job and he felt at peace since he was doing everything he could to get his letter for Mariana. He didn't even worry when, in his first month, he was sent to *Section K*, where envelopes are very carefully screened for explosives.

It's true that on the third day, a fellow worker had his right hand blown off by a letter, but the division chief claimed it was sheer negligence on the victim's part. Juan and the other employees were allowed to go back to their work, albeit feeling less secure. After work, one of them tried to organize a strike to demand higher wages for the unhealthy work, but Juan didn't join in; after thinking it over, he reported him to his superiors and thus got promoted.

You don't form a habit by doing something once, he told himself as he left his boss's office. And when he was transferred to *Section J*, where letters are carefully checked for poison dust, he felt he had climbed a rung in the ladder.

By working hard, he quickly reached *Section E*, where the work was more interesting, for he could now read and analyze the letters' contents. Here he could even hope to get hold of his letter which, judging by the time that had elapsed, had gone through the other sections and was probably floating around in this one.

Soon his work became so absorbing that his noble mission blurred in his mind. Day after day he crossed out whole paragraphs in red ink, pitilessly chucking many letters into the censored basket. These were horrible days when he was shocked by the subtle and conniving ways employed by people to pass on subversive messages; his instincts were so sharp that he found behind a simple "the weather's unsettled" or "prices continue to soar" the wavering hand of someone secretly scheming to overthrow the Government.

His zeal brought him swift promotion. We don't know if this made him happy. Very few letters reached him in *Section B*—only a handful passed the other hurdles—so he read them over and over again, passed them under a magnifying glass, searched for microprint with an electronic microscope, and tuned his sense of smell so that he was beat by the time he made it home. He'd barely manage to warm up his soup, eat some fruit, and fall into bed, satisfied with having done his duty. Only his darling mother worried, but she couldn't get him back on the right road. She'd say, though it wasn't always true: Lola called, she's at the bar with the girls, they miss you, they're waiting for you. Or else she'd leave a bottle of red wine on the table. But Juan wouldn't overdo it: any distraction could make him lose his edge and the perfect censor had to be alert, keen, attentive, and sharp to nab cheats. He had a truly patriotic task, both self-denying and uplifting.

His basket for censored letters became the best fed as well as the most cunning basket in the whole *Censorship Division.* He was about to congratulate himself for having finally discovered his true mission, when his letter to Mariana reached his hands. Naturally, he censored it without regret. And just as naturally, he couldn't stop them from executing him the following morning, another victim of his devotion to his work.

Kong at the Seaside
by Arnold Zweig

Kong got his first glimpse of the sea as he ran on the beach, which stretched like a white arc along the edge of the cove. He barked vociferously with extravagant enthusiasm. Again and again, the bluish-white spray came dashing up at him and he was forbidden to hurl himself into it! A tall order for an Airedale terrier with a wiry brown coat and shaggy forelegs. However, Willie, his young god, would not permit it; but at any rate he could race at top speed across the firm sand, which was still damp from the ebbing waters, Willie following with lusty shouts. Engineer Groll, strolling after, noticed that the dog and his tanned, light-haired, eight-year-old master were attracting considerable attention among the beach-chairs and gaily striped bathing-houses. At the end of the row, where the sky was pale and dipped into the infinite—whereas it was vividly blue overhead and shed relaxation, happiness, and vigor on all these city people and their games in the sand—some controversy seemed to be in progress. Willie was standing there, slim and defiant, holding his dog by the collar. Groll hurried over. People in bathing-suits looked pretty much alike, social castes and classes intermingled. Heads showed more character and expression, though the bodies which supported them were still flabby and colorless, unaccustomed to exposure and pale after a long winter's imprisonment within the darkness of heavy clothing. A stoutish man was sitting in the shade of a striped orange tent stretched over a blue framework; he was bending slightly forward, holding a cigar.

"Is that your dog?" he asked quietly.

A little miss, about ten years old, was with him; she was biting her underlip, and a look of hatred for the boy and the dog flashed between her tear-filled narrow lids.

"No," said Groll with his pleasant voice, which seemed to rumble deep down in his chest, "the dog belongs to the boy, who, to be sure, is mine."

"You know dogs aren't allowed off the leash," the quiet voice continued. "He frightened my daughter a bit, has trampled her canals, and is standing on her spade."

"Pull him back, Willie," laughed Groll. "You're quite right, sir, but the dog broke away and, after all, nothing serious has happened."

Willie pushed Kong aside, picked up the spade and, bowing slightly, held it out to the group. Its third member was a slender, remarkably pretty young lady, sitting in the rear of the tent; Groll decided she was too young to be the mother of the girl and too attractive to be her governess. Well gotten up, he reflected; she looks like Irish with those auburn eyebrows.

No one took the spade from the boy, and Willie, with a frown, stuck the toy into the sand in front of the girl.

"I think that squares it, especially on such a beautiful day," Groll smiled and lay down. His legs behind him, his elbows on the sand, and his face resting on his hands, he looked over at the hostile three. Willie has behaved nicely and politely; how well he looks with his Kong. The dog, evidently not as ready to make peace, growled softly, his fur bristling at the neck; then he sat down.

"I want to shoot his dog, Father," the girl suddenly remarked in a determined voice; "he frightened me so." Groll noticed a gold bracelet of antique workmanship about her wrist—three strands of pale greengold braided into the semblance of a snake. . . . These people need a lesson. I shall give it to them.

Groll nodded reassuringly at his boy, who was indignantly drawing his dog closer to him. Those grown-ups seemed to know that the girl had the upper hand of them, or, as Groll told himself, had the right to give orders. So he quietly waited for the sequel of this charming conversation; after all, he was still there to reprimand the brat if the gentleman with the fine cigar lacked the courage to do so because the sweet darling was not accustomed to proper discipline.

"No one is going to shoot my dog," threatened Willie, clenching his fists; but, without deigning to look at him, the girl continued:

"Buy him from the people, Father; here is my checkbook." She actually took the thin booklet and a fountain pen with a gold clasp from a zipper bag inside the tent.

"If you won't buy him for me, I'll throw a soup plate right off the table at dinner; you know I will, Father." She spoke almost in a whisper and was as white as chalk under her tan; her blue eyes, over which the sea had cast a greenish glint, flashed threateningly.

The gentleman said: "Ten pounds for the dog."

Groll sat up on the sand and crossed his legs. He was awaiting developments with curiosity.

"The dog is not mine; you must deal with my boy. He's trained him."

"I don't deal with boys. I offer fifteen pounds, a pretty neat sum for the cur."

Groll realized that this was an opportunity of really getting to know his eldest. "Willie," he began, "this gentleman offers you fifteen pounds for Kong so he may shoot him. For the money, you could buy the bicycle you have been wanting since last year. I won't be able to give it to you for a long time, we're not rich enough for that."

Willie looked at his father, wondering whether he could be in earnest. But the familiar face showed no sign of jesting. In answer he put an arm about Kong's neck, smiled up at Groll, and said: "I won't sell him to you, Father."

The gentleman in the bathing-suit with his still untanned, pale skin turned to Groll. Apparently the argument began to interest him. "Persuade him; I offer twenty pounds."

"Twenty pounds," Groll remarked to Willie, "that would buy you the bicycle and the canoe, which you admired so much this morning, Willie. A green canoe with double paddles for the water, and for the land a fine nickel-plated bicycle with a headlight, storage battery, and new tires. There might even be money left over for a watch. You only have to give up this old dog by handing the leash to the gentleman."

Willie said scornfully: "If I went ten steps away, Kong would pull him over and be with me again."

The beautiful and unusual young lady spoke for the first time. "He would hardly be able to do that," she said in a clear, sweet, mocking voice—a charming little person, thought Groll—and took a small Browning, gleaming with silver filigree work, out of her handbag. "This would prevent him from running very far."

Foolish of her, thought Groll. "You see, sir, the dog is a thoroughbred, pedigreed, and splendidly trained."

"We've noticed that!"

"Offer fifty pounds, Father, and settle it."

"Fifty pounds," repeated Groll, and his voice shook slightly. That would pay for this trip, and if I handled the money for him, his mother could at last regain her strength. The sanatorium is too expensive, we can't afford it. "Fifty pounds, Willie! The bicycle, the watch, the tent—you remember the brown tent with the cords and tassels—and you would have money left to help me send mother to a sanatorium. Imagine, all that for a dog! Later on, we can go to the animal welfare society, pay three shillings, and get another Kong."

Willie said softly: "There is only one Kong. I will not sell him.

"Offer a hundred pounds, Father. I want to shoot that dog. I shouldn't have to stand such boorishness."

The stoutish gentleman hesitated a moment, then made the offer. "A hundred pounds, sir," he said huskily. "You don't look as though you could afford to reject a small fortune."

"Indeed, sir, I can't," said Groll, and turned to Willie. "My boy," he continued earnestly, "a hundred pounds safely invested will within ten years assure you of a university education. Or, if you prefer, you can buy a small car to ride to school in. What eyes the other boys would make! And you could drive mother to market; that's a great deal of money, a hundred pounds for nothing but a dog."

Willie, frightened by the earnestness of the words, puckered up his face as though to cry. After all, he was just a small boy of eight and he was being asked to give up his beloved dog. "But I love Kong, and Kong loves me," he said, fighting down the tears in his voice. "I don't want to give him up."

"A hundred pounds—do persuade him, sir! Otherwise my daughter will make life miserable for me. You have no idea"—he sighed—"what a row such a little lady can kick up."

If she were mine, thought Groll, I'd leave the marks of a good lesson on each of her dainty cheeks; and after glancing at his boy, who, with furrowed brow, was striving to hold back his tears, he said it aloud, quietly, clearly, looking sternly into the eyes of the girl. "And now, I think, the incident is closed."

Then a most astounding thing happened. The little girl began to laugh. Evidently the tall, brown man pleased her, and the idea that anyone could dare to slap her, the little lady, for one of her whims fascinated her by its very roughness.

"All right, Father," she cried; "he's behaved well. Now we'll put the checkbook back in the bag. Of course, Father, you knew it was all in fun!"

The stoutish gentleman smiled with relief and said that, of course, he had known it and added that such a fine day was just made to have fun. Fun! Groll didn't believe it. He knew too much about people.

Willie breathed more freely and, pretending to blow his nose, wiped away two furtive tears. He threw himself down in the sand next to Kong, happily pulled the dog on top of himself, and began to wrestle with him; the shaggy brown paws of the terrier and the slim tanned arms of the boy mingled in joyful confusion.

However, Groll, while he somewhat reluctantly accepted a cigar and a light from the strange gentleman and silently looked out into the blue-green sea, which lay spread before him like shimmering folds of silk with highlights and shadows—Groll thought: Alas for the poor! If this offer had come to me two years ago when my invention was not yet completed and when we lived in a damp flat dreaming of the little house we now have, then—poor Willie!—this argument might have had a different outcome, this struggle for nothing more than a dog, the love, loyalty, courage, and generosity in the soul of an animal and a boy. Yet, speaking in terms of economics, a little financial security was necessary before one could indulge in the luxury of human decency. Without it—he reflected—no one should be asked to make a decision similar to the one which has just confronted Willie and me; everyone was entitled to that much material safety, especially in an era which was so full of glittering temptations.

The little girl with the spade put her slim bare feet into the sand outside of the tent and called to Willie: "Help me dig new ones." But her eyes invited the man Groll, for whose approval she was striving.

She pointed to the ruined canals. Then, tossing her head, she indicated Kong, who lay panting and lazy in the warm sunshine, and called merrily: "For all I care, he can trample them again."

The whistle of an incoming steamboat sounded from the pier.

Poetry

"Out, Out—"
by Robert Frost

The buzz saw snarled and rattled in the yard
And made dust and dropped stove-length sticks of wood,
Sweet-scented stuff when the breeze drew across it.
And from there those that lifted eyes could count
Five mountain ranges one behind the other
Under the sunset far into Vermont.
And the saw snarled and rattled, snarled and rattled,
As it ran light, or had to bear a load.
And nothing happened: day was all but done.
Call it a day, I wish they might have said
To please the boy by giving him the half hour
That a boy counts so much when saved from work.
His sister stood beside them in her apron
To tell them "Supper." At the word, the saw,
As if to prove saws knew what supper meant,
Leaped out at the boy's hand, or seemed to leap—
He must have given the hand. However it was,
Neither refused the meeting. But the hand!
The boy's first outcry was a rueful laugh,
As he swung toward them holding up the hand
Half in appeal, but half as if to keep
The life from spilling. Then the boy saw all—
Since he was old enough to know, big boy
Doing a man's work, though a child at heart—
He saw all spoiled. "Don't let him cut my hand off—
The doctor, when he comes. Don't let him, sister!"
So. But the hand was gone already.
The doctor put him in the dark of ether.
He lay and puffed his lips out with his breath.
And then—the watcher at his pulse took fright.
No one believed. They listened at his heart.
Little—less—nothing!—and that ended it.
No more to build on there. And they, since they
Were not the one dead, turned to their affairs.

A Man Said to the Universe
by Stephen Crane

A man said to the universe:
"Sir, I exist!"
"However," replied the universe,
"The fact has not created in me
A sense of obligation."

In the Name of Humanity
by V. Andrea Northcott, student

Amidst chaos and destruction,
One being, with outstretched hand,
Befriends another.
Comrades—if only for a moment—
Struggling for survival
In hope of creating a better world for future generations.
Sharing a common goal, despite all odds.
A delicately balanced scale,
Weighting Humanity's worth.
Confusion. Shock. Outrage. Contempt.
The scale tips, and all is lost.
Farewell my brother.

Ruth
by Pauli Murray

Brown girl chanting Te Deums on Sunday
Rust-colored peasant with strength of granite,
Bronze girl welding ship hulls on Monday,
Let nothing smirch you, let no one crush you.

Queen of ghetto, sturdy hill-climber,
Walk with the lilt of ballet dancer,
Walk like a strong down-East wind blowing,
Walk with the majesty of the First Woman.

Gallant challenger, millioned-hope bearer,
The stars are your beacons, earth your inheritance,
Meet blaze and cannon with your own heart's passion,
Surrender to none the fire of your soul.

Guitarreros [Guitar Players]
by Americo Paredes

Black against twisted black
The old mesquite
Rears up against the stars
Branch bridle hanging,
While the bull comes down from the mountain
Driven along by your fingers,
   Twenty nimble stallions prancing up and down the *redil*   [sheepfold]
    of the guitars.
One leaning on the trunk, one facing—
Now the song:
Not cleanly flanked, not pacing,
But in a stubborn yielding that unshapes
And shapes itself again,
Hard-mounted, zigzagged, thrusting,
Thrown, not sung,
One to the other.
The old man listens in his cloud
Of white tobacco smoke.
"It was so," he says,
"In the old days it was so."

Not Waving But Drowning
By Stevie Smith

Nobody heard him, the dead man,
But still he lay moaning:
I was much further out than you thought
And not waving but drowning.

Poor chap, he always loved larking
And now he's dead
It must have been too cold for him his heart gave way,
They said.

Oh, no no no, it was too cold always
(Still the dead one lay moaning)
I was much too far out all my life
And not waving but drowning.

Small Wire
by Anne Sexton

My faith
is a great weight
hung on a small wire,
as doth the spider
hang her baby on a thin web,
as doth the vine,
twiggy and wooden,
hold up grapes
like eyeballs,
as many angels
dance on the head of a pin.
God does not need
too much wire to keep Him there,
just a thin vein,
with blood pushing back and forth in it,
and some love.
As it has been said:
Love and a cough
cannot be concealed.
Even a small cough.
Even a small love.
So if you have only a thin wire,
God does not mind.
He will enter your hands
as easily as ten cents used to
bring forth a Coke.

For Poets
Al Young

Stay beautiful
but dont stay down underground too long
Dont turn into a mole
or a worm
or a root
or a stone

Come on out into the sunlight
Breathe in trees
Knock out mountains
Commune with snakes
& be the very hero of birds

Dont forget to poke your head up
& blink
Think
Walk all around
Swim upstream

Dont forget to fly

Drama

Dentist and Patient
by William Saroyan

(Note: "Dentist and Patient" is a segment from William Saroyan's *Anybody and Anybody Else*, an evening of theater made up of thirty-one separate episodes.)

Characters

ANYBODY

ANYBODY ELSE

ANYBODY: I'm this dentist in this little cubbyhole of an office, and you're in the chair. Open wider, please.

ANYBODY ELSE: Why are you a dentist?

A: Everybody's got to be something. I always liked teeth.

AE: That's strange; why should anybody like teeth?

A: Just a little wider, please. Teeth have form, and no two teeth are alike. A new customer comes here and opens his mouth, and I get a new surprise. This variety makes me stop and think.

AE: Stop and think about what?

A: This won't hurt, but it may put your nerves on end. It will take only a moment or two. I have seen some amazing mouths.

AE: What can possibly be amazing about a mouth? Isn't a mouth a mouth?

A: Yes, of course, but there are mouths and mouths, and each is unique. The alignment of the teeth, the size of the whole mouth, the coloration of the gums and cheek walls, the size and shape of the tongue, the tonsils—it is all fascinating.

AE: I wouldn't be a dentist for all the money in the world.

A: I am not a dentist for money. I thought I was making that clear. It is more a matter of art, or even philosophy. What are you?

AE: Well, what do you think?

A: Judging from your mouth, I'd say you are a professional man, perhaps a lawyer.

AE: Wrong. Guess again.

A: Doctor?

AE: Try again.

A: The whole mouth suggests a man of intelligence, is it possible you are in trade? A grocer, perhaps?

AE: No, try again.

A: Just a little more of this drilling, and then the annoying part will be over. Annoying to you, to me it could never be annoying, it is always fascinating. Are you a tailor?

AE: No, perhaps you had better not try any more.

A: Your mouth definitely suggests you enjoy food, the molars are quite worn from heavy chewing. Do you own a restaurant?

AE: No, you're not even warm. Give up?

A: Perhaps I'd better.

AE: I'm a millionaire, retired.

A: The mouth doesn't suggest that at all.

AE: Perhaps not, but I would never imagine the mouth could suggest anything more than itself.

A: Gold or silver?

AE: My money? It's in gold, silver, paper, stocks, bonds, and in all of the other forms it takes.

A: Shall the filling be gold or silver?

AE: Gold of course, I'm a millionaire.

A: I have heard they are thrifty. The price of gold filling has gone up; the price for this filling will be ten dollars.

AE: The best quality gold?

A: The very best. How did you ever become a millionaire? I have always wanted to ask a millionaire that question. How in the world did you ever manage such a difficult thing?

AE: Cheating.

A: That's not easy to believe. Your mouth is not the mouth of a cheater. The cheater tends to have a small tight mouth which he very much dislikes opening wide. Just a little wider, please, so I can pack the gold properly. Yours is a large, open, easy, and comfortable mouth, not the narrow, tight, small mouth of a cheater.

AE: Every millionaire I know is a cheater, most of them bigger cheaters than I am, even. I try to cheat only the rich who can afford it, but some millionaires cheat widows and orphans, and fathers and mothers who have many children, and ignorant old people.

A: Why do millionaires cheat poor people?

AE: I don't believe they know why. I don't believe they even know they cheat; I believe they believe they are doing business, that's all.

A: Do they perhaps deceive themselves?

AE: They don't seem to know the difference between cheating and not cheating, so of course it isn't necessary to deceive themselves. They just go right on cheating and getting more and more money.

A: For what?

AE: To have.

A: And then what do they do, when they are old, when they are very old and know they must soon die? What do they do?

AE: They have already taught their children how to cheat, and so they leave their money to their children.

A: Clench your teeth, please.

AE: Are you finished?

A: Almost. And it's perfect.

AE: I expect the best.

A: Rinse your mouth, please.

AE: Tastes good; what is that red stuff?

A: Lavoris, dentists have been using it for fifty years.

AE: I thought I had tasted it before.

A: You may step down, now.

AE: Thank you.

A: Why—please don't misunderstand my asking—how did it happen that you came here?

AE: I was told I could get a gold filling for ten dollars here. Other dentists charge twenty, some thirty, and a few millionaire dentists charge fifty.

A: Millionaire dentists? Is such a thing possible?

AE: There are many millionaire dentists.

A: How do they do it?

AE: By overcharging, by not keeping books, and by not paying taxes.

A: Amazing.

AE: Please accept your payment, and thank you very much. Good day. *(He goes.)*

A: Good day, come back again. Fifty dollars for a gold filling. Imagine the audacity of the rascals. Ten is the most I have ever charged. And he paid in crisp new one-dollar bills—one, two, three, four, five, six, seven, eight, nine. I guess two were stuck together. One, two, three, four, five, six, seven, eight, nine. Ah, well, new currency does stick together. It could happen to anybody.

THE LIGHTS FADE

C. Suggested Topics for Writing Literary Essays

Fiction

1. The last paragraph of "Their Mother's Purse" suggests the story's theme. State this theme in your own words and explain how elements of the story—especially plot and dialogue—bring out the theme.

2. Near the end of "Their Mother's Purse," Joe has an opportunity to tell his mother about Mary's situation. Instead he says, "I just wanted to know if she was going my way, and she wasn't." State whether you think Joe was right or wrong not to tell his mother about Mary. Support your position with details and quotations from the story.

3. "The Censors" is a kind of fable about how people in a totalitarian country can become corrupt—and even bring about their own corruption. Write a moral for this fable and show how elements of the story support the moral.

4. At the end of "The Censors," Juan is described as "another victim of his devotion to his work." Explain whether this phrase should be taken at face value or whether it has an ironic meaning. Support your interpretation with details and quotations from the story. (Consider especially that Juan is called a "victim" just after he censors his own letter to Mariana.)

5. Near the end of "Kong at the Seaside," the father reflects that "a little financial security was necessary before one could indulge in the luxury of human decency." Explain how the story can be understood as a conflict between human decency and the desire for security.

6. Choose a character in one of the stories that you consider to be an archetypal character. (See page 99.) Explain what this character represents and compare the character both to other fictitious characters and real people you know or have read about that represent the same archetype.

7. Analyze the conflict or conflicts in one of the stories and relate the conflict to the story's theme.

8. Analyze the tone of one of the stories. Remember that tone is "the author's attitude toward the plot and characters as revealed through his or her words" (page 98). Cite words and phrases that reveal tone. Explain how the story's tone influenced your own attitude toward the plot and characters.

9. If any of the stories have enriched or changed your understanding of any aspect of life, write a literary essay explaining how and why.

Poetry

10. Explain what "A Man Said to the Universe" suggests about the relationship of people to the universe. If you have read other works by Stephen Crane, such as *The Red Badge of Courage* and "The Open Boat," you might wish to compare the theme of this poem to the themes of other works by this author.

11. The title of "Out, Out—" comes from William Shakespeare's *Macbeth*, act V, scene v. The phrase occurs in the famous soliloquy beginning "Tomorrow and tomorrow and tomorrow. . . ." Tell why you think Frost chose this phrase as the title of his poem. Consider what the poem and the soliloquy have in common as commentaries on the tragic aspect of life.

12. "In the Name of Humanity" traces a relationship. In what way is the relationship universal? Why do you think the relationship broke down? Support your answers with specific quotations from the poem.

13. Explain how Pauli Murray's poem "Ruth" uses both similes and a strong rhythm to suggest the strength of the girl to whom the poem is addressed.

14. Comment on the use of metaphors in Americo Paredes's poem "Guitarreros" and of their relationship to the tone, mood, and emotion of the poem.

15. State the theme of "Small Wire" and show how the poem's basic metaphor (which is introduced in the poem's first three lines) expresses the theme.

16. "Not Waving But Drowning" suggests a great deal more than it explicitly tells about one man's life. Tell what the poem suggests, especially through the repeated phrase that is also used as the title of Stevie Smith's poem.

17. "For Poets" expresses its meaning through metaphoric language. (Obviously Al Young does not want poets literally to "breathe in trees" or "knock out mountains" or "be the very hero of birds.") Tell what each metaphor suggests. Then decide which is more effective—your literal paraphrase or the poem's metaphoric statement—and explain why.

18. Analyze a poem in terms of its use of one of the following: language, imagery, sound, rhythm, symbols. For a discussion of these terms, see page 101.

19. Samuel Taylor Coleridge, the poet and critic, defined poetry as "the best words in the best order." Show how a particular poem exemplifies Coleridge's definition.

Drama

20. Discuss the ending of "Dentist and Patient." Did it surprise you or did you expect it? Point out dialogue in the play that prepares for the ending.

21. Tell what you learn about the two characters in "Dentist and Patient," which of the two you find the more sympathetic, and why. Support what you say with specific references to the play's plot and quotations from the play's dialogue.

22. As William Saroyan wrote it, "Dentist and Patient" has no description of the set (scenery) and virtually no stage directions (indicating what actions the characters should perform and how they should speak particular lines). Assume you are going to direct this play. Write a description of the set (a dentist's office) and tell what stage directions you would add for an effective performance.

Glossary

allusion: a **figurative comparison** that refers to something (often a work of literature) that a writer expects readers to recognize (pages 317, 326)

analogy: an extended **figurative comparison** (pages 322, 324)

archetypal character: in a literary work of art, a character representing a general, universal type (page 99)

archetypal conflict: in a literary work of art, a conflict which occurs frequently in literature and which is common in human experience (page 99)

audience: a **writing variable**; the intended reader or readers of a piece of writing (page 5)

balanced sentence: a **rhetorical device**; a sentence in which each part has a similar pattern (page 317)

bibliography: in a research paper, a list of the sources of information (pages 114, 121, 357)

brainstorming: a term used to name a group of methods for generating ideas and supporting details, either by oneself or in a group (pages 208–233)

chronological order: a method of organizing events in a piece of writing by arranging them in the order they occur (page 254)

cliché: a figurative expression or other phrase that has become stale and lost its effect through overuse (page 323)

climactic order: a method of organizing details in a piece of writing by arranging them in order of importance, with the most important coming last (page 254)

climax: the decisive moment or turning point in a narrative (pages 23, 65)

conflict: a physical or mental struggle against someone or something or within oneself (pages 21, 63, 99)

connotation: the ideas or impressions connected with a word, in addition to its dictionary meaning (page 32)

dead metaphor: a **metaphor** which, through overuse, is no longer thought of as a **figurative comparison** (page 323)

demand essay: a piece of writing that must be completed within a specific period of time; often an answer to a question on an essay test (page 139)

description: a picture in words; a piece of writing that depicts a person, place, or object (pages 30, 37)

dialogue: the words that characters speak in narrative or dramatic writing (page 64)

documenting: backing up all the information and quotations in a research paper by listing their sources (page 355)

drafting process: the second stage of the writing process during which a writer composes one or more preliminary drafts (page 3)

editing and revising process: the stage of the writing process in which a writer rewrites a paper on the basis of peer editors' and teacher/editor's comments (page 3)

exaggeration (hyperbole): a **rhetorical device** using overstatement for effect (page 316)

exposition: a piece of writing that presents ideas, information, and/or opinions (page 37)

familiar-to-unfamiliar order: a method of organizing details in a piece of writing by introducing an unfamiliar item, explaining it in terms of something familiar, and concluding with the unfamiliar item (page 255)

figurative comparison: one in which two objects or concepts not usually considered alike are compared (pages 317, 320)

figurative language: language that relies on comparison, either stated or implied (page 320)

firsthand sources: sources of information that come from the writer's own experience and what she or he learns from other people (page 127)

focus: an idea or statement that leads to a **thesis statement** (page 238)

format: a **writing variable**, the form in which a piece of writing will be presented to its audience; for example, an essay (page 6)

freewriting: writing what you think about any topic without trying to order your ideas; a potential source of ideas (page 206)

graphic: something (such as a **mandala**) that shows relationships in visual form (page 249)

imagery: word pictures that appeal to the senses (page 101)

instant writing: writing at a specific time for a specific number of minutes (page 204)

invective: harsh, abusive, insulting speaking or writing (page 338)

irony: the use of words in a way that expresses their opposite meaning (page 340)

journal: a book in which one jots down one's feelings, thoughts, and experiences; an excellent source of topics for writing (pages 201–202)

literary essay: an essay interpreting what a work of art, or a part of it, means (page 97)

mandala: an ancient circular design that represents wholeness and harmony, all the pie-shaped parts fitting together to make a whole; a visual form that can be used to organize the details in a piece of writing (page 249)

memo: a concise message from one person to another in the same school, club, or business (page 150)

metaphor: a **figurative comparison** stating or implying that one thing is something else (pages 101, 321)

minor sentence: a **sentence fragment** which is understood as containing a complete thought (page 314)

narration: a piece of writing that tells a story; an account of one or more events (pages 21, 37, 63)

narrative illustration: a brief story that serves as an example of a **thesis statement** (page 50)

opposites: a **rhetorical device** used to contrast two opposing ideas (page 317)

organization: the arrangement of a piece of writing depending on how details are ordered, how the sentences in a paragraph are linked, and how the writing progresses from one paragraph to the next (page 272)

outline: a plan indicating the arrangement of ideas which are or will be contained in a written work (pages 112, 121, 283)

overall impression: the final effect that all the details of a piece of writing combine to create (page 32)

paraphrase: a restatement of a piece of writing in one's own words (page 283)

parenthetical citation: a method of documenting information in a research or scholarly paper by citing the last name of the source's author and the number of the page on which a fact or quotation appears (pages 113, 356)

parody: a form of speaking or writing that makes fun of its subject through exaggeration (page 339)

peer-editing: editing by one's classmates to be followed by revisions made on the basis of peer editors' comments and suggestions (page 275)

periodic sentence: a **rhetorical device**; withholding an important part of a sentence until the end (page 317)

persona: a fictitious **voice** a writer adopts (page 6)

personification: a **figurative comparison** giving an inanimate object human characteristics (page 322)

plagiarism: trying to pass off another writer's words or ideas as your own, a serious offense for a writer (page 49)

point of view: in a narrative work of art, the perspective from which the author chooses to tell the story (page 98)

précis: the condensation of a piece of writing to about half of its original length (page 284)

prewriting: the first stage of the **writing process** in which ideas and supporting details are generated (page 2)

publishing: as this book uses the term, presenting a piece of writing to its intended audience (page 281)

purpose: a **writing variable**, the reason for writing (page 6)

repetition: a **rhetorical device**; restating key words or phrases for emphasis and rhythm (page 316)

research paper: an expository paper that presents information that is documented through parenthetical citations (or footnotes) and a bibliography (page 110)

résumé: a summary of a job applicant's work experience, education, and other qualifications (page 190)

reversal: a **rhetorical device;** reversing the order of a phrase or clause to make a balanced sentence even more memorable (page 317)

review: a kind of argumentative essay presenting an opinion, with reasons to back it up, about a particular work of art (page 87)

rhetorical devices: techniques used to create a certain effect upon the audience of a piece of writing (page 315)

rhetorical question: a **rhetorical device;** asking a question to which the answer is already known or implied (page 315)

rhyme: the similarity of sounds at the ends of words such as *take* and *make* (page 101)

rhythm: the regular beat or pulse of poetry or music (page 101)

satire: a form of writing in which persons or institutions are ridiculed in order to convey to an audience the necessity for change (page 336)

sentence combining: various techniques of achieving a better style by combining short, jerky sentences into smoother long ones (page 307)

sentence fragment: a group of words punctuated as a complete sentence, but that does not contain both a complete subject and a complete predicate (page 313)

sequential order: a method of organizing details in a composition by placing items in the order in which they should be or have been carried out (page 255)

simile: a **figurative comparison** that uses a word of comparison, such as *like* (pages 101, 321)

situation: a **writing variable;** the circumstances of the writer and the **audience** that influence the way a piece of writing is written (page 7)

slant: a choice of words made by a writer to achieve a favorable (positive) or unfavorable (negative) reaction from a reader to an idea (page 330)

spatial order: a method of organizing descriptive details in a composition by placing the details in the order (such as near to far) one wants a reader to see them (page 253)

style: the choice of words and sentences as well as the effectiveness, arrangement, and appropriateness of the words and sentences; also the choice and arrangement of words as they reflect the personality of the writer (pages 273, 294)

symbol: in a literary work of art, a person or object representing both itself and a larger idea (page 100)

textual evidence: evidence from a literary work of art—such as quotations, details from the plot, or the recurrent use of symbols—to support the interpretation of that work in a literary essay (page 104)

theme: the idea behind all the characters and events in a literary work (page 100)

thesis statement: a sentence that controls the content of an entire piece of writing (pages 10, 234)

tone: in a literary work, the author's attitude toward the plot and characters as revealed through her or his words (page 98)

topic: a **writing variable,** the subject of a piece of writing (page 5)

topic sentence: a sentence that controls the content of a paragraph (page 234)

transitional device: a word or phrase that links one part of a piece of writing to another (page 264)

understatement (litotes): a **rhetorical device** that makes a fact seem less significant; often used for **irony** (page 316)

unity: the final impression to which all the details in a piece of writing contribute (pages 102, 248)

unwriting: reducing a piece of writing to its main points as a guide to revising it (page 282)

visual organization: methods of organizing details in a composition by using a visual form such as a **mandala** (page 249)

voice: a **writing variable** that reveals the kind of person a writer is. See also **persona.** (page 6)

writing process: the stages (**prewriting, drafting, editing and revising**) in which a piece of writing is composed (page 2)

writing variables: the circumstances influencing the composition of any piece of writing. The writing variables include **topic, audience, purpose, format, voice, situation, point of view,** and **thesis statement.** (page 2)

Index

AAA/BBB Method, 251–252
ABA/BAB Method, 251–252
Abbreviations for states, 167
Abnormal word order, 315–316
Absurd analogies, 73, 214–215
Advertising, 333
Alliteration, 317
Allusion, 317, 321, 326–327
Almanacs, 352
Analogy, 73, 214–215, 245, 324–325
Appendix (in a research paper), 121
Archetypal characters, 99–100
Archetypal conflicts, 99
Argumentation, 50
Aristotle's Topics, 9–10, 222
Assign/Write, 211–212
Atlases, 352
Attention-getting tactic, 244
Autobiography, 71
Audience, 5–6

Basic essay structure, 50–51
Beginning, 22–23, 243–245
Bibliography, 114, 121, 357–361
Biographical reference works, 352
Biography, 78
Balanced sentence, 317
Body of letter, 166, 176
Brainstorming, 8–10, 208–233
Broad topic, 5

Call number, 346
Card catalogue, 343, 345–347
Cause and effect, 229–233, 252
Cause-and-Effect Flowchart, 229–233
Character, 99–100
Checklists for revising, 271–274
Chiasmus, 317
Chronological order, 254
Classification Flowchart, 225–226
Climactic order, 254–255
Climactic parallelism, 316
Climax, 23, 65
Coherence, 264–269
Comics, 294–295
Comparison/contrast, 228–229, 251–252
Comparison/Contrast Ladders, 228–229
Complimentary close of a letter, 166, 176
Conclusion, 40, 41, 51
Conflict, 21–22, 63, 64, 99
Connotation, 32
Content, 4, 271–272
Cover letter, 190

Dead metaphor, 323–324
Degrees of slant, 332–333
Demand essay, 139
Description, 30, 65, 247, 331

397

Descriptive details, 31, 248
Development, 40, 41, 51
Dewey decimal system, 347–349
Dialogue, 64
Division Flowchart, 226–228
Documenting, 113–114, 123–124, 355–361
Drafting process, 3, 10–11
Drama, 101–103

Editing and revising process, 3, 13–16, 270–281
Encyclopedias, 351–352
Emphasis in sentence combining, 309
Ending, 245–246
Evaluating thesis statements and topic sentences, 241
Exaggeration, 316
Examples, 41
Expanding a sentence, 311–312
Experience/Write, 211
Exposition, 37

Facts, 41
Familiar-to-unfamiliar order, 255–256
Feature article, 126
Fiction, 98–100
Figurative comparison, 317, 320–329
First-person narrative, 63
Firsthand sources, 127
Five parts of a personal letter, 166
Flowcharts, 225–228, 229–233
Following up a peer editing session, 280
Format, 6, 40
Found poetry, 207
Fragment, 313–314, 316
Free Association Cluster, 212–213

Gazetteers, 352
Generalization, 244
Graphic, 288

Haiku, 205–206
Heading of a letter, 166, 175
Hyperbole, 316

Imagery, 65
Index cards, use of in research, 112, 119, 353–354

Indexes (reference works) 349–351
Inside address of a business letter, 175
Instant writing, 204–207
Instructions, 132
Introduction, 40, 51
Invective, 338–339
Irony, 340–341

Journal writing, 201–204

Key terms in essay tests, 141–143
Key words, 268–269
Kinds of sentences, 313

Letter to the editor, 182
Library of Congress system, 347
Limited topic, 8, 38–39
Limiting a topic, 118–119, 238–240
Literary essay, 97
Litotes, 316

Mandala, 249–250
Metaphor, 101, 321, 323–324
Minor sentence, 313–314, 316

Narrative, 21, 63, 247
Narrative illustration, 50
Narrator, 98
Negative Cluster, 219
Newspaper Reporter's Questions, 222–225
Newspapers, style in, 296
Note-taking, 112, 119

Onomatopoeia, 318
Opposites, 317
Organization, 272–273
Outline, 112–113, 121, 283
Overall impression, 32

Paraphrase, 283–284
Parenthetical citations, 113–114, 355–357
Parody, 339–340
Peer editing, 270, 275–280
Peer editing sessions, 278–280
Pentad Cluster, 220
Periodic sentence, 314
Persona, 6–7, 72, 77, 299–301

Personal letter, 164
Personification, 321
Placement of topic sentence, 237–238
Plagiarism, 49
Poetry, 100–101
Point of view, 8, 98–99
Positive Cluster, 218
Positive/Negative/Neutral Pigeonholes, 217–218
Précis, 283, 284–286
Predicate, 10
Prewriting process, 2, 5–10
Pro/Con Ladders, 221–222
Proofreaders' symbols, 13, 364–366
Propaganda, 333–334
Proposal, 156
Publishable, definition of, 3
Publishing, 3, 281
Purpose, 6

Question, 274
Quotation, as a beginning, 245
Quotations, use of, 104

Random List, 215
Read/Write, 211
Readers' Guide to Periodical Literature, 349–351
Rearranging a sentence, 308–309
Reasons, 41, 248
Reference works, 343–344, 349–353
Reforming a sentence, 312–313
Repetition, 316
Report, 156
Research paper, 110–124, 343–355
Research skills, 343–355
Résumé, 190
Reversals, 317
Review, 87
Revising, 270–274, 287–288
Rhetorical devices, 315–319
Rhetorical question, 315
Rhyme, 101, 318
Rhythm, 101

Salutation of a letter, 166, 175
Sardonic satire, 338
Satire, 336–342
See/Write, 210–211
Senses Cluster, 216

Sentence combining, 307–312
Sentence variety, 65, 305–314
Sequential order, 253
Simile, 101, 321
Situation, 7
Slant, 330–335
Spatial order, 253–254
Statement, 244
Style, 4, 73–74, 273, 294–304; and topic, 296–298; in comics, 294–295; in newspapers, 296
Subject, 10
Subtracting in sentence combining, 310–311
Summary, 244, 288–289
Symbols, 100, 101

Talk/Write, 210
Textual evidence, 104
Theme, 100
Thesis statement, 10, 234, 235–236, 238–241
Think/Write, 209–210
Third-person narrative, 63
Thread, unifying, 72, 79
Titles, 246–247
Tone, 98
Topic, 5, 8; and style, 296–298
Topic sentence, 234–242
Transitional expressions and conjunctions, 264–268
Twenty-five word summary, 288–289

Underlining, 318
Understatement, 316
Unity, 72, 79, 102–103, 248–263
Unwriting, 282–289; and graphics, 288
Usage and mechanics, 274

Vertical file, 344
Visual organization, 249–251
Voice, 6–7, 72

"Works Cited," 114, 357
Write/Write, 212
Writing variables, 2, 5–10, 12, 42, 238–240

ACKNOWLEDGMENTS

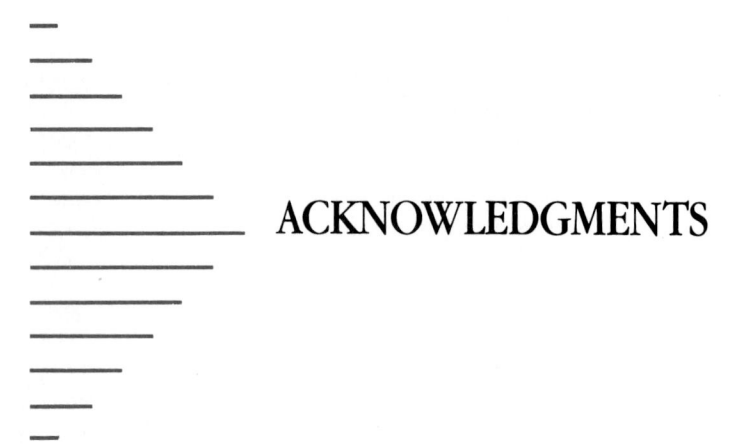

Chapter 1
    From *Barrio Boy* by Ernesto Galarza. © 1971 by University of Notre Dame Press.
    From *Intermission* by Anne Baxter. Copyright © G.P. Putnam's Sons.
    "Shopping" by Shirley Friesen, student.
    "The Weekend Chore" by Keith Wagner, student.
    "Queen of the Mountain" by Janelle McGrath, student.

Chapter 2
    "This Is All I Need" by Young-Mi Song, student.
    "The Little Black Boy" by Raymond Schow, student.
    From *Barrio Boy* by Ernesto Galarza. © 1971 by University of Notre Dame Press.
    "Moving In" by Chris Moffat, student.

Chapter 3
    "The Problem of Acid Rain" by Frank Brown, student.
    "Caring for Your New Aquarium" by Marc Attinasi. Reprinted by permission.
    "Daydreams" by Wun Yue Au, student.
    "Smokers Beware" by Tracey Rockwell, student.

Chapter 4
    "Bacterium" by Dora Anyfantis, student.
    "Before the Audition" by Rita Ringle, student.

Chapter 5
"The High Price of Soft-Sell" by Dr. Ken MacMillan, Vancouver, B.C. Reprinted by permission.
"Smoking in Public Places" by Meldon Ellis, student.

Chapter 6
"Winter Morning" by Mira Mignon, student.
"The Fight" by Bill Rasmussen, student.

Chapter 7
Excerpted from *One Writer's Beginnings* by Eudora Welty. Copyright © 1983, 1984 by Eudora Welty. Reprinted by permission of Harvard University Press.
"Footloose" by Gino Nasato, student.
"Memories" by John Parker.

Chapter 8
"Personality Salesman" by Kristin Nelson, student.
Excerpted from "Who Is Whoopi Goldberg and What Is She Doing on Broadway???" by Pamela Noel. Reprinted by permission of *Ebony* Magazine, © 1985 Johnson Publishing Company, Inc.
Excerpted from "Fernando Valenzuela: El Titan del Pitcheo" by Katharine A. Diaz. Copyright © 1981 *Caminos* Magazine. Reprinted by permission.

Chapter 9
"John F. Kennedy Re-examined" by Heather Hamill, student.
"Review of *Watership Down*" by Alexander Targ, student.
"Review of *Brave New World*" by Linda Brown, student.

Chapter 10
"The Theme of Temptation in 'Their Mother's Purse' and 'Kong at the Seaside' " by Anna Deliganis, student.

Chapter 11
"Under the Eaves" by Judy Chapelsky, student.
"The Dynamic Duo" by Steven Greenaway, student.

Chapter 12
"Acupuncture" by Lynn Stefonovich, student.

Chapter 13
"The Fascinating World of Dreams" by Mike Chan, student.

Chapter 14
"How to Throw a Frisbee" from *Made In America* by Murray Suid and Ron Harris. Copyright © 1978 by Addison-Wesley Publishing Company, Inc. Reprinted by permission of Murray Suid and Ron Harris. "Preparation is the Key to Success" is taken from *Writer's Workshop* by John F. Parker.

Chapter 15
"Four Essays from a History Class." Teacher comments by George O. Walsh, teacher Social Studies, Shorewood High School, Seattle, Washington.

Chapter 20
"Hitting the Mark," by Karla Jackson as appeared in "Letters to the Editor," Pacific Magazine, *Seattle Times*, March 4, 1984.

Chapter 24
Paragraph from *Fifth Chinese Daughter* by Jade Snow Wong. Copyright © 1945, 1948, 1950 by Jade Snow Wong. Harper & Row, Publishers Inc.

Chapter 26
"Two Plays as Different as Onions and Dirt." A review by Joe Adcock, Theater Critic, Seattle Post-Intelligencer as appeared in the Seattle Post-Intelligencer on October 19, 1982.

Chapter 29
Excerpts from "'I Dream for a Living'" (TIME, July 15, 1985) Copyright 1985 Time Inc. All rights reserved. Reprinted by permission from TIME.
"The Last Chance Energy Book" from *The Last Chance Energy Book* by Owen Phillips. Reprinted by permission of The Johns Hopkins University Press.

Chapter 30
"Autobiography of a Tumbleweed" by John McLean, student.
The following excerpt is reprinted courtesy of SPORTS ILLUSTRATED from the July 13, 1981 issue. © 1981 Time Inc. "Heck, Mes Amis, It's Only Ol' Cale" by Bob Ottum.

Specified excerpt from *Pilgrim at Tinker Creek* by Annie Dillard. Copyright © 1974 by Annie Dillard. Reprinted by permission of Harper & Row, Publishers, Inc.

Chapter 32

"The Shape of Things to Come" by Patricia Davies, student.

Chapter 33

Paragraph from *Life Before Man* by Margaret Atwood. Copyright © 1983 Warner Books and McClelland & Stewart Ltd., (Canada).
"Drowning" by Gordon Bookey, student.
"Why" by M.A. Clarkson, student.
"The March" by Mike Hawkins, student.

Chapter 34

"The Thirties" by John Parker.

Chapter 35

Excerpt from pages 115–116 of "The Fran Lebowitz High Stress Diet and Exercise Program," from *Social Studies,* by Fran Lebowitz. Copyright © 1981 by Fran Lebowitz. Published by Random House, Inc.
Paragraph from page 112 of *With All Disrespect: More Uncivil Liberties* by Calvin Trillin. Copyright © 1985 by Calvin Trillin. Published by Ticknor & Fields, New York.

Chapter 36

2 entries from page 649 from the May 1985 issue of *Reader's Guide to Periodical Literature.* Copyright © 1985 by the H. W. Wilson Company. Material reproduced by permission of the publisher.

Appendix

"The Censors." From the collection "Donde viven las aguilas," Bs. As. 1983. Editorial Celtia. Reprinted by permission of Luisa Valenzuela.
Their Mother's Purse by Morley Callaghan. Copyright © 1959 by Morley Callaghan. Reprinted by permission of Don Congdon Associates. In Canada, reprinted by permission of Macmillan of Canada, a Division of Canada Publishing Corporation.
"Kong at the Seaside" by Arnold Zweig. Every reasonable effort has been made to locate the holder of copyright, but this regrettably has not been possible.

"Not Waving But Drowning." Stevie Smith, *Collected Poems*. Copyright © 1972 by Stevie Smith. Reprinted by permission of New Directions Publishing Corp.

"Ruth." From *Dark Testament and Other Poems* by Pauli Murray. Copyright © 1970 by Pauli Murray. Reprinted by permission of The Estate of the Author. Marie Rodell-Frances Collin Literary Agency.

"For Poets" by Al Young. Copyright © 1968 by Al Young; reprinted by permission of the author.

"Small Wire" from *The Awful Rowing Toward God* by Anne Sexton. Copyright © 1975 by Loring Conant, Jr., Executor of the Estate of Anne Sexton. Reprinted by permission of Houghton Mifflin Company.

"In the Name of Humanity" by V. Andrea Northcott, student.

"Guitarreros" by Americo Paredes / First published in *Southwest Review*, Autumn 1964.

"Out, Out—" from *The Poetry of Robert Frost* edited by Edward Connery Lathem. Copyright 1916, © 1969 by Holt, Rinehart and Winston. Copyright 1944 by Robert Frost. Reprinted by permission of Holt, Rinehart and Winston, Publishers.

"Dentist and Patient" from William Saroyan's *Anybody and Anybody Else*. Every reasonable effort has been made to locate the holder of the copyright, but this regrettably has not been possible.

Photographs
- P. XII   Mark Antman/The Image Works
- P. 18   Kosti Ruohomaa/Black Star
- P. 198   NASA
- P. 290   Ray Atkeson/Black Star